MAKERS OF WORLD HISTORY

Volume 1

SECOND EDITION

MAKERS OF WORLD HISTORY

Volume 1

SECOND EDITION

J. Kelley Sowards, editor
Wichita State University

St. Martin's Press

New York

Editor: Louise H. Waller
Managing editor: Patricia Mansfield-Phelan
Project editor: Alda D. Trabucchi
Production supervisor: Joe Ford
Art director: Sheree Goodman
Photo research: Elnora Bode
Cover design: Eileen Burke

For information, write:
St. Martin's Press, Inc.
175 Fifth Avenue
New York, NY 10010

ISBN: 0–312–09650–X

Acknowledgments

Hammurabi: From *Ancient Near Eastern Texts: Relating to the Old Testament*, 3/e, by James
Pritchard, ed. Copyright © 1969 Princeton University Press. Reprinted by permission of
Princeton University Press. "The Age of Hammurabi" from *The Conquest of Civilization* by
James H. Breasted. Copyright © 1926, 1937 by Harper & Row, Publishers, Inc. Copy-
right renewed. Reprinted by permission of HarperCollins Publishers, Inc. From *The Face
of the Ancient Orient* by Sabatino Moscati. Copyright © 1961 Routledge Kegan & Paul Ltd.
Reprinted by permission.
Sappho: From *Sappho's Lyre: Archaic Lyric and Women Poets of Ancient Greece* by Diane Rayor,
"The Poet of Lesbian Love," poems 1, 4, 8, 14, 34, 35, 36, 37. Copyright © Diane Rayor.
Reprinted by permission of University of California Press. From *Sappho of Lesbos: Her Life
and Times* by Arthur Weigall (Frederick A. Stokes Co., New York, 1933, pp. 288–301,
305–309). From "Sappho of Lesbos," pp. 2–27, *The Woman and the Lyre: Women Writers in
Classical Greece and Rome* by Jane McIntosh Snyder. Copyright © 1989 by the Board of
Trustees, Southern Illinois University.

Acknowledgments and copyrights are continued at the back of the book on pages
332–333, which constitute an extension of the copyright page.
It is a violation of the law to reproduce these selections by any means whatsoever without the written permission of the copyright holder.

To my dear daughters-in-law Cindy and Jane.

Preface

Are men and women able to force change upon history by their skill and wits, their nerve and daring? Are they capable of altering history's course by their actions? Or are they hopelessly caught in the grinding process of great, impersonal forces over which they have no real control?

Historians—like theologians, philosophers, and scientists—have long been fascinated by this question. People of every age have recognized great forces at work in their affairs, whether they perceived those forces as supernatural and divine, climatological, ecological, sociological, or economic. Yet obviously at least a few individuals—Alexander, Suleiman—were able to seize the opportunity their times offered and compel the great forces of history to change course. Still others—Confucius, Muhammad, Gandhi—were able, solely by the power of their thoughts or their visions, to shape the history of their periods and of all later times even more profoundly than conquerors or military heroes.

The purpose of *Makers of World History* is to examine the careers and the impact of a number of figures who have significantly influenced world history or embodied much that is significant about the periods in which they lived. At the same time the book introduces students to the chief varieties of historical interpretation. Few personalities or events stand without comment in the historical record; contemporary accounts and documents, the so-called original sources, no less than later studies, are written by people with a distinct point of view and interpretation of what they see. Problems of interpretation are inseparable from the effort to achieve historical understanding.

The basic skeleton of all history is political history, and the "names" that occur most often are those of rulers, political figures, and other kinds of "movers and shakers." Hence, the figures loom large in the historical narrative, a fact that is reflected in the contents of *Makers of World History.*

The readings in this book have been chosen for their inherent interest and their particular way of treating their subjects. Typically, three selections are devoted to each figure. The first selection is usually an autobiographical or contemporary biographical account; in a few instances, differing assessments by contemporaries are included. Next, a more or less orthodox interpretation is presented; it is often a selection from the "standard work" on the figure in question. The final selection offers a more recent view, which may reinforce the standard interpretation, revise it in light of new evidence, or dissent from it completely. In some cases, two very different recent views are set side by side.

A book of this size cannot hope to include full-length biographies of all the individuals studied. Instead, each chapter focuses on an important interpretive issue. In some chapters the figure's relative historical importance is at issue; in others the significance of a major revealed point in the sources is discussed; in still others the general meaning of the figure's career, as debated in a spread of interpretive positions, is weighed. In every chapter the question examined is interesting and basic to an understanding of the figure's place in history.

Makers of World History is an alternative version of an earlier book, *Makers of the Western Tradition,* and has been adapted for use in World History, as opposed to Western Civilization, courses. The breakpoint between the two volumes lies in the late sixteenth/early seventeenth centuries, a fairly common dividing line between the two terms of World History courses. Each volume contains fourteen chapters; thus each fits into the fifteen weeks of a typical college semester. Each volume is also divided equally between Western and non-Western figures. This, I believe, reflects the usual subject emphasis of World History courses.

An effort was made to represent a spread of regional civilizations, resulting in three Chinese, three Indian, three Middle Eastern, two Japanese, two African, and one Native American among the non-Western figures. There is also a spread among subject areas—twenty political leaders, four philosophers or religious leaders, two literary figures, one explorer, and one scientist.

This revised second edition was prepared in response to suggestions from users of the first edition. Thus, we have eleven new figures in the second edition of this text—Hammurabi, Sappho, Cleopatra, Genghis Khan, Joan of Arc, Christopher Columbus, Clive of India, Catherine the Great, Simón Bolívar, Gandhi, and Golda Meir. We have retained the Review and Study Questions for each chapter, and have updated all the chapter bibliographies.

The second edition of *Makers of World History* is based on responses to a questionnaire by colleagues across the country who used the first edition in their classes. Their suggestions about which historical figures ought to be deleted and which added were extremely helpful in the revision. The author would especially like to thank: Norman R. Bennett, Boston University; John B. Guarino, Northern Essex Community College; Ellwood B. Hannum, University of South Alabama; Joseph P. Huffman, Westmont College; Karen L. Jolly, University of Hawaii at Manoa; Irving A. Kelter, University of St. Thomas; Lisa M. Lane, Mira Costa College; Stephen Morillo, Wabash College; Elsa Nystrom, Kennesaw State College; Joseph R. Peden, CUNY, Baruch College; Thomas D. Reins, California State University at Fullerton; Gary W. Shanafelt, McMurray University; J. Lee Shneidman, Adelphi University; and Lawrence Squeri, East Stroudsburg University.

J. K. S.

Contents

MAKERS OF
WORLD
HISTORY

Volume 1

SECOND EDITION

HAMMURABI: THE KING OF JUSTICE

?	Born
c. 1792 B.C.	Began reign
c. 1790 B.C.	Promulgated law code, though this was likely an earlier version
c. 1785 B.C.	First significant military campaign, against Erech
c. 1763 B.C.	Defeated Assyrians and Elamites, established Babylonian hegemony in Mesopotamia
c. 1750 B.C.	Died

Civilization began in Mesopotamia, in the fertile flood plain of the Tigris-Euphrates rivers, with the Sumerians, who were then conquered by the Akkadians and they by the Amorites. It was the Amorites who established their capital city at the site of Babylon, and it was from Babylon that King Hammurabi ruled. With the reign of Hammurabi (c. 1792–1750 B.C.), the Babylonian state reached its pinnacle of imperial power and Babylonian civilization its classical period.

The enormous distance in time that separates us from the ancient Near East has obliterated the human features of individual people as it has reduced their magnificent cities to anonymous tells of rubble (ancient mounds composed of remains of successive settlements) scattered across the plain of Iraq. We have an occasional striking portrait statue of some great king—Gudea of Lagash or Sargon of Akkad—and many fragments of royal inscriptions. But even for such kingly figures, we have little in the way of historical information that can help us reconstruct a picture of the kings themselves or of their times. An exception is the case with Hammurabi of Babylon, the greatest of Amorite kings. A considerable number of letters and political and business documents from his reign have come to light in the last century and a half, and they provide a wealth of detail about the life and history, customs, and commercial and diplomatic practices of

1

Hammurabi's court and a picture of the king himself at work. To a remarkable extent the work of the king was guided by a concept of law derived from yet another historical source of extraordinary value, the so-called Code of Hammurabi. The code is inscribed on a stone column in 3,600 lines of cuneiform writing. It now resides in a museum in Paris.

The Code of Hammurabi

The Code of Hammurabi, the longest and most complete document of its kind found among the remains of ancient Near Eastern civilization, contains, even more clearly than the letters of Hammurabi, a self-revealing account of the king and his accomplishments. In its prologue and epilogue, he claims the favor of a host of gods, not only Marduk, the tutelary god of Babylon, but the gods of the various other cities that have come under his sway, even the old nature gods of heaven and earth. Hammurabi claims that he has brought all the surrounding lands under the domination of Babylon, that he has destroyed the wicked and the evil and caused justice to prevail, that he has brought political order, peace, and prosperity to the people of his empire. But most of all, he claims, "I, Hammurabi, am the king of justice."

And to an astonishing extent, this claim is borne out by the detailed provisions of the code itself. While the king refers to the favor of the gods and prevails upon them from time to time, the code gives the overall impression of secular practicality. It reveals not only the king's justice but also the pulsing life of a busy, hard-working, prosperous, and orderly people. Many of the provisions of the code will strike us as startlingly modern—the detailed rules of evidence and testimony; the equity proceedings and contracts; the highly developed commercial law and regulated interest rates; laws governing the trades and professions; and some recognition of the rights of women, particularly their rights in marriage and divorce.

Yet the people who lived under these laws, like the king who codified them, exist within their own historic time and place. And the code reveals this as well. Babylonian society, like all ancient societies, was rigidly stratified, and even the provisions of the law were applied differently to people of one class or another. Babylonians believed in sorcery and witchcraft and in the trial by ordeal, and their law embraced the principle of retaliation and punishment in kind. Nevertheless, "the idea that justice was something to which man had a right began slowly to take form, and in the second millennium . . . justice as right rather than justice as favor seems to have become the general conception."[1]

---

[1]Henri Frankfort et al., *The Intellectual Adventure of Ancient Man, An Essay on Speculative Thought in the Ancient Near East* (Chicago and London: University of Chicago Press, 1946), p. 208.

That general conception is enshrined in the Code of Hammurabi, excerpts from which follow.

The Prologue

WHEN LOFTY ANUM, king of the Anunnaki,
(and) Enlil, lord of heaven and earth,
the determiner of the destinies of the land,
determined for Marduk, . . .[2]
the Enlil functions over all mankind, . . .
called Babylon by its exalted name,
made it supreme in the world,
established for him in its midst an enduring kingship,
whose foundations are as firm as heaven and earth—
at that time Anum and Enlil named me
to promote the welfare of the people,
me, Hammurabi, the devout, god-fearing prince,
to cause justice to prevail in the land,
to destroy the wicked and the evil,
that the strong might not oppress the weak,
to rise like the sun over the black-headed (people),[3]
and to light up the land.

Hammurabi, the shepherd, called by Enlil, am I;
the one who makes affluence and plenty abound;
who provides in abundance all sorts of things . . .
the ancient seed of royalty, the powerful king, the sun of Babylon,
who causes light to go forth over the lands of Sumer and Akkad;
the king who has made the four quarters of the world
    subservient; . . .
When Marduk commissioned me to guide the people aright,
to direct the land,
I established law and justice in the language of the land,

---

[2]These are all Babylonian gods. Anum was the sky god and chief among the gods. The Anunnaki were his attending lesser deities. Enlil was the god of the storm and rivaled Anum in importance. Notice that in the terms expressed here, they have given over their functions to Marduk, the chief god of Babylon and the protector god of Hammurabi the king.—ED.

[3]An old Sumerian expression to describe themselves, taken over by the Babylonians: it simply means the subjects of the state.—ED.

thereby promoting the welfare of the people.
At that time (I decreed):

The Laws

1: If a seignior accused a(nother) seignior and brought a charge of murder against him, but has not proved it, his accuser shall be put to death.[4]

2: If a seignior brought a charge of sorcery against a(nother) seignior, but has not proved it, the one against whom the charge of sorcery was brought, upon going to the river, shall throw himself into the river, and if the river has then overpowered him, his accuser shall take over his estate; if the river has shown that seignior to be innocent and he has accordingly come forth safe, the one who brought the charge of sorcery against him shall be put to death, while the one who threw himself into the river shall take over the estate of his accuser.

3: If a seignior came forward with false testimony in a case, and has not proved the word which he spoke, if that case was a case involving life, that seignior shall be put to death.

4: If he came forward with (false) testimony concerning grain or money,[5] he shall bear the penalty of that case. . . .

9: When a seignior, (some of) whose property was lost, has found his lost property in the possession of a(nother) seignior, if the seignior in whose possession the lost (property) was found has declared, "A seller sold (it) to me; I made the purchase in the presence of witnesses," and the owner of the lost (property) in turn has declared, "I will produce witnesses attesting to my lost (property)"; the purchaser having then produced the seller who made the sale to him and the witnesses in whose presence he made the purchase, and the owner of the lost (property) having also produced the witnesses attesting to his lost (property), the judges shall consider their evidence, and the witnesses in whose presence the purchase was made, along with the witnesses attesting to the lost (property), shall declare what they know in the presence of god, and since the seller was the thief, he shall be put to death, while the owner of the lost (property) shall take his lost (property), with the purchaser obtaining from the estate of the seller the money that he paid out.

10: If the (professed) purchaser has not produced the seller who

---

[4]*Seignior* is a term chosen by the translator to designate a male of the upper Babylonian social class.—Ed.

[5]While the term *money* is used here, it has reference more particularly to weights of silver, occasionally gold. The concept of money as such had not yet developed.—Ed.

made the sale to him and the witnesses in whose presence he made the purchase, but the owner of the lost property has produced witnesses attesting to his lost property, since the (professed) purchaser was the thief, he shall be put to death, while the owner of the lost property shall take his lost property.

11:   If the (professed) owner of the lost property has not produced witnesses attesting to his lost property, since he was a cheat and started a false report, he shall be put to death.

12:   If the seller has gone to (his) fate, the purchaser shall take from the estate of the seller fivefold the claim for that case.

13:   If the witnesses of that seignior were not at hand, the judges shall set a time-limit of six months for him, and if he did not produce his witnesses within six months, since that seignior was a cheat, he shall bear the penalty of that case. . . .

88:   If a merchant [lent] grain at interest, he shall receive sixty *qu* of grain per *kur* as interest. If he lent money at interest, he shall receive one-sixth (shekel) six *še* (i.e., one-fifth shekel) per shekel of silver as interest.[6]

89:   If a seignior, who [incurred] a debt, does not have the money to pay (it) back, but has the grain, [the merchant] shall take grain for his money [with its interest] in accordance with the ratio fixed by the king.

90:   If the merchant increased the interest beyond [sixty *qu*] per *kur* [of grain] (or) one-sixth (shekel) six *še* [per shekel of money] and has collected (it), he shall forfeit whatever he lent.

91:   If a merchant [lent] grain at interest and has collected money [for the full interest] on the grain, the grain along with the money may not [*be charged to the account*].

92:   (not preserved)

93:   [If the merchant] . . . or he has not had the full amount of grain [which he received] deducted and did not write a new contract, or he has added the interest to the principal, that merchant shall pay back double the full amount of grain that he received.

94:   If a merchant lent grain or money at interest and when he lent (it) at interest he paid out the money by the small weight and the grain by the small measure, but when he got (it) back he got the money by the [large] weight (and) the grain by the large measure, [that merchant shall forfeit] whatever he lent.

99:   If a merchant lent money at interest to a trader for the purpose of trading [and making purchases] and sent him out on the road, the trader shall . . . on the road [the money which was entrusted] to him.

---

[6]These are standard weights of measures and of silver.—ED.

100: If he has realized a profit where he went, he shall write down the interest on the full amount of money that he borrowed and they shall count up the days against him and he shall repay his merchant.

101: If he has not realized a profit where he went, the trader shall repay to the merchant double the money that he borrowed.

102: If a merchant has lent money to a trader as a favor and he has experienced a loss where he went, he shall pay back the principal of the money to the merchant.

103: If, when he went on the road, an enemy has made him give up whatever he was carrying, the trader shall (so) affirm by god and then he shall go free.

104: If a merchant lent grain, wool, oil, or any goods at all to a trader to retail, the trader shall write down the value and pay (it) back to the merchant, with the trader obtaining a sealed receipt for the money which he pays to the merchant. . . .

108: If a woman wine seller, instead of receiving grain for the price of a drink, has received money by the large weight and so has made the value of the drink less than the value of the grain, they shall prove it against that wine seller and throw her into the water.

109: If outlaws have congregated in the establishment of a woman wine seller and she has not arrested those outlaws and did not take them to the palace, that wine seller shall be put to death. . . .

128: If a seignior acquired a wife, but did not draw up the contracts for her, that woman is no wife.

129: If the wife of a seignior has been caught while lying with another man, they shall bind them and throw them into the water. If the husband of the woman wishes to spare his wife, then the king in turn may spare his subject.

130: If a seignior bound the (betrothed) wife of a(nother) seignior, who had had no intercourse with a male and was still living in her father's house, and he has lain in her bosom and they have caught him, that seignior shall be put to death, while that woman shall go free.

131: If a seignior's wife was accused by her husband, but she was not caught while lying with another man, she shall make affirmation by god and return to her house.

132: If the finger was pointed at the wife of a seignior because of another man, but she has not been caught while lying with the other man, she shall throw herself into the river for the sake of her husband.

133: If a seignior was taken captive, but there was sufficient to live on in his house, his wife [shall not leave her house, but she shall take care of her person by not] entering [the house of another].

133a: If that woman did not take care of her person, but has entered the house of another, they shall prove it against that woman and throw her into the water.

134: If the seignior was taken captive and there was not sufficient to live on in his house, his wife may enter the house of another, with that woman incurring no blame at all.

135: If, when a seignior was taken captive and there was not sufficient to live on in his house, his wife has then entered the house of another before his (return) and has borne children, (and) later her husband has returned and has reached his city, that woman shall return to her first husband, while the children shall go with their father.

136: If, when a seignior deserted his city and then ran away, his wife has entered the house of another after his (departure), if that seignior has returned and wishes to take back his wife, the wife of the fugitive shall not return to her husband because he scorned his city and ran away. . . .

138: If a seignior wishes to divorce his wife who did not bear him children, he shall give her money to the full amount of her marriage-price and he shall also make good to her the dowry which she brought from her father's house and then he may divorce her. . . .

142: If a woman so hated her husband that she has declared, "You may not have me," her record shall be investigated at her city council, and if she was careful and was not at fault, even though her husband has been going out and disparaging her greatly, that woman, without incurring any blame at all, may take her dowry and go off to her father's house. . . .

168: If a seignior, having made up his mind to disinherit his son, has said to the judges, "I wish to disinherit my son," the judges shall investigate his record, and if the son did not incur wrong grave (enough) to be disinherited, the father may not disinherit his son.

169: If he has incurred wrong against his father grave (enough) to be disinherited, they shall let him off the first time; if he has incurred grave wrong a second time, the father may disinherit his son. . . .

196: If a seignior has destroyed the eye of a member of the aristocracy, they shall destroy his eye.

197: If he has broken a(nother) seignior's bone, they shall break his bone.

198: If he has destroyed the eye of a commoner or broken the bone of a commoner, he shall pay one mina of silver.

199: If he has destroyed the eye of a seignior's slave or broken the bone of a seignior's slave, he shall pay one-half his value.

200: If a seignior has knocked out a tooth of a seignior of his own rank, they shall knock out his tooth.

201: If he has knocked out a commoner's tooth, he shall pay one-third mina of silver.

202: If a seignior has struck the cheek of a seignior who is superior to him, he shall be beaten sixty (times) with an oxtail whip in the assembly.

203:   If a member of the aristocracy has struck the cheek of a(nother) member of the aristocracy who is of the same rank as himself, he shall pay one mina of silver.

204:   If a commoner has struck the cheek of a(nother) commoner, he shall pay ten shekels of silver.

205:   If a seignor's slave has struck the cheek of a member of the aristocracy, they shall cut off his ear. . . .

218:   If a physician performed a major operation on a seignior with a bronze lancet and has caused the seignior's death, or he opened up the eye-socket of a seignior and has destroyed the seignior's eye, they shall cut off his hand.

219:   If a physician performed a major operation on a commoner's slave with a bronze lancet and has caused (his) death, he shall make good slave for slave.

220:   If he opened up his eye-socket with a bronze lancet and has destroyed his eye, he shall pay one-half his value in silver.

221:   If a physician has set a seignior's broken bone, or has healed a sprained tendon, the patient shall give five shekels of silver to the physician. . . .

228:   If a builder constructed a house for a seignior and finished (it) for him, he shall give him two shekels of silver per *sar*[7] of house as his remuneration.

229:   If a builder constructed a house for a seignior, but did not make his work strong, with the result that the house which he built collapsed and so has caused the death of the owner of the house, that builder shall be put to death.

230:   If it has caused the death of a son of the owner of the house, they shall put the son of that builder to death.

231:   If it has caused the death of a slave of the owner of the house, he shall give slave for slave to the owner of the house.

232:   If it has destroyed goods, he shall make good whatever it destroyed; also, because he did not make the house strong which he built and it collapsed, he shall reconstruct the house which collapsed at his own expense.

233:   If a builder constructed a house for a seignior and has not done his work properly so that a wall has become unsafe, that builder shall strengthen that wall at his own expense.

234:   If a boatman calked a boat of sixty *kur* for a seignior, he shall give him two shekels of silver as his remuneration.

---

[7]A unit of square measurement.—Ed.

235:   If a boatman calked a boat for a seignior and did not do his work well with the result that that boat has sprung a leak in that very year, since it has developed a defect, the boatman shall dismantle that boat and strengthen (it) at his own expense and give the strengthened boat back to the owner of the boat.

236:   If a seignior let his boat for hire to a boatman and the boatman was so careless that he has sunk or wrecked the boat, the boatman shall make good the boat to the owner of the boat.

237:   When a seignior hired a boatman and a boat and loaded it with grain, wool, oil, dates, or any kind of freight, if that boatman was so careless that he has sunk the boat and lost what was in it as well, the boatman shall make good the boat which he sank and whatever he lost that was in it.

238:   If a boatman sank the boat of a seignior and has then refloated it, he shall give one-half its value in silver. . . .

244:   If a seignior hired an ox or an ass and a lion has killed it in the open, (the loss) shall be its owner's.

245:   If a seignior hired an ox and has caused its death through carelessness or through beating, he shall make good ox for ox to the owner of the ox.

246:   If a seignior hired an ox and has broken its foot or has cut its neck tendon, he shall make good ox for ox to the owner of the ox.

247:   If a seignior hired an ox and has destroyed its eye, he shall give one-half its value in silver to the owner of the ox.

248:   If a seignior hired an ox and has broken its horn, cut off its tail, or injured the flesh of its back, he shall give one-quarter its value in silver.

249:   If a seignior hired an ox and god struck it and it has died, the seignior who hired the ox shall (so) affirm by god and then he shall go free. . . .

274:   If a seignior wishes to hire an artisan, he shall pay per day as the wage of a . . . five [*še*] of silver; as the wage of a *brickmaker* five *še* of silver; [as the wage of] a *linen-weaver* . . . [*še*] of silver; [as the wage] of a *seal-cutter* . . . [*še*] of silver; [as the wage of] a *jeweller* . . . [*še* of] silver; [as the wage of] a *smith* . . . [*še* of] silver; [as the wage of] a carpenter four *še* of silver; as the wage of a leatherworker . . . *še* of silver; as the wage of a basketmaker . . . *še* of silver; [as the wage of] a builder . . . *še* of silver.

The Epilogue

The laws of justice, which Hammurabi, the efficient king, set up, and by which he caused the land to take the right way and have good government.

I, Hammurabi, the perfect king,
was not careless (or) neglectful of the black-headed (people),
whom Enlil had presented to me,
(and) whose shepherding Marduk had committed to me;
I sought out peaceful regions for them;
I overcame grievous difficulties;
I caused light to rise on them.
With the mighty weapon which Zababa and Inanna entrusted to
     me,
with the insight that Enki[8] allotted to me,
with the ability that Marduk gave me,
I rooted out the enemy above and below;
I made an end of war;
I promoted the welfare of the land;
I made the peoples rest in friendly habitations;
I did not let them have anyone to terrorize them.
The great gods called me,
so I became the beneficent shepherd whose scepter is righteous;
my benign shadow is spread over my city.
In my bosom I carried the peoples of the land of Sumer and
     Akkad;
they prospered under my protection;
I always governed them in peace;
I sheltered them in my wisdom.
In order that the strong might not oppress the weak,
that justice might be dealt the orphan (and) the widow,
in Babylon, the city whose head Anum and Enlil raised aloft,
in Esagila,[9] the temple whose foundations stand firm like heaven
     and earth,
I wrote my precious words on my stela,[10]
and in the presence of the statue of me, the king of justice,
I set (it) up in order to administer the law of the land,
to prescribe the ordinances of the land,
to give justice to the oppressed.

I am the king who is preeminent among kings;
my words are choice; my ability has no equal.
By the order of Shamash, the great judge of heaven and earth,
may my justice prevail in the land;

---

[8]Three more Babylonian gods.—Ed.

[9]Another term for the temple of Marduk in Babylon.—Ed.

[10]A stone slab or pillar inscribed for commemorative purposes.—Ed.

by the word of Marduk, my lord,
my statutes have no one to rescind them; . . .

Let any oppressed man who has a cause
come into the presence of the statue of me, the king of justice,
and then read carefully my inscribed stela,
and give heed to my precious words,
and may my stela make the case clear to him;
may he understand his cause;
may he set his mind at ease!
"Hammurabi, the lord,
who is like a real father to the people,
bestirred himself for the word of Marduk, his lord,
and secured the triumph of Marduk above and below,
thus making glad the heart of Marduk, his lord,
and he also ensured prosperity for the people forever,
and led the land aright"—
let him proclaim this,
and let him pray with his whole heart for me
in the presence of Marduk, my lord. . . .

In the days to come, for all time,
let the king who appears in the land observe
the words of justice which I wrote on my stela;
let him not alter the law of the land which I enacted,
the ordinances of the land which I prescribed;
let him not rescind my statutes!
If that man has intelligence
and is able to guide his land aright,
let him heed the words which I wrote on my stela,
and may this stela show him the road (and) the way,
the law of the land which I enacted,
the ordinances of the land which I prescribed;
and let him guide aright his black-headed (people)!
Let him enact the law for them;
let him prescribe the ordinances for them!
Let him root out the wicked and the evil from his land;
let him promote the welfare of his people!

I, Hammurabi, am the king of justice,
to whom Shamash committed law.
My words are choice; my deeds have no equal;
it is only to the fool that they are empty;

to the wise they stand forth as an object of wonder.
If that man heeded my words which I wrote on my stela,
and did not rescind my law,
has not distorted my words,
did not alter my statutes,
may Shamash make that man reign
as long as I, the king of justice;
may he shepherd his people in justice!

If that man did not heed my words which I wrote on my stela,
and disregarded my curses,
and did not fear the curses of the gods,
but has abolished the law which I enacted,
has distorted my words,
has altered my statutes,
effaced my name inscribed (thereon),
and has written his own name,
(or) he has commissioned another (to do so) because of these
     curses—
as for that man, whether king or lord,
or governor or person of any rank,
may mighty Anum, the father of the gods, who proclaimed my
     reign,
deprive him of the glory of sovereignty,
may he break his scepter, may he curse his fate!
May Enlil, the lord, the determiner of destinies,
whose orders cannot be altered,
who made my kingdom great,
incite revolts against him in his abode which cannot be
     suppressed,
misfortune leading to his ruin!
May he determine as the fate for him a reign of woe,
days few in number, years of famine,
darkness without light, sudden death!
May he order by his forceful word the destruction of his city,
the dispersion of his people, the transfer of his kingdom,
the disappearance of his name and memory from the land!

The Age of Hammurabi

JAMES H. BREASTED

It was only in the 1840s that Near Eastern archaeology began, following by a generation or so the birth of Egyptology. The French scholar Paul Emile Botta began to excavate the ruins of Nineveh in 1841. The English archaeologist Austen Henry Layard began his excavations at Nimrud in 1845. And the German Robert Koldewey began work at Babylon only in 1898. The cuneiform writing system and the several ancient languages that used it began to be reliably deciphered in the late 1850s. Each new discovery was greeted enthusiastically by a growing community of scholars in the new science of archaeology as well as by biblical scholars, ancient historians, the press, and the public. Among the finds of early Near Eastern archaeology were many contracts and other obviously legal documents, even fragments of what were clearly law codes. Then in the winter of 1901–1902, the French archaeologist Jacques de Morgan, excavating at Susa in Iran, unearthed a black basalt stela nearly eight feet tall containing the Code of Hammurabi, carved in more than thirty-six hundred lines of cuneiform script around the column below a relief carving of the king receiving the laws from Shamash, the sun god and god of justice. It had been carried off by some later conqueror of Hammurabi's Babylon, probably the Elamite king Shutruk-Nahhunte, about 1200 B.C. and reerected in the Elamite capital of Susa. The Elamite king had apparently not been bothered by the solemn curses on the stela against those who would efface "my name inscribed [thereon] and has written his own name." Hammurabi's name was indeed effaced, but the name of the effacer was never substituted: there is only a blank space.

The stela was taken to the Louvre in Paris, where it remains. It was exhaustively studied by Assyriologists, translated, edited, and publicized. One of the publicists was the American Egyptologist James H. Breasted. Breasted was a popularizer not only of Egyptian but of Near Eastern scholarship as well. He was interested in constructing a convincing picture of all preclassic antiquity. His *The Conquest of Civilization*, from which the following selection is taken, reflects his enthusiasm for the Ancient Near East, and the selection is a statement of the scholarly consensus about Hammurabi, his age, and his code in the mid-1920s.

As the "Kings of Sumer and Akkad" slowly weakened, a new tribe of Semites began descending the Euphrates, just as the men of Akkad had done under Sargon. These newcomers were the Semitic Amorites of Syria by the Mediterranean. About a generation after 2200 B.C. this new tribe of western Semites seized the little town of Babylon, which was at that time still an obscure village on the Euphrates. The Amorite kings of Babylon at once began to fight their way toward the leadership of Sumer and Akkad.

After a century of such warfare there came to the throne as the sixth in the Amorite line of kings at Babylon one Hammurabi, 2067–2025 B.C.[11] In the now feeble old Sumerian cities of the South, Hammurabi found the warlike Elamites, who had come in from Elam in the eastern mountains. They fought him for over thirty years before he succeeded in driving them out and capturing the Sumerian towns. Victorious at last, Hammurabi then made his city of Babylon for the first time supreme throughout the land. It was therefore not until the 21st century B.C. that Babylon finally gained such a position of power and influence that we may call the land "Babylonia."

Hammurabi survived his triumph twelve years, and in those years of peace, as he had done in war, he proved himself the ablest of his line. He was the second great Semitic ruler, as Sargon had been the first. Only a few generations earlier his ancestors, like those of Sargon, had been drifting about the desert, without any organization. He still betrayed in his shaven upper lip, a desert custom, the evidence of his desert ancestry. But he now put forth his powerful hand upon the teeming life of the Babylonian towns, and with a touch he brought in order and system such as Babylonia had never seen before. Two chief sources of information have survived over four thousand years to reveal to us the deeds and the character of this great king: these are a group of his letters, and the splendid monument bearing his laws.

Hammurabi's letters afford us for the first time in history a glimpse into the busy life of a powerful oriental ruler in Asia. They disclose him to us sitting in the executive office of his palace at Babylon with his secretary at his side. In short, clear sentences the king begins dictating his brief letters, conveying his commands to the local governors of the old Sumerian cities which he now rules. The secretary draws a reed stylus from a leathern holder at his girdle, and quickly

---

[11]These dates are now considered much too early. But there are still difficulties with Near Eastern chronology, and three sets of dates are possible. A high chronology produces the dates 1848–1806, a middle chronology gives 1792–1750, and a low chronology gives 1728–1686. They are based on comparisons with contemporary events among other neighboring peoples, such as the Assyrians, and upon astronomical data. Most scholars prefer the middle chronology.—ED.

covers the small clay tablet with its lines of wedge groups. The writer then sprinkles over the soft wet tablet a handful of dry powdered clay. This is to prevent the clay envelope, which he now deftly wraps about the letter, from adhering to the written surface. On this soft clay envelope he writes the address and sends the letter out to be put into the furnace and baked.

Messengers constantly hand him similarly closed letters. This secretary of Hammurabi is a trusted confidential clerk. He therefore breaks to pieces the hard clay envelopes in the king's presence and reads aloud to him letters from his officials all over the kingdom. The king quickly dictates his replies. The flood has obstructed the Euphrates between Ur and Larsa, and of course a long string of boats have been tied up and are waiting. The king's reply orders the governor of Larsa to clear the channel at the earliest moment and make it navigable again.

The king is much interested in his vast flocks of sheep, as if the nomad instinct had not altogether vanished from the blood of his line. He orders the officials to appear in Babylon to celebrate the spring sheep-shearing as if it were a great feast. . . . Delinquent tax gatherers are firmly reminded of their obligations and called upon to settle without delay. Prompt punishment of an official guilty of bribery is authorized, and we can see the king's face darken as he dictates the order for the arrest of three officials of the palace gate who have fallen under his displeasure. More than once the governor of Larsa is sharply reminded of the king's orders and bidden to see that they are carried out at once.

Many a petitioner who has not been able to secure justice before the board of judges in his home city is led in before the king, confident of just treatment; and he is not disappointed. The chief of the temple bakers finds that royal orders to look after a religious feast at Ur will call him away from the capital city just at the time when he has an important lawsuit coming on. He easily obtains an order from the king postponing the lawsuit. The king's interest in the religious feast is here as much concerned as his sense of justice, for many of the letters which he dictates have to do with temple property and temple administration, in which he constantly shows his interest.

With his eye upon every corner of the land, alert, vigorous, and full of decision, the great king finally saw how necessary it was to bring into uniformity all the various and sometimes conflicting laws and business customs of the land. He therefore collected all the older written laws and usages of business and social life, and arranged them systematically. He improved them or added new laws where his own judgment deemed wise, and he then combined them into a great code or body of laws. It was written, not in Sumerian, as some of the old laws were, but in the Semitic speech of the Akkadians and Amorites. He then had it engraved upon a splendid shaft of stone. At the top was a sculptured scene in which the king was shown receiving the law from the Sun-god. The new code was then set up in the temple of the great god Marduk in Babylon. This shaft has survived to our day, the oldest preserved code of ancient law. Fragments of other copies on clay tablets, the copies used by the local courts, have also been found.

Hammurabi's code insists on justice to the widow, the orphan, and the poor; but it also allows many of the old and naïve ideas of justice to stand. Especially prominent is the principle that the punishment for an injury should require the infliction of the same injury on the culprit—the principle of "an eye for an eye, a tooth for a tooth." Injustice often resulted. For example, when a house fell and killed the son of the householder, the guilty builder must also suffer the loss of *his* son, and the innocent son was therefore condemned to die. Marriage was already a relation requiring legal agreements between the man and his wife, and these are carefully regulated in Hammurabi's code. Indeed the position of women in this early Babylonian world, as in Egypt, was a high one. Women engaged in business on their own account, and even became professional scribes. . . .

Thus regulated, the busy Babylonian communities prospered as never before.

A Modern Hammurabi

SABATINO MOSCATI

The processes of scholarship continue, in Near Eastern studies as in every other discipline. New materials come to light, older documents are reinterpreted, former conclusions are revised. The following selection, taken from Sabatino Moscati's *The Face of the Ancient Orient, A Panorama of Near Eastern Civilizations in Pre-Classical Times,* represents the view of Hammurabi and his code in this generation as the selection from Breasted represents the view of a past generation. Assyriologist and one-time director of the Center of Semitic Studies, the University of Rome, Moscati provides the best modern introduction to the ancient Near East, reflecting his substantial scholarship, up-to-date research, and judicious conclusions.

The student should take note of a few important points of difference with Breasted. For example, other earlier law codes have now been discovered, such as the Lipit-Ishtar Code, predating Hammurabi by more than a century and a half, or the Laws of Eshnunna, predating him by some two and a half centuries. These findings tend to diminish the originality of Hammurabi's code if not its importance and to link the Babylonians more closely to the earlier Sumerians in legal matters as in so many other areas of culture. The ordeal by water, for instance, is a Sumerian survival. But there are Babylonian innovations. Hammurabi's code reflects a more complex society and such practices as the marriage contract and legalized polygamy, unknown to the Sumerians. And on the darker side, the principle of retaliation or punishment in kind is a new Semitic principle of the penal law, not an "old and naive idea," as Breasted thought.

As we now know, this code is not the only, nor the oldest one in Mesopotamia, and we can no longer count on its originality; but it still remains the most complete and organic synthesis of law that we possess, and therefore it most fully documents its epoch and environment.

In its literary form, the Code follows the scheme of Sumerian times: prologue, laws, epilogue. The laws still have that analytic, piecemeal quality characteristic of the Sumerians; we find enunciated not general principles, but individual cases with their appropriate solutions. But considerable differences are to be noted in the content of the laws. Those relating to persons reveal a society divided into three classes, which approximate to the conceptions embodied in the modern terms: patricians, plebeians, and slaves.[12] Patricians and slaves correspond to the two classes already found among the Sumerians, but the concept of plebeians is new, in that the distinctive feature of their state is no longer dependence upon the palace, as in the case of the "partly free" Sumerians, but a different legal status:

> If a patrician put out another's eye, his eye shall be put out. If he break another's bone, his bone shall be broken. If he put out the eye or break the bone of a plebeian, he shall pay a mina of silver.

The law relating to the family treats the father as its head. Marriage is preceded by a betrothal gift from the bridegroom to the

---

[12]These are the same terms that are rendered in the text of the code by the terms *seigniors, commoners,* and *slaves.* There are also minor differences in the rendering of the quoted passages below.—ED.

bride, the so-called "acquisition price," something of which there is no evidence in Sumerian law. A further innovation, or, at least, something that cannot be traced back to Sumerian times, is the written contract:

> If a patrician has taken a wife, but has not made a contract with her, that woman is not his wife.

Polygamy is permitted, whereas Sumerian marriage was monogamic. Divorce is granted for an adequate reason. For example:

> If a patrician has been taken prisoner and there is not sufficient in his house to live on, his wife may enter the house of another; that woman shall incur no blame at all.

The law of inheritance is based on legitimate succession. The inheritance is divided between the male heirs, and daughters have no rights except when there are no sons; but they do have the right to share in usufruct, and to a dowry. Wills are not made, but their place is often taken by contracts of adoption.

Property rights are highly developed and organized, as one would expect in an evolved sedentary society. There are deeds of sale and purchase, hire and lease, commercial partnerships, loans on interest, and so on.

The penal law is dominated, so far as patricians are concerned, by the law of retaliation. We have already noted the application of this law: an eye for an eye, a tooth for a tooth; and we have observed that the most recent discoveries lead us to regard this law as of Semitic introduction; at any rate, it is unknown to the more ancient Sumerian legal provisions, which explicitly stipulate the payment of damages. An interesting feature of the Hammurabi Code is the punishment inflicted on medical practitioners for any ill consequences arising from their operations:

> If a surgeon has operated on a patrician with a bronze knife, and has killed him . . . his hands shall be cut off.

The penalty prescribed for negligence in an architect is more in line with our own legal conception:

> If a builder has constructed a house for anyone and has not made his work solid, so that a wall has fallen down, that builder shall repair the wall at his own cost.

Judicial proceedings take place before judges, to whom the litigants apply when they cannot reach a private solution of their dispute. Thus the law is subjective, not objective: if there is no private plaintiff there is no trial. During the hearing, both documentary and oral evidence are admissible. In the absence of evidence, recourse is made to trial by ordeal, the river test, already known to the Sumerians: the accused plunges into the water; if he survives, he is acquitted; if he succumbs, he is adjudged guilty:

> If a patrician accuses another of sorcery, but has no proofs, the accused man shall go to the river and plunge into it. If the river bears him away, the accuser shall take possession of his house. If the river shows him to be innocent and he comes forth safe, the accuser shall be slain, and the other shall take his house.

The Hammurabi Code is only a stage in the juridical tradition of Mesopotamia, but it is a particularly significant one. In the Babylonia of the great kings, under the aegis of a prosperous and powerful state, literature, art, and economic and social organization flourish as never before; and, as never before, the Sumerian heritage and the Semitic contribution achieve a harmonious synthesis. For this reason, the times of Hammurabi constitute the acme of Babylonian and Assyrian civilization; and the great king, warrior and diplomat, builder of temples and digger of canals, personifies this civilization better than any other.

Review and Study Questions

1. What sort of society do you see reflected in the Code of Hammurabi?
2. What does the code reveal about interpersonal relations among the Amorites?
3. What is the status of women in this society?
4. Does the code tell us anything about the character and personality of Hammurabi himself? Discuss.

Suggestions for Further Reading

There are two definitive English translations of the Code of Hammurabi and other Near Eastern codes, the one excerpted for this chapter from *Ancient Near Eastern Texts Relating to the Old Testament*, tr. Theophile J. Meek, ed. James B. Pritchard, 3rd ed. with supplement (Princeton: Princeton University Press, 1969), and *The Babylonian Laws*, ed. with translation and commentary by G. R. Driver and John C. Miles, 2 vols. (Oxford: Clarendon Press, 1952), the first volume the legal commentary, the second the texts. An interesting collection of ancient Near Eastern letters is *Letters from Mesopotamia: Official, Business, and Private Letters on Clay Tablets from Two Millennia,* tr. with an introduction by A. Leo Oppenheim (Chicago and London: University of Chicago Press, 1967). The continuity of Sumerian influence is illustrated in Samuel Noar Kramer, *History Begins at Sumer* (New York: Doubleday, 1959).

Most of the serious works on the ancient Near East are written by or reflect the emphasis of either archaeologists or linguistic scholars, called Assyriologists. Among the former are recommended two comprehensive surveys: Jack Finegan, *Archaeological History of the Ancient Near East* (Boulder, Colorado, and Folkstone, England: Westview Press and Dawson, 1979), and Seton Lloyd, *The Archaeology of Mesopotamia, From the Old Stone Age to the Persian Conquest* (London: Thames and Hudson, 1978). Also recommended are M. E. L. Mallowan, *Early Mesopotamia and Iran* (New York: McGraw-Hill, 1965), in which the distinguished field archaeologist deals largely with the earlier, especially Sumerian subculture of Mesopotamia, and a brilliant and readable synoptic work by Jacquetta Hawkes, *The First Great Civilizations, Life in Mesopotamia, the Indus Valley, and Egypt* (New York: Knopf, 1973). Probably the best general work on Mesopotamia is by the great Assyriologist A. Leo Oppenheim, *Ancient Mesopotamia, Portrait of a Dead Civilization,* rev. ed. completed by Erica Reiner (Chicago and London: University of Chicago Press, 1977). Also recommended is H. W. F. Saggs, *The Greatness That Was Babylon: A Survey of the Ancient Civilization of the Tigris-Euphrates Valley* (New York and Washington: Praeger, 1969). Saggs' *Civilization before Greece and Rome* (New Haven: Yale University Press, 1989) is a masterful work of synthesis and updating.

Thorkild Jacobsen, *The Treasures of Darkness: A History of Mesopotamian Religion* (New Haven: Yale University Press, 1976) is a thorough and sensitive treatment of its subject by a renowned ancient Near Eastern scholar. Robert McCormick Adams, *Heartland of Cities, Surveys of Ancient Settlement and Land Use on the Central Floodplain of the Euphrates* (Chicago and London: University of Chicago Press, 1981) is a learned treatment of the pattern of irrigation that underlies the land use of Hammurabi's Amorite Empire and other earlier and later states of Mesopotamia. In Joan Oates, *Babylon* (London: Thames and Hudson, 1979) the author emphasizes the culture of Hammurabi's city and empire.

Finally, there are two more general interpretive works: James Wellard, *Babylon* (New York: Saturday Review Press, 1972), also published in England under the title *By the Waters of Babylon* (London: Hutchinson, 1972), a readable and exciting survey by an able popularizer; and Henri Frankfort et al., *The Intellectual Adventure of Ancient*

Man, An Essay on Speculative Thought in the Ancient Near East (Chicago and London: University of Chicago Press, 1946), a profound and stimulating work of interpretation. See also the chapter by C. J. Gadd, Chapter V, "Hammurabi and the End of his Dynasty" in *The Cambridge Ancient History*, 3rd ed., Vol II, Part I (Cambridge: Cambridge University Press, 1973).

SAPPHO:
THE DIVINE LYRE

c. 612 B.C.	Born
c. 600–592 B.C.	Exile in Sicily
c. 557 B.C.	Died

The Greek society of the Archaic Age, the period between the end of the Bronze Age and the Persian Wars of the early fifth century B.C., was a rich and widespread society, bursting with creative energy. It was a society and a world dominated everywhere by a warrior aristocracy. In the fleeting moments of peace, these soldier aristocrats enjoyed a luxurious social life of which a central feature was the *symposium*—an informal gathering for eating, drinking, and entertainment. A principal part of the entertainment was a poetic competition in which successive performers vied with each other in composing and singing spontaneous verses that celebrated their warlike deeds, the offices they held or aspired to, the elements of their moral code, or the simple pleasures of food, wine, and sex.

This competition in art, as in war, "always to be best and preeminent over others"[1] was the beginning of Greek lyric poetry. We know the names and have some of the verses of a dozen or so of these warrior poets. Yet the best and most famous of the lyric poets was not a man at all, but Sappho: Plato called her the tenth muse.[2]

What we know about her life is little enough and is derived almost

---

[1] *Iliad* 6.208.

[2] *Ant. Palatina* 9.506.

entirely from the fragments of her own poetry. Of the some five hundred poems she wrote, only one complete poem remains. The rest we have only in bits and pieces, scattered shards of verse, or in admiring excerpts from later ancient writers. Sappho was born on the north Aegean island of Lesbos, only a few miles off the coast of the great Asiatic Kingdom of Lydia, probably in Mitylene, the principal town of the island. She almost surely belonged to the aristocracy. Her father's name, Skamandronymos, suggests the river Skamander on the plains of Troy and some ancestor who could claim kinship with the Homeric heroes who fought there. One of her brothers held the noble office of wine steward in the town hall of Mitylene. She herself moved easily in the circle of the aristocracy and was accepted by its members, like her fellow poet Alcaeus. Even the fact that her family suffered a period of exile in Sicily during her childhood may reflect the social prominence of the family, because this was a common punishment against powerful or politically dangerous nobles.

She returned from exile to Lesbos, the standing of her family unaffected by the exile, and resumed her place in Lesbian society. She was shortly married, and married well, to a wealthy merchant, Cercylas of the island of Andros. He apparently died soon after the birth of their daughter, of whom Sappho wrote:

> I have a beautiful child,
>   her form like golden flowers,
> beloved Kleis whom I would not trade for all of Lydia . . .[3]

By tradition, Sappho was a small, dark, and somewhat plain woman, although that tradition is of late Roman origin. On the contrary, her contemporary and friend Alcaeus called her "violet-decked, virtuous, honey-sweet smiling Sappho."[4] The story of her death by suicide for unrequited love is clearly apocryphal.

We know almost nothing else about her, except that she was the first figure in Western literature to praise female homosexual love in her poetry and to practice it in her life.[5]

---

[3]*Sappho's Lyre: Archaic Lyric and Women Poets of Ancient Greece,* tr. and ed. Diane J. Rayor (Berkeley and Los Angeles: University of California Press, 1991), p. 72.

[4]*Poetarum Lesbiorum Fragmenta,* ed. Edgar Lobel and Denys Page (Oxford: Clarendon Press, 1963), p. 261.

[5]The universality of this interpretive view is expressed by Joan DeJean in *Fictions of Sappho, 1546–1937* (Chicago: University of Chicago Press, 1989), p. 306: "The vision most Hellenists today seem to take for granted [is] that of a homosexual Sappho."

The Poet of Lesbian Love

A number of themes run through Sappho's poems, but the clearly predominant theme is that of female homoeroticism. This might not have been the case had a larger corpus of her work survived. She may have written more solemn choral odes or even heroic poems but, if she did, there is no trace of them. What has survived is a body of highly personal love poetry.

The context in which these poems were written was that of a *thiasos*, or religious guild or confraternity of women of which Sappho was the leader, that operated also as a kind of "school." The purpose of her school—and apparently of others, for Mitylene was famous for them—was to prepare aristocratic young girls for marriage, to cultivate their femininity, and literally to increase their value to their fathers, who could then boast to fathers of marriageable sons about their daughters' accomplishments. Sappho taught them proper deportment, style, and fashion, how to dress and bear themselves. After all, most of them were little more than children in their early teens. And, of course, she taught them to play the lyre, the cithara, the barbitos, and the pipe, and to sing and make songs—songs for the wedding eve, for the wedding night, for the convoy of the bride and groom to their couch. She probably also taught them the practices appropriate to a variety of women's cults sacred to Aphrodite or Hera. Sappho loved her students, openly and passionately, and her poems celebrate the twists and turns of that love—her appeal to Aphrodite to soften the heart of a reluctant lover, her lament over another lover who has left her, her jealousy over yet another who has chosen a different mistress, or her simple adoration of their young, unspoiled beauty.

1

On the throne of many hues, Immortal Aphrodite,
child of Zeus, weaving wiles—I beg you
not to subdue my spirit, Queen,
with pain or sorrow

but come—if ever before
having heard my voice from far away
you listened, and leaving your father's
golden home you came

in your chariot yoked with swift, lovely
sparrows bringing you over the dark earth
thick-feathered wings swirling down
from the sky through mid-air

arriving quickly—you, Blessed One,
with a smile on your unaging face
asking again what have I suffered
and why am I calling again

4

Some say an army of horsemen, others
say foot-soldiers, still others, a fleet,
is the fairest thing on the dark earth:
I say it is whatever one loves.

Everyone can understand this—
consider that Helen, far surpassing
the beauty of mortals, leaving behind
the best man of all,

sailed away to Troy. She had no
memory of her child or dear parents,
since she was led astray
[by Kypris] . . .
. . . .
. . . lightly
. . . reminding me now of Anaktoria
being gone,

I would rather see her lovely step
and the radiant sparkle of her face
than all the war-chariots in Lydia
and soldiers battling in shining bronze.

8

To me it seems
that man has the fortune of gods,
whoever sits beside you, and close,

who listens to you sweetly speaking
and laughing temptingly;
my heart flutters in my breast,
whenever I look quickly, for a moment—

I say nothing, my tongue broken,
a delicate fire runs under my skin,
my eyes see nothing, my ears roar,
cold sweat rushes down me,
trembling seizes me,
I am greener than grass,
to myself I seem
needing but little to die.

But all must be endured, since . . .

14

"I simply wish to die."
Weeping she left me
and said this too:
"We've suffered terribly
Sappho I leave you against my will."
I answered, go happily
and remember me,
you know how we cared for you,
if not, let me remind you
. . . the lovely times we shared.

Many crowns of violets,
roses and crocuses
. . . together you set before me
and many scented wreaths
made from blossoms
around your soft throat . . .
　　. . . with pure, sweet oil
　　　. . . you anointed me,
and on a soft, gentle bed . . .
you quenched your desire . . .
　　　. . . no holy site . . .
we left uncovered,
no grove . . . dance
　　　　　. . . sound

34

What country woman bewitches your mind . . .
wrapped in country clothes . . .
not knowing how to draw her skirts around her ankles?

35

I loved you Atthis once long ago . . .
You seemed to me a small child and without charm.

36

Atthis, for you the thought of me has become hateful,
and you fly off to Andromeda.

37

. . . Mika
. . . but I will not allow you
. . . you chose the friendship of Penthilian women
. . . malignant, our . . .
. . . sweet song . . .
. . . soft voice . . .
. . . and high, clear-sounding . . .
. . . dewy . . .

Sappho in History

ARTHUR WEIGALL

Sappho expected her young lesbian lovers to marry and lead
ordinary heterosexual lives. Indeed, she herself, as we have
seen, was married and had a daughter she adored. This appears
not to have been unique with Sappho but to have been characteristic of the aristocratic society to which she belonged and in

which a sort of casual bisexualism was the norm of behavior for
both sexes.

In fact, this tended to be the case throughout Greek history but
was more marked in the Archaic Age. In this period, more than in
later ones, well-born young boys, as well as girls, were usually sent
from their homes to the tutelage of adults outside their families.
Here the young boys were trained in deportment and taught to
make poetry in *gymnasia,* not unlike the *thiasos* of Sappho for young
girls. They associated with their peers and their elders in the socializ-
ing and exercises of the *gymnasia* and the drills and common meals
of their warrior bands. Like the young girls, the young boys were
expected eventually to marry and establish homes. But, in the meantime, in both the *gymnasia* and the warrior bands, homosexuality
was commonly accepted. It has been suggested that, because aristocratic marriages were invariably matters of property and family alliance in which the betrothed couple had little or nothing to say, they
were marriages in which heterosexual attraction and romantic love
played almost no role. Certainly heterosexuality played little role in
the lyric poetry of the age, which celebrated homosexual love as
true love.

The following selection emphasizes the bisexual nature of Sappho's emotional life. It is from her 1930's biography, the standard
work on the subject, Arthur Weigall's *Sappho of Lesbos: Her Life and
Times.*

Her childhood was passed . . . at a time when all the young men of
Lesbos were away at the wars; and when they came rollicking back at
the conclusion of peace their rough manners seem to have offended
her fastidious taste, for she did not marry until, considerably later,
she met the wealthy and presumably elegant young merchant from
Andros. Even the cultured Alkaios evoked from her no response to
his passionate love: he was too violent in his sentiments, and he
drank too much—a habit which she evidently disliked, since she
never sings the usual praises of the vine in her verses. In her widowhood it was towards the youth of her own sex that her heart opened,
for here the extreme delicacy of her nature found a more congenial
atmosphere. It is true that her brief married life had been happy,
and that, as she says, her husband's role of lover had not been
unattractive to her; but it is evident enough that the virginal, feminine grace of a girl was nearer to her ideal than either the rough
masculinity or the foppish effeminacy of the average young man of
her time.

There is clear evidence that, in the abstract, the male character and form could arouse her emotions; but in actuality she seems to have feared or disliked the usual masculine temperament, and to have dreaded that physical mastery of man over woman from which . . . the feminine mind so often derives a certain instinctive pleasure. She was, as Athenæus says, a thorough woman, and her verses are essentially feminine; but this does not mean that therefore she was attracted by the thorough man. On the contrary, her nature, as I read it, was one which was repelled by those qualities usually dominant in the male; and though her physical being was normal to the extent that it demanded—if seldom with overwhelming insistence—its physical completion in the uniting of the sexes, it was abnormal in its almost habitual rejection of that very union because of a dislike of the mental attitude of the generality of men towards women. In a word, she shunned in actuality the male moved by male instinct, yet in thought shunned not the masculine as the physical completion of the feminine. . . .

In 560 B.C., when Solon was struggling in Athens against the new tyranny of his cousin Pisistratos, when at Sardis the old King Alyattes at last died and his son Crœsus became sole monarch of Lydia, Sappho was fifty-two years of age. Her black hair was touched with gray, and her face, in spite of the creams and perfumed oils which doubtless she used, was beginning to show those faint lines which are the dread of every woman's middle age. Yet her heart was young, and the fire within her passionate breast had not died down. She was bitterly conscious of her years, and the slow process of the departure of her charms was watched by her in her mirror with increasing despair. There was still left to her, however, her personal magnetism, her grace, her graciousness, her elegance, her wit, and her brains; and these qualities, together with her fame and her wealth, evidently retained for her her social leadership in Mitylene, and filled her house with her friends and admirers.

It must have been at this time that one of the men who frequented her society asked her to marry him; and it would seem that for a while she entertained the proposal with some interest, for, as I have pointed out, she was not averse to men, provided that they conformed to her exceptional requirements and approximated to her ideal. At length, however, she decided to reject the offer, for, being a woman of very clear sight, she knew that she could not much longer hold the physical love of a man, even though she might retain his admiration. She had no illusions about herself: she was growing old, and sorrowfully she realized the fact. She therefore wrote to this personage an answer in verse, part of which has been found in Egypt amongst the scraps of her published poems. It is the saddest of letters. It reads:

If my breasts were still capable of giving suck, and my womb were able to bear children, then to another marriage-bed not with trembling feet would I come; but now on my skin age is already causing innumerable lines to go about, and Love hastens not to fly to me with his gift of pain . . . of the illustrious . . . taking for your own . . . and sing to us of her of the violet-scented breast . . .

The last sentences seem to contain her advice to him to seek a wife amongst the noble young ladies of Mytilene, and thus to be able to come to Sappho and sing to her the praises of his bride.

Yet though she declares, in one of those exquisite phrases which characterize her work, that Love with his gift of pain is in no haste any longer to come to her, it seems that there was another man who at about this time made a proposal of marriage to her. He was evidently much younger than she; and it may well be that she had amused herself with him, not realizing that she was still capable of infatuating a young man by those brilliant qualities which sometimes in the case of famous women endure long after the summer of their life is past. Here is the surviving fragment of the verses she wrote to him: ". . . but if you love me, choose a more youthful companion of your bed, for I cannot endure to be married to a young man. I am too old."

Athenæus tells us that one of Sappho's poems was addressed to a man who was greatly admired for his good looks, and he quotes two lines from it, which read: "Stand up and look me in the face as friend to friend, and unveil the beauty that is in your eyes." These words seem to have been written to a youth who was shy of her, for they suggest a certain condescension on her part; and one imagines her, thus, greatly attracted by the handsome appearance of this young man with the beautiful eyes who, either because of his youth or his humble social standing, had bowed himself before so famous a lady. Perhaps it was this selfsame personage who, having been led on by her and allowed to become intimate with her, lost his head and asked her to marry him, thus evoking that sad cry from her: "I am too old." She could not, like the Moon-goddess, enchant him into an eternal sleep so that he might be her Endymion; she could not halt the process of her decline and be forever a part of his dreams: she knew that soon he would wake up and see her as she really was, a woman whose hair was turning gray, and this she could not endure.

Her age was a torment to her, but, knowing that her malady could not be cured, she faced the situation boldly. When her girls called her the fairest of women, the sweetest player upon the lyre, she wrote to them frankly telling them that to praise her now that her prime was past was to cast a slight upon the Muses. The fragments of a poem of hers to this effect have been found, but only the ends of the lines have survived, the beginnings having been torn away; yet even so we can get the sense of it by the aid of the words which I have placed in brackets, and which will serve to make the theme intelligible.

> [*You dishonor*] the good gifts [*of the Muses*], children, [*when you say*] . . . 'dear [*Sappho*], . . . player of the clear, sweet lyre' . . . [*for*] . . . my skin with age is [*lined, and turned is*] my hair from its blackness . . . nor do my legs speed about [*as formerly when we used to dance*] like the little fawns. But who can cure it? . . . It is not possible. [*As surely as night follows*] the rose-armed dawn, [*and darkness*] . . . speeds [*to the ends*] of the earth, [*Death*] overtakes [*us; and as Death would not restore*] the beloved wife [*of Orpheus to him, so every*] woman who dies he expects [*to keep prisoner, though he should*] let her follow [*her rescuer*]. . . .

Her occasional interest in men did not deflect her thoughts from her *hetæræ.* These girls still came to her from far and near, and her delight in them, if not as great as formerly, was still considerable. "Toward you, my beautiful ones, this mind of mine will not change," she wrote; and perhaps to this period of her life may be attributed the line: "To-day for my *hetæræ* these songs right well will I sing." She still was enthralled by the beauty of the young girls of Lesbos whom she met, or whom she saw as she took her daily walks in fields or woods; and thus she begins a poem: "I saw one day gathering flowers a very dainty little girl. . . ."

There is some reason to suppose that she had a serious illness at this time. . . .

It may be that, as a result of this serious illness, she was obliged to send her *hetæræ* away, for there is a scrap of a poem of hers which seems to have been written as a farewell to them. Again part of each of the surviving lines is lost, and a guess at the missing words (given here in brackets) has had to be made. The fragment reads:

> . . . [*To them*] I replied: "Gentle [*ladies*], you will ever remember [*till you are old*] our life together in [*the splendor*] of your youth. For [*many things*] both [*pure*] and beautiful we then did [*together*]. And now that [*you depart hence, love*] wrings [*my heart*]. . . ."

In the old days she had been torn by jealousy at the thought that a girl whom she loved should transfer her affections elsewhere; but now, that magnanimity which is middle age's great compensation, enabled her to contemplate such an eventuality without pain. Thus she could write to one of her *hetæræ:* "May you sleep in the bosom of a tender companion. . . ."

The word "companion" is the feminine *hetæra*, "girlfriend"; and it is characteristic of Sappho's outlook that though she might lose her heart from time to time to a male lover, she could wish to one of her own sex no greater happiness than that she might experience the tenderness of a feminine comradeship. . . .

She was tired, I dare say, of the presence of these girls in her house now that she was no longer young enough to be the absolute mistress of their emotional life. Her house had gradually become a sort of institute, almost an Academy for Young Ladies; for as her years increased there must have been a tendency in her *hetæræ*, her comrades, to become merely pupils and protégées. In the lines written when she was ill, she spoke of the unseemliness of mourning "in a house that serves the Muses," *en moisopolo oikia;* but *oikia* is not merely "a house"—it means a group of buildings, the word being sometimes used, in fact, to signify a palace or headquarters. Thus one pictures it now as a villa surrounded by guest-houses, work-rooms, and other out-buildings—a school, in fact, over which she presided; and it is not difficult to imagine her as becoming suddenly tired of her responsibilities, and as being overwhelmed by the desire to shake herself free of the whole thing. There were still left to her, she must have felt, a few years in which her heart's emotions would animate a body not yet wholly bereft of its attractions, there were still a few years left for love and for love's excitement; and it may have been in this spirit of adventure that she turned her no longer fettered attention to the search for that happiness which a creative artist always looks for, and seldom finds, outside his work. . . .

In 557 B.C., Sappho must have been fifty-five years old, and is to be pictured as a small, dark-skinned woman, upon whose face the signs of age were almost, but not quite, concealed by the perfection of her toilet, whose smile still retained its enchantment and whose eyes reflected the undying fires of her heart. Her figure, one may suppose, had preserved its shapeliness and grace by reason of the care she had always given it in her capacity as a dancer and as a model of deportment; and in her clothes and general turnout there was now, no doubt, as always, that daintiness and *chic* which was characteristic of her. . . .

Now in Mitylene at this time there happened to live a certain young sailor, Phaon by name, who was the master of a small sailing-ship which plied for hire between Lesbos and the mainland of Asia Minor. Suidas says that he was a very beautiful young man, and that many women were in love with him; and, indeed, Ælian tells us that in the end he was caught in adultery with another man's wife and was murdered. . . .

History does not tell us how Sappho made the acquaintance of this handsome young sailor; but one can imagine her finding reason to hire his ship, and, on some warm summer's night, under the stars or by the light of the moon, drawing him into conversation as she sat by his side at the helm. We know only that she fell in love with him to a degree almost of madness, and that, as Ovid said of her in words very probably taken from one of her own poems, she seemed to be burnt up by her passion for him as when a field of ripened corn is attacked by flames driven onwards by the wind. This was indeed the harvest-time of her life, and in the fires of love was consumed all that her years had brought to perfection. . . .

Only for a little while her dream lasted; and then her lover grew tired of her, or felt that he was unable to cope with her fever. . . . There was a ship in the harbor about to sail with merchandise for Sicily; and upon it Phaon secretly took his departure from Lesbos without bidding fare-well to Sappho. One can hardly blame him; and, in view of the peculiar circumstances of the case, he may well have believed that he was acting in her best interests in taking himself out of her life. . . .

At last, being unable to endure a life bereft of his presence, she made up her mind to follow him to Sicily. There was nothing here in Lesbos to keep her: her *hetæræ* were disbanded, she hated her brother, her daughter could not understand, her friends despised her. A lonely old age faced her; and even her Muse had forsaken her. She therefore boarded a vessel which, I suppose, was bound for Corinth; for there she would be able to find a ship which would carry her by the usual Corfu-route to southern Italy and thence to Sicily. She could have had no definite plans: her only purpose was to reach the land whither Phaon had gone, and there to search for him, and, having found him, to bring him once more into her arms.

Nothing is known of her journey by way of the islands of Chios and Andros to the eastern port of Corinth; but the misery and anxiety of it may be imagined. From the western port of Corinth she sailed on in another vessel, and so came at length to the southern end of the island of Leucas which lay just to the north of Ithaca and Cephallenia, and some fifty miles south of Corfu whence the crossing to Italy was to be made; and it was here in Leucas, at the famous Leucadian Cliff which rises sheer out of the sea in a narrow promontory like a monstrous wall of white stone, that her destiny was accomplished.

The ship had put in near this headland to obtain fresh water or provisions; and Sappho, it would seem, had walked up onto the grassy top of these white cliffs, perhaps to visit a little shrine of Apollo which stood there, and at which she might offer a prayer to that god who, as the patron of music, had always been revered by her. . . . Now . . . she stood before the shrine of Apollo, looking down the white precipices to the surging sea far below. At any rate, the idea of suicide suddenly entered her head, and took possession of her overwrought thoughts. . . .

She was seized with panic. In a frenzy of terror and despair, she made the quick decision to kill herself, and, running like a mad thing across the grass, she flung herself from the cliff's dizzy edge, and fell to her death in the blue waters far below.

A few fragmentary lines of a poem written by Alkaios have survived which, I think, may have reference to the death of Sappho whom once he had loved; for he appears to have outlived her, since in another verse he speaks of himself as a white-haired old man. These fragments read:

> . . . Misfortune . . . me, a woman miserable, me a sharer in all sorrows . . . house . . . unhappy destiny . . . disgrace . . . for the incurable decline of life is at hand. But panic springs up in the terror-stricken breast of the hart . . . madness . . . ruin . . . the cold sea-waves. . . .

Sappho's broken body was eventually recovered from the sea, and was cremated, her ashes being carried back to Mitylene for burial. . . .

Sappho as Poet and Woman

JANE McINTOSH SNYDER

Much of the contemporary revisionist scholarship on Sappho and her age has come out of the women's movement, which tends to see her as a champion of women's rights in a society that granted few rights to women. And antifeminism was, indeed, a major current of Greek social history. In the otherwise enlightened golden age of Greek culture in fifth-century Athens, for example, women were kept in virtually haremlike seclusion; had almost no standing in the courts, even with regard to their own property; and (at least respectable women) were barred from participation in most of the cultural activities of this most cultured of cities.

It has been argued that this generally inferior status of women had been less oppressive in the Archaic Age, at the courts and in the entertainments of Archaic society. It is an argument based almost entirely on Sappho's case and, indeed, it may have been true in her case. On the other hand, it may be equally true that Sappho's eminence as a poet made her case a special one. It is certainly true that other sources reflect, for this period of Greek history as for later ones, not only an inferior but a despised status for women. The misanthropic poet Hesiod, who flourished about 700 B.C., pronounced women "a great pain for mortals." And Sappho's near contemporary, the poet Semonides of Amorgos, who wrote in about the middle of the seventh century B.C., was even more condemnatory, saying at the end of his poem on women:

Yes, this is the worst plague Zeus has made—women; if they seem to be some use to him who has them, it is to him especially that they prove a plague. The man who lives with a woman never goes through all his day in cheerfulness. . . .[6]

The work from which the following selection is taken, Jane McIntosh Snyder, *The Woman and the Lyre: Women Writers in Classical Greece and Rome,* is part of an excellent series of books of feminist criticism devoted to uncovering "a neglected female tradition along with a heretofore hidden history of the literary dialogue between men and women."[7] Snyder not only manifests an identity with this tradition, she brings to her work the status of a respected classical scholar. As far as Sappho is concerned, her work updates the scholarship of such books as the older biography by Weigall, excerpted above. She stays much closer to the text of Sappho's poems, arguing persuasively that these fragments alone are as valid a guide to the poet's life as to her work. And, though she admits in passing the bisexual nature of Sappho's emotional life, she emphasizes the lesbian character of both her work and her life, taking it as the main line of interpretation.

Our understanding of Sappho might perhaps be deepened if we had the kind of sources of information about the society in which she lived that we do for the writers who worked in fifth-century Athens— extensive inscriptions, the remains of everyday utensils, pictures of daily life on vase paintings, and literary sources encompassing many different aspects of Athenian customs. In contrast, what we know of Archaic Lesbos comes primarily from the fragments of her two most famous poets—Sappho and Alcaeus. Any claims about the social customs of the island in the seventh and sixth centuries not based on these two sources are either mere conjectures or deductions based on knowledge of Greek society in other times and places, which may or may not bear any relationship to the Lesbos of Sappho's day. Nevertheless, Sappho's own accomplishments as a poet, and also the kind of world that she describes, do at least suggest that the women of Lesbos

---

[6]*Females of the Species: Semonides on Women,* ed. and tr. Hugh Lloyd-Jones (Park Ridge, N.J.: Noyes Press, 1975), p. 54.

[7]Foreword, p. x.

(or at any rate, those of the aristocracy) "enjoyed a freedom found elsewhere only in Sparta and an opportunity for self-development without parallel in Greek history."[8]

What do the ancient biographers have to say of Sappho herself? Here we must be wary of certain recently established characteristics of ancient biographies of writers, especially poets. Such ancient "lives" are generally likely to preserve more fiction than fact, drawing as they do on the authors' own works as though they were autobiographical statements and on unreliable sources such as comedy. In addition, ancient biographies of poets display suspiciously uniform characteristics, often conforming to a pattern involving anecdotes of a miraculous nature, the notion of the isolation of the writer from society (often via exile), and accounts of an unusual or violent manner of death.[9] Keeping these tendencies in mind, we may reduce the possibly accurate biographical data about Sappho to the following details.

Sappho's name, which she herself mentions in the "Hymn to Aphrodite," was, properly, Psappho. Her parents were Skamandronymos and Kleis, of Mytilene on Lesbos, and she had three brothers: Erigyios, about whom nothing is known; Charaxos, who had business connections with Egypt; and Larichos, whose government service on the council (*prytaneion*) in Mytilene suggests that the family was aristocratic. She was married to Kerkylas of Andros, who is never mentioned in any of the extant fragments of her poetry, and she may have had a daughter, named after her own mother (Kleis), who appears to be mentioned in two fragments (the crucial word in one of them, "pais," can mean either "daughter" or simply "child," "girl"). The husband is often assumed by twentieth-century scholars to be fictitious (either, on the one hand, because the homoerotic nature of some of Sappho's poetry is assumed to preclude a husband or, on the other, because she is claimed to be too pure and virginal to have married!); nevertheless, there is no good reason to doubt the report of his existence. Two other details emerge. She was born just at the close of the seventh century, perhaps about 610 B.C., and at some point during a period of political unrest on Lesbos, she is supposed to have taken refuge for a while in faraway Sicily.[10]

---

[8]P. N. Ure, "The Outer Greek World in the Sixth Century," in *Cambridge Ancient History* (Cambridge: Cambridge University Press, 1926), 4:99.

[9]See Janet A. Fairweather, "Biographies of Ancient Writers," *Ancient Society* 5 (1974): 231–75 and Mary R. Lefkowitz, *The Lives of the Greek Poets* (Baltimore: Johns Hopkins University Press, 1981).

[10]For summaries of the biographical tradition (and, in some cases, uncritical acceptance of it), see W. Aly, "Sappho," in *Real-Encylopädie der Klassischen Altertumswissenschaft*

Besides these biographical details—all, it must be remembered, drawn from sources much later than Sappho herself and therefore open to question—we have one reference to her among the fragments of poetry written by her contemporary compatriot, Alcaeus: "O weaver of violets, holy, sweet-smiling Sappho. . . ."[11] The first word of the fragment, "ioplok'," is often translated as "lady of the violet hair" on the basis of a later use of the word, but in view of the widespread use of weaving imagery in Greek literature to refer to the creative process of making song, it seems preferable to keep to the literal meaning of the word and suppose that Alcaeus is complimenting Sappho in a metaphorical way on her divine abilities as a poet, not on her hairdo.[12] At any rate, the fragment suggests Alcaeus' admiration and respect for his fellow Lesbian.

When we leave this bare outline, we quickly find ourselves in the realm of legend. The most famous tale about Sappho, which seems to have gotten its start sometime at least two centuries after her life, concerns her death-leap from the White Rock of Leukas (off the west coast of the Greek mainland) into the sea in pursuit of a handsome ferryman named Phaon, with whom she was supposed to have fallen passionately in love.[13] Now Phaon is clearly a mythological figure; the ancients told stories of his transformation—via the application of a magic salve—from an old man into an attractive youth with whom Aphrodite herself fell in love, subsequently hiding him in a bed of lettuce so that no rival could find him. The leap off Cape Leukas also has mythological analogies; the same story is told, for example, of Aphrodite leaping off the cliffs out of love for another youth, Adonis.[14]

If Sappho mentioned Phaon in her poetry, it was probably in some metaphorical or mythological context (perhaps in connection with the longing for regained youth), which may then eventually have

---

and Wilhelm Schmid and Otto Stählin, *Geschichte der Griechischen Literatur* (Munich: Beck, 1929), 1:417–29.

[11]Alcaeus, Z 61, in *Poetarum Lesbiorum Fragmenta*, ed. Edgar Lobel and Denys Page (Oxford: Clarendon Press, 1963). The adjective that I have translated as *holy* ("*agnos*") also carries the sense of "pure."

[12]See Jane McIntosh Snyder, "The Web of Song: Weaving Imagery in Homer and the Lyric Poets," *Classical Journal* 76 (1981): 193–96 and Denys Page, *Sappho and Alcaeus* (Oxford: Clarendon Press, 1955), 296 n. 2.

[13]My interpretation owes much to Gregory Nagy, "Phaethon, Sappho's Phaon, and the White Rocks of Leukas," *Harvard Studies in Classical Philology* 77 (1973): 137–77.

[14]The motif of the bed of lettuce found in the Aphrodite-Phaon story also appears in some versions of the Aphrodite-Adonis story. See Marcel Detienne, *The Gardens of Adonis: Spices in Greek Mythology* (Sussex: Harvester, 1977) 67–71, who points out that the Greeks connected lettuce with impotence.

given rise to the pseudobiographical tale of her lover's leap.[15] . . .
Only in recent years have the fragments of Sappho begun to be read
again for what they actually say rather than for what the reader would
like them to say. The same scholarly approach that has led to an
enlightened understanding of nineteenth- and twentieth-century
women poets needs to be applied to women writers of the more
distant past. What Adrienne Rich has said of Emily Dickinson, for
example, pertains equally well to several of the writers in [*The Woman
and the Lyre*], particularly Sappho: "We will understand Emily Dickinson better, read her poetry more perceptively, when Freudian imputa-
tion of scandal and aberrance in women's love for women has been
supplanted by a more informed, less misogynistic attitude toward
women's experience with each other."[16] . . .

The following poem, usually called the "Hymn to Aphrodite," is
written in imitation of the standard form of a Greek prayer, in which
the deity is first addressed and identified, reminded of a past relationship with the speaker, and then called upon to perform some service,
in this case to aid in the fulfillment of some unspecified pursuit by
Sappho on the battlefield of love.

1

O immortal Aphrodite of the many-colored throne,
child of Zeus, weaver of wiles, I beseech you,
do not overwhelm me in my heart
with anguish and pain, O Mistress,

But come hither, if ever at another time
hearing my cries from afar
you heeded them, and leaving the home of your father
came, yoking your golden

Chariot: beautiful, swift sparrows
drew you above the black earth
whirling their wings thick and fast,
from heaven's ether through mid-air.

---

[15]There is some evidence that Sappho did mention Phaon; cf. fragment 211, in
Poetarum Lesbiorum Fragmenta, ed. Edgar Lobel and Denys Page (Oxford: Clarendon
Press, 1963).

[16]Adrienne Rich, "Vesuvius at Home: The Power of Emily Dickinson," in *On Lies,
Secrets, and Silence: Selected Prose 1966–1978* (New York: Norton, 1979), 163. See also
Mary R. Lefkowitz, "Critical Stereotypes and the Poetry of Sappho," *Greek, Roman, and
Byzantine Studies* 14 (1973): 113–23.

Suddenly they had arrived; but you, O Blessed Lady,
with a smile on your immortal face,
asked what I had suffered again and
why I was calling again

And what I was most wanting to happen for me
in my frenzied heart: "Whom again shall I persuade
to come back into friendship with you? Who,
O Sappho, does you injustice?

"For if indeed she flees, soon will she pursue,
and though she receives not your gifts, she will give them,
and if she loves not now, soon she will love,
even against her will."

Come to me now also, release me from
harsh cares; accomplish as many things as my heart desires
to accomplish; and you yourself
be my fellow soldier.[17]

One of the characteristics of Sappho as a writer is her ability to adapt traditional forms (such as the prayer) to suit her own purposes. In the case of the "Hymn to Aphrodite," the goddess' presence is made remarkably vivid through the central description—which occupies all but the first and last stanzas of the poem—of her "epiphany" at some time in the past. The report of the goddess' words within the description, first indirectly and then directly (through quotation), not only pays tribute to Aphrodite's wonderful power but also implies, through the repetition of the word "again," that she has exerted that power on Sappho's behalf many times in the still more distant past. Oddly, then, the poem continually moves backwards into the past, and yet the vividness of the description evokes the image of the goddess as a real force in the immediate present, who is being called upon to assist Sappho now. Whether the piece was actually offered

---

[17]My translations of Sappho throughout this chapter are based on the Greek text in a standard edition, *Poetarum Lesbiorum Fragmenta,* ed. Edgar Lobel and Denys Page (Oxford: Clarendon Press, 1963). The translations are numbered according to this edition as well. I use ellipses to indicate where gaps in the text occur and square brackets to show where I have added words to fill out the sense. For excellent summaries of recent scholarly articles on Sappho's poetry, see Douglas E. Gerber, "Studies in Greek Lyric Poetry: 1967–1975," *Classical World* 70 (1976): 106–15. On the importance of recognizing the fragmentary nature of most Greek lyric, see W. R. Johnson, *The Idea of Lyric* (Berkeley: University of California Press, 1982), 24–26.

up as a prayer is dubious, especially in view of the artfulness in emphasizing the past relationship by making it occupy the bulk of the poem, but we can be certain, on the basis of the treatment of the gods in Archaic literature and art, that Aphrodite is no literary nicety, no symbol of some abstract notion of love: she is a real and potent force in Sappho's world. While we need not approach the poem with the sort of literalmindedness that would assume that it refers to an actual day in the poet's life, the sheer power of the description, with the emphasis on the swiftness of Aphrodite's descent, precludes the recent assumptions that the goddess is merely Sappho's projection of herself or that the poet is using the figure of Aphrodite as a device for lighthearted self-mockery.[18] Aphrodite's smile (in the fourth stanza) is the smile of power and benevolence and serenity (like the so-called Archaic smile on statues of the period), not of humor or amusement or derision.

Much has been written on whether the goddess' past service centered on problems of unrequited love or estrangement or infidelity. But as far as the poem itself is concerned, the question is moot; the emphasis is not on the nature of the discrepancy between Sappho and her woman friend but on Aphrodite's absolute power to transform the situation: to change flight into pursuit, refusal into desire, rejection into love. . . .

31

He seems to me to be like the gods
—whatever man sits opposite you
and close by hears you
talking sweetly

And laughing charmingly; which
makes the heart within my breast take flight;
for the instant I look upon you, I cannot anymore
speak one word,

But in silence my tongue is broken, a fine
fire at once runs under my skin,
with my eyes I see not one thing, my ears
buzz,

---

[18]For the former view, see Paul Friedrich, *The Meaning of Aphrodite* (Chicago: University of Chicago Press, 1978) 108; for the latter, Page, 16. Tilmar Krischer ("Sapphos Ode on Aphrodite," *Hermes* 96 [1968]: 1–14) rightly concludes that Aphrodite is presented as offering real—if more psychological than pragmatic—help.

Cold sweat covers me, trembling
seizes my whole body, I am more moist than grass;
I seem to be little short
of dying. . . .

But all must be ventured. . . .

The man of the opening line has been magnified in importance ever since the publication in 1913 of a book on Sappho by the German scholar Wilamowitz. He was an enormously influential scholar, and rightly so, but his blindness with respect to Sappho has profoundly distorted the modern view of her and particularly of this poem. To paraphrase his interpretation: The woman sits opposite a man and jokes and laughs with him. Who can he be other than her bridegroom? The wedding guests enter, and Sappho takes up the barbitos[19] and sings a song similar to the ones she has composed for the weddings of so many of her pupils. This time she sings of her passionate love for the bride. But, contrary to the remark in the *Suda* about Sappho's 'shameful friendships,' this love is completely honorable because she is not embarrassed to mention it openly and because she sings of it in the context of a wedding.[20] So Wilamowitz "proves"—by mere assertion—that 31 is a wedding song! And thus Sappho's homoeroticism is diluted and placed into a context which offers no offense to Victorian morality. (Interestingly, homoeroticism in male Greek writers like Solon or Theognis does not seem to have provoked the same kind of prudishness among Victorian scholars.)

The absurdity of Wilamowitz' explanation of 31 has been amply noted in recent years and the obvious pointed out—that a wedding song must have chiefly to do with the bride and groom, not with the speaker's passion for one of them.[21] Yet the wedding-song theory persists. . . .

One of the reasons that the wedding-song theory has continued to enjoy so much acceptance is that some scholars felt it necessary to explain the man of the opening line. As recently as 1977, an attempt was made to suggest that the man is the object of attention not only of the presumed "bride," but even of the speaker of the poem: "Two girls grow up together or they become friends early in their lives. What happens if some day one of them is attracted to a man and must as a result desert her friend? What happens if both girls realize they

---

[19]A many-stringed musical instrument similar to the lyre.—Ed.

[20]Wilamowitz-Moellendorff, 58–59.

[21]Page, 30–33.

love the same man but one of them succeeds in winning him?"[22] Few scholars seem to be aware—as Catullus and "Longinus" were—that the man (*whatever* man) is simply not important in the poem except as part of the background for the poem's setting and as a foil for the exposition of the speaker's feelings. He is calmly "godlike" in response to the woman's sweet talk and charming laugh, whereas the speaker, in the same situation, is instantly struck dumb.

Some critics, while not necessarily subscribing to the wedding-song theory, nevertheless continue to attribute undue importance to the man by assuming that the poem is about jealousy. This interpretation, which rests on the supposition that the "which" of the first line of stanza 2 refers to the sight of the man and woman together, is contradicted by the third line of the stanza ("for the instant I look upon you . . . ," the "you" in the Greek clearly being singular). Also the remainder of the fragment clearly indicates that the speaker is describing her reaction upon seeing the woman. Hence the "which" in question must refer to the woman's talk and laughter, not to the sight of some tête-à-tête that provokes in the speaker an attack of jealousy, or even more absurdly, a homosexual "anxiety attack."[23] The heart of the poem is a description not of jealousy or anxiety but of overwhelming passion.

We might also usefully take note of the female language of the song. For example, the emphasis in the description of the woman is on her activity, not on specific physical characteristics (height, hair color, etc.). Instead, the speaker focuses on the woman's speaking and laughing, much in the same way that the narrator of 16 (see below) calls to her mind Anaktoria's "lovely walk and the bright sparkle of her face." In addition, the detailed, introspective picture of the narrator's feelings on seeing and hearing the beloved woman, concludes—just before the narrator's illusion of near-death—with a comparison drawn from nature. The speaker is "chlorotera de poias," "paler" or "moister" than grass. (The phrase is usually translated as "greener than grass" by those who want to read the poem as one about envy and jealousy.) In Greek the adjective *chloros* is often used of young shoots, and also describes wood, honey, and the pale yellow-green band in the spec-

---

[22]Odysseus Tsagarakis, *Self-Expression in Early Greek Lyric, Elegiac, and Iambic Poetry* (Wiesbaden: Franz Steiner, 1977), 75–76.

[23]George Devereux, "The Nature of Sappho's Seizure in Fr. 31 LP as Evidence of Her Inversion," *Classical Quarterly* 20 (1970): 27–34; for opposing views, see M. Marcovich, "Sappho: Fr. 31: Anxiety Attack or Love Declaration?," *Classical Quarterly* 22 (1972): 19–32 and G. L. Koniaris, "On Sappho, Fr. 31 (L.-P.)," *Philologus* 112 (1968): 173–86. The interpretation presented here owes much to Mary R. Lefkowitz, "Critical Stereotypes."

trum of a rainbow. Thus the word is connected with youth and life—
not the death seemingly experienced by the speaker in the very next
line. The death is only apparent, as emphasized in the opening word of
line 16, "I seem. . . ." Far from being an absurd exaggeration, as many
have taken the phrase, "chlorotera de poias" anchors the speaker's
experience firmly in the natural world, a world of freshness, growth,
and moisture. Just as nature quickens with the advent of spring, so the
speaker quickens even as she seems to die.[24]

16

Some say that the most beautiful thing
upon the black earth is an army of horsemen;
others, of infantry, still others, of ships;
but I say it is what one loves.

It is completely easy to make this
intelligible to everyone; for the woman
who far surpassed all mortals in beauty,
Helen, left her most brave husband

And sailed off to Troy, nor did she
remember at all her child
or her dear parents; but [the Cyprian]
led her away. . . .

[All of which] has now reminded me
of Anaktoria, who is not here.

Her lovely walk and the bright sparkle of her face
I would rather look upon than
all the Lydian chariots
and full-armed infantry.   [*This may be the end of the poem.*]

Fragment 16, whose cyclical structure through the military references at the beginning and end of the fragment suggests that it may
be a nearly complete poem, illustrates Sappho's ability to interweave

---

[24]On the association of love and death in Sappho, see D. D. Boedeker, "Sappho and
Acheron," in *Arktouros: Hellenic Studies Presented to Bernard M. W. Knox*, ed. Glen W.
Bowersock, Walter Burkert, and Michael C. J. Putnam (Berlin: Walter de Gruyter,
1979), 40–52. On *chloros*, see Eleanor Irwin, *Colour Terms in Greek Poetry* (Toronto:
Hakkert, 1974), 31–78.

the personal with the mythological, as well as the abstract with the concrete. The underlying form of the piece is one found in many Greek and Roman poems: the catalog, or more specifically, the priamel, in which a list of items is presented, followed by a concluding statement which somehow ties the items together.[25] In this instance, three items are presented as potentially "the most beautiful thing upon the black earth"; then all are rejected in favor of the speaker's assertion that the most beautiful thing is "what one loves." This generalization is then illustrated both through the allusion to Helen, who left her home in Sparta to accompany the object of her desire, Paris, back to Troy, and through the speaker's similar longing for the one she loves, Anaktoria.

The poem's conclusion, with its return to military imagery and the implicit comparison between Anaktoria's appearance and the splendor of the military display, strikes at least one critic as "a little fanciful."[26] But physical beauty is elsewhere in Archaic poetry expressed in terms of motion and brightness (as in Alkman's poems) rather than mere static shape. The military imagery of the poem reinforces Sappho's definition of Anaktoria's beauty; it is the movement of her body and the brightness of her facial expression that the speaker calls to her mind, not static qualities like shape or size or coloring. Thus there is nothing particularly odd in the speaker's statement that she would much prefer to behold Anaktoria's "lovely walk" and "bright sparkle" than watch the movement of troops and the gleam of their weaponry. In effect, the poem both accepts and rejects the splendor of military might; it is beautiful—but it is nothing when set against the splendor of the person one loves.

Some scholars have searched for stark logic in the poem's examples and, finding it wanting, have criticized the song as too loosely tied together. After all, they say, how does the fact that Helen left her husband and child and went off to Troy prove the narrator's thesis that what is most beautiful is what one loves?[27] If we look for association of ideas and images, rather than strict logic, however, we can see the poem as highly coherent. The emphasis of the song is on the concept of "kalliston" (line 3)—the power of whatever is

---

[25]See William H. Race, *The Classical Priamel from Homer to Boethius, Mnemosyne.* suppl. 74 (Leiden: E. J. Brill, 1982).

[26]Page, 57.

[27]See, for example, Gary Wills, "The Sapphic 'Umvertung aller Werte,'" *American Journal of Philology* 88 (1967): 434–42. Cf. Page, 53: "The sequence of thought might have been clearer." In the view of Jack Winkler, "there is a charming parody of logical argumentation in these stanzas" ("Gardens of Nymphs: Public and Private in Sappho's Lyrics," *Women's Studies* 8 [1981]: 74).

"most beautiful," and Helen, as the most beautiful woman in the world, is the supreme exemplum of "kallos" (line 7, the corresponding line in the next stanza). Although the gap in the text of stanza 4 prevents us from seeing the exact connection, it appears to be the thought of Helen that reminds the narrator of the absent Anaktoria (lines 15–16). Even if Helen represents par excellence what is "most beautiful," to the narrator the most beautiful thing in the world is the sight of Anaktoria. And again through association and implication, the epic-scale naval expedition and displays of military might connected with the abduction of Helen pale in significance to the splendor of one face—the face that by the narrator's standard is the most beautiful.

Thus the myth of Helen, while it does not "prove" the thesis of the song, incorporates all of the elements of the catalog—ships, foot soldiers, cavalry, and an object of love, Helen herself—and at the same time provides the poem with a foil for the speaker's own redefinition of "to kalliston." The most beautiful thing in the world is not Helen, but Anaktoria, who represents for the narrator "what one loves." Beauty is defined not in a cosmic way in mythical terms, but in a particular way in terms of a single individual's perception. Through that perception, the myth of Helen has been transformed, for Helen is no longer a passive object of others' attentions. Like the narrator, who actively seeks the sight of Anaktoria, Helen evidently chooses to leave behind her husband and forget her child and parents. Just as the narrator seeks Anaktoria, so Helen here seeks her voyage to Troy to be with Paris.[28]

94

. . . .
"Honestly, I wish I were dead!"
Weeping many tears she left me,

Saying this as well:
"Oh, what dreadful things have happened to us,
Sappho! I don't want to leave you!"

I answered her:
"Go with my blessings, and remember me,
for you know how we cherished you.

---

[28]On Sappho's emphasis on the active choices made by Helen, see Page DuBois, "Sappho and Helen," *Arethusa* 11 (1978): 89–99.

"But if you have [forgotten], I want
to remind you . . .
of the beautiful things that happened to us:

"Close by my side you put around yourself
[many wreaths] of violets and roses and saffron. . . .

"And many woven garlands
made from flowers . . .
around your tender neck,

"And . . . with costly royal
myrrh . . .
you anointed . . . ,

"And on a soft bed
. . . tender . . .
you satisfied your desire. . . .

"Nor was there any . . .
nor any holy . . .
from which we were away,

. . . nor grove. . . ."

Fragment 94, although badly mutilated, contains enough detail to reveal the more calmly sensual side of Sappho's poetry. Known to modern readers only since its publication at the turn of the century, it is a description of past intimacy recalled—rather than passion experienced in the present tense, as in 31, previously discussed. Like 31, however, this piece was also subjected to Wilamowitz' purifying interpretations, though fortunately with less impact on succeeding views of the fragment than in the case of his so-called marriage song. Wilamowitz read the poem as follows (to paraphrase his German). Sappho will perform the song for her pupils, to tell them how her feelings are hurt when her pupils go off into the world and forget their teacher. The poem reveals to us what her circle of girls delighted in—picking flowers, dressing up, and sleeping sweetly when they were tired out from dancing. Sappho's school trained aristocratic girls in the value of good manners. No doubt the food was plentiful, though I have no proof of that.[29]

Despite the very sensual language and setting of the poem (the

---

[29]Wilamowitz-Moellendorff, 51.

garlands, the anointing of bodies with perfumed oil, cushions, a bed, etc.), Wilamowitz chose to render the obvious sexual undertones of "exies potho[n]" ("you satisfied your desire") with the bland phrase "you stilled your need for rest," a need that he takes to have been brought on by excessive dancing. (Notice that what is left of the poem itself makes no mention at all of dancing, much less of plentiful food.) The other fragments in which Sappho uses the word *pothos* (desire) establish clearly that the word is erotic.

More recent interpretations generally acknowledge the sensual aspect of the poem even if the subject matter is sometimes played down with descriptions such as a "long list of girlish pleasures."[30] But some scholars seem to have pursued Wilamowitz' notion of "hurt feelings" by assigning the opening line of the fragment (at least one line is missing from the poem's beginning) to the speaker. Since quotation marks were not used in ancient Greek texts, the line could be assigned either to the speaker or to the other woman. Scholars who attribute the line to the speaker see the whole piece as a sort of confessional lament of an anguished Sappho who wishes she were dead. Burnett has recently shown in detail that it is more reasonable to assume that the first extant line should be assigned to the departed friend, whose youthful tendency towards exaggerated language reveals an "affectionately melodramatic" kind of person whose "raw emotion" is set against Sappho's own "perfected meditation." As Burnett demonstrates, Sappho's memory of the bed of lovemaking and of fulfilled desire "has taken from blunt objects and fleeting sensations their enduring essence."[31] The poem, then, is hardly a "confession," but rather a recapturing of past pleasures through memory, by which the "dreadful things" mentioned by the girl—that is, the impending separation—are transformed into Sappho's "beautiful things" beginning in stanza 4.

The imagery in the second half of the fragment is worthy of May Sarton: violets, roses, and saffron (a type of crocus with purple flowers). The female associations of flowers in Sappho's poetry are well

---

[30]Page, 83.

[31]Anne Burnett, "Desire and Memory (Sappho Frag. 94)," *Classical Philology* 74 (1979): 25; she notes (26 n. 37) that "it is hard to avoid the conclusion that the scholarly determination to discover a miserable woman behind Sappho's poems is connected with the scholarly recognition of the nature of the love she refers to. The unexpressed reasoning seems to be unnatural, therefore unhappy." Burnett expands her ideas on the role of memory in Sappho's songs in general in *Three Archaic Poets* (Cambridge: Harvard University Press, 1983), 277–313. On the importance of the memory of past intimacies in fragment 94, see also Eva Stehle Stigers, "Sappho's Private World," *Women's Studies* 8 (1981): 54–56.

established through references in other fragments to a woman who is like a mountain hyacinth trampled by shepherds (105c), the roses around Aphrodite's temple (2), the many-flowered fields in Lydia where Atthis' departed friend roams (96, line 11), the wreaths of flowers worn by the yellow-haired girl of 98, and the golden flowers connected with Kleis (132). The predominance of such flower imagery in Sappho is all the more striking when we note its rarity in her compatriot, Alcaeus, whose favorite imagery involves the sea. The anthological list here in Sappho 94 is filled out by further references to natural beauty in the form of myrrh, a resin produced by certain trees and shrubs, and the grove alluded to (line 27) as the fragment breaks off. Just as the departed woman in 96 (another poem concerned with the theme of separation . . .) is described through a simile involving the moon, flowery fields, the sea, and dew, so here the past relationship between the two women is depicted through recollection and recreation of their mutual enjoyment of especially sensuous aspects of nature—her flowers and her exotic perfumes. Like 96, this fragment, too, is primarily concerned with private human emotions set within the context of selected aspects of the natural environment.

Review and Study Questions

1. How do Sappho's poems reflect the warrior aristocracy to which she belonged?
2. Speculate on why homosexuality was so prevalent and widely accepted in ancient Greek society.
3. In your opinion, is her lesbianism the main interpretive framework for explaining Sappho?

Suggestions for Further Reading

The definitive text of Sappho's work is that established by Edgar Lobel and Denys Page (eds.), *Poetarum Lesbiorum Fragmenta* (Oxford: Clarendon Press, 1963 [1955]). But this is a scholar's edition, with the text in Greek and the apparatus in Latin. Denys Page, however, in his *Sappho and Alcaeus: An Introduction to the Study of Ancient Lesbian Poetry* (Oxford: Clarendon Press, 1979 [1955]), does present his text, but it is not a complete translation: the Greek is reproduced and then the text is paraphrased in prose lines. There are several other editions and translations available. The most authoritative, besides Page and Lobel, is the four-volume *Greek Lyric* (Cambridge, Mass.: Harvard

University Press, 1982). I have chosen to use for this chapter the latest and one of the best modern translations, by Diane J. Rayor, *Sappho's Lyre: Archaic Lyric and Women Poets of Ancient Greece* (Berkeley and Los Angeles: University of California Press, 1991). There are a number of other popular, rather than scholarly, editions, including *The Songs of Sappho in English Translation by Many Poets* (Mt. Vernon, N.Y.: Peter Pauper Press, 1942), *Sappho: A New Translation* by Mary Barnard, foreword by Dudley Fitts (Berkeley and Los Angeles: University of California Press, 1958), and *The Poems of Sappho*, ed. Suzy Q. Groden (Indianapolis: Bobbs-Merrill, 1966). Her individual poems have been collected or anthologized in dozens of collections, such as *The Oxford Book of Greek Verse* (Oxford: Clarendon Press, n.d.), *The Greek Poets*, ed. Moses Hadas (New York: Modern Library, 1953), and *Greek Lyric Poetry*, ed. and tr. Willis Barnstone (Bloomington: Indiana University Press, 1987).

The only comprehensive biography of Sappho in English is Arthur Weigall, *Sappho of Lesbos: Her Life and Times* (New York: Frederick A. Stokes, 1933), excerpted for this chapter. But there are a number of works that deal primarily with her poetry and, to some extent, with Sappho and the setting in which she wrote. Anthony J. Podlecki, *The Early Greek Poets and Their Time* (Vancouver: University of British Columbia Press, 1984) is a capable critical survey that includes a brief but perceptive chapter on Sappho. A similar work is Anne Pippin Burnett, *Three Archaic Poets: Archilochus, Alcaeus, Sappho* (Cambridge, Mass.: Harvard University Press, 1983). J. A. Davison, *From Archilochus to Pindar: Papers on Greek Literature of the Archaic Period* (New York: St. Martin's Press, 1968) is a collection of learned papers containing one on Sappho that can be read with some profit though it is somewhat technical. In Richard Jenkyns, *Three Classical Poets: Sappho, Catullus, and Juvenal* (Cambridge, Mass.: Harvard University Press, 1982), in the portion of the book dealing with Sappho, one finds a close reading of all her extant verse and, secondarily, some interpretation of her poetry, less of her biography. One of the standard works of interpretation is C. M. Bowra, *Greek Lyric Poetry from Alcman to Simonides*, 2nd rev. ed. (Oxford: Clarendon Press, 1961).

Judy Grahn, *The Highest Apple: Sappho and the Lesbian Poetic Tradition* (San Francisco: Spinsters, Ink., 1985) is not really about Sappho the poet or the historical personality but about Sappho as the first in a long line of lesbian poets who, in the view of the author, have always formed a special part of an underground community. Mary R. Lefkowitz, *Heroines and Hysterics* (New York: St. Martin's Press, 1981) contains two chapters on Sappho in a book essentially about women poets, much like the preceding book, but less focused on lesbianism.

For the historical setting, an indispensable book is K. J. Dover, *Greek*

Homosexuality (Cambridge, Mass.: Harvard University Press, 1978), the standard work on its subject. More specific period histories are Chester G. Starr, *The Origins of Greek Civilization 1100–650 B.C.* (New York: Knopf, 1961), Anthony Snodgrass, *Archaic Greece: The Age of Experiment* (London: J. M. Dent and Sons, 1980), and Michael Grant, *The Rise of the Greeks* (New York: Collier, 1987).

More general histories are the brief and lucid A. R. Burn, *The Warring States of Greece: From Their Rise to the Roman Conquest* (New York: McGraw-Hill, 1968) and Carol G. Thomas, *The Earliest Civilizations: Ancient Greece and the Near East, 3000–200 B.C.* (Washington: University Press of America, 1982), a modest little book especially designed for undergraduate students.

THE BUDDHA:
THE ENLIGHTENED ONE

c. 563 B.C.	Born
c. 547 B.C.	Married to Princess Yasodhara
c. 534 B.C.	Renounced princely life and began his religious mission
c. 528 B.C.	Received the enlightenment
c. 483 B.C.	Died

Almost no fact about the Buddha is indisputably true, except that he did live and that he founded Buddhism, one of the world's great religions. What we know about him as a person is hopelessly lost in the tangle of pious legends that began to surround him during his lifetime and continued for centuries.

The following approaches as nearly as possible a coherent account of the Buddha's life. He was probably born about 563 B.C. in Sakaya in northeast India, near the border of Nepal, in the capital city of Kapilavastua. His given name was Siddartha Gautama. He was a prince, the son of the Sakaya king Suddhodana and his queen Mahamaya, who died a few days after her son was born. In midlife, after a long spiritual journey, he passed through the ultimate transcendental experience of self-awakening that made him the Buddha or "enlightened one."

The Buddha: Who Was He?

THE BUDDHA-KARITA OF ASVAGHOSHA

The traditional account of the Buddha's life, like those of other early religious leaders, is a blend of the historical and the legendary. Moreover, the biography of the Buddha became part of an enormous, pious accretion surrounding his teachings. These teachings, or "sayings," of the Buddha were supposed to have been put together in five collections or "baskets" by Ananda, a cousin and devoted early disciple, shortly after the Buddha's death. This is doubtful, however, since the opening words of the canon, "Thus have I heard," form a timeworn, formulaic phrase for reporting the Buddha's words within the framework of a long tradition of oral transmission. In fact, there is no trace of any authentic contemporary text; the texts all appear in later languages and dialects, and all bear the marks of an oral tradition.

The text from which the following selection is taken is one of several canonical or "official" biographical accounts, some written in Pali and some in Sanskrit. This one, the *Buddha-Karita*, was written in Sanskrit by a Buddhist scholar named Asvaghosha, who probably lived in the first century of the Christian era. It takes the form of a long epic poem, thirteen books of which survive. The poem itself bears many of the marks of long oral transmission typical of epic literature: it repeats titles and epithets; it makes lavish use of omens and supernatural foreshadowing of events; and it endows its central figure with a range of divine and heroic attributes that virtually conceal the historic personality. It is, nevertheless, the best ancient version we have.

The account begins by describing the Buddha's parents and his miraculous birth.

There was a city, the dwelling-place of the great saint Kapila, having its sides surrounded by the beauty of a lofty broad table-land as by a line of clouds, and itself, with its high-soaring palaces, immersed in the sky. . . .

A king, by name Suddhodana, of the kindred of the sun, anointed to stand at the head of earth's monarchs,—ruling over the city, adorned it, as a bee-inmate a full-blown lotus.

The very best of kings with his train ever near him,—intent on liberality yet devoid of pride; a sovereign, yet with an ever equal eye thrown on all,—of gentle nature and yet with wide-reaching majesty. . . .

To him there was a queen, named Mâyâ, as if free from all deceit (mâyâ)—an effulgence proceeding from his effulgence, like the splendour of the sun when it is free from all the influence of darkness,—a chief queen in the united assembly of all queens. . . .

Then falling from the host of beings in the Tushita heaven, and illumining the three worlds, the most excellent of Bodhisattvas suddenly entered at a thought into her womb, like the Nâga-king entering the cave of Nandâ.[1]

Assuming the form of a huge elephant white like Himâlaya, armed with six tusks, with his face perfumed with flowing ichor, he entered the womb of the queen of king Suddhodana, to destroy the evils of the world. . . .

Then one day by the king's permission the queen, having a great longing in her mind, went with the inmates of the gynaeceum[2] into the garden Lumbinî.

As the queen supported herself by a bough which hung laden with a weight of flowers, the Bodhisattva suddenly came forth, cleaving open her womb. . . .

Having thus in due time issued from the womb, he shone as if he had come down from heaven, he who had not been born in the natural way,—he who was born full of wisdom, not foolish,—as if his mind had been purified by countless aeons of contemplation. . . .

The wandering sage Asita appears and is entertained by the king.

Then the king, having duly honoured the sage, who was seated in his seat, with water for the feet and an arghya offering, invited him (to speak) with all ceremonies of respect. . . .

The sage, being thus invited by the king, filled with intense feeling as was due, uttered his deep and solemn words, having his large eyes opened wide with wonder: . . .

---

[1]The term *Bodhisattva* means "Buddha to be." It later came to mean all the previous lives of the Buddha. The other terms—*Tushita heaven, the three worlds,* and *the Nâga-king*—are later Hindu terms and concepts that came to permeate Buddhist literature.—ED.

[2]*Gynaeceum* is a term for women's quarters or harem.—ED.

'But hear now the motive for my coming and rejoice thereat; a heavenly voice has been heard by me in the heavenly path, that thy son has been born for the sake of supreme knowledge. . . .'

'Having forsaken his kingdom, indifferent to all worldly objects, and having attained the highest truth by strenuous efforts, he will shine forth as a sun of knowledge to destroy the darkness of illusion in the world.'

'He will deliver by the boat of knowledge the distressed world, borne helplessly along, from the ocean of misery which throws up sickness as its foam, tossing with the waves of old age, and rushing with the dreadful onflow of death. . . .'

Having heard these words, the king with his queen and his friends abandoned sorrow and rejoiced; thinking, 'such is this son of mine,' he considered that his excellence was his own.

But he let his heart be influenced by the thought, 'he will travel by the noble path,'—he was not in truth averse to religion, yet still he saw alarm at the prospect of losing his child. . . .

When he had passed the period of childhood and reached that of middle youth, the young prince learned in a few days the various sciences suitable to his race, which generally took many years to master.

But having heard before from the great seer Asita his destined future which was to embrace transcendental happiness, the anxious care of the king of the present Sâkya race turned the prince to sensual pleasures.

Then he sought for him from a family of unblemished moral excellence a bride possessed of beauty, modesty, and gentle bearing, of wide-spread glory, Yasodharâ by name, having a name well worthy of her, a very goddess of good fortune. . . .

In course of time to the fair-bosomed Yasodharâ,—who was truly glorious in accordance with her name,—there was born from the son of Suddhodana a son named Râhula, with a face like the enemy of Râhu.

Then the king who from regard to the welfare of his race had longed for a son and been exceedingly delighted [at his coming],—as he had rejoiced at the birth of his son, so did he now rejoice at the birth of his grandson. . . .

Having heard of the delightful appearance of the city groves beloved by the women, [the prince] resolved to go out of doors, like an elephant long shut up in a house.

The king, having learned the character of the wish thus expressed by his son, ordered a pleasure-party to be prepared, worthy of his own affection and his son's beauty and youth.

He prohibited the encounter of any afflicted common person in the highroad; 'heaven forbid that the prince with his tender nature should even imagine himself to be distressed.'

Then having removed out of the way with the greatest gentleness all those who had mutilated limbs or maimed senses, the decrepit and the sick and all squalid beggars, they made the highway assume its perfect beauty. . . .

But then the gods, dwelling in pure abodes, having beheld that city thus rejoicing like heaven itself, created an old man to walk along on purpose to stir the heart of the king's son.

The prince having beheld him thus overcome with decrepitude and different in form from other men, with his gaze intently fixed on him, thus addressed his driver with simple confidence:

'Who is this man that has come here, O charioteer, with white hair and his hand resting on a staff, his eyes hidden beneath his brows, his limbs bent down and hanging loose,—is this a change produced in him or his natural state or an accident?'

Thus addressed, the charioteer revealed to the king's son the secret that should have been kept so carefully, thinking no harm in his simplicity, for those same gods had bewildered his mind:

'That is old age by which he is broken down,—the ravisher of beauty, the ruin of vigour, the cause of sorrow, the destruction of delights, the bane of memories, the enemy of the senses.

'He too once drank milk in his childhood, and in course of time he learned to grope on the ground; having step by step become a vigorous youth, he has step by step in the same way reached old age.'

Being thus addressed, the prince, starting a little, spoke these words to the charioteer, 'What! will this evil come to me also?' and to him again spoke the charioteer:

'It will come without doubt by the force of time through multitude of years even to my long-lived lord; all the world knows thus that old age will destroy their comeliness and they are content to have it so.' . . .

Then the same deities created another man with his body all afflicted by disease; and on seeing him the son of Suddhodana addressed the charioteer, having his gaze fixed on the man:

'Yonder man with a swollen belly, his whole frame shaking as he pants, his arms and shoulders hanging loose, his body all pale and thin, uttering plaintively the word "mother," when he embraces a stranger,—who, pray, is this?'

Then his charioteer answered, 'Gentle Sir, it is a very great affliction called sickness, that has grown up, caused by the inflammation of the (three) humours, which has made even this strong man no longer master of himself.'

Then the prince again addressed him, looking upon the man compassionately, 'Is this evil peculiar to him or are all beings alike threatened by sickness?'

Then the charioteer answered, 'O prince, this evil is common to all; thus pressed round by diseases men run to pleasure, though racked with pain.' . . .

But as the king's son was thus going on his way, the very same deities created a dead man, and only the charioteer and the prince, and none else, beheld him as he was carried dead along the road.

Then spoke the prince to the charioteer, 'Who is this borne by four men, followed by mournful companions, who is bewailed, adorned but no longer breathing?'

Then the driver,—having his mind overpowered by the gods who possess pure minds and pure dwellings,—himself knowing the truth, uttered to his lord this truth also which was not to be told:

'This is some poor man who, bereft of his intellect, senses, vital airs and qualities, lying asleep and unconscious, like mere wood or straw, is abandoned alike by friends and enemies after they have carefully swathed and guarded him.'

Having heard these words of the charioteer he was somewhat startled and said to him, 'Is this an accident peculiar to him alone, or is such the end of all living creatures?'

Then the charioteer replied to him, 'This is the final end of all living creatures; be it a mean man, a man of middle state, or a noble, destruction is fixed to all in this world.'

Then the king's son, sedate though he was, as soon as he heard of death, immediately sank down overwhelmed, and pressing the end of the chariot-pole with his shoulder spoke with a loud voice,

'Is this end appointed to all creatures, and yet the world throws off all fear and is infatuated! Hard indeed, I think, must the hearts of men be, who can be self-composed in such a road.

'Therefore, O charioteer, turn back our chariot, this is no time or place for a pleasure-excursion; how can a rational being, who knows what destruction is, stay heedless here, in the hour of calamity?' . . .

Later that same night

Having awakened his horse's attendant, the swift *Kham*daka, he thus addressed him: 'Bring me quickly my horse Ka*m*thaka, I wish to-day to go hence to attain immortality.

'Since such is the firm content which to-day is produced in my heart, and since my determination is settled in calm resolve, and since even in loneliness I seem to possess a guide,—verily the end which I desire is now before me.'. . .

The city-roads which were closed with heavy gates and bars, and which could be with difficulty opened even by elephants, flew open of their own accord without noise, as the prince went through.

Firm in his resolve and leaving behind without hesitation his father who turned ever towards him, and his young son, his affectionate people and his unparalleled magnificence, he then went forth out of his father's city.

Then he with his eyes long and like a full-blown lotus, looking back on the city, uttered a sound like a lion, 'Till I have seen the further shore of birth and death I will never again enter the city called after Kapila.'. . .

For six years, vainly trying to attain merit, he practised self-mortification, performing many rules of abstinence, hard for a man to carry out. . . .

'Wearied with hunger, thirst, and fatigue, with his mind no longer self-possessed through fatigue, how should one who is not absolutely calm reach the end which is to be attained by his mind?

'True calm is properly obtained by the constant satisfaction of the senses; the mind's self-possession is only obtained by the senses being perfectly satisfied.

'True meditation is produced in him whose mind is self-possessed and at rest,—to him whose thoughts are engaged in meditation the exercise of perfect contemplation begins at once.

'By contemplation are obtained those conditions through which is eventually gained that supreme calm, undecaying, immortal state, which is so hard to be reached.'. . .

Then he sat down on his hams in a posture, immovably firm and with his limbs gathered into a mass like a sleeping serpent's hood, exclaiming, 'I will not rise from this position on the earth until I have obtained my utmost aim.'

Then the dwellers in heaven burst into unequalled joy; the herds of beasts and the birds uttered no cry; the trees moved by the wind made no sound, when the holy one took his seat firm in his resolve.

When the great sage, sprung from a line of royal sages, sat down there with his soul fully resolved to obtain the highest knowledge, the whole world rejoiced; but Mâra,[3] the enemy of the good law, was afraid.

Then, having conquered the hosts of Mâra by his firmness and

---

[3]Mâra was the Hindu god of evil. He brought an assortment of threats and temptations to the Buddha at this time.—ED.

calmness, he the great master of meditation set himself to meditate, longing to know the supreme end.

And having attained the highest mastery in all kinds of meditation, he remembered in the first watch the continuous series of all his former births. . . .

And having remembered each birth and each death in all those various transmigrations, the compassionate one then felt compassion for all living beings. . . .

When the second watch came, he, possessed of unequalled energy, received a pre-eminent divine sight, he the highest of all sight-gifted beings.

Then by that divine perfectly pure sight he beheld the whole world as in a spotless mirror.

As he saw the various transmigrations and rebirths of the various beings with their several lower or higher merits from their actions, compassion grew up more within him. . . .

The all-knowing Bodhisattva, the illuminated one, having thus determined, after again pondering and meditating thus came to his conclusion:

'This is pain, this also is the origin of pain in the world of living beings; this also is the stopping of pain; this is that course which leads to its stopping.' So having determined he knew all as it really was.

Thus he, the holy one, sitting there on his seat of grass at the root of the tree, pondering by his own efforts attained at last perfect knowledge.

The Buddha: What Did He Teach?

H. SADDHATISSA

Having thus attained "perfect knowledge," the Buddha had two choices. He could devote himself to contemplation or to teaching others how to attain the perfection he had achieved. While he pondered these choices the Brahman (Hindu) gods Indra and Brahma, according to legend, appeared to him and pleaded that he go out into the world and teach his doctrine. That was the decision he made, and the result was the creation of Buddhism.

Buddhism has been variously described as a form of meditation or yoga, a profound ethical system, a full-scale philosophy, and a salvationist religion. It is all these. Its origin, however, was relatively simple. It was a nontheistic religion, having no central god figure, although in later times the Buddha himself came to be worshipped as a god. Nor did it recognize the existence of an immortal soul. Rather, human beings as substantive creatures were seen as being caught up in an endless, miserable cycle of birth and death, re-birth and re-death. To free them from this cycle the Buddha formulated the Four Noble Truths: the truth of misery; the truth that misery comes from the desire for pleasure; the truth that this desire can be eliminated; and the truth that this elimination is the result of an Eightfold Path that people may follow to attain the ultimate goal of Nibbana, or Nirvana—an obscure condition that has been described by various terms such as enlightenment, non-being, and forgetfulness, although the Buddha himself never fully explained what he meant by it.

The following selection is a discussion of the Eightfold Path by a learned Indian Buddhist scholar, H. Saddhatissa, who is especially concerned to explain his religion in a way that westerners can understand. Saddhatissa's book has become a kind of standard "primer" of Buddhism.

The path leading to the release from suffering is said to be eight-fold. These are not consecutive steps. The eight factors are interdependent and must be perfected simultaneously, the fulfillment of one factor being unlikely without at least the partial development of the others. These eight factors are:

1. *sammā diṭṭhi*   right understanding or views
2. *sammā saṅkappa*   right thought or motives
3. *sammā vācā*   right speech
4. *sammā kammanta*   right action
5. *sammā ājīva*   right means of livelihood
6. *sammā vāyāma*   right effort
7. *sammā sati*   right mindfulness
8. *sammā samādhi*   right concentration.

It is important to realize that the word *sammā* prefixing each of the eight factors has a wide range of meaning. In this context it can mean right as opposed to wrong, or it can, in the developed follower of the path, come to mean completed or perfected.

The initial task of one wishing to follow the eight-fold path is to observe oneself carefully and see which factors have already been developed to a certain extent and which are still in a very rudimentary condition. (Some people, for example, have developed their thinking faculty but their ability to communicate with other people is almost non-existent. Others, on the contrary, find it easy to form relationships but have an undeveloped reflective faculty.) The weak aspects of character or of life will then have to be brought into balance and harmony with the strong.

We shall proceed now to consider each factor of the path in turn.

1. *Sammā diṭṭhi* (right understanding or views) in the initial stages of one's practice of the path need mean little more than a vague recognition that 'all is not what it seems'. Right understanding implies in the first instance having seen through the delusion that material security automatically brings peace of mind, or that ceremonies and ritual can wipe out the effects of a past act. Gradually, as the path is perfected, right views, based on knowledge, replace the previous delusions or superstitions that were based on ignorance and lack of insight. . . .

2. *Sammā saṅkappa,* usually translated as right thought or right motives, seems to apply to the emotional basis of thought rather than to thinking itself. As the first factor of the path is concerned with the content and direction of thought, the second factor is concerned with the quality of the drive behind the thinking. . . .

This means that one's mind should be pure, free from carnal 'thirst' (*rāga*), malevolence (*vyāpāda*), cruelty (*vihiṃsā*) and the like. At the same time, one should be willing to relinquish anything that obstructs one's onward march.

3. *Sammā vācā* (right speech). By not indulging in, or listening to, lying, back-biting, harsh talk and idle gossip, we can establish a connecting link between 'right thought' and 'right action'. *Sammā vācā* is free from dogmatic assertions and from hypnotic suggestions; it is an instrument whereby one can learn and teach, comfort and be comforted. We are practising right speech when we use conversation as a means of coming to know people, to understand them and ourselves. . . .

4. *Sammā kammanta* (right action). . . . Right action is any action that proceeds from an unobstructed mind. Whereas morality, in the usual sense of the word, can be practised by one who is blind to the motives behind this behaviour right action is impossible without a clear and deep understanding.

The *path* of right action involves abstaining from unwholesome *kamma* and performing only those actions which will lead to beneficial results. The *goal* of right action, however, is to transcend even *kusala* (wholesome) *kamma,* for once the enlightenment experience has arisen in life, actions will cease to produce any *kammic* results, harmful or beneficial. . . .

5. *Sammā ājīva* (right means of livelihood). The simplest interpretation of this factor of the path is based on the five precepts. Conscientious observance of the five precepts automatically vetos certain trades and professions. The first precept—not to harm living things— requires that we do not earn our living by means of butchering cattle, dealing in flesh, fishing, hunting and so forth. Neither may one make or use weapons, nor engage in any form of warfare. Similarly the fifth precept—not to indulge in drinks or drugs that tend to cloud the mind—prevents us not only from trafficking in drugs, but also from engaging in the manufacture or distribution of alcohol. . . .

Even if one manages more or less to avoid the wrong means of livelihood, the problems are not yet over. *Sammā ājīva* implies much more than the mere avoiding of wrong means of livelihood. It implies a careful weighing up of our attributes and potentialities, and the selecting of a job that will use the talents we have and at the same time help to develop our weak points. . . .

6. *Sammā vāyāma* (right effort). Although the canonical division of right effort into four categories seems at first sight to be rather pedantic and meaningless it has, if one studies it more closely, a sound practical and psychological validity. The four-fold division of right effort consists of:

1. the effort to cut off unwholesome states that have already arisen;
2. the effort to prevent the arising of unwholesome states that have not yet arisen;
3. the effort to preserve wholesome states that have already arisen;
4. the effort to encourage wholesome states that have not yet arisen.

Right effort requires the development of insight, intuition and will power. We need to develop insight in order to perceive which of the states of mind habitually present are to be preserved and which are to be weeded out. We need to develop intuition so that we can gauge when we are sailing close to a hitherto unknown state of mind and whether we should go ahead or withdraw from it. . . .

7. *Sammā sati* (right mindfulness) is the pivotal factor of the path. Without it none of the other factors can be brought to completion. Right mindfulness serves too as a control over the other factors, preventing the excessive development of one at the expense of the others. In Christian terminology *sammā sati* might be translated as 'the practice of the presence of God'; it implies gradually extending one's

awareness until every action, thought and word is performed in the full light of consciousness. . . .

8. *Sammā samādhi.* Right concentration or meditation is the last factor of the path leading to the cessation of suffering. Meditation and its counterpart in daily life—mindfulness (*sati*)—form together the essence of the Buddha's teaching. . . .

It has been said of the mind that it is like a pool. Too often that pool is agitated and muddy, reflecting nothing but its own turbidity. Buddhist meditation is designed to quieten the mind until it becomes perfectly still. Then the deep recesses of the pool can be seen clearly, and it will reflect a true picture of whatever is presented to it. There are many hindrances in the way of one who seeks to quieten the mind in this way: violent emotions of desire or of hatred, restlessness and discontent, hesitation and doubt, laziness, weariness and sloth.

The Buddha in History

SIR PERCIVAL SPEAR

Neither the Buddha himself nor his followers thought very deeply about history. Buddhism is transcendental and hence oriented to the eternal rather than the historical. Nevertheless, the Buddha lived in historical time and acted upon historical events. Further, the Buddha and Buddhism are invariably treated in any history of India because of their immense historical importance.

The following selection is taken from probably the best one-volume survey of Indian history, *India: A Modern History,* by Sir Percival Spear, an established scholar who spent most of his life and professional career in India. This survey, unlike many others of its kind, gives thorough coverage to the earlier history of "classical India." The selection deals with the setting of the Age of Buddha and with the revolutionary impact of the man and his ideas upon that age.

Buddhism was one of several movements which arose in a period of unrest and ferment from about the year 600 B.C. Three causes may be hazarded for this ferment, one material, one moral, and one racial. On the material side there was the transition from a pastoral to an agricultural economy. The Indo-Aryan tribes were settling down, becoming tillers of the soil instead of shepherds of flocks. They were developing cities and becoming attached to the soil. Tribal groups were becoming territorial kingdoms. With crop-raising there began to be a surplus production which led to the development of arts and crafts, to exchange in the form of trade and commerce. Such a transition inevitably meant social tension. The merchant or *vaishya* class rose in importance and resented the privileges claimed by the upper two orders. To put it in modern terms, here was a situation which provided material for middle-class discontent with aristocratic privilege and priestly domination. Bourgeois aggressiveness bred anticlerical feelings.

The second force at work (in what proportions the two combined we cannot say at this distance of time) was a religious and intellectual ferment comparable with that of contemporary Greece. There was a striving after spiritual truth in a ferment of minds and much dissatisfaction with the current Brahminical order. In the thousand years or so since the Indo-Aryans had arrived the Brahmins or hereditary priests (worshipers of Brahma the creator) had seized the leadership of society from the nobles and had already established the most subtle and powerful domination of all, that of the mind. They had progressed, it is true, from the Vedic religion of hymns to the powers of nature and spells to secure boons and ward off dangers. They had developed the doctrine of *karma* or the law of consequences and the complementary doctrine of transmigration of souls from life to life. But the conditions governing the working of these laws were nonmoral and ritualistic. Reliance was placed on *mantras* or spells, on sacrifice, and on priestly ritual. The law of consequences was not yet a law of *moral* consequences. The developing conscience of the age revolted against this mechanistic religiosity. There grew up a longing for *moksha* or freedom or release from rebirth, the conscience demanding something more than ritual and the mind something more than formulae. With these gropings schools of asceticism and moral discipline and schools of philosophy or intellectual apprehension developed. From the former came movements like Buddhism. . . .

Another element should be added to this ferment. It was the tension between the non-Aryans admitted to the Hindu fold, and the Brahmins. For example, the tribe in the Nepal hills from which the Buddha came is thought to have been of Mongolian stock. The nobles of such groups had little relish for the Brahmin superiority which they found established in the new society. To sum up, we may say that a period of heart-searching and change was introduced by class tension caused by the economic transition and the rise of a mercantile class, by intellectual and spiritual tension caused by the mechanistic character of the Brahmin ascendancy, and by race tension caused by the expansion of Hindu society to include non-Aryan groups. . . .

Siddhartha Gautama, the Buddha or Enlightened One, also known as Sakyamuni or Savior of the Sakyas, was born into a noble family of the Sakya tribe at Kapilavastu on the borders of Nepal. The date now most generally accepted is about 567 B.C., though the Buddhists of Ceylon put it as early as 623 B.C. He died around 487 B.C. at the age of eighty. Around his life there has grown a tangle of pious legend, through which it is very difficult to penetrate to the flowers of historic truth. On the main outline of the story, however, there is general agreement. Gautama grew up in an atmosphere of ease and luxury, married within his class, and had a son. In some way he became aware of the sorrow and suffering of the world and of the transitoriness of life. In his twenty-ninth year he left his palace and family, donned the yellow robe, and commenced to wander, a homeless ascetic. For six years he wandered, seeking wisdom and the secret of sorrow. He trod the well-worn path of asceticism and austerities without achieving his goal. He then gave up these practices, so that his disciples deserted him saying "the ascetic Gautama has become luxurious; he has ceased from striving and turned to a life of comfort." It was then that, sitting under a *bodhi* tree under a full moon at Gaya, he attained enlightenment or Buddhahood. The meaning of sorrow, the arising of sorrow, and the conquest of sorrow became clear to him. From Gaya he went to Sarnath near Banaras where, sitting in a deer park, he gave his first sermon. From that time he moved up and down north India, preaching the Path and organizing his followers.

The Buddha's teaching concerned the nature of sorrow, which for him was the manifestation of evil in the world. Sorrow arose from desire, and desire from attachment to the transitory features of an illusive world. Desire or attachment was the cause of rebirth in successive lives. Desire in its turn was fostered by illusion, the belief that the material, changing world was real. For the Buddha it was a dancing fantasm, tempting men with its glitter and movement to bind themselves to the ever-revolving wheel of life. Desire meant sorrow in life after life. The way of escape was to conquer desire. This would bring freedom from rebirth and absorption into the All, a state called Nirvana. Whether, in the Buddha's mind, this meant extinction or conscious bliss is uncertain; what is certain is that he considered this enlightenment infinitely preferable to the only alternative of enduring sorrow. It can thus be said that the doctrine of the Buddha amounted to a spiritual and mental discipline for the attainment of right views about life. About ultimates he was agnostic. There was no personal God in the original system. It would be a mistake, however, to picture the Buddha as a late-nineteenth-century rationalist, founding an Ethical Society and lecturing in rationalist halls. The accounts of his enlightenment have in them the marks of universal mystical experience, the feeling of oneness with the universe. It was this experience toward which the Buddha's doctrine and discipline led, and it was this experience which attracted his followers and dispensed with the need for theistic worship. Meditation took the place of prayer and inner peace of divine worship.

For a time the Buddha thought that his doctrine was "too profound and subtle" for "this race of mankind, who only seek and revel in pleasure." But he repented and persevered with his teaching. There developed during his life a double way. The first was the way of renunciation for those who aspired to Buddhahood and freedom or release from the wheel of life. These disciples were organized in the *Sangha* or order, containing both men and women. They renounced the world and donned the saffron robe, lived in communities of monks and nuns, and had no possessions but their robes, their staves, and begging bowls. The modern state name of Behar derives from the word *vihara*, a Buddhist monastery, for it was once famous for these establishments.

The second way was for the householder, who, while continuing to live in the world, sought, as it were, to improve his ultimate prospects by right living. This was the Middle Way of historic Buddhism, eschewing all extremes, whose code was the "noble eightfold path." This is the ethic of popular Buddhism, and consists of right views, right resolves, right speech, right action, right living, right effort, right recollectedness, and right meditation. Without going further into these rules we may note the spirit which underlay them. One thread was that of ahimsa or nonviolence. The spirit of life was in all creatures and all creatures were therefore akin. While the Christian prays for all men, the Buddhist prays for all sentient beings. There follow such practices as vegetarianism and the refusal to take life. Another thread was compassion, which may be called the characteristic and pervasive virtue of the original system. It is this feeling, together with that of abstraction, which irradiates the countenance of the Buddha in his Indian statues. It marked a distinction from the Brahmins of the time, for whom knowledge was the supreme gift. In the personality and message of the Buddha there is a serenity and spiritual calm which charms and subdues the student after two and a half millennia. Like the silver rays of a full moon on a calm night, the Buddha's words still shed their gentle light on the face of troubled humanity. "Now monks, I have nothing more to tell you than this; decay is inherent in all compounded things. Work out your salvation energetically." . . . The Buddha, on the other hand, while accepting some basic Hindu ideas such as *karma*, separated himself from current Hinduism in a number of ways. He discountenanced caste, the keystone of the Hindu social arch. He had no place for Brahmins, replacing them in his system with monks. Agnostic in ultimate belief, he could not support the gods of the populace. Like a later Protestant, he believed that the scriptures should be understood by the people. He taught in the current speech of the Gangetic plain, a dialect akin to the Pali which later became the Buddhist sacred language. He was an opponent of the priesthood, of magic and sacrifice, of privileges, and of hiding truth in the mystery of a strange language and unintelligible books. His message was for all equally. The Middle Path provided a way of life for all, the Discourses of the Buddha a holy book for all, and the life of renunciation a way of release for all. In some respects, Buddhism was a democratic protest against Brahmin supremacy. It had therefore to separate itself from Brahminism or perish. When and where it later reunited with Brahminism it did perish.

Review and Study Questions

1. In the account from the *Buddha-Karita of Asvaghosha* what elements suggest that Buddha was a supernatural being?

2. Do you consider the teachings of the Buddha primarily to be a salvationist religion or a moral philosophy? Why?

3. Why do you suppose Buddhism never gained a wide following in the Buddha's native India?

4. How reliable are essentially religious writings as historical sources?

Suggestions for Further Reading

As with most religions, there is an enormous literature of Buddhism, including a considerable amount of biographical material—though much of it legendary and unhistorical—on the Buddha himself. The rest of the *Buddha-Karita*, excerpted for this chapter, can be read with considerable profit. The version used here is the *Buddha-Karita of Asvaghosha*, tr. B. B. Cowell in *Buddhist Mahayara Texts*, "The Sacred Books of the East," vol. 49 (New York: Dover, 1969 [1894]). Also useful are such canonical works as the "Discourse on the Aryan Quest," the "Greater Discourse to Saccaka," the "Great Discourse on the Lion's Roar," and "The Book of the Discipline," all in *Sacred Books of the Buddhists Series,* ed. F. Max Müller, 3 vols. (London: Luzac and Co., 1969 [1899]). Other useful works include *Buddhist Wisdom Books, Containing the Diamond Sutra and the Heart Sutra,* tr. and ed. Edward Conze (London: Allen and Unwin, 1958), *The Perfection of Wisdom in Eight Thousand Lines and Its Verse Summary,* tr. Edward Conze (Berkeley: Bolinas, 1973), *The Large Sutra on Perfect Wisdom,* tr. Edward Conze (Berkeley, Los Angeles, London: University of California Press, 1975), and H. Saddhatissa, *The Buddha's Way* (New York: Braziller, 1971), excerpted for this chapter. There are also a number of excellent anthologies: one of the best is *Buddhist Texts through the Ages,* ed. Edward Conze, in the Harper Torchbooks series (New York: Harper & Row, 1964). See also *Buddhism, a Religion of Infinite Compassion: Selections from Buddhist Literature,* ed. Clarence H. Hamilton (New York: The Liberal Arts Press, 1952), and *The Buddhist Philosophy of Man: Early Indian Buddhist Dialogues,* ed. Trevor Ling (London et al.: Everyman's Library, 1981). An excellent interpretive guide to Buddhist sacred literature is Edward Conze, *Buddhist Thought in India* (London: Allen and Unwin, 1962), and a basic interpretive work is Helmuth von Glasenapp, *Buddhism: A Non-theistic Religion,* tr. Irmgard Schloegl (New York: Braziller, 1966). Edward Conze, *Buddhism: Its Essence and Development* (New York and Evanston: Harper, 1959) is a readable, understandable analysis.

Of the many biographies of the Buddha, most are conventional and pietistic, written by "true believers" such as H. Saddhatissa, *The Life of Buddha* (New York: Harper & Row, 1976). Of the more recent and critical, two brief biographies can be recommended: Betty Kelen, *Gautama Buddha: In Life and Legend* (New York: Lothrop, Lee and Shepart, 1967), simple, charming, and reliable, and Michael Carrithers, *The Buddha* (Oxford and New York: Oxford University Press, 1983), in the "Past Masters" series.

Of the interpretive studies of Buddhism the most important is probably Govind Chandra Pende, *Studies in the Origins of Buddhism* (Allahabad: University Allahabad, 1957). An old standard work is Edward J. Thomas, *The History of Buddhist Thought* (New York: Barnes and Noble, 1971 [1933]). A more recent and authoritative work is Richard H. Robinson and Willard L. Johnson, *The Buddhist Religion: A Historical Introduction,* 3rd ed., in "The Religious Life of Man Series" (Belmont, Cal.: Wadsworth, 1982). Two brief standard treatments are Edward Conze, *A Short History of Buddhism* (London: Allen and Unwin, 1980) and Christmas Humphreys, *Buddhism* (Baltimore: Penguin, 1969).

On the history of India the massive old standard *Cambridge History of India,* 6 vols. (Cambridge: Cambridge University Press, 1919–69), even with its supplementary volume on the Indus Civilization, is now seriously outdated. An essential work, though difficult and demand-ing, is A. L. Basham, *The Wonder That Was India: A Survey of the Culture of the Indian Sub-Continent Before the Coming of the Muslims* (New York: Grove Press, 1954). Of the briefer works that devote some attention to the age of the Buddha, one can recommend Percival Spear, *India: A Modern History*, excerpted for this chapter; the classic and still useful W. H. Moreland and Atul Chandra Chatterjee, *A Short History of India*, 4th ed. (London: Longmans, Green and Co., 1969 [1936]); and the excellent recent book by Stanley Wolpert, *A New History of India*, 3rd ed. (New York and Oxford: Oxford University Press, 1989).

CONFUCIUS: THE MOST SAGELY ANCIENT TEACHER

C. 551 B.C.	Born
C. 530 B.C.	Opened his school in Lu
C. 497 B.C.	Voluntary exile
C. 482 B.C.	Returned to Lu
C. 479 B.C.	Died

Chinese civilization was already more than a thousand years old by the time of Confucius. In the middle of the second millennium B.C. the first historical dynasty, the Shang, established itself in the basin of the Yellow River and its tributary system. It was united by common ancestry, a common language and script, and a common religion based on the cult of ancestors and carried on through elaborate state rituals. In the late twelfth century B.C. a new dynasty, the Chou, under King Wu and his brother Tan the Duke of Chou, came to dominate the Shang lands. They adopted the Shang political and religious systems and raised both to new heights. But by the time of Confucius in the mid-sixth century B.C., the Chou dynasty was in decline. A Chou king still reigned, but the concept of the dynastic state had been successfully challenged by regional political leaders, quarreling and fighting among themselves. This is the age known in Chinese tradition as the "Spring and Autumn Period."

Confucius looked back to the age of the early Chou as a kind of formative golden age—the Duke of Chou was his cultural hero—and he diligently studied the accumulated wisdom of that golden age, which had been handed down in poetry, history, customary law, and ritual. He hoped to find in the traditional wisdom the fundamental principles on which to organize the life of the state, the family, and the individual. He hoped also to find an administrative position in the state that would permit him to apply those fundamental principles. But he never attained a sufficiently powerful position to realize this hope. Failing to become a political force himself, he became a teacher—the first private individual in Chinese history to do so. If he could not apply his principles himself then perhaps his students could. That is precisely what happened. Confucius's teachings became for his students the essential blueprint for good government, order, public welfare, and peace; and Confucius himself became "the most sagely ancient teacher," in the phrase of one of the Sung emperors of the twelfth century.

For more than two thousand years he has been regarded as China's great teacher, and his teachings have, for most of those two thousand years, been accepted as the orthodox way of life by both scholars and officials. One of his disciples wrote of him, "It would be as hard to equal our Master as to climb up on a ladder to the sky. Had our Master ever been put in control of a State or of a great Family it would have been described in the words: 'He raised them, and they stood, he led them and they went. He steadied them as with a rope, and they came. He stirred them, and they moved harmoniously. His life was glorious, his death bewailed. How can such a one ever be equalled?' "[1]

---

[1] *The Analects of Confucius,* tr. and ed. Arthur Waley (New York: Random House, 1938), 19:25, p. 230.

Who Confucius Was

SSU-MA CH'IEN

Despite the reverence for Confucius that has made him indisputably the most famous person in Chinese history, almost nothing is known about the man himself. His name has been Anglicized from the Chinese *Kung fu-tzu,* "Master Kung," but we do not know the family to which he actually belonged—the legendary account is entirely fictitious on this point. The traditional date and place of his birth, 551 B.C. in the minor state of Lu, are probably reasonably correct, as is the fact that he belonged to the lower nobility, the *Shih* or gentleman class. His own statement informs us that his father died shortly after Confucius's birth and that he was raised in relative poverty by his mother. Given these circumstances, it is not known how he received his education. Mencius *(Meng-tzu),* an important Confucian scholar of the fourth century B.C., tells us that, as a young man, Confucius served as a clerk of the state granaries of Lu and was later appointed to check on the pasture land belonging to the state. At nineteen he married, but nothing is known of his wife's family. He had a son and a daughter.

He continued to study to prepare himself for state service, but high office eluded him. His studies convinced him that good government could only be achieved by the application of the principles that were becoming clear in his own thinking—and those principles were unacceptable to the men of power who might have employed him. Moreover, it is likely that Confucius himself was too honest, blunt, and forthright to flatter them for the sake of a position.

He seems to have spent some time in the neighboring state of Ch'i but found no greater success there and returned to Lu. It was in this period that he established himself as a teacher. Between 501 and 495 B.C. he was employed by the government of Lu, though again not in a commanding position. He resigned in frustration and traveled in neighboring states for some ten years; virtually nothing is known of this period of his life. At the age of nearly seventy he returned to Lu, where he enjoyed some access to those in power because of his great reputation—though he still had no real authority. He continued to teach and to collate the ancient texts he had collected. Now old age was beginning to come upon him. He was grieved by the death of his son and several of his favorite disciples. There is no reliable account of his own death.

The foregoing sketchy account is gleaned from occasional personal references in the *Analects,* a collection of his sayings, and from the few credible details that can be sifted out of the legendary traditional account that is our only biographical source for Confucius. The following account is from a work entitled *The Historical Records,* written by Ssu-Ma Ch'ien about the turn of the second century B.C., some four hundred years after the time of Confucius. While it is called a work of history, it is far from our western notions of historical accuracy and relevancy. It does repeat most of the instances of personal reminiscence from the *Analects,* but it also reports as fact much of the miraculous lore and pure supposition that had already accumulated to obscure the historical character of Confucius. The English translators, George H. Danton and Annina Periam Danton, worked from an earlier German translation by the German scholar Richard Wilhelm, but collated it with an authoritative French translation by Edouard Chavanne, with the standard English text of the *Confucian Classics* by James Legge, and with the Chinese text itself.

Confucius was born in the State of Lu, in the District of Ch'ang P'ing, in the city of Chou. His ancestor was from the State of Sung and was called K'ung Fang-shu. Fang-shu begat Po-hsia. Po-hsia begat Shu-Liang Ho. Late in life, Ho was united in matrimony with the daughter of the man, Yen, and begat Confucius. His mother prayed to the hill, Ni, and conceived Confucius.[2] It was in the twenty-second year of Duke Hsiang of Lu that Confucius was born (551 B.C.). At his birth, he had on his head a bulging of the skull, whence he is said to have received the name "Hill" (Ch'iu). His style or appellation was Chung Ni, his family name K'ung. When he was born, his father, Shu-Liang Ho, died. . . . Confucius was poor and of low estate, and when he grew older he served as a petty official of the family Chi, and while he was in office his accounts and the measures were always correct. Thereupon, he was made Chief Shepherd, then the beasts grew in numbers and multiplied.

Therefore he was appointed Minister of Public Works. Finally he left Lu, was abandoned in Ch'i, was driven out of Sung and Wei, suffered want between Ch'ên and Ts'ai. Thereupon he returned to Lu. Confucius was nine feet six inches tall. All the people called him a giant and marvelled at him. Lu again treated him well; so he returned to Lu. . . .

People of Ch'i spoke of him with praise; Duke Ching thereupon

---

[2] This entire genealogy is fictitious.—ED.

questioned him regarding the government. Confucius said: "Let the prince be prince, the servant servant, the father father, the son son." Duke Ching replied: "That is an excellent answer: if the prince be not prince, and the servant not servant; if the father be not father, and the son not son; even though I have my revenue, how could I enjoy it!"

On another day, he again questioned Confucius about the government. Confucius replied: "Governing consists in being sparing with the resources." Duke Ching rejoiced, and wished to grant Confucius the fields of Ni Ch'i as a fief. Then Yen Ying interfered and said: "Scholars are smooth and sophisticated; they cannot be taken as a norm; they are arrogant and conceited; they cannot be used to guide the lower classes. They attach a great importance to mourning; they emphasize the lamentations, and waste their substance on magnificent funerals; they cannot be used as regulators of manners. They travel about as advisers in order to enrich themselves; they cannot be used in the ruling of the state. Since the great sages have passed away and the House of Chou has degenerated, rites and music have become defective and incomplete. Now Confucius splendidly forms the rules of behaviour, increases the ceremonies of reception and departure, and the customs in walking and in bowing, so that many generations would not be enough to exhaust his teachings. Years would not suffice to plumb his rules of decorum. If you wish to use him to change the manners of Ch'i, this is not the correct way to lead the common people." After that time, Duke Ching continued to receive Confucius, always, to be sure, with great respect, but he no longer questioned him concerning decorum. . . .

After a while, Confucius departed from Lu and held a number of distinguished positions in neighboring states. These are recounted in great detail and are completely fabricated. Finally, hearing of the death of the ruler of Lu, Confucius decided to return.

Confucius gave instruction in four subjects: Literature, Conduct, Conscientiousness, and Loyalty. He was free from four things: he had "no foregone conclusions, no arbitrary predeterminations, no obstinacy, and no egoism." The matters in which he exercised the greatest caution were the periods of fasting, of warfare, of illness. The Master seldom spoke of fortune, of fate, of "perfect virtue."

He gave no help to him who was not zealous. If he presented one corner of a subject as an example, and the pupil could not transfer what he had learned to the other three corners, Confucius did not repeat.

In everyday life, Confucius was altogether modest, as though he were not able to speak. In the ancestral temple and at court, he was eloquent, yet his speeches were always cautious. At court, he conversed with the upper dignitaries in exact and definite terms; with the lower dignitaries he was free and open. Whenever he entered in at the duke's door, he walked as though bowed over, with quick steps; he approached as if on wings. Whenever the Prince commanded his presence at a reception of guests, his appearance was serious. Whenever a command of the Prince summoned him, he left his house without waiting for the horses to be put to his chariot. . . .

Confucius was ill. Tze Kung asked permission to visit him. Then Confucius walked back and forth in the courtyard, supporting himself on his staff, and said: "Tzu, why are you so late?" Then Confucius sighed and sang:

> "The Sacred Mountain caves in,
> The roof beam breaks,
> The Sage will vanish."

Then he shed tears and said to Tze Kung: "For a long time the world has been unregulated; no one understood how to follow me. The people of Hsia placed the coffin upon the east steps, the people of Chou placed it on the west steps, the people of Yin placed it between the two pillars. Last night I dreamed that I was sitting before the sacrificial offerings between the two pillars. Does that mean that I am a man of Yin?" Seven days later, Confucius died. Confucius had attained an age of seventy-three years, when he died, in the fourth month of the sixteenth year of Duke Ai of Lu (479 B.C.).

What Confucius Said

THE *ANALECTS* OF CONFUCIUS

There is no convincing evidence that Confucius wrote anything at all. Quite the contrary: he himself is reported to have said, "I have transmitted what was taught to me without making up anything of my own."[3] Nevertheless, stubborn tradition ascribes to his authorship or editorship a list of so-called Confucian Classics—the Classics

---

[3]*Analects*, 7:1–3, Waley ed. p. 123.

of Poetry, History, Changes, Spring and Autumn Annals, and the Rites. This tradition holds that he wrote the Spring and Autumn Classic, that he selected the 305 poems in the *Book* of Poetry *from some 3,000 items, that he edited the Book of History,* and that he perhaps collated the *Book of Rites.* But the book called the *Analects* of Confucius, *Lun Yü,* is probably closer to the authentic words of Confucius than any other. It is a collection of his "sayings" compiled many years after Confucius's death from the recollections of his disciples. The traditional books of the work contain material from very different periods, but books III–IX represent the oldest part of the work. It is from these books that the following excerpts are taken.

The *Analects*—or at least some of their contents—were known to Mencius in the fourth century B.C., but it was in the second century A.D. that they received something like their present form at the hands of the Confucian scholar Cheng Hsüan. By this time many of the sayings attributed to Confucius were actually much older proverbial maxims or those of his disciples that had a Confucian flavor to them. Some of the older traditional sayings, however, may actually have been appropriated by Confucius and thus may be attributed to him, as the sayings of his disciples may contain a kernel of what "the Master" said. But with all their faults and textual problems, the *Analects* preserve the words of Confucius better than any other source we have.

Even if this is the case, we shall labor in vain in the *Analects* to find a systematic statement of Confucius's philosophy. The *Analects* have neither unity nor logical order. They are a seemingly random collection of sayings. Some are autobiographical, some philosophical; some give practical advice, others relate trivial anecdotes. They often reflect genuine wisdom, insight, or compassion; almost as often they are perfectly ordinary in sentiment. Some are so cryptic as to be nearly incomprehensible. There are, to be sure, central themes, but the sayings that bear on them are scattered through the work and we are compelled to construct a system to set them in.

The Confucian system is fundamentally a moral philosophy with almost no reference to religion. Confucius apparently did not believe in a personal deity. Of course, he honored the "will of Heaven," the traditional gods, and the rituals of their worship—but he had no concept of life after death and he contemptuously rejected traditional belief in ghosts and prodigies. Yet he did believe in transcendental values, in love and righteousness as cosmic virtues, and in "the way of Heaven" as directive of the way of humans. The *tao* or "way" in its broadest implications refers to the entire sociopolitical order, with its public and familial roles, statuses, and ranks; the *tao* governs this order. But it also refers to the inner moral life of the individual. Confucius found that "the *tao* does not prevail in the

world"[4] and saw himself as its restorer. It meant to him not only
"the traditional" but "the good." A related concept is *li,* which refers
to all the rites, ceremonies, and forms of behavior that join people
to each other. One of the most important Confucian principles is
jen, "true manhood" or "perfect virtue"—the quality of a "gentleman" or a "superior person." This was also a traditional idea, but
Confucius opened it up to ordinary people and attached to it a
moral rather than a hierarchical meaning. One could achieve *jen* by
study, zeal, and self-cultivation whatever one's status in society. In an
ethical sense *jen* is inner serenity and indifference to fortune and
misfortune. It is, in Confucius's own phrase, "human heartedness,"
and it brings a happiness that comes only from the possession of
virtue. Probably the most influential of Confucius's principles was
filial piety. It is in the family that *li* and *jen* are found. It is there that
one learns how to exercise authority and submit to authority, and
from the family these virtues are translated to the state. Though
Confucius saw himself as a political reformer, his concept of government was quite simple. Government should exist to serve the needs
of its people. Government should not unnecessarily interfere in the
lives of its people; it should allow them scope for their own moral
autonomy. A ruling class that does not enjoy the trust of its people
will not endure.

   Most of these concepts and principles are represented in the following selection of the sayings of Confucius, from the *Analects.*

III.

   3. The Master said, A man who is not Good, what can he have to
do with ritual? A man who is not Good, what can he have to do with
music?
   4. Lin Fang asked for some main principles in connexion with
ritual. The Master said, A very big question. In ritual at large it is a
safe rule always to be too sparing rather than too lavish; and in the
particular case of mourning-rites, they should be dictated by grief
rather than by fear. . . .
   18. The Master said, Were anyone to-day to serve his prince according to the full prescriptions of ritual, he would be thought a
sycophant. . . .
   26. The Master said, High office filled by men of narrow views,
ritual performed without reverence, the forms of mourning observed
without grief—these are things I cannot bear to see!

---

[4]*Analects,* 12:2, Waley ed. p. 204.

IV.

1. The Master said, It is Goodness that gives to a neighbourhood its beauty. One who is free to choose, yet does not prefer to dwell among the Good—how can he be accorded the name of wise?

2. The Master said, Without Goodness a man

> Cannot for long endure adversity,
> Cannot for long enjoy prosperity.

The Good Man rests content with Goodness; he that is merely wise pursues Goodness in the belief that it pays to do so.

3, 4. Of the adage 'Only a Good Man knows how to like people, knows how to dislike them,' the Master said, He whose heart is in the smallest degree set upon Goodness will dislike no one.

5. Wealth and rank are what every man desires; but if they can only be retained to the detriment of the Way he professes, he must relinquish them. Poverty and obscurity are what every man detests; but if they can only be avoided to the detriment of the Way he professes, he must accept them. The gentleman who ever parts company with Goodness does not fulfil that name. Never for a moment does a gentleman quit the way of Goodness. He is never so harried but that he cleaves to this; never so tottering but that he cleaves to this.

6. The Master said, I for my part have never yet seen one who really cared for Goodness, nor one who really abhorred wickedness. One who really cared for Goodness would never let any other consideration come first. One who abhorred wickedness would be so constantly doing Good that wickedness would never have a chance to get at him. Has anyone ever managed to do Good with his whole might even as long as the space of a single day? I think not. Yet I for my part have never seen anyone give up such an attempt because he had not the *strength* to go on. It may well have happened, but I for my part have never seen it. . . .

9. The Master said, A Knight[5] whose heart is set upon the Way, but who is ashamed of wearing shabby clothes and eating coarse food, is not worth calling into counsel.

10. The Master said, A gentleman in his dealings with the world has neither enmities nor affections; but wherever he sees Right he ranges himself beside it. . . .

14. The Master said, He does not mind not being in office; all he

---

[5]This translates as *shih*, or "gentleman".—Ed.

minds about is whether he has qualities that entitle him to office. He does not mind failing to get recognition; he is too busy doing the things that entitle him to recognition.

15. The Master said, Shên! My Way has one (thread) that runs right through it. Master Tsêng said, Yes. When the Master had gone out, the disciples asked, saying What did he mean? Master Tsêng said, Our Master's Way is simply this: Loyalty, consideration.

V.

5. The Master gave Ch'i-tiao K'ai leave to take office, but he replied, 'I have not yet sufficiently perfected myself in the virtue of good faith.' The Master was delighted. . . .

19. Chi Wên Tzu used to think thrice before acting. The Master hearing of it said, Twice is quite enough. . . .

27. The Master said, In a hamlet of ten houses you may be sure of finding someone quite as loyal and true to his word as I. But I doubt if you would find anyone with such a love of learning. . . .

VI.

16. The Master said, When natural substance prevails over ornamentation you get the boorishness of the rustic. When ornamentation prevails over natural substance, you get the pedantry of the scribe. Only when ornament and substance are duly blended do you get the true gentleman.

17. The Master said, Man's very life is *honesty*, in that without it he will be lucky indeed if he escapes with his life. . . .

20. Fan Ch'ih asked about wisdom. The Master said, He who devotes himself to securing for his subjects what it is right they should have, who by respect for the Spirits keeps them at a distance, may be termed wise. He asked about Goodness. The Master said, Goodness cannot be obtained till what is difficult has been duly done. He who has done this may be called Good. . . .

25. The Master said, A gentleman who is widely versed in letters and at the same time knows how to submit his learning to the restraints of ritual is not likely, I think, to go far wrong.

28. Tzu-kung said, If a ruler not only conferred wide benefits upon the common people, but also compassed the salvation of the whole State, what would you say of him? Surely, you would call him Good? The Master said, It would no longer be a matter of 'Good.' He would without doubt be a Divine Sage. Even Yao and Shun could hardly criticize him. . . .

VII.

6. The Master said, Set your heart upon the Way, support yourself by its power, lean upon Goodness, seek distraction in the arts.

7. The Master said, From the very poorest upwards—beginning even with the man who could bring no better present than a bundle of dried flesh—none has ever come to me without receiving instruction.

8. The Master said, Only one who bursts with eagerness do I instruct; only one who bubbles with excitement, do I enlighten. If I hold up one corner and a man cannot come back to me with the other three, I do not continue the lesson. . . .

11. The Master said, If any means of escaping poverty presented itself, that did not involve doing wrong, I would adopt it, even though my employment were only that of the gentleman who holds the whip. But so long as it is a question of illegitimate means, I shall continue to pursue the quests that I love. . . .

15. The Master said, He who seeks only coarse food to eat, water to drink and bent arm for pillow, will without looking for it find happiness to boot. Any thought of accepting wealth and rank by means that I know to be wrong is as remote from me as the clouds that float above. . . .

19. The Master said, I for my part am not one of those who have innate knowledge. I am simply one who loves the past and who is diligent in investigating it. . . .

21. The Master said, Even when walking in a party of no more than three I can always be certain of learning from those I am with. There will be good qualities that I can select for imitation and bad ones that will teach me what requires correction in myself. . . .

24. The Master took four subjects for his teaching: culture, conduct of affairs, loyalty to superiors and the keeping of promises.

25. The Master said, A Divine Sage I cannot hope ever to meet; the most I can hope for is to meet a true gentleman. The Master said, A faultless man I cannot hope ever to meet; the most I can hope for is to meet a man of fixed principles. Yet where all around I see Nothing pretending to be Something, Emptiness pretending to be Fullness, Penury pretending to be Affluence, even a man of fixed principles will be none too easy to find. . . .

27. The Master said, There may well be those who can do without knowledge; but I for my part am certainly not one of them. To hear much, pick out what is good and follow it, to see much and take due note of it, is the lower of the two kinds of knowledge. . . .

33. The Master said, As to being a Divine Sage or even a Good Man, far be it from me to make any such claim. As for unwearying effort to learn and unflagging patience in teaching others, those are

merits that I do not hesitate to claim. Kung-hsi Hua said, The trouble is that we disciples cannot learn!

VIII.

8. The Master said, Let a man be first incited by the *Songs,* then given a firm footing by the study of ritual, and finally perfected by music. . . .

10. The Master said, One who is by nature daring and is suffering from poverty will not long be law-abiding. Indeed, any men, save those that are truly Good, if their sufferings are very great, will be likely to rebel. . . .

13. The Master said, Be of unwavering good faith, love learning, if attacked be ready to die for the good Way. Do not enter a State that pursues dangerous courses, nor stay in one where the people have rebelled. When the Way prevails under Heaven, then show yourself; when it does not prevail, then hide. When the Way prevails in your own land, count it a disgrace to be needy and obscure; when the Way does not prevail in your land, then count it a disgrace to be rich and honoured. . . .

IX.

24. The Master said, First and foremost, be faithful to your superiors, keep all promises, refuse the friendship of all who are not like you; and if you have made a mistake, do not be afraid of admitting the fact and amending your ways.

What Confucius Meant

H. G. CREEL

As we have already seen, there is no inherent thematic unity in the philosophy of Confucius. This, in combination with the enormous authority of his name and his sayings, has made it possible for Confucius to mean many things to many people over the centuries. He has been a sage, a prophet, a magician, a teacher, a philosopher, even a religious figure. To some extent, of course, he was a multifaceted thinker who truly did mean many things. But when we ask what his primary emphasis was, we can best answer that he was primarily a political reformer and that everything else in his thought stemmed from that emphasis. This view is reflected in the book, excerpted below, by H. G. Creel, *Confucius the Man and the Myth*. Creel was a longtime professor at the University of Chicago and one of the most distinguished American Sinologists. This book, among many that he wrote, is one of the seminal works of twentieth-century Confucian interpretation. Indeed, John K. Fairbank, himself a distinguished Orientalist, wrote that "there is no doubt that we have in this book the most scholarly, vivid, and all-around view of Confucius the man now available."[6] It is as authoritative now as when it was written a generation ago, to a large extent because it is a fundamental reinterpretation of Confucius. Creel rejects the entire Chinese Confucian tradition as historically unreliable, and goes back to contemporary records and to his own expert evaluation of them. In the selection below he begins with the political environment of Confucius's own age and his reaction to it.

The rulers and their powerful ministers were scions of hereditary noble houses. With rare exceptions, they were prey to the degeneration usually suffered by families in which power and luxury are bequeathed from father to son for many generations. They needed two virtues, prowess in war and skill in intrigue, and these they cultivated to the utmost. The result was a world that no man who cared for human dignity and human happiness could contemplate with equanimity.

Confucius was such a man, and he was profoundly disturbed. He dedicated his life to the attempt to make a better world. . . .

Confucius himself said that he was the intellectual heir of King Wên, the father of the founder of the Chou dynasty. He also implied, in a passage which is somewhat vague, that he looked upon the Duke of Chou, a son of Wên, as his inspiration. Chinese tradition, from a very early time, has regarded the Duke of Chou as a source of Confucian ideas and sometimes even as the founder of Confucianism, notwithstanding the fact that he lived more than five hundred years before Confucius. . . .

In China, the effect was to leave an ideal of kingship as a form of stewardship, in which the test of a good king was whether or not he brought about the welfare of the people. Since the Chou legitimized their title by the claim that they had replaced an oppressive sovereign, justice and kindness became the duty of every later ruler. The ac-

---

[6]*New York Times*, May 8, 1949, p. 7.

cepted theory was that every person in authority must regard his office as a sacred and difficult trust. As we have abundantly seen, it was almost universally honored in the breach rather than the observance. Yet the mere fact that such a code existed was of the highest importance. In it Confucius found ready to his hand much that was very useful for his undertaking. The fact that (like the teachings of Jesus) it was almost universally acknowledged to be right, though considered impracticable, gave to his doctrines a support they could have obtained in no other way. . . .

Since his own world was far from ideal, it is natural that he thought of the best state as one that had those things in which his own was conspicuously lacking; in which, that is, the whole people should enjoy peace, security, and plenty. When we speak of peace, it is not to be supposed that Confucius was a pacifist; clearly he was not. But needless war was against his principles, and since most of the war in his day was internecine and an aspect of the general lawlessness, the governmental reforms he advocated would, if successful, have automatically eliminated it.

"Tzŭ-kung asked about government. The Master replied, 'An effective government must have sufficient food, sufficient weapons, and the confidence of the common people.' 'Suppose,' Tzŭ-kung said, 'that one of these three had to be dispensed with; which should it be?' The Master said, 'Weapons.' 'And what if one of the remaining two must be let go?' 'Then,' replied the Master, 'let the food go. For, from of old, death has been the lot of all men; but if the people have no confidence in the government, the state cannot stand.' ". . .

This last statement is extremely important. It does not mean that a government should starve its people to death in order to maintain itself; that would be absurd and very un-Confucian. What it does mean is that rulers should not drive and exploit their people unmercifully for the sake of economic gain, while giving the excuse that it is "for the people's own good" although they are too stupid to realize it. Even more important, it is an assertion that a state is a cooperative enterprise in which all, rulers and ruled alike, must share in the understanding of its purposes and the enjoyment of its benefits. . . .

"The Master said, 'If one tries to guide the people by means of rules, and keep order by means of punishments, the people will merely seek to avoid the penalties without having any sense of moral obligation. But if one leads them with virtue [both by precept and by example], and depends upon *li* to maintain order, the people will then feel their moral obligation and correct themselves.' " Here is the essence of Confucius' political philosophy. Not negative punishment but positive example; not tirades about what the people should not do but education as to what they should do. Not a police state dominated by fear but a cooperative commonwealth in which there is mutual understanding and good will between the rulers and the ruled. On this point he agreed with the most modern democratic theory. . . .

Once the people's poverty has been relieved, Confucius said, they should then be educated. We have already seen that he advocated at least some education for all the people. He once declared that if any man, no matter how humble, came to him seeking truth he was prepared to spend all the time that was necessary in helping him solve his problem. He boasted that he had never turned away a student, and in fact he seems to have accepted them, for training in the art of government, without regard to qualifications of birth or wealth, if only they were intelligent and industrious.

In thus advocating some education for all, and undertaking to make educated "gentlemen" out of ambitious commoners, Confucius was striking a blow that was ultimately fatal to the hereditary aristocratic order. . . . He undertook to take any intelligent student, of whatever background, and educate him to the point where he should be capable of making his own moral judgments. But he did not depend, to secure acceptance for his views, on any divine revelation or any claim of special authority for himself. Like the scientist, he believed that he could convince men through an appeal to their reason. This seems to be the sense of a somewhat obscure passage in the *Analects* in which he declares that the common people are the standard by which the justice of his actions may be tested.

Confucius conceived the highest political good to be the *happiness* of the people. This is of the utmost importance and is quite different from aiming merely at their welfare. . . .

The claim that a government brings about the welfare of the people may mean anything. But happiness is something else. "The Duke of Shê asked about government. The Master said, 'When there is good government, those who are near are made happy and those who are distant come.' " Another time he said that when the people of other states heard of a really good government they would be so eager to live under it that they would "come carrying their children on their backs." The important point about such statements is that they make the common people, and nobody else, the judges of what is good and what is bad government. Men can be forced to be orderly and to be productive, but they cannot be forced to be happy any more than a horse can be made to drink. They can be made happy only by a government that is good by their own standards. . . .

He appears to have believed that:

The proper aim of government is the welfare and happiness of the whole people.

This aim can be achieved only when the state is administered by those most capable of government.

Capacity to govern has no necessary connection with birth, wealth, or position; it depends solely on character and knowledge.

Character and knowledge are produced by proper education.

In order that the best talents may become available, education should be widely diffused.

It follows that the government should be administered by those persons, chosen from the whole population, who prove themselves to have profited most by the proper kind of education.

It is evident that this is not the same thing as saying that the people as a whole should control the government. But it does say that every man should have the opportunity to show whether he is capable of taking part in its control and its administration, and that if he proves himself so capable he should be not only permitted but urged to participate. This is in effect an aristocratic system, of government by an aristocracy not of birth or wealth but of virtue and ability.

Review and Study Questions

1. Why do you suppose the teachings of Confucius came to play so fundamental a role in Chinese civilization?

2. How does Confucius's emphasis on regulation and order translate into a political philosophy?

3. Why was the family so central to Confucius's philosophy? Why has it remained so central in Chinese life?

4. What elements of moral philosophy stand out in the precepts of Confucius?

5. Confucius was convinced that the character and knowledge necessary to rule are produced by proper education. To what extent has this basic Confucian conviction been adopted by the rulers of China?

Suggestions for Further Reading

The standard English text of Confucius's *Analects* as well as of the other so-called Confucian classics is the massive seven-volume *The Chinese Classics,* ed. and tr. James Legge (Oxford: Clarendon Press, 1893). This series also reproduces the Chinese text. There is a reprint of the first volume of this series, *The Four Books, Confucian Analects, the Great Learning, the Doctrine of the Mean, and the Works of Mencius,* ed.

and tr. James Legge (New York: Paragon Books, 1966). *The Living Thoughts of Confucius,* ed. Alfred Doeblin (London et al.: Cassell, 1948) is a brief selection of translated passages from most of the important Confucian texts. *The Analects of Confucius,* ed. and tr. Arthur Waley (New York: Vintage Books, 1938), excerpted for this chapter, is a more modern and readable translation, the best available. The only English version of the Ssu-Ma Ch'ien historical biography is the one used in this chapter, Richard Wilhelm, *Confucius and Confucianism,* tr. George H. Danton and Annina Periam Danton (London: Routledge and Kegan Paul, 1972 [1931]).

On Confucius in Chinese literature, one of the most learned and readable works is Benjamin I. Schwartz, *The World of Thought in Ancient China* (Cambridge, Mass., and London: Harvard University Press, 1985). Burton Watson, *Early Chinese Literature* (New York and London: Columbia University Press, 1962) is one of the series "Companions to Asian Studies" and is an extremely useful handbook.

The best biography of Confucius is the one used in this chapter, H. G. Creel, *Confucius the Man and the Myth* (Westport, Conn.: Greenwood Press, 1972 [1949]), which is also available in the "Harper Torchbooks" series under the title *Confucius and the Chinese Way* (New York: Harper & Row, 1960). Two important interpretive works are Herbert Fingarette, *Confucius: The Secular as Sacred* (New York: Harper & Row, 1972) and Pierre Do-Dinh, *Confucius and Chinese Humanism,* tr. Charles Lam Markmann (New York: Funk and Wagnalls, 1969). D. Howard Smith, *Confucius* (New York: Scribner, 1973) and Liu Wu-Chi, *Confucius: His Life and Time* (New York: Philosophical Library, 1955) are competent standard biographies, as is the briefer Raymond Dawson, *Confucius* (New York: Hill and Wang, 1981) in the reliable "Past Masters" series. An interesting book is Kam Louie, *Critiques of Confucius in Contemporary China* (New York: St. Martin's Press, 1980), on how the Chinese Communists have dealt with the revered Confucian tradition. A book that goes to the other end of that tradition is John K. Shryock, *The Origins and Development of the State Cult of Confucius* (New York: Paragon Books, 1966 [1932]).

On the general history of the period, L. Carrington Goodrich, *A Short History of the Chinese People* (New York and London: Harper, 1943) is an excellent introduction to Chinese civilization and social history, largely based on original sources. Of the same sort is C. P. Fitzgerald and Norman Kotker, *The Horizon History of China* (New York: American Heritage Publishing Co., 1969). Charles O. Hucker, *China's Imperial Past* (Stanford: Stanford University Press, 1975) is a modern classic. John K. Fairbank, Edwin O. Reischauer, Albert M. Craig, *East Asia: Tradition and Transformation,* new impression (Boston et al.: Houghton Mifflin, 1978) is an authoritative and respected general survey.

THE IMAGE OF SOCRATES: MAN OR MYTH?

c. 470 B.C.	Born
c. 431–424 B.C.	Served in Peloponnesian War
406–405 B.C.	Served as a member of Athenian executive council
399 B.C.	Trial and death

By the lifetime of Socrates, in the late fifth century B.C., Greek civilization was almost at an end. This historic civilization was centered in Socrates' own city of Athens, which Pericles proudly called "the school of Hellas." But that magnificent city, which has so captivated our imagination, was widely regarded by its fellow city-states as a threat to their own independence—and with more than a little justification.

This threat led to the great Peloponnesian War, so vividly recounted in the pages of Socrates' contemporary, the historian Thucydides. Athens and its subject states were set against her arch-rival Sparta and Sparta's allies, the Peloponnesian League. It was a long, costly, and enervating war of almost thirty years' duration. And Athens finally lost it. Athens was humiliated, forced to accept its enemies' terms, and stripped of its subject states, its wealth, its navy. The buoyant optimism that had earlier characterized the city was one of the prime casualties of the war, along with confidence in its institutions and even in many of the presuppositions of its public life and private morality. It is in the backwash of these events that we must seek the life, and the death, of Socrates.

Socrates was surely the most famous Athenian of his age. Yet despite that fame, the facts of his life remain stubbornly vague. He was not a public official; hence we do not have archival records to rely on. And though he is a famous figure in literature, he actually wrote

93

nothing himself to which we can refer. There are scattered references to him in Aristotle; a substantial (though prosaic) account in the works of Xenophon, who knew him; and, of course, the principal source of our information about him, the dialogues of the great philosopher Plato, who was Socrates' adoring pupil and disciple and made him the main character in most of his dialogues. And there are references and anecdotes from a considerable number of near contemporary accounts of Socrates that have been preserved, although the original sources are now lost.

What we know about Socrates is this. He was born an Athenian citizen about 470 B.C. His family belonged to the class of small artisans; his mother was a midwife and his father a stone mason. Socrates himself followed his father's trade. Rather late in life he married Xanthippe, and they had three sons, two of them still very young at the time of their father's death. Like most able-bodied Athenians of his time, Socrates was a veteran of the Peloponnesian War and even served with some distinction. On two occasions he seems to have held office on the large civic boards and commissions that carried on the business of the city. But generally he avoided public life. From a number of surviving descriptions and portrait busts we know what Socrates looked like—small and balding, anything but the lofty Greek ideal of physical beauty. And we also know that he spent most of his time going about the city, trailed by a delighted and curious crowd of bright young aristocrats, asking often embarrassing questions of people who interested him, usually public officials and individuals of substance and position. This practice was to the detriment of his own family and his own trade. Socrates was a poor man.

The Clouds

ARISTOPHANES

The preceding bare account of Socrates is supplemented—one must almost say contradicted—by a single additional source, *The Clouds* of Aristophanes. This work is of considerable value in that it is the only really substantial account of Socrates by a mature contemporary. Even Plato, our principal source of information, was forty years younger than Socrates, knew him only as an old man, and wrote *The Dialogues* many years after Socrates' death. *The Clouds* is, of course, not a biography. It is a play, by the greatest of Greek comic dramatists, in which Socrates is not only one of its chief characters but also the object of its satire.

Aristophanes was a conservative, and his plays are a catalog of his objections to the management of the war and public policy, the state of literature and philosophy, the subversion of the stern old virtues "of our forefathers," and the "new morality" that he saw about him. In *The Clouds* he accused Socrates of being a professional teacher who received, nay extracted, money for his "lessons"—which was not true. He denounced him as a cynical, opportunistic atheist—which was also apparently not the case. He attributed to him an expert competence in natural philosophy—which was highly unlikely. And in what was perhaps the most unfounded of all his charges, he portrayed Socrates as being the chief of the Sophists.

The Sophists were a school of professional teachers, then very popular in Athens, who taught young men of wealth and position (usually for substantial fees) the techniques of public life, mostly logic and oratorical persuasion. The Sophists also tended to a flexible morality in which success was to be preferred to virtue, victory to either morality or philosophic consistency. It is a more than Socratic irony that Socrates should have been depicted as one of them, for it was squarely against the Sophists and their moral relativism that he had taken his stand. The whole point of his life, the reason he engaged other people in his famous questioning and endured their animosity, the entire "Socratic method" was an attempt to make people understand that there are moral absolutes, unchanging abstract principles of conduct to which they must ultimately resort.

Why Aristophanes portrayed Socrates in this fashion we do not know. Perhaps he genuinely believed that Socrates was a Sophist. Or

perhaps he knew the truth but simply did not care, and made use
of Socrates' notoriety in Athens to score his own point about the
scandalous decline of education and what he regarded as philosophic quackery.

In any event, the play is cruel, mean, and malicious, but it is out-
rageously funny. And it gives us a view, however hostile, of the historic Socrates.

The Clouds opens in the house of Strepsiades, a foolish old farmer,
whose son Pheidippides' extravagant passion for racehorses has
piled up so many debts that the old man is faced with ruin. One
night, unable to sleep, Strepsiades decides to enroll the boy in the
Sophist's school down the street. He calls it the "Thinkery." But
Pheidippides will have nothing to do with "those filthy charlatans
you mean—those frauds, those barefoot pedants with the look of
death, Chairephon and that humbug, Sokrates."

The old man then decides to go to the school himself. He kicks
on the door, and a student-doorman answers. As they stand at the
door, the student extols the wisdom of his master Socrates, citing a
number of examples, not the least of which is Socrates' resolution of
the problem of how the gnat hums. "According to him, the intesti-
nal tract of the gnat is of puny proportions, and through this di-
minutive duct the gastric gas of the gnat is forced under pressure
down to the rump. At that point the compressed gases, as through
a narrow valve, escape with a whoosh, thereby causing the characteristic tootle or cry of the flatulent gnat."

Strepsiades is suitably impressed. "Why, Thales himself was an
amateur compared to this! Throw open the Thinkery! Unbolt the
door and let me see this wizard Sokrates in person. Open up! I'm
MAD for education!" And Strepsiades enters the school.

STREPSIADES

Look: who's that dangling up there in the basket?

STUDENT

Himself.

STREPSIADES

Who's Himself?

STUDENT

Sokrates.

STREPSIADES

SOKRATES!

Then call him down. Go on. Give a great big shout.

STUDENT

Hastily and apprehensively taking his leave.

Er . . . *you* call him. I'm a busy man.

Exit Student.

STREPSIADES

O Sokrates!

No answer from the basket.

Yoohoo. Sokrates!

SOKRATES

From a vast philosophical height.

Well, creature of a day?

STREPSIADES

What in the world are you doing up there?

SOKRATES

Ah, sir,

I walk upon the air and look down upon the sun
from a superior standpoint.

STREPSIADES

Well, I suppose it's better

that you sneer at the gods from a basket up in the air
than do it down here on the ground.

SOKRATES

Precisely. You see,

only by being suspended aloft, by dangling
my mind in the heavens and mingling my rare thought
with the ethereal air, could I ever achieve strict
scientific accuracy in my survey of the vast empyrean.
Had I pursued my inquiries from down there on the ground,
my data would be worthless. The earth, you see, pulls down
the delicate essence of thought to its own gross level.

As an afterthought.

Much the same thing happens with watercress.

STREPSIADES

Ecstatically bewildered.

You don't say?
Thought draws down . . . delicate essence . . . into
watercress. O dear little Sokrates, please come down.
Lower away, and teach me what I need to know!

Sokrates is slowly lowered earthwards.

SOKRATES

What subject?

STREPSIADES

Your course on public speaking and debating techniques.
You see, my creditors have become absolutely ferocious.
You should see how they're hounding me. What's more,
Sokrates, they're about to seize my belongings.

SOKRATES

How in the
world could you fall so deeply in debt without realizing it?

STREPSIADES

How? A great, greedy horse-pox ate me up, that's how.
But that's why I want instruction in your second Logic,
you know the one—the get-away-without-paying argument.
I'll pay you *any* price you ask. I swear it.
By the gods.

SOKRATES

By the gods? The gods, my dear simple fellow,
are a mere expression coined by vulgar superstition.
We frown upon such coinage here.

STREPSIADES

What do *you* swear by?
Bars of iron, like the Byzantines?

SOKRATES

Tell me, old man,
would you honestly like to learn the truth, the *real* truth,
about the gods?

STREPSIADES

By Zeus, I sure would. The *real* truth. . . .

[*At this point the chorus of clouds enters, singing.*]

STREPSIADES

Holy Zeus, Sokrates, who were those ladies that sang
that solemn hymn? Were they heroines of mythology?

SOKRATES

No, old man.
Those were the Clouds of heaven, goddesses of men of
leisure and philosophers. To them we owe our repertoire of
verbal talents: our eloquence, intellect, fustian, casuistry,
force, wit, prodigious vocabulary, circumlocutory skill—

. . . .

[*The leader of the chorus greets them.*]

KORYPHAIOS

Hail, superannuated man!
Hail, old birddog of culture!

To Sokrates.

And hail to you, O Sokrates,
high priest of poppycock!
Inform us what your wishes are.
For of all the polymaths on earth, it's you we most prefer—

. . . .

sir, for your swivel-eyes, your barefoot swagger down the
street, because you're poor on our account and terribly
affected.

STREPSIADES

Name of Earth, what a voice! Solemn and holy and awful!

SOKRATES

These are the only gods there are. The rest are but figments.

STREPSIADES

Holy name of Earth! Olympian Zeus is a figment?

SOKRATES

Zeus?
    What Zeus?
        Nonsense.
            There is no Zeus.

STREPSIADES

                            No Zeus?
Then *who* makes it rain? Answer me that.

SOKRATES

                        Why, the Clouds,
of course.
        What's more, the proof is incontrovertible.
                            For instance,
have you ever yet seen rain when you didn't see a cloud?
But if your hypothesis were correct, Zeus could drizzle
    from an empty sky
while the clouds were on vacation.

STREPSIADES

                        By Apollo, you're right. A pretty
    proof.
And to think I always used to believe the rain was just Zeus
pissing through a sieve.
                    All right, *who* makes it thunder?
Brrr. I get goosebumps just saying it.

SOKRATES

                            The Clouds again,
of course. A simple process of Convection.

STREPSIADES

                        I admire you,
but I don't follow you.

SOKRATES

    Listen. The Clouds are a saturate water-solution.

Tumescence in motion, of necessity, produces precipitation.
When these distended masses collide—*boom!*
                                        Fulmination.

STREPSIADES

But who makes them move before they collide? Isn't that
Zeus?

SOKRATES

Not Zeus, idiot. The Convection-principle!

STREPSIADES

                                        Convection? That's
a new one.
Just think. So Zeus is out and Convection-principle's in.
Tch, tch.
        But wait: you haven't told me who makes it thunder.

SOKRATES

But I just *finished* telling you! The Clouds are water-packed;
they collide with each other and explode because of the
pressure.

STREPSIADES

        Yeah?
And what's your proof for *that?*

SOKRATES

                        Why, take yourself as example.
You know that meat-stew the vendors sell at the Panathenaia?[1]
How it gives you the cramps and your stomach
starts to rumble?

STREPSIADES

                                Yes,
by Apollo! I remember. What an awful feeling! You feel
sick and your belly churns and the fart rips loose like
thunder. First just a gurgle, *pappapax;* then louder,

---

[1]The quadrennial festival of Athena, the patron goddess of Athens.—ED.

pappaPAPAXapaX, and finally like thunder,
PAPAPAPAXAPAXAPPAPAXapap!

SOKRATES

Precisely.
First think of the tiny fart that your intestines make.
Then consider the heavens: their infinite farting is thunder.
For thunder and farting are, in principle, one and the same.

[*Strepsiades is convinced and is initiated into Socrates' school. But, alas, he is incapable of learning the subtleties Socrates sets out to teach him and is contemptuously dismissed from the school. Then the leader of the chorus suggests that he fetch his son to study in his place. A splendid idea! As Strepsiades drags his son on to the scene, Pheidippides protests.*]

PHEIDIPPIDES

But Father,
what's the matter with you? Are you out of your head?
Almighty Zeus, you must be mad!

STREPSIADES

"Almighty Zeus!"
What musty rubbish! Imagine, a boy your age
still believing in Zeus!

PHEIDIPPIDES

What's so damn funny?

STREPSIADES

It tickles me when the heads of toddlers like you
are still stuffed with such outdated notions. Now then,
listen to me and I'll tell you a secret or two
that might make an intelligent man of you yet.
But remember: you mustn't breathe a word of this.

PHEIDIPPIDES

A word of what?

STREPSIADES

Didn't you just swear by Zeus?

PHEIDIPPIDES

I did.

STREPSIADES

Now learn what Education can do for *you:*
Pheidippides, there is no Zeus.

PHEIDIPPIDES

There is no Zeus?

STREPSIADES

No Zeus. Convection-principle's in power now.
Zeus has been banished.

PHEIDIPPIDES

Drivel!

STREPSIADES

Take my word for it,
it's absolutely true.

PHEIDIPPIDES

Who says so?

STREPSIADES

Sokrates.
And Chairephon too. . . .

PHEIDIPPIDES

Are you so far gone on the road to complete insanity
you'd believe the word of those charlatans?

STREPSIADES

Hush, boy.
For shame. I won't hear you speaking disrespectfully
of such eminent scientists and geniuses. And, what's more,
men of such fantastic frugality and Spartan thrift,
they regard baths, haircuts, and personal cleanliness
generally as an utter waste of time and money—whereas
you, dear boy, have taken me to the cleaner's so many times,
I'm damn near washed up. Come on, for your father's sake,
go and learn.

[Some time later]
Enter Strepsiades from his house, counting on his fingers.

STREPSIADES

Five days, four days, three days, two days, and then
that one day of the days of the month
I dread the most that makes me fart with fear—
the last day of the month, Duedate for debts,
when every dun in town has solemnly sworn
to drag me into court and bankrupt me completely.
And when I plead with them to be more reasonable—
"But PLEASE, sir. Don't demand the whole sum now.
Take something on account. I'll pay you later."—
they snort they'll never see the day, curse me
for a filthy swindler and say they'll sue.
                                              Well,
let them. If Pheidippides has learned to talk,
I don't give a damn for them and their suits.
                                              Now then,
a little knock on the door and we'll have the answer.

He knocks on Sokrates' door and calls out.

Porter!
            Hey, porter!

Sokrates opens the door.

SOKRATES

                        Ah, Strepsiades. Salutations.

STREPSIADES

Same to you, Sokrates.

He hands Sokrates a bag of flour.

                        Here. A token of my esteem.
Call it an honorarium. Professors always get honorariums.

Snatching back the bag.

But wait: has Pheidippides learned his rhetoric yet—. . . .

SOKRATES

Taking the bag.

He has mastered it.

STREPSIADES

O great goddess Bamboozle!

SOKRATES

Now, sir, you can evade any legal action you wish to.

*[But instead of help with his creditors, Strepsiades gets a very different kind
of treatment from his son.]*

*With a bellow of pain and terror, Strepsiades plunges out of his house, hotly
pursued by Pheidippides with a murderous stick.*

STREPSIADES

OOOUUUCH!!!
                HALP!
                        For god's sake, help me!

Appealing to the Audience.

                                                Friends!
Fellow-countrymen! Aunts! Uncles! Fathers! Brothers!
To the rescue!
                He's beating me!
                                Help me!
                                        Ouuch!
O my poor head!
                Ooh, my jaw!

To Pheidippides.

                                —You great big bully,
Hit your own father, would you?

PHEIDIPPIDES

                                Gladly, Daddy.

STREPSIADES

You hear that? The big brute *admits* it.

PHEIDIPPIDES

                                Admit it? Hell,
I *proclaim* it. . . .
                Would a logical demonstration
convince you?

STREPSIADES

A logical demonstration? You mean to tell me
you can *prove* a shocking thing like that?

PHEIDIPPIDES

Elementary, really.
What's more, you can choose the logic. Take your pick.
Either one.

STREPSIADES

Either *which?*

PHEIDIPPIDES

Either *which?* Why,
Socratic logic or pre-Socratic logic. Either logic.
Take your pick.

STREPSIADES

Take my pick, damn you? Look,
who do you think paid for your shyster education anyway?
And now you propose to convince *me* that there's nothing
wrong in whipping your own father?

PHEIDIPPIDES

I not only propose it:
I propose to *prove* it. Irrefutably, in fact. Rebuttal
is utterly inconceivable. . . .

[*Pheidippides then "proves" that since his father beat him as a child "for your
own damn good" "because I loved you," then it is only "a fortiori" logic that
the father be beaten by the son, since "old men logically deserve to be beaten
more, since at their age they have clearly less excuse for the mischief that they
do."*]

*There is a long tense silence as the full force of this
crushing argument takes its effect upon Strepsiades.*

STREPSIADES

What?
But how. . . ?
Hmm,
by god, you're right!

To the Audience.

—Speaking for the older generation, gentlemen, I'm compelled to admit defeat. The kids have proved their point: naughty fathers should be flogged. . . .

[*But this arrogance is too much, logic or no logic, for Strepsiades.*]

STREPSIADES

O Horse's Ass, Blithering Imbecile, Brainless Booby, Bonehead that I was to ditch the gods for Sokrates!

He picks up Pheidippides' stick and savagely smashes the potbellied model of the Universe in front of the Thinkery. He then rushes to his own house and falls on his knees before the statue of Hermes.

—Great Hermes, I implore you!

[*Strepsiades and his slave set fire to the Thinkery and he beats the choking, sputtering Socrates and his pallid students off the stage.*]

The Apology

PLATO

In 399 B.C., twenty-five years after *The Clouds,* Socrates stood before the great popular court of Athens. He was accused of much the same charges that had been leveled at him by Aristophanes, specifically "that Socrates is a doer of evil, who corrupts the youth; and who does not believe in the gods of the state, but has other new divinities of his own." The charges were brought by three fellow Athenians, Meletus, Lycon, and Anytus. Although only one of the accusers, Anytus, was a person of any importance, and he only a minor political figure, the charges carried the death penalty if the court so decided. Indeed, this was the intent of the accusers.

Socrates, now seventy years old, rose to speak in his own defense; he was not the pettifogging buffoon of *The Clouds.* Perhaps that man never really existed. By the same token, did the speaker at the trial ever exist? The trial is Socrates', but the account of it is Plato's. *The Apology,* from *The Dialogues of Plato,* is the "defense" of Socrates at his trial.

How you, O Athenians, have been affected by my accusers, I cannot tell; but I know that they almost made me forget who I was—so persuasively did they speak; and yet they have hardly uttered a word of truth. But . . . first, I have to reply to the older charges and to my first accusers, and then I will go on to the later ones. For of old I have had many accusers, who have accused me falsely to you during many years; and I am more afraid of them than of Anytus and his associates, who are dangerous, too, in their own way. But far more dangerous are the others, who began when you were children, and took possession of your minds with their falsehoods, telling of one Socrates, a wise man, who speculated about the heaven above, and searched into the earth beneath, and made the worse appear the better cause. The disseminators of this tale are the accusers whom I dread; for their hearers are apt to fancy that such enquirers do not believe in the existence of the gods. And they are many, and their charges against me are of ancient date, and they were made by them in the days when you were more impressible than you are now—in childhood, or it may have been in youth— and the cause when heard went by default, for there was none to answer. And hardest of all, I do not know and cannot tell the names of my accusers; unless in the chance case of a Comic poet. . . .

I dare say, Athenians, that some one among you will reply, 'Yes, Socrates, but what is the origin of these accusations which are brought against you; there must have been something strange which you have been doing? All these rumours and this talk about you would never have arisen if you had been like other men: tell us, then, what is the cause of them, for we should be sorry to judge hastily of you.' Now I regard this as a fair challenge, and I will endeavour to explain to you the reason why I am called wise and have such an evil fame. . . .

. . . I will refer you to a witness who is worthy of credit; that witness shall be the God of Delphi—he will tell you about my wisdom, if I have any, and of what sort it is. You must have known Chaerephon; he was early a friend of mine. . . .Well, Chaerephon, as you know, was very impetuous in all his doings, and he went to Delphi and boldly asked the oracle to tell him whether—as I was saying, I must beg you not to interrupt—he asked the oracle to tell him whether any one was wiser than I was, and the Pythian prophetess answered, that there was no man wiser. Chaerephon is dead himself; but his brother, who is in court, will confirm the truth of what I am saying.

Why do I mention this? Because I am going to explain to you why I have such an evil name. When I heard the answer, I said to myself, What can the god mean? and what is the interpretation of his riddle? for I know that I have no wisdom, small or great. What then can he mean when he says that I am the wisest of men? And yet he is a god, and cannot lie; that would be against his nature. After long consideration, I thought of a method of trying the question. I reflected that if I could only find a man wiser than myself, then I might go to the god with a refutation in my hand. I should say to him, 'Here is a man who is wiser than I am; but you said that I was the wisest.' Accordingly I went to one who had the reputation of wisdom, and observed him— his name I need not mention; he was a politician whom I selected for examination—and the result was as follows: When I began to talk with him, I could not help thinking that he was not really wise, although he was thought wise by many, and still wiser by himself; and thereupon I tried to explain to him that he thought himself wise, but was not really wise; and the consequence was that he hated me, and his enmity was shared by several who were present and heard me. So I left him, saying to myself, as I went away: Well, although I do not suppose that either of us knows anything really beautiful and good, I am better off than he is,—for he knows nothing, and thinks that he knows; I neither know nor think that I know. In this latter particular, then, I seem to have slightly the advantage of him. Then I went to another who had still higher pretensions to wisdom, and my conclusion was exactly the same. Whereupon I made another enemy of him, and of many others besides him. . . .

This inquisition has led to my having many enemies of the worst and most dangerous kind, and has given occasion also to many calumnies. And I am called wise, for my hearers always imagine that I myself possess the wisdom which I find wanting in others: but the truth is, O men of Athens, that God only is wise, and by his answer he intends to show that the wisdom of men is worth little or nothing; he is not speaking of Socrates, he is only using my name by way of illustration, as if he said, He, O men, is the wisest, who, like Socrates, knows that his wisdom is in truth worth nothing. And so I go about the world, obedient to the god, and search and make enquiry into the wisdom of any one, whether citizen or stranger, who appears to be wise; and if he is not wise, then in vindication of the oracle I show him that he is not wise, and my occupation quite absorbs me, and I have no time to give either to any public matter of interest or to any concern of my own, but I am in utter poverty by reason of my devotion to the god.

There is another thing:—young men of the richer classes, who have not much to do, come about me of their own accord; they like to hear the pretenders examined, and they often imitate me, and proceed to examine others; there are plenty of persons, as they quickly discover, who think they know something, but really know little or nothing; and then those who are examined by them instead of being angry with themselves are angry with me: This confounded Socrates, they say; this villainous misleader of youth—and then if somebody asks them, Why, what evil does he practise or teach? they do not know, and cannot tell; but in order that they may not appear to be at a loss, they repeat the ready-made charges which are used against all philosophers about teaching things up in the clouds and under the earth, and having no gods and making the worse appear the better cause. . . .

Turning to the formal charges against him, Socrates dismisses them almost contemptuously, returning to the main charges as he sees them and his lifelong "argument" with his city and its citizenry.

And now, Athenians, I am not going to argue for my own sake, as you may think, but for yours, that you may not sin against the God by condemning me, who am his gift to you. For if you kill me you will not easily find a successor to me, who, if I may use such a ludicrous figure of speech, am a sort of gadfly, given to the state by God; and the state is a great and noble steed who is tardy in his motions owing to his very size, and requires to be stirred into life. I am that gadfly which God has attached to the state, and all day long and in all places am always fastening upon you, arousing and persuading and reproaching you. You will not easily find another like me, and therefore I would advise you to spare me. I dare say that you may feel out of temper (like a person who is suddenly awakened from sleep), and you think that you might easily strike me dead as Anytus advises, and then you would sleep on for the remainder of your lives, unless God in his care of you sent you another gadfly. When I say I am given to you by God, the proof of my mission is this:—if I had been like other men, I should not have neglected all my own concerns or patiently seen the neglect of them during all these years, and have been doing yours, coming to you individually like a father or elder brother, exhorting you to regard virtue; such conduct, I say, would be unlike human nature. If I had gained anything, or if my exhortations had been paid, there would have been some sense in my doing so; but now, as you will perceive, not even the impudence of my accusers dares to say that I have ever exacted or sought pay of any one; of that they have no witness. And I have a sufficient witness to the truth of what I say—my poverty. . . .

The jury returns the verdict of guilty.

There are many reasons why I am not grieved, O men of Athens, at the vote of condemnation. I expected it, and am only surprised that the votes are so nearly equal; for I had thought that the majority against me would have been far larger; but now, had thirty votes gone over to the other side, I should have been acquitted. And I may say, I think, that I have escaped Meletus. I may say more; for without the assistance of Anytus and Lycon, any one may see that he would not have had a fifth part of the votes, as the law requires, in which case he would have incurred a fine of a thousand drachmae.

And so he proposes death as the penalty. . . .

Some one will say: Yes, Socrates, but cannot you hold your tongue, and then you may go into a foreign city, and no one will interfere with you? Now I have great difficulty in making you understand my answer to this. For if I tell you that to do as you say would be a disobedience to the God, and therefore that I cannot hold my tongue, you will not believe that I am serious; and if I say again that daily to discourse about virtue, and of those other things about which you hear me examining myself and others, is the greatest good of man, and that the unexamined life is not worth living, you are still less likely to believe me. Yet I say what is true, although a thing of which it is hard for me to persuade you. Also, I have never been accustomed to think that I deserve to suffer any harm. Had I money I might have estimated the offence at what I was able to pay, and not have been much the worse. But I have none, and therefore I must ask you to proportion the fine to my means. Well, perhaps I could afford a mina, and therefore I propose that penalty: Plato, Crito, Critobulus, and Apollodorus, my friends here, bid me say thirty minae, and they will be the sureties. Let thirty minae be the penalty; for which sum they will be ample security to you. . . .

Socrates is condemned to death.

And now, O men who have condemned me, I would fain prophesy to you; for I am about to die, and in the hour of death men are gifted with prophetic power. And I prophesy to you who are my murderers, that immediately after my departure punishment far heavier than you have inflicted on me will surely await you. Me you have killed because you wanted to escape the accuser, and not to give an account of your lives. But that will not be as you suppose: far otherwise. For I say that there will be more accusers of you than there are now; accusers whom hitherto I have restrained: and as they are younger they will be more inconsiderate with you, and you will be more offended at them. If you think that by killing men you can prevent some one from censuring your evil lives, you are mistaken; that is not a way of escape which is either possible or honourable; the easiest and the noblest way is not to be disabling others, but to be improving yourselves. This is the prophecy which I utter before my departure to the judges who have condemned me.

Friends, who would have acquitted me, I would like also to talk with you about the thing which has come to pass, while the magistrates are busy, and before I go to the place at which I must die. Stay then a little, for we may as well talk with one another while there is time. You are my friends, and I should like to show you the meaning of this event which has happened to me. O my judges—for you I may truly call judges—I should like to tell you of a wonderful circumstance. Hitherto the divine faculty of which the internal oracle[2] is the source has constantly been in the habit of opposing me even about trifles, if I was going to make a slip or error in any matter; and now as you see there has come upon me that which may be thought, and is generally believed to be, the last and worst evil. But the oracle made no sign of opposition, either when I was leaving my house in the morning, or when I was on my way to the court, or while I was speaking, at anything which I was going to say; and yet I have often been stopped in the middle of a speech, but now in nothing I either said or did touching the matter in hand has the oracle opposed me. What do I take to be the explanation of this silence? I will tell you. It is an intimation that what has happened to me is a good, and that those of us who think that death is an evil are in error. For the customary sign would surely have opposed me had I been going to evil and not to good. . . .

Wherefore, O judges, be of good cheer about death, and know of a certainty, that no evil can happen to a good man, either in life or after death. He and his are not neglected by the gods; nor has my own approaching end happened by mere chance. But I see clearly that the time had arrived when it was better for me to die and be released from trouble wherefore the oracle gave no sign. For which reason, also, I am not angry with my condemners, or with my accusers; they have done me no harm, although they did not mean to do me any good; and for this I may gently blame them.

Still I have a favour to ask them. When my sons are grown up, I would ask you, O my friends, to punish them; and I would have you trouble them, as I have troubled you, if they seem to care about riches, or anything, more than about virtue; or if they pretend to be something when they are really nothing,—then reprove them, as I

---

[2]This was Socrates' famous "daimon," more than a conscience, less perhaps than a separate "in-dwelling" god, but, as he claimed, at least a guiding voice.—Ed.

have reproved you, for not caring about that for which they ought to care, and thinking that they are something when they are really nothing. And if you do this, both I and my sons will have received justice at your hands.

The hour of departure has arrived, and we go our ways—I to die, and you to live. Which is better God only knows.

Socrates: A Modern Perspective

MOSES HADAS AND MORTON SMITH

Which Socrates are we to choose? Is it even possible to reconstruct the real man from either the idealized, "gospel"-like account of Plato or the malicious parody of Aristophanes, or from both together? Two distinguished American professors, Moses Hadas (d. 1966) and Morton Smith, do not think so. They state their case in the following selection from their book *Heroes and Gods: Spiritual Biographies in Antiquity.*

As surely as the figure of Achilles is the paradigm for heroic epic, so surely is Socrates the paradigm for aretalogy.[3] He is manifestly the point of departure for the development of the genre after his time, but he is also the culmination of antecedent development. It is likely that the historical Achilles (assuming there was one) was both more and less than Homer's image of him, but even if he was exactly as the image represents him, without it he could never have served posterity as a paradigm. Nor could Socrates have served posterity except through the image Plato fashioned. It is not, strictly speaking, a developed aretalogy that Plato presents; that is to say, he does not provide a single systematic account of a career that can be used as a sacred text. Indeed, Plato's treatment made it impossible for others to elaborate the image plausibly or to reduce it to a sacred text. But the whole image, full and consistent and unmistakable, is presupposed in every Platonic dialogue which contributes to it. Undoubtedly the historical

---

[3]The worship of, or reverence for, nobility or virtue; from the Greek *areté*, "virtue."—Ed.

Socrates was an extraordinarily gifted and devoted teacher, and his image does undoubtedly reflect the historical figure, but the image clearly transcends the man, and the image is the conscious product of Plato's art.

Because of Plato, and only Plato, Socrates' position in the tradition of western civilization is unique. Other fifth-century Greeks have won admiration bordering on adulation for high achievement in various fields, but only Socrates is completely without flaw; the perfect image leaves no opening for impugning his wisdom or temperance or courage or wholehearted devotion to his mission. We might expect that a dim figure out of the imperfectly recorded past, an Orpheus or Pythagoras or even Empedocles, might be idealized, but Socrates lived in the bright and merciless light of a century that could ostracize Aristides, deny prizes to Sophocles, throw Pericles out of office. Perhaps the nearest approach to Plato's idealization of Socrates is Thucydides' idealization of Pericles; some critics have thought that Thucydides' main motive in writing his history was to glorify Pericles. But Thucydides never claimed for Pericles the kind of potency that Plato suggests for Socrates, and on the basis of Thucydides' own history the world has accepted Pericles as a farseeing but not preternaturally gifted or wholly successful statesman. Only in the case of Socrates has the idealized image effaced the reality.

What makes Plato's share in the idealization obvious is the existence of parallel accounts of Socrates that are less reverent. Plato's reports are indeed the fullest: the larger part of his extensive writings purports to be an exposition of Socrates' thought. But there are other witnesses. . . . In the *Clouds* of Aristophanes, Socrates is the central figure, and the boot is on a different foot, for it was produced in 423, when Socrates was not yet fifty and therefore in the prime of his career but not yet shielded by the extraordinary eminence later bestowed upon him. Nor was Aristophanes' comedy the only caricature of Socrates. Also in 423 a comic Socrates figures in a play of Amipsias and two years later in one of Eupolis. These poets, it must be remembered, were dealing with a personality that was familiar to them and also, perhaps more important, to their audiences.

The caricature, certainly Aristophanes' and presumably the others' also, is of course grossly unfair: Socrates did not meddle with natural science or receive pay for his teaching, as the *Clouds* alleges he did: the most carping critic could not question his probity. The very absurdity of the charges and the topsy-turvy carnival atmosphere of the festival eliminated the possibility of rancor; in the *Symposium*, of which the fictive date is a decade after the presentation of the *Clouds*, Plato represents Aristophanes and Socrates as consorting on the friendliest of terms. And yet it is plain that Aristophanes' large audience was not outraged by the frivolous treatment of a saint, and in the *Apology*, which Socrates is presumed to have pronounced at his defense twenty-five years later, the point is made that the caricature had seriously prejudiced the public against Socrates. To some degree, then, the caricature is a significant corrective to later idealization. . . .

Really to know where the truth lies, . . . we should have his actual words or a public record of his deeds, but Socrates wrote nothing and was not, like Pericles, a statesman. The image is therefore not subject to correction on the basis of his own works. Aristophanes also deals harshly with Euripides, but we have Euripides' own plays to read, so that the caricature tells us more of Aristophanes than it does of Euripides. Isocrates wrote an encomium of Evagoras and Xenophon of Agesilaus, but the praise of these statesmen carries its own corrective. Of Socrates we know, or think we know, much more than of those others—what he looked like, how he dressed and walked and talked, and most of all, what he thought and taught. . . .

Actually the only significant datum in the inventory which is beyond dispute is that Socrates was condemned to death in 399 B.C. and accepted his penalty when he might have evaded it. The magnanimity of this act no one can belittle; it is enough to purify and enhance even a questionable career, and it is certainly enough to sanctify a Socrates. For Plato it clearly marked a decisive turn, as he himself records in his autobiographical *Seventh Epistle*. For him it undoubtedly crystallized the image of Socrates that fills the early dialogues. . . . All of Plato's earlier dialogues, and the more plainly in the degree of their earliness, are as much concerned with the personality of Socrates as with his teachings. His pre-eminence in reason, his devotion to his mission, his selfless concern for the spiritual welfare of his fellow men, the purity of his life, even his social gifts, are made prominent. The *Apology*, quite possibly the earliest of the Socratic pieces, is concerned with the man and his personal program, not his doctrines. Here he is made to present, without coyness or swagger or unction, his own concept of his mission to sting men, like a gadfly, to self-examination and to serve as midwife to their travail with ideas. The *Apology* also illustrates the devotion of his disciples to Socrates and the surprisingly large proportion of his jurors who were willing to acquit him. Again, in the short early dialogues, which are mainly concerned with questioning common misconceptions of such abstract nouns as "piety" or "friendship," it is the man as defined by his program, not the abstract doctrine, that is being presented. In the great central group—*Protagoras, Gorgias, Symposium, Republic*—the proportion of doctrinal content is larger, but the doctrine requires the personality of Socrates to make it plausible. The moral significance of education may emerge from the rather piratical dialectic in the *Protagoras*, but the argument takes on special meaning from Socrates' wise and tender treatment of the eager and youthful disciple who is enamored of Protagoras' reputation. That it is a worse thing for a man to inflict than to receive an injury and that a good man is incapable of being injured is the kind of doctrine which absolutely requires that its promulgator be a saint, as Socrates is pictured in the *Gorgias;* on the lips of a lesser man it would be nothing more than a rhetorical paradox. A great weight of individual prestige must similarly be built up to enable a man to enunciate the grand scheme of the *Republic,* and the occasional playfulness of the tone only emphasizes the stature of the individual who enunciates it. People too earth-bound to recognize such stature, like Thrasymachus in Book I, can only find the whole proceeding absurd. And only from a man whose special stature was recognized could the vision of Er be accepted as other than an old wives' tale.

In the *Symposium* more than in other dialogues the individuality of Socrates is underscored. It is not a trivial matter, for establishing the character of Socrates, that he could be welcome at a party of the fashionable wits of Athens, could get himself respectably groomed for the occasion, and engage in banter with his fellow guests without compromising his spiritual ascendancy one whit. We hear incidentally of his absolute bravery in battle and his disregard of self in the service of a friend, of his extraordinary physical vitality that enabled him to stand all night pondering some thought while his fellow soldiers bivouacked around him to watch the spectacle, of how he could lose himself in some doorway in a trance and so make himself late for his appointment until he had thought through whatever was on his mind. The subject of the *Symposium* is love, and love had been conceived of, in the series of speeches praising it, in a range from gross homosexuality to romantic attachment, to a cosmic principle of attraction and repulsion, to Socrates' own concept . . . of an ascent to union with the highest goodness and beauty. . . .

But it is in the *Phaedo* that Socrates comes nearest to being translated to a higher order of being. In prison, during the hours preceding his death, Socrates discourses to his devoted followers on the most timely and timeless of all questions, the immortality of the soul. The *Phaedo* is the most spiritual and the most eloquent of all dialogues; the account of Socrates' last moments is surely the second most compelling passion in all literature. If Plato's object was to inculcate a belief in immortality, there are of course sound practical reasons for giving the spokesman of the doctrine extraordinary prestige. In such an issue it is the personality of the teacher rather than the cogency of his arguments that is most persuasive. . . .

But the saintliness with which Socrates is endowed in the *Phaedo* seems more than a mere device to promote belief in the immortality of the soul. If belief is being inculcated, it is belief in Socrates, not in immortality. Only an occasional reader of the *Phaedo* could rehearse its arguments for immortality years or months after he had laid the book down; the saintliness of Socrates he can never forget. It is his image of Socrates rather than any specific doctrine that Plato wished to crystallize and perpetuate. From the tenor of all his writing it is clear that Plato believed that the welfare of society depended upon leadership by specially endowed and dedicated men. Ordinary men following a prescribed code would not do. Indeed, Plato conceived of his own effectiveness as teacher in much the same way; in the autobiographical *Seventh Epistle* he tells us that no one could claim to have apprehended his teachings merely from study of his writings: long personal contact with a master spirit is essential.

In the centuries after Plato the images of certain saintly figures who, like Socrates, had selflessly devoted themselves to the spiritual improvement of the community and had accepted the suffering, sometimes the martyrdom, these efforts entailed, played a considerable role in the development of religious ideas and practices. In some cases the image may have masked a character negligible or dishonest, and the men who created and exploited the image may have done so for selfish motives; but in some cases, surely, the man behind the image was a devoted teacher whose disciples embroidered his career in good faith into a kind of hagiology[4] that they then used for moral edification. Whatever the motivation, there can be little doubt that the prime model for the spiritual hero was Socrates. . . .

Review and Study Questions

1. How did Socrates respond to the charges brought against him at his trial?

2. By his conduct at his trial was Socrates seeking martyrdom? Explain your answer.

3. Is there any historical validity in the image of Socrates presented by Aristophanes in *The Clouds?*

4. Do you consider Plato's image of Socrates in *The Apology* more historically valid than Aristophanes' image of him in *The Clouds?* Why?

---

[4]Veneration of a saint or saints.—ED.

5. What part did the temper of the times play in the trial and execution of Socrates?
6. Was Socrates a spiritual hero? Give reasons for your answer.

Suggestions for Further Reading

Socrates is a maddeningly elusive historical figure: he exists only in the works of others. Luis E. Navia, *Socratic Testimonies* (Lanham, Md.: University Press of America, 1987), is a convenient outline of the sources of historical information we do have for Socrates and of the major critical problems in Socratic studies. Because of the lack of historical sources there is a nearly irresistible urge to create a "historical Socrates," which has produced a number of biographical or semibiographical works on him. The preeminent modern account is A. E. Taylor, *Socrates* (New York: Anchor, 1953 [1933]), in which the great British Platonist argues that the striking figure of Socrates as derived from Plato's dialogues is essentially an accurate historical account. The book is clear and readable as well as authoritative. An almost equally good account is Jean Brun, *Socrates*, tr. Douglas Scott (New York: Walker, 1962), in which the author, writing for young people, simplifies and sorts out the leading elements in the traditional view of Socrates—i.e., the Delphic dictum "Know thyself," Socrates' "in-dwelling Daimon," and the Socratic irony. At the other extreme are Alban D. Winspear and Tom Silverberg, *Who Was Socrates?* (New York: Russell and Russell, 1960 [1939]), and Norman Gulley, *The Philosophy of Socrates* (London and New York: Macmillan and St. Martin's, 1968). Winspear and Silverberg argue—not entirely convincingly—for a complete revision of the tradition and make Socrates evolve in the course of his career from a democratic liberal to an aristocratic conservative. And Gulley argues for the rejection of Plato's view of Socrates as a skeptic and agnostic in favor of a more constructive role for Socrates in ancient philosophy. Laszlo Versényi, *Socratic Humanism* (New Haven, Conn.: Yale University Press, 1963), while not going as far as Gulley, does advocate a separation between the often paired Socrates and Plato in favor of tying Socrates more closely to the sophists, especially Protagoras and Gorgias. Students should find especially interesting Alexander Eliot, *Socrates: A Fresh Appraisal of the Most Celebrated Case in History* (New York: Crown, 1967). It is less a fresh appraisal than a popular and extremely readable review of Socrates' background, life, and the evidence brought to his trial. The second part of the book is what the author calls "a free synthesis" of all the Platonic dialogues touching on the trial and death of Socrates—essentially a new, dramatic dialogue account in fresh, modern English. On the matter of "the case" of Socrates—i.e., his trial and the evidence and testimony presented—two essays in Gregory Vlastos (ed.), *The Philosophy of Socrates: A Collection of Critical Essays* (South Bend, Ind.: University of Notre Dame Press, 1980 [1971]), Kenneth J. Dover, "Socrates in the *Clouds*" and A. D. Woozley, "Socrates on Disobeying the Law," are of considerable interest. On the two dialogues most pertinent to the trial and death of Socrates, *The Apology* and *The Crito*, two books are recommended. R. E. Allen, *Socrates and Legal Obligation* (Minneapolis, Minn.: University of Minnesota Press, 1980) is a clear and penetrating analysis of the dialogues as is Richard Kraut, *Socrates and the State* (Princeton, N.J.: Princeton University Press, 1984), which also makes the case for Socrates' conscious civil disobedience: it is the best modern treatment of Socrates before the law. Thomas C. Brickhouse and Nicholas D. Smith, *Socrates on Trial* (Princeton, N.J.: Princeton University Press, 1989) judiciously surveys all the evidence for the trial. On the other hand, I. F. Stone, *The Trial of Socrates* (New York: Anchor, 1989) is a muckraking attempt to portray Socrates as an antidemocratic reactionary—an outrageous book, but an interesting one. Mario Montuori, *Socrates: Physiology of a Myth*, tr. J. M. P. and M. Langdale (Amsterdam: J. C. Gieben, 1981) is an account paralleling that of Hadas and Smith in the chapter, but more detailed.

Of somewhat larger scope is the important scholarly work of Victor Ehrenberg, *The People of Aristophanes: A Sociology of Old Attic Comedy* (New York: Schocken, 1962 [1943]), a study not only of the characters in the plays but also of the audiences; see especially ch. 10, on religion and education, for Socrates. Of larger scope still is T. B. L. Webster, *Athenian Culture and Society* (Berkeley and Los Angeles: University of California Press, 1973), a superb analysis of the linkage between the culture of Athens and its society—the background to an understanding of the place of Socrates in that society and culture. For this sort of analysis, students may prefer Rex Warner, *Men of Athens* (New York: Viking, 1972), a brilliant popularization which sees Socrates as the end product as well as the victim of fifth-century Athenian culture. J. W. Roberts, *City of Sokrates: A Social History of Classical Athens* (London: Routledge and Kegan Paul, 1984), however, is the best modern historical treatment of Socrates' Athens.

The standard work on the system of Athenian government is A. H. M. Jones, *Athenian Democracy* (Oxford, England: Oxford University Press, 1957), which should be updated by reference to W. R. Connor, *The New Politicians of Fifth Century Athens* (Princeton, N.J.: Princeton University Press, 1971).

THE "PROBLEM" OF ALEXANDER THE GREAT

356 B.C.	Born
336 B.C.	Became king of Macedonia
334 B.C.	Began conquest of Persia
333 B.C.	Battle of Issus
331 B.C.	Battle of Gaugamela and death of Darius, the Persian king
326 B.C.	Battle of Hydaspes in India
323 B.C.	Died

If Alexander had simply been a successful conqueror, no matter how stupefying his conquests, there would really be no "Alexander problem." But, from his own lifetime, there lingered about Alexander the sense that there was something more to him, that he was "up to something," that he had great, even revolutionary, plans. The conviction of manifest destiny that Alexander himself felt so strongly contributed to this, as did his instinct for the unusual, the cryptic, the dramatic in political and religious, as well as in strategic and military, decisions. But most of all, his death at age thirty-three, in the year 323 B.C.—his conquests barely completed and his schemes for the future only hinted at or imperfectly forecast—led the ancient writers to speculate about the questions, "What if Alexander had lived on?" "What plans would his imperial imagination have conceived?" and to sift and resift every scrap of information available—and to invent a few that were not!

The problem of the ancient sources themselves has added greatly to the difficulty of interpretation. And this is surely ironic. For Alexander's own sense of his destiny made him unusually sensitive to the need for keeping records of his deeds. A careful log or journal was maintained, but it exists today only in the most useless fragments, if indeed the "fragments" in question even came from that record. Alexander's staff included at least two scholar-secretaries to keep records.

One was Callisthenes, the nephew of Alexander's old friend and tutor Aristotle. The other was the scientist-philosopher Aristobulus. Callisthenes subsequently fell out with Alexander and was executed for complicity in a plot in 327 B.C. But, while nothing of his work remains it was clearly the basis for a strongly anti-Alexandrian tradition that flourished in Greece, especially in Athens. This hostile tradition is best represented in Cleitarchus, a Greek rhetorician of the generation following Alexander, who never knew him but who became "the most influential historian of Alexander."[1] The account of Aristobulus, who was apparently much closer and more favorable to Alexander than was Callisthenes or Cleitarchus, is also lost. Ptolemy, one of Alexander's most trusted generals and later founder of the Hellenistic monarchy in Egypt, wrote a detailed memoir based in part on Alexander's own *Journal,* but this did not survive either.

Later ancient writers like Diodorus, Plutarch, Curtius, and Justin did know these sources and used them. But of the accounts of Alexander surviving from antiquity, the best one is that of the Greek writer Arrian, of the second century—thus over four hundred years removed from his sources! Furthermore, while Arrian's account is our fullest and most detailed and is based scrupulously on his sources, it is terribly prosaic: we miss precisely what we most want to have, some sense of the "why" of Alexander. Despite Arrian's devotion to his subject, he tends to tell the story—mainly the military side of it at that—without significant comment. And where we would like to have him analyze, he moralizes instead.

Modern scholars have continued to be fascinated by the puzzle of what Alexander was "up to," and none more than William W. Tarn (d. 1957). Tarn was one of those brilliant English "amateurs" of independent means and equally independent views who have contributed so uniquely to scholarship in a score of fields. He was a lawyer by profession, but he devoted most of his scholarly life—more than half a century—to Greek history. Tarn practically invented Hellenistic scholarship, that is, the study of the post-Alexandrian period in the history of Greek civilization. He authored numerous books and studies, beginning with his "Notes on Hellenism in Bactria and India," which appeared in the *Journal of Hellenic Studies* for 1902, through his first important book, *Antigonos Gonatas* (1913), to *Hellenistic Civilization* (1928), *Hellenistic Military and Naval Developments* (1930), *The Greeks in Bactria and India* (1938), and chapters in the first edition of the *Cambridge Ancient History* (1924–1929).

---

[1]N. G. L. Hammond, *Alexander the Great: King, Commander and Statesman* (Park Ridge, N.J.: Noyes Press, 1980), p. 2.

Because the springboard of the Hellenistic age was Alexander, Tarn devoted special attention to him. He adopted the stance of a scholar-lawyer, in a sense, taking Alexander as his "client" and setting out to make a case for the defense. And Alexander was badly in need of such defense. The trend of modern scholarship before Tarn had been to view Alexander as an archtyrant, arbitrary and megalomaniac, a drunken murderer, and the oppressor of Greek political freedom and philosophic independence—a view derived ultimately from the Callisthenes-Cleitarchan tradition of antiquity.

Tarn was brilliantly successful in turning opinion around in his defense of Alexander, so much so that the "traditional" view of Alexander today is still essentially that created by Tarn. His authority has been so great that it has even affected the way in which we interpret the ancient sources themselves, whether they seem to be "for" or "against" Tarn's case.

The Ancient Sources:
Arrian, Eratosthenes, and Plutarch

In the first selection of this chapter, we present the five "proof texts" on which Tarn built his defense of Alexander: one from Arrian, one from Eratosthenes (preserved in Strabo), and three from Plutarch.

This passage, from *The Life of Alexander the Great by Arrian*, took place near the end of Alexander's incredible journey of conquest. In 324 B.C. Alexander assembled his Macedonian troops at Opis in Mesopotamia and announced that he proposed to discharge and send home, with lavish rewards, all those who were disabled or overage. But, instead of gratitude, a smoldering resentment surfaced, and the entire Macedonian force began to clamor to be sent home. Arrian attributes the resentment to Alexander's "orientalizing," his adoption of Persian dress and customs, and his attempt to incorporate Persians and other peoples in his army. This had offended the Macedonians' stubborn pride and sense of exclusiveness, and they now threatened a mutiny. Alexander was furious. After having the ringleaders arrested, he addressed the Macedonians in a passionate, blistering speech, reminding them of their own accomplishments, as well as his, and of what he had done for them. Alexander's speech had a profound effect upon the Macedonians, as did the plans, immediately put into effect, for reorganizing the army in the event that they defected. But instead of deserting, the Macedonians repented.

Alexander, the moment he heard of this change of heart, hastened out to meet them, and he was so touched by their grovelling repentance and their bitter lamentations that the tears came into his eyes. While they continued to beg for his pity, he stepped forward as if to speak, but was anticipated by one Callines, an officer of the mounted Hetaeri, distinguished both by age and rank. "My lord," he cried, "what hurts us is that you have made Persians your kinsmen— Persians are called 'Alexander's kinsmen'—Persians kiss you. But no Macedonian has yet had a taste of this honour."

"Every man of you," Alexander replied, "I regard as my kinsman, and from now on that is what I shall call you."

Thereupon Callines came up to him and kissed him, and all the others who wished to do so kissed him too. Then they picked up their weapons and returned to their quarters singing the song of victory at the top of their voices.

To mark the restoration of harmony, Alexander offered sacrifice to the gods he was accustomed to honour, and gave a public banquet which he himself attended, sitting among the Macedonians, all of whom were present. Next to them the Persians had their places, and next to the Persians distinguished foreigners of other nations; Alexander and his friends dipped their wine from the same bowl and poured the same libations, following the lead of the Greek seers and the Magi. The chief object of his prayers was that Persians and Macedonians might rule together in harmony as an imperial power. It is said that 9,000 people attended the banquet; they unanimously drank the same toast, and followed it by the paean of victory.

After this all Macedonians—about 10,000 all told—who were too old for service or in any way unfit, got their discharge at their own request.

Eratosthenes of Cyrene, who lived about 200 B.C., was head of the great Library of Alexandria and one of the most learned individuals of antiquity. But his works exist only in fragments and in citations in the writings of others, such as the following, from *The Geography* by the Greek scientist Strabo, of the first century B.C.

Now, towards the end of his treatise—after withholding praise from those who divide the whole multitude of mankind into two groups, namely, Greeks and Barbarians, and also from those who advised Alexander to treat the Greeks as friends but the Barbarians as enemies—Eratosthenes goes on to say that it would be better to make such divisions according to good qualities and bad qualities; for not only are many of the Greeks bad, but many of the Barbarians are refined—Indians and Arians, for example, and, further, Romans and Carthaginians, who carry on their governments so admirably. And this, he says, is the reason why Alexander, disregarding his advisers, welcomed as many as he could of the men of fair repute and did them favours—just as if those who have made such a division, placing some people in the category of censure, others in that of praise, did so for any other reason than that in some people there prevail the law-abiding and the political instinct, and the qualities associated with education and powers of speech, whereas in other people the opposite characteristics prevail! And so Alexander, not disregarding his advisers, but rather accepting their opinion, did what was consistent with, not contrary to, their advice; for he had regard to the real intent of those who gave him counsel.

Two of the Plutarch passages are from his essay "On the Fortune of Alexander," which is one of the pieces comprising the collection known as the *Moralia*.

Moreover, the much-admired *Republic* of Zeno, the founder of the Stoic sect, may be summed up in this one main principle: that all the inhabitants of this world of ours should not live differentiated by their respective rules of justice into separate cities and communities, but that we should consider all men to be of one community and one polity, and that we should have a common life and an order common to us all, even as a herd that feeds together and shares the pasturage of a common field. This Zeno wrote, giving shape to a dream or, as it were, shadowy picture of a well-ordered and philosophic commonwealth; but it was Alexander who gave effect to the idea. For Alexander did not follow Aristotle's advice to treat the Greeks as if he were their leader, and other peoples as if he were their master; to have regard for the Greeks as for friends and kindred, but to conduct himself toward other peoples as though they were plants or animals; for to do so would have been to cumber his leadership with numerous battles and banishments and festering seditions. But, as he believed that he came as a heaven-sent governor to all, and as a mediator for the whole world, those whom he could not persuade to unite with him, he conquered by force of arms, and he brought together into one body all men everywhere, uniting and mixing in one great loving-cup, as it were, men's lives, their characters, their marriages, their very habits of life. He bade them all consider as their fatherland the whole inhabited earth, as their stronghold and protection his camp, as akin to them all good men, and as foreigners only the wicked; they should not distinguish between Grecian and foreigner by Grecian cloak and targe, or scimitar and jacket; but the distinguishing mark of the Grecian should be seen in virtue, and that of the foreigner in iniquity; clothing and food, marriage and manner of life they should regard as common to all, being blended into one by ties of blood and children.

After dwelling on the wisdom of Alexander in affecting a mixed Graeco-Macedonian and Persian costume, Plutarch continues.

For he did not overrun Asia like a robber nor was he minded to tear and rend it, as if it were booty and plunder bestowed by unexpected good fortune. . . . But Alexander desired to render all upon earth subject to one law of reason and one form of government and to reveal all men as one people, and to this purpose he made himself conform. But if the deity that sent down Alexander's soul into this world of ours had not recalled him quickly, one law would govern all mankind, and they all would look toward one rule of justice as though toward a common source of light. But as it is, that part of the world which has not looked upon Alexander has remained without sunlight.

This passage from the famous "Life of Alexander" in *Plutarch's Lives* deals with an incident early in Alexander's career, after his conquest of Egypt—his journey across the desert to the oracle of Ammon at Siwah.

When Alexander had passed through the desert and was come to the place of the oracle, the prophet of Ammon gave him salutation from the god as from a father; whereupon Alexander asked him whether any of the murderers of his father had escaped him.[2] To this the prophet answered by bidding him be guarded in his speech, since his was not a mortal father. Alexander therefore changed the form of his question, and asked whether the murderers of Philip had all been punished; and then, regarding his own empire, he asked whether it was given to him to become lord and master of all mankind. The god gave answer that this was given to him, and that Philip was fully avenged. Then Alexander made splendid offerings to the god and gave his priests large gifts of money. . . . We are told, also, that he listened to the teachings of Psammon[3] the philosopher in Egypt, and accepted most readily this utterance of his, namely, that all mankind are under the kingship of God, since in every case that which gets the mastery and rules is divine. Still more philosophical, however, was his own opinion and utterance on this head, namely that although God was indeed a common father of all mankind, still, He made peculiarly His own the noblest and best of them.

---

[2]Alexander had come to the throne of Macedonia upon the murder of his father, Philip II, in 336 B.C.—ED.

[3]This is the only reference in antiquity to such a person.—ED.

Alexander the Great
and the Unity of Mankind

W. W. TARN

We turn now to the thesis that W. W. Tarn built in defense of Alexander. He had begun to develop his characteristic view in a number of journal articles and anticipated it in fairly complete form in his contributions to the 1927 edition of the *Cambridge Ancient History*. He was later to state it most completely in his monumental two-volume *Alexander the Great* (Cambridge: Cambridge University Press, 1948). But the most succinct statement of the Tarn thesis is that contained in his Raleigh Lecture on History, read before the British Academy in 1933. It is entitled "Alexander the Great and the Unity of Mankind."

What I am going to talk about is one of the great revolutions in human thought. Greeks of the classical period, speaking very roughly, divided mankind into two classes, Greeks and non-Greeks; the latter they called barbarians and usually regarded as inferior people, though occasionally some one, like Herodotus or Xenophon, might suggest that certain barbarians possessed qualities which deserved consideration, like the wisdom of the Egyptians or the courage of the Persians. But in the third century B.C. and later we meet with a body of opinion which may be called universalist; all mankind was one and all men were brothers, or anyhow ought to be. Who was the pioneer who brought about this tremendous revolution in some men's way of thinking? Most writers have had no doubt on that point; the man to whom the credit was due was Zeno, the founder of the Stoic philosophy. But there are several passages in Greek writers which, *if* they are to be believed, show that the first man actually to think of it was not Zeno but Alexander. This matter has never really been examined; some writers just pass it over, which means, I suppose, that they do not consider the passages in question historical; others have definitely said that it is merely a case of our secondary authorities attributing to Alexander ideas taken from Stoicism. I want to consider to-day whether the passages in question are or are not historical and worthy of credence; that is, whether Alexander was or was not the first to believe in, and to contemplate, the unity of mankind. This will entail, among other things, some examination of the concept which Greeks called Homonoia, a word which meant more than its Latin translation, Concord, means to us; it is more like Unity and Concord, a being of one mind together, or if we like the phrase, a union of hearts; ultimately it was to become almost a symbol of the world's longing for something better than constant war. For convenience of discussion I shall keep the Greek term Homonoia.

Before coming to the ideas attributed to Alexander, I must sketch very briefly the background against which the new thought arose, whoever was its author; and I ought to say that I am primarily talking throughout of theory, not of practice. It may be possible to find, in the fifth century, or earlier, an occasional phrase which looks like a groping after something better than the hard-and-fast division of Greeks and barbarians; but this comes to very little and had no importance for history, because anything of the sort was strangled by the idealist philosophies. Plato and Aristotle left no doubt about their views. Plato said that all barbarians were enemies by nature; it was proper to wage war upon them, even to the point of enslaving or extirpating them. Aristotle said that all barbarians were slaves by nature, especially those of Asia; they had not the qualities which entitled them to be free men, and it was proper to treat them as slaves. His model State cared for nothing but its own citizens; it was a small aristocracy of Greek citizens ruling over a barbarian peasantry who cultivated the land for their masters and had no share in the State—a thing he had seen in some cities of Asia Minor. Certainly neither Plato nor Aristotle was quite consistent; Plato might treat an Egyptian priest as the repository of wisdom, Aristotle might suggest that the constitution of Carthage was worth studying; but their main position was clear enough, as was the impression Alexander would get from his tutor Aristotle.

There were, of course, other voices. Xenophon, when he wanted to portray an ideal shepherd of the people, chose a Persian king as shepherd of the Persian people. And there were the early Cynics. But the Cynics had no thought of any union or fellowship between Greek and barbarian; they were not constructive thinkers, but merely embodied protests against the vices and follies of civilization. When Diogenes called himself a cosmopolite, a horrible word which he coined and which was not used again for centuries, what he meant was, not that he was a citizen of some imaginary world-state—a thing he never thought about—but that he was not a citizen of any Greek city; it was pure negation. And the one piece of Cynic construction, the ideal figure of Heracles, labouring to free Greece from monsters, was merely shepherd of a *Greek* herd till after Alexander, when it took colour and content from the Stoics and became the ideal benefactor of humanity. All that Xenophon or the Cynics could supply was the figure of an ideal shepherd, not of the human herd, but of some national herd.

More important was Aristotle's older contemporary Isocrates, because of his conception of Homonoia. The Greek world, whatever its practice, never doubted that in theory unity in a city was very desirable; but though the word Homonoia was already in common use among Greeks, it chiefly meant absence of faction-fights, and this rather negative meaning lasted in the cities throughout the Hellenistic period, as can be seen in the numerous decrees in honour of the judicial commissions sent from one city to another, which are praised because they tried to compose internal discord. There was hardly a trace as yet of the more positive sense which Homonoia was to acquire later—a mental attitude which should make war or faction impossible because the parties were at one; and Isocrates extended the application of the word without changing its meaning. He took up a suggestion of the sophist Gorgias and proposed to treat the whole Greek world as one and the futile wars between city and city as faction fights—to apply Homonoia to the Greek race. For this purpose he utilized Plato's idea that the barbarian was a natural enemy, and decided that the way to unite Greeks was to attack Persia; "I come," he said, "to advocate two things: war against the barbarian, Homonoia between ourselves." But somebody had to do the uniting; and Isocrates bethought him of the Cynic Heracles, benefactor of the Greek race, and urged King Philip of Macedonia, a descendant of Heracles, to play the part. But if Philip was to be Heracles and bring about the Homonoia of the Greek world, the way was being prepared for two important ideas of a later time; the essential quality of the king must be that love of man, φιλανθρωπία,[4] which had led Heracles to perform his labours, and the essential business of the king was to promote Homonoia; so far this only applied to Greeks, but if its meaning were to deepen it would still be the king's business. The actual result of all this, the League of Corinth[5] under Philip's presidency, was not quite what Isocrates had dreamt of.

This then was the background against which Alexander appeared. The business of a Macedonian king was to be a benefactor of Greeks to the extent of preventing inter-city warfare; he was to promote Homonoia among Greeks and utilize their enmity to barbarians as a bond of union; but barbarians themselves were still enemies and slaves by nature, a view which Aristotle emphasized

---

[4]Literally "philanthropy."—ED.

[5]The league Philip formed after defeating the Greek states at Chaeronea in 338 B.C.—ED.

when he advised his pupil to treat Greeks as free men, but barbarians as slaves.

I now come to the things Alexander is supposed to have said or thought; and the gulf between them and the background I have sketched is so deep that one cannot blame those who have refused to believe that he ever said or thought anything of the sort. There are five passages which need consideration: one in Arrian; one from Eratosthenes, preserved by Strabo; and three from Plutarch, one of which, from its resemblance to the Strabo passage, has been supposed by one of the acutest critics of our time to be taken in substance from Eratosthenes,[6] and as such I shall treat it. The passage in Arrian says that, after the mutiny of the Macedonians at Opis and their reconciliation to Alexander, he gave a banquet to Macedonians and Persians, at which he prayed for Homonoia and partnership in rule between these two peoples. What Eratosthenes says amounts to this. Aristotle told Alexander to treat Greeks as friends, but barbarians like animals; but Alexander knew better, and preferred to divide men into good and bad without regard to their race, and thus carried out Aristotle's real intention. For Alexander believed that he had a mission from the deity to harmonize men generally and be the reconciler of the world, mixing men's lives and customs as in a loving cup, and treating the good as his kin, the bad as strangers; for he thought that the good man was the real Greek and the bad man the real barbarian. Of the two Plutarch passages, the first says that his intention was to bring about, as between mankind generally, Homonoia and peace and fellowship and make them all one people; and the other, which for the moment I will quote without its context, makes him say that God is the common father of all men.

It is obvious that, wherever all this comes from, we are dealing with a great revolution in thought. It amounts to this, that there is a natural brotherhood of all men, though bad men do not share in it; that Homonoia is no longer to be confined to the relations between Greek and Greek, but is to unite Greek and barbarian; and that Alexander's aim was to substitute peace for war, and reconcile the enmities of mankind by bringing them all—all that is whom his arm could reach, the peoples of his empire—to be of one mind together: as men were one in blood, so they should become one in heart and spirit. That such a revolution in thought did happen is unquestioned; the question is, was Alexander really its author, or are the thoughts attributed to him those of Zeno or somebody else? . . .

---

[6]The reference is to the German scholar E. Schwarz.—ED.

"To try to answer that question," Tarn follows with a long and complex analysis of Homonoia and kingship in Graeco-Roman history,
leading to the universalism of the late Roman empire.

The belief that it was the business of kings to promote Homonoia
among their subjects without distinction of race thus travelled down
the line of kingship for centuries; but the line, you will remember,
had no beginning. . . . It must clearly have been connected with
some particular king at the start, and that king has to be later than
Isocrates and Philip and earlier than Diotogenes and Demetrius.[7] It
would seem that only one king is possible; we should have to postu-
late Alexander at the beginning of the line, even if there were not a
definite tradition that it *was* he. This means that Plutarch's statement, that Alexander's purpose was to bring about Homonoia between men generally—that is, those men whom his arm could
reach—must be taken to be true, unless some explicit reason be
found for disbelieving it; and I therefore now turn to the Stoics, in
order to test the view that the ideas attributed to him were really
taken from Stoicism. . . . We have seen that it was the business of
kings to bring about Homonoia; but this was not the business of a
Stoic, because to him Homonoia had already been brought about by
the Deity, and it existed in all completeness; all that was necessary
was that men should see it. . . .
    This is the point I want to make, the irreconcilable opposition
between Stoicism and the theory of kingship, between the belief that
unity and concord existed and you must try and get men to see it, and
the belief that unity and concord did not exist and that it was the
business of the rulers of the earth to try and bring them to pass. . . .
Consequently, when Eratosthenes says that Alexander aspired to be
the harmonizer and reconciler of the world, and when Plutarch attributes to him the intention of bringing about fellowship and Homonoia between men generally—those men whom his arm reached—
then, wherever these ideas came from, they were not Stoic; between
them and Stoicism there was a gulf which nothing could bridge. This
does not by itself prove that Alexander held these ideas; what it does
do is to put out of court the only alternative which has ever been
seriously proposed, and to leave the matter where I left it when

---

[7]Isocrates (436–338 B.C.), the Athenian orator; Philip II of Macedonia (355–336
B.C.); Diotogenes, an early Hellenistic author of uncertain date; Demetrius (336–283
B.C.), an early Hellenistic ruler.—ED.

considering the theory of kingship, that is, that there is a strong presumption that Alexander *was* their author. . . .

Before leaving Stoicism, I must return for a moment to Zeno's distinction of the worthy and the unworthy; for Alexander, as we saw, is said to have divided men into good and bad, and to have excluded the bad from the general kinship of mankind and called them the true barbarians. Might not *this* distinction, at any rate, have been taken from Stoicism and attributed to him? The reasons against this seem conclusive, apart from the difficulty of discarding a statement made by so sound and scientific a critic as Eratosthenes. First, no Stoic ever equated the unworthy class with barbarians; for to him there were no barbarians. . . . Secondly, while the unworthy in Zeno, as in Aristotle, are the majority of mankind, Alexander's "bad men" are not; they are, as Eratosthenes says, merely that small residue everywhere which cannot be civilized. One sees this clearly in a story never questioned, his prayer at Opis, when he prayed that the Macedonian and Persian races (without exceptions made) might be united in Homonoia. And thirdly, we know where the idea comes from: Aristotle had criticized some who said that good men were really free and bad men were really slaves (whom he himself equated with barbarians), and Alexander is in turn criticizing Aristotle; as indeed Eratosthenes says, though he does not quote this passage of Aristotle. The matter is not important, except for the general question of the credibility of Eratosthenes, and may conceivably only represent that period in Alexander's thought when he was outgrowing Aristotle; it does not conflict, as does Zeno's conception of the unworthy, with a general belief in the unity of mankind. . . .

There is just one question still to be asked; whence did Zeno get his universalism? Plutarch says that behind Zeno's dream lay Alexander's reality; and no one doubts that Alexander was Zeno's inspiration, but the question is, in what form? Most writers have taken Plutarch to mean Alexander's *empire;* but to me this explains nothing at all. One man conquers a large number of races and brings them under one despotic rule; how can another man deduce from this that distinctions of race are immaterial and that the universe is a harmony in which men are brothers? It would be like the fight between the polar bear and the parallelepiped. The Persian kings had conquered and ruled as large an empire as Alexander, including many Greek cities; why did Darius never inspire any one with similar theories? It does seem to me that what Plutarch really means is not Alexander's empire but Alexander's ideas; after all, the frequent references in antiquity to Alexander as a philosopher, one at least of which is contemporary, must mean *something.* Zeno's inspiration, then, was Alexander's idea of the unity of mankind; and what Zeno himself did was to carry this idea to one of its two logical conclusions. Judging by his prayer at Opis for the Homonoia of Macedonians and Persians, Alexander, had he lived, would have worked through national groups, as was inevitable in an empire like his, which comprised many different states and subject peoples; Theophrastus,[8] who followed him, included national groups in his chain of progress towards world-relationship. But Zeno abolished all distinctions of race, all the apparatus of national groups and particular states, and made his world-state a theoretic whole. His scheme was an inspiration to many; but in historical fact it was, and remained, unrealizable. But Alexander's way, or what I think was his way, led to the Roman Empire being called one people. I am not going to bring in modern examples of these two different lines of approach to world-unity, but I want to say one thing about the Roman Empire. It has been said that Stoic ideas came near to realization in the empire of Hadrian and the Antonines, but it is quite clear, the moment it be considered, that this was not the case; that empire was a huge national state, which stood in the line of kingship and was a partial realization of the ideas of Alexander. When a Stoic *did* sit on the imperial throne, he was at once compelled to make terms with the national state; to Marcus Aurelius, the Stoic world-state was no theoretic unity, but was to comprise the various particular states as a city comprises houses. And there is still a living reality in what he said about himself: "As a man I am a citizen of the world-state, but as the particular man Marcus Aurelius I am a citizen of Rome."

I may now sum up. We have followed down the line of kingship the theory that it was the business of a king to promote Homonoia among his subjects—all his subjects without distinction of race; and we have seen that this theory ought to be connected at the start with some king, who must be later than Philip and earlier than Demetrius; and there is a definite tradition which connects the origin of the theory with Alexander. We have further seen that the intention to promote Homonoia among mankind, attributed in the tradition to Alexander, is certainly not a projection backwards from Stoicism, or apparently from anything else, while it is needed to explain certain things said by Theophrastus and done by Alexarchus.[9] Lastly, we have seen the idea of the kinship or brotherhood of mankind appearing suddenly in Theophrastus and Alexarchus; their common source can be no one but Alexander, and again tradition supports this. Only one conclusion from all this seems possible: the things which, in the tradition, Alexander is

---

[8] The philosopher-scientist who followed Aristotle as head of his school.—ED.

[9] A minor Macedonian princeling, following Alexander, who set up his small state apparently on the model of Alexander's ideas.—ED.

supposed to have thought and said are, in substance, true. He did say that all men were sons of God, that is brothers, but that God made the best ones peculiarly his own; he did aspire to be the harmonizer and reconciler of the world—that part of the world which his arm reached; he did have the intention of uniting the peoples of his empire in fellowship and concord and making them of one mind together; and when, as a beginning, he prayed at Opis for partnership in rule and Homonoia between Macedonians and Persians, he meant what he said—not partnership in rule only, but true unity between them. I am only talking of theory, not of actions; but what this means is that he was the pioneer of one of the supreme revolutions in the world's outlook, the first man known to us who contemplated the brotherhood of man or the unity of mankind, whichever phrase we like to use. I do not claim to have given you exact proof of this; it is one of those difficult border-lands of history where one does not get proofs which could be put to a jury. But there is a very strong presumption indeed that it is true. Alexander, for the things he *did,* was called The Great; but if what I have said to-day be right, I do not think we shall doubt that this idea of his—call it a purpose, call it a dream, call it what you will—was the greatest thing about him.

The New Alexander

N. G. L. HAMMOND

Despite Tarn's enormous scholarly reputation and his lordly dismissal of critics, his own interpretive view of Alexander was bound to be challenged, and it has been. Tarn massively overstated his case. As Mary Renault put it, "the defence was pushed too far."[10] And Ernst Badian, probably Tarn's most effective critic among this generation of scholars, has called the Alexander of Tarn's vision a "phantom" that "has haunted the pages of scholarship" for "a quarter of a century."[11] In reaction against Tarn's view of Alexander not only as a stunning conqueror but as a conqueror of stunning philosophic profundity as well, scholars have again depicted him "as a ruthless murderer, an

---

[10]Mary Renault, *The Nature of Alexander* (New York: Pantheon, 1975), p. 23.

[11]Ernst Badian, "Alexander the Great and the Unity of Mankind," *Historia* 7 (1958), 425.

autocratic megalomaniac, even a bisexual profligate."[12] Even more careful and moderate scholars like R. D. Milns hold that such an idea as the kinship of mankind was quite beyond Alexander and must be attributed to "later thinkers and philosophers."[13]

Now the reaction seems to be moving back toward the Tarn view. The "new" Alexander is more anchored in his own times and mores, and none of the more recent authorities attribute to Alexander the "great revolution in thought" that Tarn did. But the Alexander we see today is considerably more cerebral and innovative both in thought and action. This new image of Alexander is nowhere better represented than in the work of the distinguished Cambridge classicist N. G. L. Hammond, *Alexander the Great: King, Commander and Statesman,* from which the following excerpt is taken.

We have the advantage of hindsight. We can see that it was Alexander's leadership and training which made the Macedonians incomparable in war and in administration and enabled them as rulers of the so-called Hellenistic kingdoms to control the greater part of the civilised world for a century or more. In a reign of thirteen years he brought to Macedonia and Macedonians the immense wealth which maintained their strength for generations. All this was and is an unparalleled achievement. Moreover, as king of Macedonia he did not drain his country unduly in his lifetime, since Antipater had enough men to defeat the Greeks in 331 B.C. and 322 B.C. Yet the system he was creating—quite apart from any further conquests he had in mind in 323 B.C.—was certain to put an immense strain on present and future Macedonians. They were spread dangerously thin at the time of his death, and the prolonged absence of so many Macedonians abroad was bound to cause a drop in the birth-rate in Macedonia itself. Of course Alexander expected his Macedonians to undertake almost superhuman dangers and labours, and it was their response to his challenge that made them great. But the dangers and labours were being demanded for the sake of a policy which was not Macedonian in a nationalistic sense, which the Macedonians did not wholly understand, and which they never fully implemented. Philip's singlemindedness made him the greatest king of Macedonia. Alexander's wider vision made him at the same time something more and something less than the greatest king of Macedonia. . . .

As constitutionally elected king, Alexander had sole right of com-

---

[12]Hammond, *Alexander the Great,* p. 5.

[13]R. D. Milns, *Alexander the Great* (London: Robert Hale, 1968), p. 265.

mand and an inherited authority. From the age of twenty onwards he appointed his deputies without let or hindrance, issued all orders, and controlled all payments, promotions, and discharges. His authority as a commander was almost absolute, his discipline unquestioned, and his position unchallenged. As religious head of the state, he interceded for his men and was seen daily to sacrifice on their behalf.

Unique in his descent from Zeus and Heracles, he was acclaimed "son of Zeus" by the oracle at Didyma, the Sibyl at Erythrae, and the oracle of Ammon (the last at least in the opinion of his men), and he fostered the idea of divine protection by having the sacred shield of Athena carried into battle by his senior Bodyguard (it saved his life against the Malli; [Arrian] 6.10.2). Before engaging at Gaugamela Alexander prayed in front of the army, raising his right hand towards the gods and saying, "If I am really descended from Zeus, protect and strengthen the Greeks." That prayer, apparently, was answered. In the eyes of most men—and most men then had faith in gods, oracles, and omens—Alexander was favoured by the supernatural powers. To those who were sceptical he had extraordinarily good luck.

The brilliance of Alexander's mind is seen most clearly in his major battles. . . . For example, he saw at once the advantages and disadvantages of Darius' position on the Pinarus river and he anticipated the effects of his own detailed dispositions and orders to a nicety. "He surpassed all others in the faculty of intuitively meeting an emergency," whether in besieging Tyre or facing Scythian tactics or storming an impregnable fortress. He excelled in speed and precision of thought, the calculation of risks, and the expectation of an enemy's reactions. Having himself engaged in every kind of action and having grappled with practical problems from a young age, he had a sure sense of the possible and extraordinary versatility in invention. Unlike many famous commanders, his mind was so flexible that at the time of his death he was creating an entirely new type of army.

A most remarkable quality of Alexander's was the concern for his men. No conqueror had so few casualties in battle, and the reason was that Alexander avoided "the battle of rats" by using his brains not just to win, but to win most economically. He made this his priority because he loved his Macedonians. He grew up among them and fought alongside them, both as a youth admiring his seniors and as a mature man competing with his companions. He honoured and rewarded courage and devotion to duty in them, paying a unique tribute to the first casualties by having bronze statues made by the leading sculptor, and he felt deeply with them in their sufferings and privations. He aroused in them an amazing response. He not only admired courage and devotion to duty in his own men but in his enemies, whom he treated with honour. In return he won the respect and loyalty of

Asians of many races whom he had just defeated in battle. . . . Some commanders may have rivalled him in the handling of his own race. None have had such a capacity for leading a multiracial army. . . .

We have already touched upon his statesmanship in enhancing the prestige of the Macedonian monarchy and advancing the power of the Macedonian state. He reduced the harshness of customary law, (for instance, he no longer required the execution of the male relatives of a convicted traitor), and he was concerned for the welfare and the birth rate of Macedonia. He provided tax reliefs for the dependants of casualties, brought up war orphans at his own expense, and sought to avoid conflicts between the European and Asian families of his Macedonians by maintaining the latter in Asia. He increased the number of young Macedonians when he legitimised the soldiers' children by Asian women, and he sent the 10,000 veterans home in the expectation of their begetting more children in Macedonia. . . .

While Philip invented and inaugurated the Greek League, it was Alexander who demonstrated its efficacy as a *modus operandi* for the Macedonians and the Greeks and used their joint forces to overthrow the Persian Empire. By opening Asia to Greek enterprise and culture Alexander relieved many of the social and economic pressures which had been causing distress and anarchy in the Greek states. At the same time he was personally concerned with affairs in Greece, as we see from the large number of embassies which came to him in Asia rather than to his deputy, Antipater, in Macedonia. . . .

Alexander's originality is seen most clearly in Asia. He set himself an unparalleled task when he decided in advance not to make the Macedonians and the Greeks the masters of the conquered peoples but to create a self-sustaining Kingdom of Asia. Within his kingdom he intended the settled peoples to conduct their internal affairs in accordance with their own laws and customs, whether in a Greek city or a native village, in a Lydian or a Carian state, in a Cyprian or a Phoenician kingdom, in Egypt, Babylonia, or Persis, in an Indian principality or republic. As his power extended, he did not introduce European administrators at a level which would inhibit native self-rule (as so-called colonial powers have so often done); instead he continued native administrators in office and raised the best of them to the highest level in civil affairs by appointing them as his immediate deputies in the post of satrap (e.g., Mazaeus at Babylon) or nomarch (e.g., Doloaspis in Egypt). . . .

What is important is the effectiveness of Alexander's system: native civilians and armed forces alike lodged complaints with Alexander, the accused were tried legally and openly, and those found guilty were executed forthwith, in order "to deter the other satraps, governors, and civil officers" and to make it known that the rulers were not permit-

ted to wrong the ruled in Alexander's kingdom. In the opinion of
Arrian, who lived at the zenith of the Roman Empire and had a standard of comparison, it was this system which "more than anything else
kept to an orderly way of life the innumerable, widely diffused peoples
who had been subjugated in war or had of their own will joined him"
(6.27.5). In the same way rebels, sometimes in the form of native
pretenders, were put on trial; and, if found guilty, they were executed,
often in the manner native to the particular area (Arrian 6.30.2).
Where the rights of his subjects were at stake, he showed no mercy or
favouritism for any Macedonian, Greek, Thracian, Persian, Median, or
Indian. . . .

What Alexander sought in his senior administrators was summed
up in the word "excellence" (*arete*). He assessed it by performance in
his own army and in that of his enemy; for he approved courage and
loyalty, wherever he found it. But a particular kind of excellence was
needed where conquerors had to accept the conquered as their equals
in administering the kingdom of Asia. The Macedonians justifiably
regarded themselves as a military élite, superior to Greeks and barbarians, and closer to their king than any foreigner; and the Greeks
despised all Asians as barbarians, fitted by nature only to be slaves.
Yet here was Alexander according equal status, regardless of race, not
only to all his administrators but also to all who served in his army!
Resentment at this was the chief factor in the mutiny of the Macedonians at Opis. On that occasion Alexander enforced his will. He celebrated the concept of equal status in an official banquet, at which the
Macedonians sat by their king, with whom they were not reconciled;
next were the Persians; and after them persons of "the other races."
All the guests were men who ranked first in reputation or in some
other form of excellence (*arete*). . . .

When Alexander encountered nomadic or marauding peoples, he
forced them, often by drastic methods of warfare, to accept his rule
and to adopt a settled way of life. Many of his new cities were founded
among these peoples so that "they should cease to be nomads," and
he encouraged the concentration of native villages to form new urban
centres. For he intended to promote peace, prosperity, and culture
within these parts of his kingdom too, and the cities and centres were
means to that end. Strongly fortified and well manned, they were
bastions of peace, and the young men in them were trained by Macedonian and Greek veterans to join Alexander's new army and maintain his peace. They were sited to become markets for agricultural
produce and interregional exchange, and their citizens, especially in
the new cities by the deltas of the Nile, the Euphrates, and the Indus,
learnt the capitalistic form of economy, which had brought such prosperity to the Greek states in the fifth and fourth centuries.

The cultural model for the new cities was the Macedonian town, itself very strongly imbued with Greek ideas and practices. The ruling element from the outset was formed by Macedonian and Greek veterans; and the Asians, although free to practise their own religion and traditions, were encouraged to learn Greek and adopt some forms of Greco-Macedonian life. According to Plutarch (*Mor.* 328e) Alexander founded 70 new cities, which started their life with 10,000 adult male citizens as the norm, and he must have envisaged a fusion of European and Asian cultures developing within and spreading out from these arteries into the body of the kingdom. . . .

The effects of a statesman's ideas, especially if he dies at the age of thirty-two, are rarely assessable within his lifetime. Yet before Alexander died his ideas bore fruit in the integration of Asians and Macedonians in cavalry and infantry units; the training of Asians in Macedonian weaponry; the association of Asians and Macedonians in each file of the army; the settling of Macedonians, Greeks, and Asians in the new cities; the spread of Greek as a common language in the army and in the new cities; the development of Babylon as the "metropolis" or capital of the kingdom of Asia; the honouring of interracial marriage; and the raising of Eurasian children to a privileged status.

Peace reigned in this kingdom of Asia, and its people now had little to fear from their neighbours. Urbanisation, trade, water-borne commerce, agriculture, flood-control, land-reclamation, and irrigation were developing fast, and exchange was stimulated by the liberation of hoarded treasure. The gold and silver coinage of Alexander, uniform in types and weights, was universally accepted because it was of real, bullion value. In the eastern satrapies especially the gold darics and silver shekels of the Persian treasuries continued to circulate, and in the western satrapies local currencies were provided by the Greek, Cyprian, and Phoenician cities. . . .

The skill with which Alexander changed the economy of Asia into that system of commercial exchange which the Greeks had invented and we call capitalism, and at that within so few years, is one of the most striking signs of his genius. . . .

The fulfilment of Alexander's plans was impaired by his early death and by the strife between the generals which ensued. Yet even so, within the span of thirteen years, he changed the face of the world more decisively and with more longlasting effects than any other statesman has ever done. He first introduced into Asia the Greco-Macedonian city within the framework of a monarchical or autocratic state, and this form of city was to be the centre of ancient and medieval civilisation in the southern Balkans, the Aegean, and the Near East. For the city provided that continuity of Greek language, literature, and culture which enriched the Roman world, fostered Christianity, and affected Western Europe so profoundly. The outlook and the achievements of Alexander created an ideal image, an apotheosis of kingship which was to inspire the Hellenistic kings, some Roman emperors, and the Byzantine rulers. And his creation of a state which rose above nationalism and brought liberators and liberated, victors and defeated into collaboration and parity of esteem puts most of the expedients of the modern world to shame. . . .

That Alexander should grow up with a sense of mission was certainly to be expected. For he was descended from Zeus and Heracles, he was born to be king, he had the career of Philip as an exemplar, and he was advised by Isocrates, Aristotle, and others to be a benefactor of Macedonians and Greeks alike. His sense of mission was inevitably steeped in religious associations, because from an early age he had been associated with the king, his father, in conducting religious ceremonies, and he was imbued with many ideas of orthodox religion and of ecstatic mysteries. Thus two observations by Plutarch (*Mor.* 342 A and F) have the ring of truth. "This desire (to bring all men into an orderly system under a single leadership and to accustom them to one way of life) was implanted in Alexander from childhood and grew up with him"; and on crossing the Hellespont to the Troad Alexander's first asset was "his reverence towards the gods." Already by then he planned to found a Kingdom of Asia, in which he would rule over the peoples, as Odysseus had done, "like a kindly father" (*Odyssey* 5.11). He promoted the fulfilment of that plan "by founding Greek cities among savage peoples and by teaching the principles of law and peace to lawless, ignorant tribes." When he had completed the conquest of "Asia" through the favour of the gods and especially that of Zeus Ammon, he went on to establish for all men in his kingdom "concord and peace and partnership with one another" (*Mor.* 329 F).

This was a practical development, springing from a religious concept and not from a philosophical theory (though it led later to the philosophical theory of the Cynics, who substituted for Asia the whole inhabited world and talked of the brotherhood of all men), and it came to fruition in the banquet at Opis, when he prayed in the presence of men of various races for "concord and partnership in the ruling" of his kingdom "between Macedonians and Persians."

What distinguishes Alexander from all other conquerors is this divine mission. He had grown up with it, and he had to a great extent fulfilled it, before he gave expression to it at the banquet at Opis in such words as those reported by Plutarch (*Mor.* 329 C). "Alexander considered," wrote Plutarch, "that he had come from the gods to be a general governor and reconciler of the world. Using force of arms when he did not bring men together by the light of reason, he harnessed all resources to one and the same end, mixing the lives, manners, marriages and customs of men, as it were in a loving-cup." This is his true claim to be called "Alexander the Great": that he did not crush or dismember his enemies, as the conquering Romans crushed Carthage and Molossia and dismembered Macedonia into four parts; nor exploit, enslave or destroy the native peoples, as "the white man" has so often done in America, Africa, and Australasia; but that he created, albeit for only a few years, a supranational community capable of living internally at peace and of developing the concord and partnership which are so sadly lacking in the modern world.

Review and Study Questions

1. In your judgment, do the ancient sources quoted in this chapter support the interpretation of W. W. Tarn? Explain.

2. Is it credible that, given the nature and temperament of Alexander, he was responsible for such a sophisticated concept as "the natural brotherhood of all men"?

3. Is it justifiable to characterize Alexander as "the great"? Give your reasons.

Suggestions for Further Reading

As is often the case, the classical sources for the biography of Alexander are among the most lively and entertaining works about him, especially Plutarch and Arrian. Plutarch's "Life of Alexander" from his *Parallel Lives of Noble Greeks and Romans* (available in several editions) is, like the rest of the biographical sketches in this famous book, a gossipy and charming account, containing most of the familiar anecdotes associated with Alexander. Arrian's work, the most substantial of the ancient sources, despite a certain stuffiness and lack of analytical daring, is solidly based on more contemporary sources now long lost—particularly Ptolemy's journal and the work of Aristobulus. And it contains the best and most detailed account of Alexander's conquests. See the excellent modern translation by Aubrey de Sélincourt, *Arrian's Life of Alexander the Great* (Harmondsworth, England: Penguin, 1958).

The views of W. W. Tarn summarized in the excerpted passage above from his Raleigh Lecture on History, "Alexander the Great and the Unity of Mankind," are spelled out in greater detail in the chapters he wrote on Alexander and his age—chs. 12–15 of the *Cambridge Ancient History*, vol. 6 (Cambridge, England: Cambridge University

Press, 1927), and in his larger *Alexander the Great*, 2 vols. (Cambridge, England: Cambridge University Press, 1948), based on the account in *Cambridge Ancient History* but expanded and updated.

Tarn's most bitter critic is Ernst Badian, who chose to challenge Tarn in particular for the views expressed in his Raleigh Lecture. Badian's article, with the same title, "Alexander the Great and the Unity of Mankind," appeared in *Historia*, 7 (1958), 425–444, and is reprinted in *Alexander the Great: The Main Problems*, ed. G. T. Griffith (New York: Barnes and Noble, 1966). This article is highly specialized, closely reasoned, and contains long passages in Greek; but it is very important and, despite the difficulties of the text, the argument can be clearly followed even by the nonspecialist. Peter Green, *Alexander the Great* (New York: Praeger, 1970), is a modern general account of Alexander's career in the same critical tradition as Badian. Two other modern works that deal more with the conquests than the conqueror are Peter Bamm, *Alexander the Great: Power as Destiny*, tr. J. M. Brownjohn (New York: McGraw-Hill, 1968), and Sir Mortimer Wheeler, *Flames over Persepolis: Turning Point in History* (New York: Morrow, 1968), the latter of particular interest because of Wheeler's expert knowledge of Near Eastern and Indian archaeology.

There is another relatively recent book that stresses the continuing work in archaeology, including the dramatic finds at Vergina in Macedonia: Robin Lane Fox, *The Search for Alexander* (Boston: Little, Brown, 1980). The most balanced and readable modern general account, however, may still be A. R. Burn, *Alexander the Great and the Hellenistic Empire* (London: The English Universities Press, 1947), although the more recent R. D. Milns, *Alexander the Great* (London: Robert Hale, 1968) is also recommended.

Finally, Alexander is the subject of two first-rate historical novels by Mary Renault, *Fire from Heaven* (New York: Pantheon, 1969), and *The Persian Boy* (New York: Pantheon, 1972), the first carrying the story through Alexander's childhood to his accession to the throne of Macedonia, the second recounting his conquests as narrated by the Persian boy-eunuch Bagoas, Alexander's companion and lover. Renault has also produced a nonfiction account, fully as readable as her novels, and based on the meticulous research she prepared for them, *The Nature of Alexander* (New York: Pantheon, 1975).

CLEOPATRA, QUEEN OF EGYPT

69 B.C.	Born
51 B.C.	Succeeded to Egyptian throne
48–45 B.C.	Caesar in Egypt
42–40 B.C.	Antony in Egypt
31 B.C.	Battle of Actium
30 B.C.	Died

Future ages would depict Cleopatra at the dark and exotic Egyptian queen who used her personal powers as much as her position to sway the two greatest Romans of her day, Caesar and Antony, to her cause. In fact, she was not an Egyptian at all but a blonde Macedonian, the descendant of Alexander's general Ptolemy, who had seized Egypt on Alexander's death and established his own dynasty there. Cleopatra had come to the throne on the death of her father in 51 B.C. and ruled successively with her two brothers, Ptolemy XIII and Ptolemy XIV, and her son Ptolemy XV.

By her lifetime Rome had become the dominant force in the Hellenistic east, having begun the diplomatic and military penetration of that region in the Second Punic War. Cleopatra realized that accommodation to Rome had to be made if she and her kingdom were to prosper. Caesar arrived in Egypt in 48 B.C. in pursuit of Pompey after his victory at Pharsalus. But Pompey had been murdered and Cleopatra was on the throne. She immediately set out to conquer Caesar, who was equally attracted to the Egyptian queen. He needed her money and resources; she needed Caesar's power to reestablish her dynasty and recover its lost provinces. Caesar dallied in Egypt with Cleopatra for some four years, giving her a son, whom she called Caesarion. Cleopatra returned to Rome with Caesar and was installed by him in regal state. With his assassination in 44 B.C.

she returned to Egypt to await the outcome of the next round of Rome's civil wars.

When Caesar's assassins were defeated at the battle of Philippi in 42 B.C., the victors were the consul Marcus Antonius (Antony) and Caesar's adopted son Octavian. These two divided the Roman Empire between them, with Antony taking the east. His intention was to pursue a war against the Parthians. Cleopatra saw the opportunity to continue with Antony the liaison she had begun with Caesar—and for the same purposes. She met him at Tarsus in Asia Minor, laden with gifts and promises. Antony was as captivated by her as Caesar had been and, abandoning his Parthian campaign, returned with her to Egypt. In 40 B.C. they were married. This step alienated Antony not only from Octavian but from the majority of Romans. This alienation continued and culminated in the battle of Actium, 31 B.C., in which the forces of Antony and Cleopatra were routed by those of Octavian. Returning to Egypt, Antony took his own life. Shortly thereafter Cleopatra committed suicide, perhaps by snakebite. She was 39 and had been queen for 22 years.

The Roman sources of her lifetime are filled with references to Cleopatra, but a full narrative account of her life and policies had to wait for the second century, in particular the works of the Greek historian Dio Cassius and the Greek essayist and biographer Plutarch, from whose lives of Caesar and Antony the following excerpt is taken.

Lives

PLUTARCH

Plutarch was a learned and aristocratic Greek who lived among the highest circles in Rome and was a great admirer of all things Roman. He is famous for a biographical series, *The Parallel Lives of Noble Greeks and Romans,* which included substantial sketches of both Caesar and Antony. We turn to these works for Plutarch's account of Cleopatra. He begins with Antony.

Such being his temper, the last and crowning mischief that could befall him came in the love of Cleopatra, to awaken and kindle to fury passions that as yet lay still and dormant in his nature, and to stifle and finely corrupt any elements that yet made resistance in him of goodness and a sound judgment. He fell into the snare thus. When making preparation for the Parthian war, he sent to command her to make her personal appearance in Cilicia, to answer an accusation, that she had given great assistance, in the late wars, to Cassius. Dellius, who was sent on this message, had no sooner seen her face, and remarked her adroitness and subtlety in speech, but he felt convinced that Antony would not so much as think of giving any molestation to a woman like this; on the contrary, she would be the first in favour with him. So he set himself at once to pay his court to the Egyptian, and gave her his advice, "to go," in the Homeric style, to Cilicia, "in her best attire," and bade her fear nothing from Antony, the gentlest and kindest of soldiers. She had some faith in the words of Dellius, but more in her own attractions; which, having formerly recommended her to Caesar and the young Caenus Pompey, she did not doubt might prove yet more successful with Antony. Their acquaintance was with her when a girl, young and ignorant of the world, but she was to meet Antony in the time of life when women's beauty is most splendid, and their intellects are in full maturity. She made great preparation for her journey, of money, gifts, and ornaments of value, such as so wealthy a kingdom might afford, but she brought with her her surest hopes in her own magic arts and charms.

She received several letters, both from Antony and from his friends, to summon her, but she took no account of these orders; and at last, as if in mockery of them, she came sailing up the river Cydnus, in a barge with gilded stern and outspread sails of purple, while oars of silver beat time to the music of flutes and fifes and harps. She herself lay all along under a canopy of cloth of gold, dressed as Venus in a picture, and beautiful young boys, like painted Cupids, stood on each side to fan her. Her maids were dressed like sea nymphs and graces, some steering at the rudder, some working at the ropes. The perfumes diffused themselves from the vessel to the shore, which was covered with multitudes, part following the galley up the river on either bank, part running out of the city to see the sight. The market-place was quite emptied, and Antony at last was left alone sitting upon the tribunal; while the word went through all the multitude, that Venus was come to feast with Bacchus, for the common good of Asia. On her arrival, Antony sent to invite her to supper. She thought it fitter he should come to her; so, willing to show his good-humour and courtesy, he complied, and went. He found the preparations to receive him magnificent beyond expression, but nothing so admirable as the great number of lights; for on a sudden there was let down altogether so great a number of branches with lights in them so ingeniously disposed, some in squares, and some in circles, that the whole thing was a spectacle that has seldom been equalled for beauty.

The next day, Antony invited her to supper, and was very desirous to outdo her as well in magnificence as contrivance; but he found he was altogether beaten in both, and was so well convinced of it that he was himself the first to jest and mock at his poverty of wit and his rustic awkwardness. She, perceiving that his raillery was broad and gross, and savoured more of the soldier than the courtier, rejoined in the same taste, and fell into it at once, without any sort of reluctance or reserve. For her actual beauty, it is said, was not in itself so remarkable that none could be compared with her, or that no one could see her without being struck by it, but the contact of her presence, if you lived with her, was irresistible; the attraction of her person, joining with the charm of her conversation, and the character that attended all she said or did, was something bewitching. It was a pleasure merely to hear the sound of her voice, with which, like an instrument of many strings, she could pass from one language to another; so that there were few of the barbarian nations that she answered by an interpreter; to most of them she spoke herself, as to the Ethiopians, Troglodytes, Hebrews, Arabians, Syrians, Medes, Parthians, and many others, whose language she had learnt; which was all the more surprising because most of the kings, her predecessors, scarcely gave themselves the trouble to acquire the Egyptian tongue, and several of them quite abandoned the Macedonian.

Antony was so captivated by her that, while Fulvia his wife maintained his quarrels in Rome against Caesar by actual force of arms, and the Parthian troops, commanded by Labienus (the king's generals having made him commander-in-chief), were assembled in Mesopotamia, and ready to enter Syria, he could yet suffer himself to be carried away by her to Alexandria, there to keep holiday, like a boy, in play and diversion, squandering and fooling away in enjoyments that most costly, as Antiphon says, of all valuables, time. They had a sort of company, to which they gave a particular name, calling it that of the Inimitable Livers. The members entertained one another daily in turn, with an extravagance of expenditure beyond measure or belief. Philotas, a physician of Amphissa, who was at that time a student of medicine in Alexandria, used to tell my grandfather Lamprias that, having some acquaintance with one of the royal cooks, he was invited by him, being a young man, to come and see the sumptuous preparations for supper. So he was taken into the kitchen, where he admired the prodigious variety of all things; but particularly, seeing eight wild boars roasting whole, says he, "Surely you have a great number of guests." The cook laughed at his simplicity, and told him there were not above twelve to sup, but that every dish was to be served up just roasted to a turn, and if anything was but one minute ill-timed, it was spoiled. "And," said he, "maybe Antony will sup just now, maybe not this hour, maybe he will call for wine, or begin to talk, and will put it off. So that," he continued, "it is not one, but many suppers must be had in readiness, as it is impossible to guess at his hour." This was Philotas's story. . . .

To return to Cleopatra; Plato admits four sorts of flattery, but she had a thousand. Were Antony serious or disposed to mirth, she had at any moment some new delight or charm to meet his wishes; at every turn she was upon him, and let him escape her neither by day nor by night. She played at dice with him, drank with him, hunted with him; and when he exercised in arms, she was there to see. At night she would go rambling with him to disturb and torment people at their doors and windows, dressed like a servant-woman, for Antony also went in servant's disguise, and from these expeditions he often came home very scurvily answered, and sometimes even beaten severely, though most people guessed who it was. However, the Alexandrians in general liked it all well enough, and joined good-humouredly and kindly in his frolic and play, saying they were much obliged to Antony for acting his tragic parts at Rome, and keeping his comedy for them. It would be trifling without end to be particular in his follies, but his fishing must not be forgotten. He went out one day to angle with Cleopatra, and, being so unfortunate as to catch nothing in the presence of his mistress, he gave secret orders to the fishermen to dive under water, and put fishes that had been already taken upon his hooks; and these he drew so fast that the Egyptian perceived it. But, feigning great admiration, she told everybody how dexterous Antony was, and invited them next day to come and see him again. So, when a number of them had come on board the fishing-boats, as soon as he had let down his hook, one of her servants was beforehand with his divers, and fixed upon his hook a salted fish from Pontus. Antony, feeling his line give, drew up the prey, and when, as may be imagined, great laughter ensued, "Leave," said Cleopatra, "the fishing-rod, general, to us poor sovereigns of Pharos and Canopus; your game is cities, provinces, and kingdoms."

Whilst he was thus diverting himself and engaged in this boy's play, two despatches arrived; one from Rome, that his brother Lucius and his wife Fulvia, after many quarrels among themselves, had joined in war against Caesar, and having lost all, had fled out of Italy; the other bringing little better news, that Labienus, at the head of the Parthians, was overrunning Asia, from Euphrates and Syria as far as Lydia and Ionia. So, scarcely at last rousing himself from sleep, and shaking off the fumes of wine, he set out to attack the Parthians, and went as far as Phoenicia; but, upon the receipt of lamentable letters from Fulvia, turned his course with two hundred ships to Italy. And, in his way, receiving such of his friends as fled from Italy, he was given to understand that Fulvia was the sole cause of the war, a woman of a restless spirit and very bold, and withal her hopes were that commotions in Italy would force Antony from Cleopatra. But it happened that Fulvia, as she was coming to meet her husband, fell sick by the way, and died at Sicyon, so that an accommodation was the more easily made. For when he reached Italy, and Caesar showed no intention of laying anything to his charge, and he on his part shifted the blame of everything on Fulvia, those that were friends to them would not suffer that the time should be spent in looking narrowly into the plea, but made a reconciliation first, and then a partition of the empire between them, taking as their boundary the Ionian Sea, the eastern provinces falling to Antony, to Caesar the western, and Africa being left to Lepidus. And an agreement was made that every one in their turn, as they thought fit, should make their friends consuls, when they did not choose to take the offices themselves. . . .

But the mischief that thus long had lain still, the passion for Cleopatra, which better thoughts had seemed to have lulled and charmed into oblivion, upon his approach to Syria gathered strength again, and broke out into a flame. And, in fine, like Plato's restive and rebellious horse of the human soul, flinging off all good and wholesome counsel, and breaking fairly loose, he sends Fonteius Capito to bring Cleopatra into Syria. To whom at her arrival he made no small or trifling present, Phoenicia, Coele-Syria, Cyprus, great part of Cilicia, that side of Judaea which produces balm, that part of Arabia where the Nabathaeans extend to the outer sea; profuse gifts which much displeased the Romans. For although he had invested several private persons in great governments and kingdoms, and bereaved many kings of theirs, as Antigonus of Judaea, whose head he caused to be struck off (the first example of that punishment being inflicted on a king), yet nothing stung the Romans like the shame of these honours paid to Cleopatra. Their dissatisfaction was augmented also by his acknowledging as his own the twin children he had by her, giving them the names of Alexander and Cleopatra, and adding, as their surnames, the titles of Sun and Moon. But he, who knew how to put a good colour on the most dishonest action, would say that the greatness of the Roman empire consisted more in giving than in taking kingdoms, and that the way to carry noble blood through the world was by begetting in every place a new line and series of kings; his own ancestor had thus been born of Hercules; Hercules had not limited his hopes of progeny to a single womb, nor feared any law like Solon's or any audit of procreation, but had freely let nature take her will in the foundation and first commencement of many families.

For assembling the people in the exercise ground, and causing two golden thrones to be placed on a platform of silver, the one for him and the other for Cleopatra, and at their feet lower thrones for their children, he proclaimed Cleopatra Queen of Egypt, Cyprus, Libya, and Coele-Syria, and with her conjointly Caesarion, the reputed son of the former Caesar, who left Cleopatra with child. His own sons by Cleopatra were to have the style of kings of kings; to Alexander he gave Armenia and Media, with Parthia, so soon as it should be overcome; to Ptolemy, Phoenicia, Syria, and Cilicia. Alexander was brought out before the people in Median costume, the tiara and upright peak, and Ptolemy, in boots and mantle and Macedonian cap done about with the diadem; for this was the habit of the successors of Alexander, as the other was of the Medes and Armenians. And as soon as they had saluted their parents, the one was received by a guard of Macedonians, the other by one of Armenians. Cleopatra was then, as at other times when she appeared in public, dressed in the habit of the goddess Isis, and gave audience to the people under the name of the New Isis.

Caesar, relating these things in the senate, and often complaining to the people, excited men's minds against Antony, and Antony also sent messages of accusation against Caesar. The principal of his charges were these: first, that he had not made any division with him of Sicily, which was lately taken from Pompey; secondly, that he had retained the ships he had lent him for the war; thirdly, that, after deposing Lepidus, their colleague, he had taken for himself the army, governments, and revenues formerly appropriated to him; and lastly, that he had parcelled out almost all Italy amongst his own soldiers, and left nothing for his. Caesar's answer was as follows: that he had put Lepidus out of government because of his own misconduct; that what he had got in war he would divide with Antony, so soon as Antony gave him a share of Armenia; that Antony's soldiers had no claims in Italy, being a possession of Media and Parthia, the acquisitions which their brave actions under their general had added to the Roman empire.

Antony was in Armenia when this answer came to him, and immediately sent Canidius with sixteen legions towards the sea; but he, in the company of Cleopatra, went to Ephesus, whither ships were coming in from all quarters to form the navy, consisting, vessels of burden included, of eight hundred vessels, of which Cleopatra furnished two hundred, together with twenty thousand talents, and provision for the whole army during the war. Antony, on the advice of Domitius and some others, bade Cleopatra return into Egypt, there to expect the event of the war; but she, dreading some new reconciliation by Octavia's means, prevailed with Canidius, by a large sum of money, to speak in her favour with Antony, pointing out to him that it was not just that one that bore so great a part in the charge of the war should be robbed of her share of glory in the carrying it on; nor would it be politic to disoblige the Egyptians, who were so considerable a part of his naval forces; nor did he see how she was inferior in prudence to any one of the kings that were serving with him; she had long governed a great kingdom by herself alone, and long lived with him, and gained experience in public affairs. These arguments (so the fate that destined all to Caesar would have it) prevailed; and when all their forces had met, they sailed together to Samos, and held high festivities. For, as it was ordered that all kings, princes, and governors, all nations and cities within the limits of Syria, the Maeotid Lake, Armenia, and Illyria, should bring or cause to be brought all munitions necessary for war, so was it also proclaimed that all stage-players should make their appearance at Samos; so that, while pretty nearly the whole world was filled with groans and lamentations, this one island for some days resounded with piping and harping, theatres filling, and choruses playing. Every city sent an ox as its contribution to the sacrifice, and the kings that accompanied Antony competed who should make the most magnificent feasts and the greatest presents; and men began to ask themselves, what would be done to celebrate the victory, when they went to such an expense of festivity at the opening of the war. . . .

The speed and extent of Antony's preparations alarmed Caesar, who feared he might be forced to fight the decisive battle that summer. For he wanted many necessaries, and the people grudged very much to pay the taxes; freemen being called upon to pay a fourth part of their incomes, and freed slaves an eighth of their property, so that there were loud outcries against him, and disturbances throughout all Italy. And this is looked upon as one of the greatest of Antony's oversights, that he did not then press the war. For he allowed time at once for Caesar to make his preparations and for the commotions to pass over. For while people were having their money called for, they were mutinous and violent; but, having paid it, they held their peace. Titius and Plancus, men of consular dignity and friends to Antony, having been ill-used by Cleopatra, whom they had most resisted in her design of being present in the war, came over to Caesar and gave information of the contents of Antony's will, with which they were acquainted. It was deposited in the hands of the vestal virgins, who refused to deliver it up, and sent Caesar word, if he pleased, he should come and seize it himself, which he did. And, reading it over to himself, he noted those places that were most for his purpose, and, having summoned the senate, read them publicly. Many were scandalised at the proceeding, thinking it out of reason and equity to call a man to account for what was not to be until after his death. Caesar specially pressed what Antony said in his will about his burial; for he had ordered that even if he died in the city of Rome, his body, after being carried in state through the forum, should be sent to Cleopatra at Alexandria. Calvisius, a dependant of Caesar's, urged other charges in connection with Cleopatra against Antony; that he had given her the library of Pergamus, containing two hundred thousand distinct volumes; that at a great banquet, in the presence of many guests, he had risen up and rubbed her feet, to fulfil some wager or promise; that he had suffered the Ephesians to salute her as their queen; that he had frequently at the public audience of kings and princes received amorous messages written in tablets made of onyx and crystal, and read them openly on the tribunal; that when Furnius, a man of great authority and eloquence among the Romans, was pleading, Cleopatra happening to pass by in her chair, Antony started up and left them in the middle of their cause, to follow at her side and attend her home. . . .

When the armaments gathered for the war, Antony had no less than five hundred ships of war, including numerous galleys of eight and ten banks of oars, as richly ornamented as if they were meant for a triumph. He had a hundred thousand foot and twelve thousand horse. He had vassal kings attending, Bocchus of Libya, Tarcondemus of the Upper Cilicia, Archelaus of Cappadocia, Philadelphus of Paphlagonia, Mithridates of Commagene, and Sadalas of Thrace; all these were with him in person. Out of Pontus Polemon sent him considerable forces, as did also Malchus from Arabia, Herod the Jew, and Amyntus, King of Lycaonia and Galatia; also the Median king sent some troops to join him. Caesar had two hundred and fifty galleys of war, eight thousand foot, and horse about equal to the enemy. Antony's empire extended from Euphrates and Armenia to the Ionian sea and the Illyrians; Caesar's, from Illyria to the westward ocean, and from the ocean all along the Tuscan and Sicilian sea. Of Africa, Caesar had all the coast opposite to Italy, Gaul, and Spain, as far as the Pillars of Hercules, and Antony the provinces from Cyrene to Ethiopia.

But so wholly was he now the mere appendage to the person of Cleopatra that, although he was much superior to the enemy in land-forces, yet, out of complaisance to his mistress, he wished the victory to be gained by sea, and that, too, when he could not but see how, for want of sailors, his captains, all through unhappy Greece, were pressing every description of men, common travellers and ass-drivers, harvest labourers and boys, and for all this the vessels had not their complements, but remained, most of them, ill-manned and badly rowed. Caesar, on the other side, had ships that were built not for size or show, but for service, not pompous galleys, but light, swift, and perfectly manned; and from his headquarters at Tarentum and Brundusium he sent messages to Antony not to protract the war, but come out with his forces; he would give him secure roadsteads and ports for his fleet, and, for his land army to disembark and pitch their camp, he would leave him as much ground in Italy, inland from the sea, as a horse could traverse in a single course. Antony, on the other side, with the like bold language, challenged him to a single combat, though he were much the older; and, that being refused, proposed to meet him in the Pharsalian fields, where Caesar and Pompey had fought before. But whilst Antony lay with his fleet near Actium, where now stands Nicopolis, Caesar seized his opportunity and crossed the Ionian sea, securing himself at a place in Epirus called the Ladle. And when those about Antony were much disturbed, their land forces being a good way off, "Indeed," said Cleopatra, in mockery, "we may well be frightened if Caesar has got hold of the Ladle!"

On the morrow, Antony, seeing the enemy sailing up, and fearing lest his ships might be taken for want of the soldiers to go on board of them, armed all the rowers, and made a show upon the decks of being in readiness to fight; the oars were mounted as if waiting to be put in motion, and the vessels themselves drawn up to face the enemy on either side of the channel of Actium, as though they were properly manned and ready for an engagement. And Caesar, deceived by this stratagem, retired. He was also thought to have shown considerable skill in cutting off the water from the enemy by some lines of trenches and forts, water not being plentiful anywhere else, nor very good. . . .

When it was resolved to stand to a fight at sea, they set fire to all the Egyptian ships except sixty; and of these the best and largest, from ten banks down to three, he manned with twenty thousand full-armed men and two thousand archers. Here it is related that a foot captain, one that had fought often under Antony, and had his body all mangled with wounds, exclaimed, "O my general, what have our wounds and swords done to displease you, that you should give your confidence to rotten timbers? . . .'

When they engaged, there was no charging or striking of one ship by another, because Antony's, by reason of their great bulk, were incapable of the rapidity required to make the stroke effectual, and on the other side, Caesar's durst not charge head to head on Antony's, which were all armed with solid masses and spikes of brass; nor did they like even to run in on their sides, which were so strongly built with great squared pieces of timber, fastened together with iron bolts, that their vessels' beaks would easily have been shattered upon them. So that the engagement resembled a land fight, or, to speak yet more properly, the attack and defence of a fortified place; for there were always three or four vessels of Caesar's about one of Antony's, pressing them with spears, javelins, poles, and several inventions of fire, which they flung among them, Antony's men using catapults also, to pour down missiles from wooden towers. Agrippa drawing out the squadron under his command to outflank the enemy, Publicola was obliged to observe his motions, and gradually to break off from the middle squadron, where some confusion and alarm ensued, while Arruntius engaged them. But the fortune of the day was still undecided, and the battle equal, when on a sudden Cleopatra's sixty ships were seen hoisting sail and making out to sea in full flight, right through the ships that were engaged. For they were placed behind the great ships, which, in breaking through, they put into disorder. The enemy was astonished to see them sailing off with a fair wind towards Peloponnesus. Here it was that Antony showed to all the world that he was no longer actuated by the thoughts and motives of a commander or a man, or indeed by his own judgment at all, and what was once said as a jest, that the soul of a lover lives in some one else's body, he proved to be a serious truth. For, as if he had been born part of her, and must move with her wheresoever she went, as soon as he saw her ship sailing away, he abandoned all that were fighting and spending their lives for him, and put himself aboard a galley of five banks of oars, taking with him only Alexander of Syria and Scellias, to follow her that had so well begun his ruin and would hereafter accomplish it.

She, perceiving him to follow, gave the signal to come aboard. So, as soon as he came up with them, he was taken into the ship. But without seeing her or letting himself be seen by her, he went forward by himself, and sat alone, without a word, in the ship's prow, covering his face with his two hands. In the meanwhile, some of Caesar's light Liburnian ships, that were in pursuit, came in sight. But on Antony's commanding to face about, they all gave back except Eurycles the Laconian, who pressed on, shaking a lance from the deck, as if he meant to hurl it at him. Antony, standing at the prow, demanded of him, "Who is this that pursues Antony?" "I am," said he, "Eurycles, the son of Lachares, armed with Caesar's fortune to revenge my father's death." Lachares had been condemned for a robbery, and beheaded by Antony's orders. However, Eurycles did not attack Antony, but ran with his full force upon the other admiral-galley (for there were two of them), and with the blow turned her round, and took both her and another ship, in which was a quantity of rich plate and furniture. So soon as Eurycles was gone, Antony returned to his posture and sat silent, and thus he remained for three days, either in anger with Cleopatra, or wishing not to upbraid her, at the end of which they touched at Taenarus. Here the women of their company succeeded first in bringing them to speak, and afterwards to eat and sleep together. And, by this time, several of the ships of burden and some of his friends began to come in to him from the rout, bringing news of his fleet's being quite destroyed, but that the land forces, they thought, still stood firm. So that he sent messengers to Canidius to march the army with all speed through Macedonia into Asia. And, designing himself to go from Taenarus into Africa, he gave one of the merchant ships, laden with a large sum of money, and vessels of silver and gold of great value, belonging to the royal collections, to his friends, desiring them to share it amongst them, and provide for their own safety. . . .

But at Actium, his fleet, after a long resistance to Caesar, and suffering the most damage from a heavy sea that set in right ahead, scarcely at four in the afternoon, gave up the contest, with the loss of not more than five thousand men killed, but of three hundred ships taken, as Caesar himself has recorded. Only a few had known of Antony's flight; and those who were told of it could not at first give any belief to so incredible a thing as that a general who had nineteen entire legions and twelve thousand horse upon the seashore, could abandon all and fly away; and he, above all, who had so often experienced both good and evil fortune, and had in a thousand wars and battles been inured to changes. His soldiers, however, would not give up their desires and expectations, still fancying he would appear from some part or other, and showed such a generous fidelity to his service that, when they were thoroughly assured that he was fled in earnest, they kept themselves in a body seven days, making no account of the messages that Caesar sent to them. . . .

When Antony came into Africa, he sent on Cleopatra from Paraetonium into Egypt, and stayed himself in the most entire solitude that he could desire, roaming and wandering about with only two friends, one a Greek, Aristocrates, a rhetorician, and the other a Roman, Lucilius, of whom we have elsewhere spoken, how, at Philippi, to give Brutus time to escape, he suffered himself to be taken by the pursuers, pretending he was Brutus. Antony gave him his life, and on this account he remained true and faithful to him to the last.

But when also the officer who commanded for him in Africa, to whose care he had committed all his forces there, took them over to Caesar, he resolved to kill himself, but was hindered by his friends. And coming to Alexandria, he found Cleopatra busied in a most bold and wonderful enterprise. Over the small space of land which divides the Red Sea from the sea near Egypt, which may be considered also the boundary between Asia and Africa, and in the narrowest place is not much above three hundred furlongs across, over this neck of land Cleopatra had formed a project of dragging her fleet and setting it afloat in the Arabian Gulf, thus with her soldiers and her treasure to secure herself a home on the other side, where she might live in peace far away from war and slavery. But the first galleys which were carried over being burnt by the Arabians of Petra, and Antony not knowing but that the army before Actium still held together, she desisted from her enterprise, and gave orders for the fortifying of all the approaches to Egypt. But Antony, leaving the city and the conversation of his friends, built him a dwelling-place in the water, near Pharos, upon a little mole which he cast up in the sea, and there, secluding himself from the company of mankind, said he desired nothing but to live the life of Timon; as indeed, his case was the same, and the ingratitude and injuries which he suffered from those he had esteemed his friends made him hate and distrust all mankind. . . . Canidius now came, bringing word in person of the loss of the army before Actium. Then he received news that Herod of Judaea was gone over to Caesar with some legions and cohorts, and that the other kings and princes were in like manner deserting him, and that, out of Egypt, nothing stood by him. All this, however, seemed not to disturb him, but, as if he were glad to put away all hope, that with it he might be rid of all care, and leaving his habitation by the sea, which he called the Timoneum, he was received by Cleopatra in the palace, and set the whole city into a course of feasting, drinking, and presents. The son of Caesar and Cleopatra was registered among the youths, and Antyllus, his own son by Fulvia, received the gown without the purple border given to those that are come of age; in honour of which the citizens of Alexandria did nothing but feast and revel for many days. They themselves broke up the Order of the Inimitable Livers, and constituted another in its place, not inferior in splendour, luxury, and sumptuosity, calling it that of the Diers Together. For all those that said they would die with Antony and Cleopatra gave in their names, for the present passing their time in all manner of pleasures and a regular succession of banquets. But Cleopatra was busied in making a collection of all varieties of poisonous drugs, and, in order to see which of them were the least painful in the operation, she had them tried upon prisoners condemned to die. But, finding that the quick poisons always worked with sharp pains, and that the less painful were slow, she next tried venomous animals, and watching with her own eyes whilst they were applied, one creature to the body of another. This was her daily practice, and she pretty well satisfied herself that nothing was comparable to the bite of the asp, which, without convulsion or groaning, brought on a heavy drowsiness and lethargy, with a gentle sweat on the face, the senses being stupefied by degrees; the patient, in appearance, being sensible of no pain, but rather troubled to be disturbed or awakened like those that are in a profound natural sleep. . . .

Caesar would not listen to any proposals for Antony, but he made answer to Cleopatra, that there was no reasonable favour which she might not expect, if she put Antony to death, or expelled him from Egypt. He sent back with the ambassadors his own freedman, Thyrsus, a man of understanding, and not at all ill-qualified for conveying the messages of a youthful general to a woman so proud of her charms and possessed with the opinion of the power of her beauty. But by the long audiences he received from her, and the special honours which she paid him, Antony's jealousy began to be awakened; he had him seized, whipped, and sent back; writing Caesar word that the man's busy, impertinent ways had provoked him; in his circumstances he could not be expected to be very patient: "But if it offend you," he added, "you have got my freedman, Hipparchus, with you; hang him up and scourge him to make us even." But Cleopatra, after this, to clear herself, and to allay his jealousies, paid him all the attentions imaginable. When her own birthday came, she kept it as was suitable to their fallen fortunes; but his was observed with the utmost prodigality of splendour and magnificence, so that many of the guests sat down in want, and went home wealthy men. Meantime, continual letters came to Caesar from Agrippa, telling him his presence was extremely required at Rome. . . .

After this, Antony sent a new challenge to Caesar to fight him hand-to-hand; who made him answer that he might find several other ways to end his life; and he, considering with himself that he could not die more honourably than in battle, resolved to make an effort both by land and sea. At supper, it is said, he bade his servants help him freely, and pour him out wine plentifully, since to-morrow, perhaps, they should not do the same, but be servants to a new master, whilst he should lie on the ground, a dead corpse, and nothing. His friends that were about him wept to hear him talk so; which he perceiving, told them he would not lead them to a battle in which he expected rather an honourable death than either safety or victory. That night, it is related, about the middle of it, when the whole city was in a deep silence and general sadness, expecting the event of the next day, on a sudden was heard the sound of all sorts of instruments, and voices singing in tune, and the cry of a crowd of people shouting and dancing, like a troop of bacchanals on its way. This tumultuous procession seemed to take its course right through the middle of the city to the gate nearest the enemy; here it became the loudest, and suddenly passed out. People who reflected considered this to signify that Bacchus, the god whom Antony had always made it his study to copy and imitate, had now forsaken him.

As soon as it was light, he marched his infantry out of the city, and posted them upon a rising ground, from whence he saw his fleet make up to the enemy. There he stood in expectation of the event; but as soon as the fleets came near to one another, his men saluted Caesar's with their oars; and on their responding, the whole body of the ships, forming into a single fleet, rowed up direct to the city. Antony had no sooner seen this, but the horse deserted him, and went over to Caesar; and his foot being defeated, he retired into the city, crying out that Cleopatra had betrayed him to the enemies he had made for her sake. She, being afraid lest in his fury and despair he might do her a mischief, fled to her monument, and letting down the falling doors, which were strong with bars and bolts, she sent messengers who should tell Antony she was dead. He, believing it, cried out, "Now, Antony, why delay longer? Fate has snatched away the only pretext for which you could say you desired yet to live." Going into his chamber, and there loosening and opening his coat of armour, "I am not," said he, "troubled, Cleopatra, to be at present bereaved of you, for I shall soon be with you; but it distresses me that so great a general should be found of a tardier courage than a woman." He had a faithful servant, whose name was Eros; he had engaged him formerly to kill him when he should think it necessary, and now he put him to his promise. Eros drew his sword, as designing to kill him, but, suddenly turning round, he slew himself. And as he fell dead at his feet, "It is well done, Eros," said Antony; "you show your master how to do what you had not the heart to do yourself; and so he ran himself into the belly, and laid himself upon the couch. The wound, however, was not immediately mortal; and the flow of blood ceasing when he lay down, presently he came to himself, and entreated those that were about him to put him out of his pain; but they all fled out of the chamber, and left him crying out and struggling, until Diomede, Cleopatra's secretary, came to him, having orders from her to bring him into the monument.

When he understood she was alive, he eagerly gave order to the servants to take him up, and in their arms was carried to the door of the building. Cleopatra would not open the door, but, looking from a sort of window, she let down ropes and cords, to which Antony was fastened; and she and her two women, the only persons she had allowed to enter the monument, drew him up. Those that were present say that nothing was ever more sad than this spectacle, to see Antony, covered all over with blood and just expiring, thus drawn up, still holding up his hands to her, and lifting up his body with the little force he had left. As, indeed, it was no easy task for the women; and Cleopatra, with all her force, clinging to the rope, and straining with her head to the ground, with difficulty pulled him up, while those below encouraged her with their cries, and joined in all her efforts and anxiety. When she had got him up, she laid him on the bed, tearing all her clothes, which she spread upon him; and, beating her breast with her hands, lacerating herself, and disfiguring her own face with the blood from his wounds, she called him her lord, her husband, her emperor, and seemed to have pretty nearly forgotten all her own evils, she was so intent upon his misfortunes. Antony, stopping her lamentations as well as he could, called for wine to drink, either that he was thirsty, or that he imagined that it might put him the sooner out of pain. When he had drunk, he advised her to bring her own affairs, so far as might be honourably done, to a safe conclusion, and that, among all the friends of Caesar, she should rely on Proculeius; that she should not pity him in this last turn of fate, but rather rejoice for him in remembrance of his past happiness, who had been of all men the most illustrious and powerful, and in the end had fallen not ignobly, a Roman by a Roman overcome.

Just as he breathed his last, Proculeius arrived from Caesar; for when Antony gave himself his wound, and was carried into Cleopatra, one of his guards, Dercetaeus, took up Antony's sword and hid it; and, when he saw his opportunity, stole away to Caesar, and brought him the first news of Antony's death, and withal showed him the bloody sword. Caesar, upon this, retired into the inner part of his tent, and giving some tears to the death of one that had been nearly allied to him in marriage, his colleague in empire, and companion in so many wars and dangers, he came out to his friends, and, bringing with him many letters, he read to them with how much reason and moderation he had always addressed himself to Antony, and in return what overbearing and arrogant answers he received. Then he sent Proculeius to use his utmost endeavours to get Cleopatra alive into his power; for he was afraid of losing a great treasure, and, besides, she would be no small addition to the glory of his triumph. She, however, was careful not to put herself in Proculeius's power; but from within her monument, he standing on the outside of a door, on the level of the ground, which was strongly barred, but so that they might well enough hear one another's voice, she held a conference with him; she demanding that her kingdom might be given to her children, and he binding her to be of good courage, and trust Caesar in everything. . . .

In the meanwhile, Caesar made his entry into Alexandria, with Areius the philosopher at his side, holding him by the hand and talking with him; desiring that all his fellow-citizens should see what honour was paid to him, and should look up to him accordingly from the very first moment. Then, entering the exercise ground, he mounted a platform erected for the purpose, and from thence commanded the citizens (who, in great fear and consternation, fell prostrate at his feet) to stand up, and told them that he freely acquitted the people of all blame, first, for the sake of Alexander, who built their city, then for the city's sake itself, which was so large and beautiful; and, thirdly, to gratify his friend Areius. . . .

Of Antony's children, Antyllus, his son by Fulvia, being betrayed by his tutor, Theodorus, was put to death; and while the soldiers were cutting off his head, his tutor contrived to steal a precious jewel which he wore about his neck, and put it in his pocket, and afterwards denied the fact, but was convicted and crucified. Cleopatra's children, with their attendants, had a guard set on them, and were treated very honourably. Caesarion, who was reputed to be the son of Caesar the Dictator, was sent by his mother, with a great sum of money, through Ethiopia, to pass into India; but his tutor, a man named Rhodon, about as honest as Theodorus, persuaded him to turn back, for that Caesar designed to make him king. Caesar consulting what was best to be done with him, Areius we are told, said,

"Too many *Caesars* are not well."

So, afterwards, when Cleopatra was dead he was killed.

Many kings and great commanders made petition to Caesar for the body of Antony, to give him his funeral rites; but he would not take away his corpse from Cleopatra by whose hands he was buried with royal splendour and magnificence, it being granted to her to employ what she pleased on his funeral. In this extremity of grief and sorrow, and having inflamed and ulcerated her breasts with beating them, she fell into a high fever, and was very glad of the occasion, hoping, under this pretext, to abstain from food, and so to die in quiet without interference. She had her own physician, Olympus, to whom she told the truth, and asked his advice and help to put an end to herself, as Olympus himself has told us, in a narrative which he wrote of these events. But Caesar, suspecting her purpose, took to menacing language about her children, and excited her fears for them, before which engines her purpose shook and gave way, so that she suffered those about her to give her what meat or medicine they pleased.

Some few days after, Caesar himself came to make her a visit and comfort her. She lay then upon her pallet-bed in undress, and, on his entering, sprang up from off her bed, having nothing on but the one garment next her body, and flung herself at his feet, her hair and face looking wild and disfigured, her voice quivering, and her eyes sunk in her head. The marks of the blows she had given herself were visible about her bosom, and altogether her whole person seemed no less afflicted than her soul. But, for all this, her old charm, and the boldness of her youthful beauty, had not wholly left her, and, in spite of her present condition, still sparkled from within, and let itself appear in all the movements of her countenance. Caesar, desiring her to repose herself, sat down by her; and, on this opportunity, she said something to justify her actions, attributing what she had done to the necessity she was under, and to her fear of Antony; and when Caesar, on each point, made his objections, and she found herself confuted, she broke off at once into language of entreaty and deprecation, as if she desired nothing more than to prolong her life. And at last, having by her a list of her treasure, she gave it into his hands; and when Seleucus, one of her stewards, who was by, pointed out that various articles were omitted, and charged her with secreting them, she flew up and caught him by the hair, and struck him several blows on the face. Caesar smiling and withholding her, "Is it not very hard, Caesar," said she, "when you do me the honour to visit me in this condition I am in, that I should be accused by one of my own servants of laying by some women's toys, not meant to adorn, be sure, my unhappy self, but that I might have some little present by me to make your Octavia and your Livia, that by their intercession I might hope to find you in some measure disposed to mercy?" Caesar was pleased to hear her talk thus, being now assured that she was desirous to live. And, therefore, letting her know that the things she had laid by she might dispose of as she pleased, and his usage of her should be honourable above her expectation, he went away, well satisfied that he had overreached her, but, in fact, was himself deceived. . . .

Having made these lamentations, crowning the tomb with garlands and kissing it, she gave orders to prepare her a bath, and, coming out of the bath, she lay down and made a sumptuous meal. And a country fellow brought her a little basket, which the guards intercepting and asking what it was, the fellow put the leaves which lay uppermost aside, and showed them it was full of figs; and on their admiring the largeness and beauty of the figs, he laughed, and invited them to take some, which they refused, and, suspecting nothing, bade him carry them in. After her repast, Cleopatra sent to Caesar a letter which she had written and sealed; and, putting everybody out of the monument but her two women, she shut the doors. Caesar, opening her letter, and finding pathetic prayers and entreaties that she might be buried in the same tomb with Antony, soon guessed what was doing. At first he was going himself in all haste, but, changing his mind, he sent others to see. The thing had been quickly done. The messengers came at full speed, and found the guards apprehensive of nothing; but on opening the doors they saw her stone-dead, lying upon a bed of gold, set out in all her royal ornaments. Iras, one of her women, lay dying at her feet, and Charmion, just ready to fall, scarce able to hold up her head, was adjusting her mistress's diadem. And when one that came in said angrily, "Was this well done of your lady, Charmion?" "Extremely well," she answered, "and as became the descendant of so many kings;" and as she said this, she fell down dead by the bedside.

Some relate that an asp was brought in amongst those figs and covered with the leaves, and that Cleopatra had arranged that it might settle on her before she knew, but, when she took away some of the figs and saw it, she said, "So here it is," and held out her bare arm to be bitten. Others say that it was kept in a vase, and that she vexed and pricked it with a golden spindle till it seized her arm. But what really took place is known to no one, since it was also said that she carried poison in a hollow bodkin, about which she wound her hair; yet there was not so much as a spot found, or any symptom of poison upon her body, nor was the asp seen within the monument; only something like the trail of it was said to have been noticed on the sand by the sea, on the part towards which the building faced and where the windows were. Some relate that two faint puncture-marks were found on Cleopatra's arm, and to this account Caesar seems to have given credit; for in his triumph there was carried a figure of Cleopatra, with an asp clinging to her. Such are the various accounts. But Caesar, though much disappointed by her death, yet could not but admire the greatness of her spirit, and gave order that her body should be buried by Antony with royal splendour and magnificence. Her women, also, received honourable burial by his directions. Cleopatra had lived nine-and-thirty years, during twenty-two of which she had reigned as queen, and for fourteen had been Antony's partner in his empire. Antony, according to some authorities, was fifty-three, according to others, fifty-six years old. His statues were all thrown down, but those of Cleopatra were left untouched; for Archibius, one of her friends, gave Caesar two thousand talents to save them from the fate of Antony's.

The Roman Reaction

HANS VOLKMANN

Two different modern assessments of the position of Cleopatra in world history are now examined. The first is taken from her most definitive modern biography, *Cleopatra, A Study in Politics and Propaganda*, by Hans Volkmann. Volkmann views the conflict between Octavian on the one side and Antony and Cleopatra on the other in the context of Roman history, where he sees this conflict as pivotal. He stresses the reaction of the great contemporary Roman literary figures, the masters of Augustan propaganda.

A resolution of the Senate declared the day on which Octavian had captured Alexandria a public holiday, 'as on this day the Imperator Caesar Augustus freed the State from the direst peril'. The month, on the first day of which Octavian had thus set the seal on his victory, had till now been known as Sextilis: from the beginning of the Principate it bore the new name of Augustus. When it had once been desired to honour Caesar in this way, it was to the month of his birth (till then Quinctilis) that the name Julius was given. In the case of the distinction conferred on Augustus, the choice did not fall on the month of his birth (September) but on the month of his greatest success. And so even now the month of August serves to remind us not only of the Emperor himself but also of his victory over Cleopatra.

Horace, too, who on the evening after the Battle of Actium had still been alarmed about the eventual outcome, found his apprehensions resolved by the events of August 30. The jubilant song of triumph which the news of victory drew from him turns about the one great theme of Cleopatra. This poem, which redounds no less to the poet's honour than to that of the defeated queen, presents us with two striking pictures. Cleopatra is in the first instance the 'fatale monstrum,' the demon of mischief. She is the queen who wanted to lay the Capitol in ruins and to destroy the Roman Empire. She is represented as maniacal and distracted, measureless in her ambitions, intoxicated with good fortune, like a drunken maenad, out of her senses. Her company are a sickly crew of men shamefully unmanned. This sketch, in which Horace devotes not one syllable to Antony, or to the participation of Romans on Cleopatra's side, takes over the leading motifs with which Octavian's propaganda prepared for the conflict. It is all the more astounding that Horace describes the fall of Rome's grim enemy with manifest respect. Heavy blows delivered by Octavian put a sudden end to her ecstasy and throw her into an agony of fear: she flees, but in her ruin she rises to true greatness. She disdains to sail away with her fleet and abandon her homeland. She sees her royal palace levelled with the ground; she refuses to suffer the dishonour of the triumph, and chooses for herself the exceptionally horrible end of death by snake-bite. Horace has no word to say about the hostile rumours of her treachery, her secret negotiations, or of the seductive arts with which it was supposed she tried to win over Octavian at the eleventh hour. For Horace she is the woman of mighty spirit ('non humilis mulier') to whom he cannot refuse his respect.

How unique was this noble attitude of Horace we can infer from Propertius' libellous effusion, an elegy written eight years later. In this he flatly insults Cleopatra as 'incesti meretrix regina Canopi', the royal whore, not of Egypt, but of Canopus, a suburb of Alexandria notorious for its immorality. The reproach of licentiousness conveyed by these words is not merely lacking in taste, it offends truth. No historian of antiquity brings definite charges of sexual excesses against Cleopatra, such as history reports of many other royal women. She gave herself to Caesar and Antony to gain political ends. Propertius himself brands her alliance with Antony with the words: 'Did she not, as the price of her shameful marriage, demand that the walls of Rome should be hers, and the Fathers made bondsmen of her kingdom?' In impressive pictures he demonstrates the significance of her defeat. Cleopatra would have made the river-god Tiber a slave to the Nile, would have replaced the Roman Jupiter with the yelping dog-headed Anubis; she, a woman, wanted to issue laws to the Romans, who had once smashed the axes of their own kings! The collapse of morality, the overthrow of the country's gods, shameful serfdom, in short a national and religious calamity—that was what Cleopatra had stood for. The battle-cry devised by Octavian's propaganda for the war echoes once again after the victory in the mouth of the poet, whom it enables to reveal the full measure of Augustus' achievements and to extol them appropriately.

'With so mighty a citizen to protect you, Rome, you had no need to fear me and my tongue drowned in perpetual wine', Cleopatra is forced to admit by Propertius. His flattery of the victory goes still further. 'These walls the gods built, these they also preserve. If Caesar is safe, Rome need hardly fear even Jupiter.' Apollo, beneath whose gaze the Battle of Actium was fought, will himself celebrate in epic song this victory surpassing all the previous achievements of Roman generals.

This poem of Propertius', which carries the attack on Cleopatra to absurd lengths, illustrates the increasing importance of the place won by her in Augustan poetry. It exalts the figure of Octavian, justifies his deeds and is closely linked to the foundation of the Principate. As time passed, Roman apprehension of the great event deepened, until it was finally lifted to the mythological plane. The central point of the legend is occupied by the Battle of Actium. The national gods of Rome themselves seize weapons. Apollo, Octavian's patron deity, aids him to achieve the victory; his presence and help transform Octavian into the agent of the divine will, the struggle with Cleopatra into a holy war.

An example of this attitude is furnished by Vergil. In the eighth book of his national Roman epic, the *Aeneid,* composed in the same period as Propertius' poem, he draws a striking contrast between West and East. At the head of the Italians stands Augustus, by his side the Senate, the people and the gods of his country. He is transfigured by supernatural phenomena. Flames stream from his temples, the star of his deified father Caesar blazes in the heaven behind his head and promises its aid. Near him marches Agrippa, adorned with the gleaming crown presented to him after his naval victory over Pompeius. From these two loyal Romans Vergil's gaze turns to Antony and his Egyptian wife who follows him. The single word 'nefas' ('O abomination!'), echoes Vergil's horror at the dishonouring alliance. Antony is no longer a Roman: he commands only the barbaric hordes of the East in all their pomp and variety. In the battle Vergil assigns him no part; in contradiction to the accounts of the historians, he places Cleopatra, the real enemy, in the midst of the mêlée: with the sistrum, the rattle of Isis, she issues orders to her multitudes. All kinds of monstrous Egyptian gods, such as the dog-headed Anubis, wrestle with the Roman deities Neptune, Venus and Minerva. Mars and his sister Bellona, the deities of war, and Discordia, the goddess of dissension, exult in the fury of the strife. Then Apollo of Actium intervenes with his bow drawn. The apparition is at an end: all the foreign peoples, Egyptians, Indians, Arabs and Sabaians flee in wild panic. Cleopatra herself pales with the presentiment of death and sets her sails for flight.

Vergil's picture of the Battle of Actium stamped itself deeply into the consciousness of his contemporaries. After him poets make repeated mention, whether briefly or fully, of the myth of Apollo's help. Propertius himself in a later poem once again practised his poetical

art on the exalted theme; but to our taste his treatment of it is artisti-
cally no better than before. Instead of painting a splendid picture, full
of movement, of the battle and the god's intervention, as Vergil did,
he makes Apollo appear to Octavian, 'the saviour of the world', before the battle, and reassure him in a long speech. 'It is the cause for
which he fights that increases or breaks down the soldier's strength: if
that is not just, shame strikes the weapon from his hand.' Consciousness of the justice of his cause was precisely what Octavian had emphasized in his declaration of war; and in the poet's song Apollo himself
asserts it. As for the fight, it is self-evident that its outcome is decided
as soon as the god discharges his arrows. The poet only needs to state
the result in the brief epigrammatic words:

'Phoebus keeps faith: Rome wins, the woman pays the price!'

Cleopatra flees to the Nile. In one thing only does she succeed: she
may choose the day on which she is to die. The gods thought it
unbefitting the dignity of the triumph that a single woman should
tread in the footsteps of the great Jugurtha. This outcome, then,
though it cheated Octavian's hopes, derived from a well-weighted
decision of the gods, and was therefore easier for the victor to bear.

Vergil and Propertius, with their legend of Actium, have glorified
the battle as the great turning-point of the fortunes of Rome. The
conviction that this is so prevails throughout the Principate. Lucan, a
contemporary of Nero, utters the cry of surprise:

'And in Leucadian waters, the issue doubtful stood
Whether the world should be ruled by a woman of alien blood!'

As an epigram preserved on a papyrus foretells, the Battle of
Actium will never cease to be talked about. As late as the beginning of
the fifth century A.D. Nonnus of Panopolis in Egypt celebrates the
victory at Actium over Cleopatra, a foe 'practised in sea-fights',
through which the Roman Empire consummated its great history and
united the world under its rule of peace. This is beyond doubt a
sound judgement. Even Oswald Spengler—who in his *Decline of the
West* obstinately refuses to accept the verdict of history and maintains
that 'Antony should have won at Actium'—concedes, despite his protest, the significance of the result. And E. Stauffer includes 31 B.C. in
his six 'great dates of ancient history', as the year in which Rome won
a total victory over the Egyptian world-monarchy and free Europe
assumed the leading place in imperial history and world-politics.

The memory of this great event, which has moulded the course of
European history, is for ever linked with Cleopatra's name. She not

only took part in what happened, but significantly influenced it. We, who look back along the lines of history and survey its entire course, can see how the age summoned Cleopatra to its service. In her the tendencies of a dying epoch could be discerned so clearly and intelligibly that they evoked and even aided the contrary forces under Octavian, and brought a new epoch into being. Cleopatra was an instrument used and then broken by the sovereign will of history. She failed tragically, and has long had to accept a picture of herself misdrawn by the propaganda of her adversary and displayed in a false light. Dante meets her in the second circle of Hell among the carnal sinners and mentions her, 'the licentious Cleopatra', along with Semiramis, Dido and Helen. Her sensuality has been heavily stressed in countless stage-pieces—plays, operas and ballets.

In fact she never sought sexual pleasure for its own sake. She was a royal woman, the last scion of a princely house, in whose exacting traditions she had consciously lived from youth up. Fate had given into her hands the vast forces that resided in the unique character of the land she ruled, in its wealth and its type of administration. It had also favoured her with the moment of opportunity—with the *kairos*, as the Greeks called the fertile hour that waits upon the great man who knows how to use it. Cleopatra perceived her opportunity with rare vigilance and readiness. Possessed by the will to power, she brought into play, among other weapons, those that are given to women alone. One thing only she was not aware of—the law that sets bounds to the actions of men, even of great men. The ancient Greek virtues of *sophrosynē* (wise prudence) and *mesotēs* (moderation)—not often to be found in politics—were alien to the Hellenistic princess who felt herself to be an Egyptian deity. She thought that if she were to prove a worthy heir to the mighty past, she must be able to shape history; and she resolutely took her place beside men of world-history, Caesar and Antony, and imparted to them impulses, whose demonic force we can in the last resort only guess at.

But the age required more of her than this. It was her fate that in Octavian she opposed a man who was not merely an heir and a successor, but also the creator of a new epoch. In history it does not matter, in the last analysis, whether an Empire is founded but how it is founded. Octavian, not Cleopatra, fulfilled the requirements of history in this respect. Knowing how to keep within the limits appointed for him, he appealed to the national consciousness of Rome and secured the general approval ('consensus universorum') for his political work. Thus he was enabled to throw the physical and moral resources of the West against the East's display of might, and to devise the individual form of constitution by which the eastern type of empire was for centuries superseded.

The contributions of human beings to history, and our final verdict on them, are certainly not dependent on the success of their efforts. Rather, their value is determined by the way in which they grasp and endure their fortune. Cleopatra's opponents were already passing judgment on her according to this standard. After her death Octavian himself acknowledged her noble bearing with admiration; and the poet Horace found the appropriate words for her greatness: 'non humilis mulier', 'a woman of mighty spirit'. As such, among the women who intervene in the masculine strife for political power, she will always occupy a special position, and ever and anon excite the imagination of mankind.

Antony and Cleopatra in World History

MICHAEL GRANT

In his biography of Cleopatra, the wide-ranging modern classical historian Michael Grant sees the positions respectively of Antony and Cleopatra on the one side and Octavian on the other in the context not only of Roman but of world history, with Octavian's victory producing the possibility of the Roman Empire that was to endure as a political entity for three more centuries and as an imperial ideal for a thousand years more.

Although Cleopatra, not Antony, had been Octavian's declared foe, all his statues at Alexandria were torn down, but hers were allowed to stand, because one of her friends, Archibius, gave the victor two thousand talents to save them from destruction. For a generation to come she was still spoken of as *the* queen, like Arsinoe II before her, and a 'Cleopatreion' mentioned in AD 4–5 at Rosetta (Rashid), like other similar buildings in different parts of the country, appears to have been a shrine erected in her honour. Sixty years after her death an Alexandrian grammarian named Apion, hated by Josephus, championed her memory. Her statue in the Temple of Venus Genetrix at Rome, set up by Julius Caesar, was still standing there in the third century AD, and the cult of Cleopatra Aphrodite remained alive more than one hundred years later still. It was said that another powerful empress Zenobia (Bat Zabbi), ruling in the Syrian desert city of Palmyra (AD 269–73), claimed descent from Cleopatra and made a collection of her drinking cups, and although the story may be fictitious it illustrates the continuing power of the Egyptian queen's name. The historian Ammianus Marcellinus (*c.* AD 330–95) suggests that the Egyptians were still flattering her memory to a scandalous extent, and a Coptic bishop of the seventh century AD, John of Nikiu, declared that it was impossible to think of any monarch or woman who had ever surpassed her. Many of Alexandria's greatest monuments and architectural masterpieces, including the palace and Pharos lighthouse, were believed to have been her work. Alone of Alexander the Great's successors she became a legend, like Alexander himself.

*

Most historians, ancient and modern alike, see a total inevitability in the defeat of Antony and Cleopatra at Octavian's hands. But their defeat was only inevitable because Agrippa was a better admiral than Antony or any of his lieutenants. To contrast the faults of their régime with the merits of that of Octavian, the later Augustus, and to conclude that the Augustan system was bound to win is an unjustifiable procedure. There were many faults and merits on both sides, and if Antony and Cleopatra had been victorious in the Actium campaigns, it would not have been their failings but Octavian's which posterity would have emphasized. The particular brand of Roman empire that he established turned out, in its own way, to be one of the great, durable success stories of history. But it has meant that all appreciation—apart from the sympathies attaching to personal melodrama—has been withheld from the losers, and that their aspirations have been lost sight of.

During the last hundred years and more there has been lively discussion about the qualities, first of the successful Julius Caesar, and then of the successful Augustus, and both their personalities have come under a sharper and colder process of inspection than before. But the cases of Caesar and Augustus are different. The trouble about withholding all sympathy from Caesar is that his 'Republican' opponents were for the most part so very unpleasant. There is a movement today, from praiseworthy motives, to get away from the cult of success, and this has even led to a certain veneration for failure, as exhibited, for example, in the downfall and death of Che Guevara. But to make similar anti-heroes out of Julius Caesar's adversaries is absurd. Caesar possessed extremely distasteful qualities, but to be ruled by him might well have appeared the lesser evil.

A comparison between Augustus and *his* opponents, Antony and Cleopatra, ought to yield a different result. As the historian Tacitus explains in his sour preface to the *Annals,* Augustus was a cold-blooded and ruthless man. Without that ruthlessness he could never have carried through the unparalleled achievements and reorganizations of his forty-five-year reign that followed Actium. But his enemies were very different from the enemies of Julius Caesar. Between the nobility who hated Caesar, and Antony and Cleopatra who fought against his heir, there is little in common. The record of the anti-Caesarian nobility is negative and brutal, especially in their later years. But Antony and Cleopatra had plans to provide a much more positive and constructive policy. Its existence has not, in general, been admitted, though W. W. Tarn in *The Cambridge Ancient History* (1934) was not unsympathetic, while Ronald Syme, in his *Roman Revolution* (1939) pointed to the wisdom of many of Antony's administrative arrangements.

But why is it that so few other historians have appreciated that Antony and Cleopatra had a serious, valid point of view? If devotees of the cult of failure can even muster sympathy for Caesar's opponents, one might have expected them to find more promising scope here. There are two main reasons why this has not been so. In the first place, the story of the lovers offers such unexampled opportunities for romantic sentiment that attention has constantly been distracted from matters of policy. Secondly, their conflict with Octavian is seen as part of the historic feud between east and west—and we are westerners. The countries of western Europe, and the United States of America, are the direct heirs of the occidental victor of Actium, and of the tradition which he deliberately implanted. Indeed, this very assertion, that Actium was part of the clash between east and west, is itself a direct echo of his propaganda—propaganda which, because of Octavian's naval victory, prevailed.

However, like so much of the best propaganda, it contains an element of truth. Many lies were told on both sides, but Actium *was* a clash between eastern and western ideologies. There is less truth, on the other hand, in the further statement, endlessly repeated, that Antony and Cleopatra stood for the queer, outlandish tribes and fetishes of the remote orient. What they really stood for was Hellenism—or rather, a partnership between Hellenism and *Romanità*. How they envisaged the shape of this partnership was suggested, in broad outline, by the territorial gifts of 37 BC, and the Donations of Alexandria in 34. Although a Roman was to remain in supreme charge, Antony and Cleopatra saw the Romans who occupied the western part of the empire, and the Greeks and Hellenized orientals who lived in the eastern provinces and client kingdoms, as more or less equal partners. This was how they interpreted the Concord between Peoples (Homonoia) which was one of the most vigorous ideals of the age, and the Sibylline Oracles and other anonymous contemporary writings showed the enthusiasm evoked by such concepts among eastern peoples.

Augustus felt otherwise. It is true that the elaborate, rather superficial apparatus of phil-Hellenism which accompanied his religious and cultural policy provided a certain mild corrective to the anti-Hellenic sentiments of his compatriots. Nevertheless, he was ultimately the heir of Roman imperialism: the Italians were unmistakably intended to be top dogs. Certainly, there was to be a great reconciliation between east and west, and it is expressed with extraordinary brilliance and subtlety by Virgil. But the prophetic words the poet ascribes to Aeneas' father Anchises reflect Augustus' belief that it might be a reconciliation presided over by Rome, which would still reign supreme over the Greeks:

> There are others, assuredly I believe,
> Shall work in bronze more sensitively, moulding
> Breathing images, or carving from the marble
> More lifelike features: some shall plead more eloquently,
> Or gauging with instruments the sky's motion
> Forecast the rising of the constellations:
> But yours, my Roman, is the gift of government,
> That is your bent—to impose upon the nations
> The code of peace; to be clement to the conquered,
> But utterly to crush the intransigent.

That is unforgettably said, but in terms of politics it is very one-sided. The Greeks and Hellenized easterners, according to Virgil, were to be excluded from the heights of government—which is precisely what continued to happen. But it was the antithesis of the intentions of Antony and Cleopatra. Under their guidance, great areas of the east were to be under the administration and overlordship of Greek monarchies, led by a nexus of Ptolemaic kingdoms. The official coinages link Antony and Cleopatra together, not only as gods united in a divine union, but as human leaders of this partnership between Romans and Greeks.

The partnership never materialized, because Agrippa proved too good an admiral. But that does not mean it was impossible. W. W. Tarn's somewhat reluctant conclusion that the Hellenistic world had already fallen victim to itself before it fell victim to Rome is the product of hindsight. It is true that the age of wholly independent Hellenistic monarchies was at an end, because their continued existence was incompatible with Rome. But the idea of great Hellenistic kingdoms in intimate and honourable association with the Romans was a novel one and the relatively high status it conceded the Greeks was by no means an unrealistic dream. That is conclusively proved by the condition of the Roman world three or four centuries later, in which the Greeks had risen to the political surface once again—with the result that the subsequent Byzantine empire was not Roman but Greek. If the events of 31 BC had gone the other way it is difficult to believe that this same sort of development would not have occurred, or at least begun to occur, three hundred years sooner.

In the foregoing discussion Antony and Cleopatra have been bracketed together, as a single political entity. This identification of their attitudes must not be carried too far, since there were certain political differences between them—for example, their disagreement about King Herod of Judaea. But the grand design belonged to them both, and both of them believed in it. Antony's methods of government, both inside and outside the Ptolemaic sphere, show a wide phil-hellenic sympathy for the concept of Greek ruling Greek. Nevertheless, it is only right to ascribe the main initiative to Cleopatra. For one thing she was Greek herself. And secondly, Antony, for all his very considerable gifts, was her inferior in drive, energy and ambition. Josephus sums up her character in a statement which seems to mean: 'if she lacked one single thing that she desired, she imagined that she lacked everything'. She was a woman of single-minded determination. Moreover, as Canidius and Crassus pointed out to Antony before Actium, she was a ruler of outstanding ability and experience.

The question of what might have happened if Actium had gone the other way raises one special, inflammable problem, which must have been constantly in Cleopatra's mind, even if Antony tried not to think of it too often. The problem is this. Once the campaign was won, what would have been her political position in the new order?

During the immediately preceding years, Antony's official Latin coinage, with unprecedented explicitness and emphasis, had declared her to be his honoured partner. If they had been victorious in 31 BC, she would have been his partner in the rulership of the entire Roman empire. The propaganda of the other side, which declared that she intended to dispense justice from the sacred Capitol itself, was surely right in supposing that she would have gone to Rome. For that is where Antony would have gone, and she would never have stayed behind permanently in Alexandria. Modern historians usually dismiss the idea of her going to Rome as an utter impossibility on the grounds that the Roman ruling class would never have tolerated such a thing. Yet her Roman supporters, though they had decreased in number, still remained fairly numerous—a fact of which little was heard, naturally enough, once she had been defeated and was dead. Moreover, after Antony had victoriously entered Rome, the opposition would have been cowed, just as the surviving Antonians were cowed after the issue went the other way. To discuss how long she might have lasted at Rome would be taking historical might-have-beens too far.

Another obscure but all-important question is the nature of the constitutional relationship which would then, following the victory, have existed between Cleopatra and Antony. Probably they would then, at last, have married, no longer merely in the theological sense of a union between gods, but as man and wife. Once Antony had become autocrat over the whole Roman world, he could have twisted Roman law to his needs—as the victorious Octavian, too, in his own way, was ready enough to give it a twist or two. In Italy, the Antonian régime would have encountered greater difficulties than the Augustan régime ever did. But Antony, on the other hand, would have received far greater and keener support from the rich and numerous populations of the east—which would thus have become a more potent political force than his opponent ever allowed them to be.

Actium set the scene for three centuries of western supremacy. If the losers had won, there would instead have been some sort of partnership between the two great populations of the empire, the Romans represented by Antony (who would have remained the supreme overlord), and the Greeks led by Cleopatra. She would never have tried to rule without Roman support, for she was faithful to her father's realistic recognition that Egypt could do no such thing. She preferred a theme of partnership. If we can forget the sentiments of occidentalism, whether conscious or unconscious, that her enemy Octavian has implanted in our hearts, Cleopatra's plan was not necessarily a less noble or even a less practicable plan than his. But she was born before her time, and her plan had to wait, as it turned out, for three hundred years.

Review and Study Questions

1. Why did Caesar and Antony go to Egypt in the first place?
2. Who played the dominant role in the alliance of Caesar and Cleopatra?
3. Who played the dominant role in the alliance of Antony and Cleopatra?
4. How would you assess the victory of Octavian at Actium in the context of the history of Rome?

Suggestions for Further Reading

There are many modern editions of Plutarch's *Lives of Noble Greeks and Romans*. The one excerpted in this chapter is the Everyman's Library edition, 3 vols., ed. Arthur Hugh Clough (London and New York: Dent and Dutton, 1910 [1962]). The other major narrative source for Cleopatra is the Greek historian Dio Cassius, Dio's *Roman History*, tr. Earnest Cary, 5 vols. (Cambridge and London: Harvard University Press and William Heinemann, Ltd., 1917 [1967]).

Among the several biographies of Cleopatra the most definitive are Hans Volkmann, *Cleopatra, A Study in Politics and Propaganda*, tr. T. J. Cadoux (New York: Sagamore Press, Inc., 1958) and Arthur Weigall, *The Life and Times of Cleopatra Queen of Egypt, A Study in the Origins of the Roman Empire*, new rev. ed. (New York: Greenwood Press, 1968). Two additional excellent modern biographies are Jack Lindsay, *Cleopatra* (New York: Coward McCann and Geoghegan, Inc., 1978) and Edwyn Bevan, *The House of Ptolemy, A History of Egypt under the Ptolemaic Dynasty* (Chicago: Argonaut Publishers, Inc., 1968).

The story of Cleopatra is part of the story of Hellenistic Greece. This story is set forth in Michael Grant, *From Alexander to Cleopatra, The Hellenistic World* (New York: Scribner's, 1982) and Peter Green, *Alexander to Actium, the Historic Evolution of the Hellenistic Age* (Berkeley and Los Angeles: The University of California Press, 1990).

It is also part of the story of the rise of the Roman Empire. Among the larger and more comprehensive Roman histories are Edward T. Salmon, *A History of the Roman World from 30 B.C. to A.D. 138*, 3 vols. (London and New York: Methuen and Barnes and Noble, 1944), T. Rice Holmes, *The Roman Republic and the Founder of the Empire*, 3 vols. (New York: Russell and Russell, 1923), and Guglielmo Ferrero, *The Greatness and Decline of Rome*, 5 vols., tr. H. J. Chaytor (New York: Putnam, n.d.).

Under special topics in Roman history can be recommended H. H. Scullard, *From the Gracchi to Nero, A History of Rome from 133 B.C. to A.D. 68* (New York: Praeger, 1959), Frank Burr Marsh, *A History of the Roman World from 146 B.C. to 30 B.C.* (London: Methuen, 1967 [1935]), and Stewart Perowne, *Death of the Roman Republic: From 146 B.C. to the Birth of the Roman Empire* (New York: Doubleday, 1968). See also Ronald Syme, *The Roman Revolution* (London: Oxford, 1960). Two excellent biographies can also be recommended, J. P. V. D. Balsdon, *Julius Caesar and Rome* (London: English Universities Press, 1967) and John Buchan, *Augustus* (Boston: Houghton Mifflin, 1937).

MUHAMMAD: THE MESSENGER OF GOD

c. 570   Born
c. 595   Married Khadijah
c. 610   Beginning of his revelations
   622   The "Hegira" flight to Medina
   624   Battle of Badr
   630   Conquest of Mecca
   632   Died

Muhammad, who was to found one of the world's most widespread religions, was born in the Arabian town of Mecca in about 570. Mecca was one of a number of merchant communities that had sprung up along the Arabian shore of the Red Sea, on the main caravan route leading from the Persian Gulf and Yemen to Syria and the Mediterranean. Muhammad was the son of a respectable Meccan family, which most likely engaged in commerce but was not of the "inner" merchant aristocracy dominating the town. Little is known of Muhammad's early life except that he was orphaned; he was probably raised first by his grandfather and then by an uncle. It is probable that Muhammad engaged in commerce.

As in the case of every great religious leader, the figure of Muhammad has been obscured by a mass of pious tradition. We know that he married a rich widow, Khadijah, who was some years older than himself. Says the Koran, "Did not He [God] find thee needy, and suffice thee?" (93:6–8). Having been thus "sufficed," Muhammad assumed the management of a considerable estate and probably lived much like any other Meccan merchant.

When he was about forty, Muhammad received the earliest of a series of divine revelations upon which he based his religious teachings. There is no record of whether this revelation came as a result of an arduous spiritual search or as an unbidden insight. At first Muhammad confined his teaching to his family; then he extended it to friends. Eventually he began to preach more widely and openly, seeking converts whom he called Muslims, "submissive to God." In contrast to the polytheism then prevalent in Arabia, Muhammad recognized only one God, Allah, and spoke of himself as God's messenger or prophet. And, like the ancient Hebrew prophets, he condemned polytheism and idolatry.

His success was modest, but it was sufficient to alarm the merchant artistocracy of Mecca. In a society in which religion and politics were inseparable, the revolutionary nature of Muhammad's religious teachings implied the possibility of political unrest. And political unrest is a threat to commerce. Moreover, Mecca was not only an economic but also a religious center for the various gods of the desert people who came to trade there. In a shrine called the Kaaba were housed the sacred stones representing the primitive gods of the Arabic tribes, and this along with other shrines attracted pilgrims, and hence, business to Mecca. It is not surprising then that public opinion mobilized against this dangerous radical who, by his attack on idolatry and other beliefs, threatened both the prosperity and the religious status of his city. He had also begun to criticize the merchant leaders for their rapacity and lack of charity.

By 621 Muhammad and his followers were in dire circumstances. They were being bitterly persecuted. The chief of the Hashimite clan, to which Muhammad himself belonged and who had protected him, died, as did Muhammad's devoted wife Khadijah. He had even sent some eighty of his disciples to Abyssinia for their own protection. Then, suddenly, a change occurred. Two of the tribes of Yathrib, a city some three hundred miles to the north of Mecca, sent for Muhammad. Some of their members had heard him speak, and they now sought him as a "wise man" and mediator to bring peace among their warring clans and factions. His followers preceded him in small groups. Then Muhammad himself fled to his new home city, which he named Medinat un Nabi, "the City of the Prophet," soon shortened to Medina. This was the "Hegira," the flight, of the year 622. It was later considered to mark the beginning of Islam—appropriately enough, for it was in Medina that Islam first became a state and a culture. Ultimately it was to become a world empire and a world religion.

The Founding of Islam

IBN ISHAQ'S *SIRAT RASUL ALLAH*

Muhammad wrote nothing himself, and none of his early disciples or immediate successors left any written record of the prophet. He declared his revelations to his followers, many of whom knew them by heart. Some of the revelations were dictated or written down later, but at his death there was no one complete and authoritative text. It was only in the following generation that Muhammad's successors commanded that the revelations be collected "from palm branches and tablets of stone and the hearts of men." This was done by the chief secretary of the prophet, and by the year 651 the collection was completed. This was the Koran, "The Reading," the one sacred book of Islam.

While devout Muslims believe that every word of the Koran is the word of God, Muhammad was the prophet through whom God's word was revealed, and there are occasional references to him in it. But such scattered references do not constitute even the outline of a biography. The enormous collections of traditions (Hadith), or stories about Muhammad that began to be assembled even before his death, are almost useless as a source of reliable biographical detail. It is only in the eighth and ninth centuries, when formal biographies begin to appear, that we have sources on which to base a true biographical account. There are several of these, but the most comprehensive and reliable is the *Sirat Rasul Allah* of Ibn Ishaq—*The Book of Campaigns and (the Prophet's) Biography.*

Ibn Ishaq was born in Medina about 707 and died in Baghdad in 773. His account of Muhammad is based on interviews with eyewitnesses and other near contemporaries, and on other largely oral records and traditions. He subjected his sources to considerable skeptical scrutiny, often saying that his informant "alleged" something to be true or that God only knows whether a particular statement is true or not. He was regarded by his Arabic contemporaries as the "best informed man" about his subject: "Knowledge will remain in Medina as long as Ibn Ishaq lives." The eminent modern western authority Alfred Guillaume agrees: "He has given us the only systematic straightforward account of the life of Muhammad which, apart from legends and stories of miracles, deserves to be accepted as history in the full sense of the word."[1] His book was edited and preserved by another scholar, Abdul-Malik ibn Hisham, about a century later.

We pick up his account with the events leading up to Muhammad's flight from Mecca to Medina.

When Quraysh[2] became insolent towards God and rejected His gracious purpose, accused His prophet of lying, and ill treated and exiled those who served Him and proclaimed His unity, believed in His prophet, and held fast to His religion, He gave permission to His apostle to fight and to protect himself against those who wronged them and treated them badly. . . .

When God had given permission to fight and this clan of the Anṣār[3] had pledged their support to him in Islam and to help him and his followers, and the Muslims who had taken refuge with them, the apostle commanded his companions, the emigrants of his people and those Muslims who were with him in Mecca, to emigrate to Medina and to link up with their brethren the Anṣār. 'God will make for you brethren and houses in which you may be safe.' So they went out in companies, and the apostle stayed in Mecca waiting for his Lord's permission to leave Mecca and migrate to Medina. . . . After his companions had left, the apostle stayed in Mecca waiting for permission to migrate. Except for Abū Bakr and 'Alī, none of his supporters were left but those under restraint and those who had been forced to apostatize. The former kept asking the apostle for permission to emigrate and he would answer, 'Don't be in a hurry; it may be that God will give you a companion.' Abū Bakr hoped that it would be Muhammad himself. . . .

Among the verses of the Quran which God sent down about that day . . . are: 'And when the unbelievers plot to shut thee up or to kill thee or to drive thee out they plot, but God plots also, and God is the best of plotters,' and 'Or they say he is a poet for whom we may expect the misfortune of fate. Say: Go on expecting for I am with you among the expectant.'

It was then that God gave permission to his prophet to migrate. Now Abū Bakr was a man of means, and at the time that he asked the apostle's permission to migrate and he replied 'Do not hurry; perhaps

---

[1] A. Guillaume, "The Biography of the Prophet in Recent Research," *Islamic Quarterly* 1 (1954), 8.

[2] Quraysh (or Koreish), the name of the leading tribe in Mecca, is used to refer to the whole city's population.—Ed.

[3] This term means "helpers" and refers to those citizens of Medina who joined his cause.—Ed.

God will give you a companion,' hoping that the apostle meant himself he bought two camels and kept them tied up in his house supplying them with fodder in preparation for departure. . . .

According to what I have been told none knew when the apostle left except 'Alī and Abū Bakr and the latter's family. I have heard that the apostle told 'Alī about his departure and ordered him to stay behind in Mecca in order to return goods which men had deposited with the apostle; for anyone in Mecca who had property which he was anxious about left it with him because of his notorious honesty and trustworthiness.

When the apostle decided to go he came to Abū Bakr and the two of them left by a window in the back of the latter's house and made for a cave on Thaur, a mountain below Mecca. . . .

The apostle ordered that a mosque should be built, and he stayed with Abū Ayyūb until the mosque and his houses were completed. The apostle joined in the work to encourage the Muslims to work and the *muhājirīn*[4] and the *anṣār* laboured hard. . . .

The apostle lived in Abū Ayyūb's house until his mosque and dwelling-houses were built; then he removed to his own quarters. . . .

The apostle stayed in Medina from the month of Rabī'u'l-awwal to Ṣafar of the following year until his mosque and his quarters were built. This tribe of the Anṣār all accepted Islam and every house of the Anṣār accepted Islam except Khaṭma, Wāqif, Wā'il, and Umayya who were the Aus Allah, a clan of Aus who clung to their heathenism.

The apostle wrote a document[5] concerning the emigrants and the helpers in which he made a friendly agreement with the Jews and established them in their religion and their property, and stated the reciprocal obligations, as follows: In the name of God the Compassionate, the Merciful. This is a document from Muhammad the prophet [governing the relations] between the believers and Muslims of Quraysh and Yathrib, and those who followed them and joined them and laboured with them. They are one community (*umma*) to the exclusion of all men. The Quraysh emigrants according to their present custom shall pay the bloodwit within their number and shall redeem their prisoners with the kindness and justice common among believers. . . .

A believer shall not take as an ally the freedman of another Mus-

---

[4]This is another term for his followers from Mecca.—Ed.

[5]This is the document known as the Constitution of Medina. It is reproduced and analyzed in W. Montgomery Watt, *Muhammad at Medina* (Oxford: The Clarendon Press, 1956), pp. 221 ff.—Ed.

lim against him. The God-fearing believers shall be against the rebellious or him who seeks to spread injustice, or sin or enmity, or
corruption between believers; the hand of every man shall be
against him even if he be a son of one of them. A believer shall not
slay a believer for the sake of an unbeliever, nor shall he aid an
unbeliever against a believer. God's protection is one, the least of
them may give protection to a stranger on their behalf. Believers are
friends one to the other to the exclusion of outsiders. To the Jew
who follows us belong help and equality. He shall not be wronged
nor shall his enemies be aided. The peace of the believers is indivisi-
ble. No separate peace shall be made when believers are fighting in
the way of God. Conditions must be fair and equitable to all. In
every foray a rider must take another behind him. The believers
must avenge the blood of one another shed in the way of God. The
God-fearing believers enjoy the best and most upright guidance. No
polytheist shall take the property or person of Quraysh under his
protection nor shall he intervene against a believer. Whosoever is
convicted of killing a believer without good reason shall be subject to
retaliation unless the next of kin is satisfied (with blood-money), and
the believers shall be against him as one man, and they are bound to
take action against him.

It shall not be lawful to a believer who holds by what is in this
document and believes in God and the last day to help an evil-doer or
to shelter him. The curse of God and His anger on the day of resurrec-
tion will be upon him if he does, and neither repentance nor ransom
will be received from him. Whenever you differ about a matter it
must be referred to God and to Muhammad.

The Jews shall contribute to the cost of war so long as they are
fighting alongside the believers. The Jews of the B. 'Auf are one
community with the believers (the Jews have their religion and the
Muslims have theirs), their freedmen and their persons except those
who behave unjustly and sinfully, for they hurt but themselves and
their families. The same applies to the Jews of the B. al-Najjār, B. al-
Ḥārith, B. Sā'ida, B. Jusham, B. al-Aus, B. Tha'laba, and the Jafna, a
clan of the Tha'laba and the B. al-Shuṭayba. Loyalty is a protection
against treachery. The freedmen of Tha'laba are as themselves. The
close friends of the Jews are as themselves. None of them shall go out
to war save with the permission of Muhammad, but he shall not be
prevented from taking revenge for a wound. He who slays a man
without warning slays himself and his household, unless it be one who
has wronged him, for God will accept that. The Jews must bear their
expenses and the Muslims their expenses. Each must help the other
against anyone who attacks the people of this document. They must
seek mutual advice and consultation, and loyalty is a protection

against treachery. A man is not liable for his ally's misdeeds. The wronged must be helped. The Jews must pay with the believers so long as war lasts. Yathrib shall be a sanctuary for the people of this document. A stranger under protection shall be as his host doing no harm and committing no crime. A woman shall only be given protection with the consent of her family. If any dispute or controversy likely to cause trouble should arise it must be referred to God and to Muhammad the apostle of God. God accepts what is nearest to piety and goodness in this document. Quraysh and their helpers shall not be given protection. The contracting parties are bound to help one another against any attack on Yathrib. If they are called to make peace and maintain it they must do so; and if they make a similar demand on the Muslims it must be carried out except in the case of a holy war. Every one shall have his portion from the side to which he belongs, the Jews of al-Aus, their freedmen and themselves have the same standing with the people of this document in pure loyalty from the people of this document.

Loyalty is a protection against treachery: He who acquires aught acquires it for himself. God approves of this document. This deed will not protect the unjust and the sinner. The man who goes forth to fight and the man who stays at home in the city is safe unless he has been unjust and sinned. God is the protector of the good and God-fearing man and Muhammad is the apostle of God. . . .

The apostle instituted brotherhood between his fellow emigrants and the helpers, and he said according to what I have heard—and I appeal to God lest I should attribute to him words that he did not say—'Let each of you take a brother in God.' He himself took ʿAlī by the hand and said, 'This is my brother.' So God's apostle, the lord of the sent ones and leader of the God-fearing, apostle of the Lord of the worlds, the peerless and unequalled, and ʿAlī b. Abū Ṭālib became brothers. . . .

When the apostle was firmly settled in Medina and his brethren the emigrants were gathered to him and the affairs of the helpers were arranged Islam became firmly established. Prayer was instituted, the alms tax and fasting were prescribed, legal punishments fixed, the forbidden and the permitted prescribed, and Islam took up its abode with them. It was this clan of the helpers who 'have taken up their abode (in the city of the prophet) and in the faith.' When the apostle first came, the people gathered to him for prayer at the appointed times without being summoned. At first the apostle thought of using a trumpet like that of the Jews who used it to summon to prayer. Afterwards he disliked the idea and ordered a clapper to be made, so it was duly fashioned to be beaten when the Muslims should pray.

The Prophet and the True Believer

SAYED AMEER ALI

From the time of Ibn Ishaq to the present, Muslim biographers have continued to write about Muhammad's life, and their accounts have tended to be uncritical and adulatory of the prophet—as are all such apologetic works. Nevertheless, these biographies form one of the strands making up the tradition of Islam. One of the most widely accepted of them is Sayed Ameer Ali, *The Spirit of Islam: A History of the Evolution and Ideals of Islam, with a Life of the Prophet,* rev. ed. (London: Chatto and Windus, 1978 [1891]. Sayed Ameer Ali was an English-trained Indian lawyer and judge in Bengal, and a devout Muslim. He was a prolific writer; some of his books dealt with his profession—he was an authority on the law of evidence—but most of them dealt with Islam. In 1873 he published *Critical Examination of the Life and Teachings of Mohammed,* in 1880 *Personal Law of the Mohammedans,* in 1893 *The Ethics of Islam,* and in 1899 *A Short History of the Saracens.* But his best-known book was *The Spirit of Islam,* from which the following passage is excerpted.

The passage deals with Muhammad's consolidation of his position in Medina, his work as a political leader and administrator, and his actions as the head of his new religion. It also deals with the increasing hostility between Muhammad and the important Jewish community of Medina. The reader should note, in the account, the pervasive tone of harshness toward the Jews, their actions, and their motives; the unfailing clemency of Muhammad; and even the intervention of angelic forces on the side of Islam at the Battle of Badr.

At this time there were three distinct parties in Medîna. The Muhâjirîn (the Exiles) and the Ansâr (the Helpers) formed the kernel of Islâm. Their devotion to the Prophet was unbounded. . . .

But the Jews, who may be said to have formed the third party, constituted the most serious element of danger. They had close business relations with the Koreish, and their ramifications extended into various parts hostile to the Faith. At first they were inclined to look with some favour on the preachings of Mohammed. He could not, of course, be their promised Messiah, but perhaps a weak dreamer, a humble preacher, dependent upon the hospitality of their old ene-

184

mies, now their patrons, the Aus and the Khazraj, might become their avenger, help them in conquering the Arabs, and found for them a new kingdom of Judah. With this aim in view, they had joined with the Medinites in a half-hearted welcome to the Prophet. And for a time they maintained a pacific attitude. But it was only for a time; for barely a month had gone by before the old spirit of rebellion, which had led them to crucify their prophets, found vent in open seditions and secret treachery. One of the first acts of Mohammed after his arrival in Medîna was to weld together the heterogeneous and conflicting elements of which the city and its suburbs were composed, into an orderly confederation. With this object he had granted a charter to the people, by which the rights and obligations of the Moslems *inter se,* and of the Moslems and Jews, were clearly defined. And the Jews, borne down for the moment by the irresistible character of the movement, had gladly accepted the Pact. . . .

No kindness or generosity, however, on the part of the Prophet would satisfy the Jews; nothing could conciliate the bitter feelings with which they were animated. Enraged that they could not use him as their instrument for the conversion of Arabia to Judaism, and that his belief was so much simpler than their Talmudic legends, they soon broke off, and ranged themselves on the side of the enemies of the new Faith. And when asked which they preferred, idolatry or Islâm, they, like many Christian controversialists, declared they preferred idolatry, with all its attendant evils, to the creed of Mohammed. . . .

And now came the moment of severest trial to Islâm. Barely had the Prophet time to put the city in a state of defence and organise the Believers, before the blow descended upon him. Medîna itself was honeycombed by sedition and treachery. And it became the duty of Mohammed to take serious measures to guard against that dreaded catastrophe which a rising within, or a sudden attack from without, would have entailed upon his followers. He was not simply a preacher of Islâm; he was also the guardian of the lives and liberties of his people. As a Prophet, he could afford to ignore the revilings and the gibes of his enemies; but as the head of the State, "the general in a time of almost continual warfare," when Medîna was kept in a state of military defence and under a sort of military discipline, he could not overlook treachery. He was bound by his duty to his subjects to suppress a party that might have led, and almost did lead to the sack of the city by investing armies. The safety of the State required the proscription of the traitors, who were either sowing the seeds of sedition within Medîna or carrying information to the common enemy. Some half a dozen were placed under the ban, outlawed, and executed. We are, however, anticipating the course of events in referring to these executions.

The Koreish army was afield before Mohammed received God's command to do battle to His enemies.

He who never in his life had wielded a weapon, to whom the sight of human suffering caused intense pain and pity, and who, against all the canons of Arab manliness, wept bitterly at the loss of his children or disciples, whose character ever remained so tender and so pathetic as to cause his enemies to call him womanish,—this man was now compelled, from the necessities of the situation, and against his own inclination, to repel the attacks of the enemy by force of arms, to organise his followers for purposes of self-defence, and often to send out expeditions to anticipate treacherous and sudden onslaughts. Hitherto, Arab warfare consisted of sudden and murderous forays, often made in the night or in the early morn; isolated combats or a general melée, when the attacked were aware of the designs of the attacking party. Mohammed, with a thorough knowledge of the habits of his people, had frequently to guard against these sudden onslaughts by sending forth reconnoitering parties.

The Meccans and their allies commenced raiding up to the very vicinity of Medîna, destroying the fruit-trees of the Moslems, and carrying away their flocks. A force, consisting of a thousand well-equipped men, marched under the noted Abû Jahl, "the Father of Ignorance," towards Medîna to destroy the Moslems, and to protect one of their caravans bringing munitions of war. The Moslems received timely notice of the movement, and a body of three hundred disciples proceeded at once to forestall the heathens by occupying the valley of Badr, upon which Abû Jahl was moving. When Mohammed saw the infidel army arrogantly advancing into the valley, raising his hands towards heaven, like the prophets of Israel, he prayed that the little band of the Faithful might not be destroyed: "O Lord, forget not Thy promise of assistance. O Lord, if this little band were to perish, there will be none to offer unto Thee pure worship."

Three of the Koreish advanced into the open space which divided the Moslems from the idolaters, and, according to Arab usage, challenged three champions from the Moslem ranks to single combat. Hamza, Ali, and Obaidah accepted the challenge, and came out conquerors. The engagement then became general. At one time the fortunes of the field wavered, but Mohammed's appeal to his people decided the fate of the battle. "It was a stormy winter day. A piercing blast swept across the valley." It seemed as if the angels of heaven were warring for the Moslems. Indeed, to the earnest minds of Mohammed and his followers, who, like the early Christians, saw God's providence "in all the gifts of nature, in every relation of life, at each turn of their affairs, individual or public,"—to them those blasts of wind and sand, the elements warring against the enemies of God, at that critical moment appeared veritable succour sent from heaven; as angels riding on the wings of the wind, and driving the faithless idolaters before them in confusion. The Meccans were driven back with great loss; many of their chiefs were slain; and Abû Jahl fell a victim to his unruly pride. . . .

The remarkable circumstances which led to the victory of Badr, and the results which followed from it, made a deep impression on the minds of the Moslems. They firmly believed that the angels of heaven had battled on their side against the unbelieving host. . . .

The defeat of the idolaters at Badr was felt as keenly by the Jews as by the Meccans. Immediately after this battle a distinguished member of their race, called Ka'b, the son of Ashraf, belonging to the tribe of Nazîr, publicly deploring the ill-success of the idolaters, proceeded towards Mecca. Finding the people there plunged in grief, he spared no exertion to revive their courage. . . . His acts were openly directed against the commonwealth of which he was a member. He belonged to a tribe which had entered into the Compact with the Moslems, and pledged itself for the internal as well as the external safety of the State. Another Jew of the Nazîr, Abû Râf'e Sallâm, son of Abu'l Hukaik, was equally wild and bitter against the Musulmans. He inhabited, with a fraction of his tribe, the territories of Khaibar, four or five days' journey to the north-west of Medîna. Detesting Mohammed and the Musulmans, he made use of every endeavour to excite the neighbouring Arab tribes, such as the Sulaim and the Ghatafân, against them. It was impossible for the Musulman Commonwealth to tolerate this open treachery on the part of those to whom every consideration had been shown, with the object of securing their neutrality, if not their support. The very existence of the Moslem community was at stake; and every principle of safety required that these traitorous designs should be quietly frustrated. The sentence of outlawry was executed upon them by the Medinites themselves—in one case by a member of the tribe of Aus, in the other by a Khazrajite. . . . The Jews had openly and knowingly infringed the terms of their compact. It was necessary to put a stop to this with a firm hand, or farewell to all hope of peace and security. Consequently Mohammed proceeded at once to the quarter of the Banî-Kainukâ', and required them to enter definitely into the Moslem Commonwealth by embracing Islâm, or to vacate Medîna. The reply of the Jews was couched in the most offensive terms. "O, Mohammed, do not be elated with the victory over thy people (the Koreish). Thou hast had an affair with men ignorant of the art of war. If thou art desirous of having any dealings with us, we shall show thee that we are men." They then shut themselves up in their fortress, and set Mohammed's authority at defiance. But their reduction was an absolute duty, and siege was accordingly laid to their stronghold without loss of time. After fifteen days they surrendered. At first it was intended to inflict some severe punishment on them, but the clemency of Mohammed's nature overcame the dictates of justice, and the Banî-Kainukâ' were simply banished.

A Western Assessment of Muhammad

WILLIAM MONTGOMERY WATT

In Medina, Muhammad made himself the head of a growing politico-religious movement. In 630 he was able to conquer Mecca and to make the city of his birth the permanent center of Islam. Two years later Muhammad died. He had formed the scattered polyglot of Arab tribes into an Arab nation and armed it with a powerful new religion.

In the course of the next generation Islam exploded out of the Near East to become a world political force. Arab armies defeated the Byzantines in Syria and Asia Minor. They swept away the weak structures of Byzantine authority in North Africa and, within a century, they had established themselves facing the western Christians in Spain and along the shores of the Mediterranean. It was in the ensuing long period of confrontation that the traditional suspicion and hostility between Islam and the West developed.

If the Muslim biographical tradition of Muhammad has been adulatory and uncritical, the western tradition has been equally unrestrained in its hostility toward him, beginning with the accounts of the twelfth century that picture him as Mahound "the great enemy," "the prince of darkness." Although it moderated somewhat over time, the fundamental hostility of this western view persisted well into the nineteenth century. Indeed, it has only been in the last generation that western scholars have seriously turned to the task of creating a reliable and sympathetic picture of the prophet of Islam.

One of the leading figures in this revisionist revolution has been William Montgomery Watt, from whose most important book, *Muhammad at Medina,* the following passage is taken. Watt is Professor of Arabic and Islamic Studies at the University of Edinburgh and past chairman of the Association of British Orientalists. It has been his life's work "to reach an objective view of Muhammad's char-

acter," as a precondition for meaningful understanding between the
Muslim world and our own.

———————————————

Several accounts have been preserved of the appearance of Muḥammad, and, as they largely agree, they are perhaps near the truth,
though there is a tendency in some of them to paint a picture of the
ideal man. According to these accounts Muḥammad was of average
height or a little above the average. His chest and shoulders were
broad, and altogether he was of a sturdy build. His arms, or perhaps
rather forearms, were long, and his hands and feet rough. His fore-
head was large and prominent, and he had a hooked nose and large
black eyes with a touch of brown. The hair of his head was long and
thick, straight or slightly curled. His beard also was thick, and he had
a thin line of fine hair on his neck and chest. His cheeks were spare,
his mouth large, and he had a pleasant smile. In complexion he was
fair. He always walked as if he were rushing downhill, and others had
difficulty in keeping up with him. When he turned in any direction,
he did so with his whole body.

He was given to sadness, and there were long periods of silence
when he was deep in thought; yet he never rested but was always busy
with something. He never spoke unnecessarily. What he said was
always to the point and sufficient to make his meaning clear, but there
was no padding. From first to last he spoke rapidly. Over his feelings
he had a firm control. When he was annoyed he would turn aside;
when he was pleased, he lowered his eyes. His time was carefully
apportioned according to the various demands on him. In his dealings with people he was above all tactful. He could be severe at times,
but in the main he was not rough but gentle. His laugh was mostly a
smile.

There are many stories illustrating his gentleness and tenderness of
feeling. Even if some of them are not true, the probability is that the
general picture is sound. There seems to be no reason, for instance,
for doubting the truth of the story of how he broke the news of the
death of Jaʿfar b. Abī Ṭālib to his widow Asmāʾ bint ʿUmays; the story
is said to have been told by Asmāʾ herself to her grand-daughter. She
had been busy one morning with her household duties, which had
included tanning forty hides and kneading dough, when Muḥammad
called. She collected her children—she had three sons by Jaʿfar—
washed their faces and anointed them. When Muḥammad entered,
he asked for the sons of Jaʿfar. She brought them, and Muḥammad
put his arms round them and smelt them (as a mother would a baby).
Then his eyes filled with tears and he burst out weeping. 'Have you

heard something about Ja'far?', she asked, and he told her that he had been killed. Later he instructed some of his people to prepare food for Ja'far's household, 'for they are too busy today to think about themselves'. About the same time the little daughter of Zayd b. Ḥārithah (who had been killed along with Ja'far) came to him in tears to be comforted, and he wept along with her; afterwards, when questioned about this, he said it was because of the great love between Zayd and himself. The memory of his first wife Khadījah could also soften his heart. After Badr the husband of his daughter Zaynab was among the prisoners taken by the Muslims, and Zaynab sent a necklace of Khadījah's to Muḥammad for a ransom, but he was so moved at the sight of it that he set the man free without payment.

Muḥammad seems to have felt especial tenderness towards children, and to have got on well with them. Perhaps it was an expression of the yearning of a man who had seen all his sons die in infancy. Much of his paternal affection went to his adopted son Zayd, who has just been mentioned. . . .

He was able to enter into the spirit of childish games and had many friends among children. 'Ā'ishah was still a child when he married her, and she continued to play with her toys. He would ask her what they were. 'Solomon's horses', she replied, and Muḥammad smiled. . . . His kindness extended even to animals, and this is something remarkable for Muḥammad's century and part of the world. As his men marched towards Mecca just before the conquest they passed a bitch with puppies, and Muḥammad not merely gave orders that they were not to be disturbed, but posted a man to see that the orders were carried out. . . .

These are interesting sidelights on the personality of Muḥammad, and fill out the picture of him we form from his conduct of public affairs. He gained men's respect and confidence by the religious basis of his activity and by such qualities as courage, resoluteness, impartiality, firmness inclining to severity but tempered by generosity. In addition to these, however, he had a charm of manner which won their affection and secured their devotion.

Of all the world's great men none has been so much maligned as Muḥammad. It is easy to see how this has come about. For centuries Islam was the great enemy of Christendom, for Christendom was in direct contact with no other organized states comparable in power to the Muslims. . . . The aim of the present discussion is to work towards a more objective attitude with regard to the moral criticisms inherited from medieval times. The main points are three. Muḥammad has been alleged to be insincere, to be sensual, and to be treacherous.

The allegation of insincerity or imposture was vigorously attacked by Thomas Carlyle over a hundred years ago, has been increasingly opposed by scholarly opinion since then, and yet is still sometimes made.

The extreme form of the view was that Muḥammad did not believe in his revelations and did not in any sense receive them from 'outside himself', but deliberately composed them, and then published them in such a way as to deceive people into following him, so gaining power to satisfy his ambition and his lust. Such a view is incredible. Above all it gives no satisfying explanation of Muḥammad's readiness to endure hardship in his Meccan days, of the respect in which he was held by men of high intelligence and upright character, and of his success in founding a world religion which has produced men of undoubted saintliness. These matters can only be satisfactorily explained and understood on the assumption that Muḥammad was sincere, that is, that he genuinely believed that what we now know as the Qur'ān was not the product of his own mind, but came to him from God and was true. . . .

When we come to the other two allegations, however, namely, that Muḥammad was morally defective in that he was treacherous and sensual, the discussion has to embrace not merely factual points, but also the question of the standard by which the acts have to be judged. . . .

The allegation of treachery may be taken to cover a number of criticisms made by European writers. It applies most clearly to such acts as the breaking of his agreements with the Jews and his one-sided denunciation of the treaty of al-Ḥudaybiyah with the Meccans. It may also, however, be taken to include the infringement either of the sacred month or of the sacred territory on the expedition to Nakhlah when the first Meccan blood was shed, the mass execution of the Jewish clan of Qurayẓah, and the orders or encouragement given to his followers to remove dangerous opponents by assassination. . . .

Now the Islamic community or *ummah* was thought of as a tribe. Towards tribes with which it had agreements, it had duties and obligations, and these were scrupulously observed according to the standards of the day; Muḥammad even paid blood-money to a man who was really but not technically responible for the death of several Muslims. Where a tribe was at war with the Muslims, however, or had no agreement, they had no obligations towards it even of what we would call common decency. If contemporaries showed some surprise at the execution of all the males of Qurayẓah, it was because Muḥammad was not afraid of any consequences of such an act; the behaviour of Qurayẓah during the siege of Medina was regarded as having cancelled their agreement with Muḥammad. Similarly, the terms of the treaty of al-Ḥudaybiyah had been broken by the Meccans before Muḥammad denounced it, and the individuals who were assassinated had forfeited any claim to friendly treatment by Muḥammad through their propaganda against him. So far were the Muslims who killed them from feeling any qualms that one of them, describing the return from the deed, wrote that they returned with the head of their victim 'five honourable men, steady and true, and God was the sixth with us'. This is so much in keeping with the spirit of pre-Islamic times that it is almost certainly authentic; but, even if not, it shows the attitude of the early Muslims. . . .

Again, the common European and Christian criticism that Muḥammad was a sensualist or, in the blunter language of the seventeenth century, an 'old lecher', fades away when examined in the light of the standards of Muḥammad's time. There was a strain in early Muslim thought which tended to magnify the common—or perhaps we should say 'superhuman'—humanity of their prophet. There is even a tradition to the effect that his virility was such that he was able to satisfy all his wives in a single night. This looks like an invention, for the usual account is that he gave his wives a night each in turn, but it shows the outlook of some at least of his followers.[6] The early Muslims looked askance at celibacy and checked any movements towards it, and even rigorous ascetics in Islam have commonly been married. . . .

In general, then, there was nothing in Muḥammad's marital relationships which his contemporaries regarded as incompatible with his prophethood. They did not consider him a voluptuary any more than they considered him a scoundrel. The sources record criticisms of him, but these are based on no moral criterion, but on a conservatism which was akin to superstition. Though later Muslims might produce colourful stories of Muḥammad's susceptibility to feminine charm, and though there is no reason to suppose that he disregarded the factor of physical attraction, it is practically certain that he had his feelings towards the fair sex well under control, and that he did not enter into marriages except when they were politically and socially desirable.

It is possible, too, to go further and, while restricting oneself to the standpoint of Muḥammad's time, to turn the alleged instances of treachery and sensuality into matter for praise. In his day and generation Muḥammad was a social reformer, indeed a reformer even in the sphere of morals. He created a new system of social security and a new family structure, both of which were a vast improvement on what went before. In this way he adapted for settled communities all that was best in the morality of the nomad, and established a religious and social framework for the life of a sixth of the human race today. That is not the work of a traitor or a lecher. . . .

---

[6]Muhammad had eleven wives in all.—ED.

Circumstances of place and time favoured Muḥammad. Various forces combined to set the stage for his life-work and for the subsequent expansion of Islam. . . . There was nothing inevitable or automatic about the spread of the Arabs and the growth of the Islamic community. But for a remarkable combination of qualities in Muḥammad it is improbable that the expansion would have taken place, and these vast forces might easily have spent themselves in raids on Syria and 'Irāq without any lasting consequences. In particular we may distinguish three great gifts Muḥammad had, each of which was indispensable to the total achievement.

First there is what may be called his gift as a seer. Through him— or, on the orthodox Muslim view, through the revelations made to him—the Arab world was given an ideological framework within which the resolution of its social tensions became possible. The provision of such a framework involved both insight into the fundamental causes of the social malaise of the time, and the genius to express this insight in a form which would stir the hearer to the depths of his being. The European reader may be 'put off' by the Qur'ān, but it was admirably suited to the needs and conditions of the day.

Secondly, there is Muḥammad's wisdom as a statesman. The conceptual structure found in the Qur'ān was merely a framework. The framework had to support a building of concrete policies and concrete institutions. . . . His wisdom in these matters is shown by the rapid expansion of his small state to a world-empire and by the adaptation of his social institutions to many different environments and their continuance for thirteen centuries.

Thirdly, there is his skill and tact as an administrator and his wisdom in the choice of men to whom to delegate administrative details. Sound institutions and a sound policy will not go far if the execution of affairs is faulty and fumbling. When Muḥammad died, the state he had founded was a 'going concern', able to withstand the shock of his removal and, once it had recovered from this shock, to expand at prodigious speed.

Review and Study Questions

1. What sort of man was Muhammad? Compare him with (a) the Buddha and (b) Confucius.

2. What was the role of the Jews of Medina in the early history of Islam?

3. What was the nature of the community Muhammad established?

Suggestions for Further Reading

The contemporary and near-contemporary sources for the life of Muhammad present all the difficulties already referred to and more. While limited as a biographic source, the Koran ought to be sampled by interested students. Of the several available English translations, the best and the one that comes closest to conveying the impression made on Muslims by the original is *The Koran Interpreted*, a translation by Arthur J. Arberry (New York: Macmillan, 1955), although the standard edition is probably still *The Koran*, tr. J. M. Rodwell (London and New York: J. M. Dent and E. P. Dutton, Everyman's Library, 1909). Another alternative edition is *The Qur'an*, tr. Richard Bell (Edinburgh: T. and T. Clark, 1937–39). A useful work is W. Montgomery Watt, *Companion to the Qur'an* (London: Allen and Unwin, 1967).

Alfred Guillaume, *The Traditions of Islam* (New York: Books for Libraries—Arno Press, 1980) is devoted to the Hadith, the traditional sayings and anecdotes about Muhammad, and includes a substantial selection from them. Of the early biographies of Muhammad, students may read further from Ibn Ishaq's *Sirat Rasul Allah* in *The Life of Muhammad, A Translation of Ishaq's Sirat Rasul Allah,* intro. A. Guillaume (Lahore, Karachi, Dacca: Oxford University Press Pakistan Branch, 1970 [1955]), excerpted for this chapter. Another early work is al-Waqidi's *Maghazi*, ed. J. M. B. Jones, dealing extensively with Muhammad's military campaigns and his relations with the people of Medina and the surrounding tribes. A good critique of the early historical sources is A. Guillaume, "The Biography of the Prophet in Recent Research," *Islamic Quarterly* 1 (1954), 5–11.

Of the traditional Muslim biographies of Muhammad, in addition to Sayed Ameer Ali, *The Spirit of Islam: A History of the Evolution and Ideals of Islam, with a Life of the Prophet*, rev. ed. (London: Chatto and Windus, 1978 [1891]), a simple and straightforward example is Muhammad Zafrulla Khan, *Muhammad: Seal of the Prophets* (London: Routledge and Kegan Paul, 1980), whose aim is to help "a seeker after truth to determine whether he was truly the divine instrument chosen for the regeneration of mankind through the ages." A somewhat more sophisticated example is Muhammad Husayn Haykal, *The Life of Mohammed*, best sampled in the extensive excerpts in a critical work, Antonie Wessels, *A Modern Arabic Biography of Muhammad, A Critical Study of Muhammad Husayn Haykal's Hayat Muhammad* (Leiden: Brill, 1972).

Among the best modern western critical biographies of Muhammad is W. Montgomery Watt, *Muhammad at Medina* (Oxford: The Clarendon Press, 1956), excerpted for this chapter. It needs to be read, however, along with his earlier companion volume, *Muhammad at Mecca* (Oxford: The Clarendon Press, 1953). The material in both these books is condensed in a smaller volume by Watt, *Muhammad Prophet and Statesman* (Oxford: Oxford University Press, 1961). Maxime Rodinson, *Mohammed,* tr. Anne Carter (New York: Pantheon, 1971) is an excellent work by an able French scholar who, however, is more interested in the ideology of Islam than in its prophet. Two interesting works, both by British military men who spent their lives in the Near East and both popular laymen's biographies, are R. V. C. Bodley, *The Messenger: The Life of Mohammed* (New York: Greenwood Press, 1946) and John Bagot Glubb, *The Life and Times of Muhammad* (New York: Stein and Day, 1970).

Among the many general works on the history and culture of the Islamic world, two in particular are recommended: Philip K. Hitti, *History of the Arabs, From the Earliest Times to the Present,* 5th ed. rev. (London: Macmillan, 1953) and Bernard Lewis, *The Arabs in History,* 3rd ed. (London: Hutchinson, 1964). Recommended also is *The Cambridge History of Islam,* 4 vols. (Cambridge: Cambridge University Press, 1979), especially vols. I and IA.

MURASAKI SHIKIBU: THE LADY OF THE SHINING PRINCE

c. 973	Born
c. 998	Married
1001	Widowed
1005–6	Entered the service of the Empress Shoshi
c. 1010	Completed most of *The Tale of Genji*
c. 1026	Died

The greatest work of Japanese prose literature, the earliest novel in any language, and one of the great novels of world literature, *The Tale of Genji,* was written by a woman, the Lady Murasaki Shikibu, in the early eleventh century. Even more remarkably, the culture of the Heian Age, to which she belonged—one of the most important periods of Japanese history—was almost totally dominated by women like Murasaki. This situation, nearly unique in the course of Japanese history, resulted from a peculiar constellation of events.

Early Japan was shaped by the older, richer culture of China. In late prehistoric times, elements of Chinese culture, including the fabrication of iron and bronze and the wet cultivation of rice, began to spread to Korea and Japan. By the fifth century A.D. Japan was ruled by a hereditary imperial dynasty, the Yamato. In the following century two important influences were introduced into Japan, both from China. One was the structural notion of central government, with its hierarchies of court ranks; the other was Buddhism. In the early eighth century the Japanese—again on the model of China—built their first capital city, at Nara. Within less than a century the capital was moved to Kyoto, where it remained for more than a thousand years. It was called Heian-kyo, "the capital of peace and tranquility," and it became a brilliant center of art and culture.

The emperor was the cultural leader of the emerging Japanese society, the focal point of its empire and its religion, and the central figure of its elaborate court pageantry; but the real political authority of the nation was in the hands of a powerful family, the Fujiwara clan. The Fujiwara ruled not as emperors but as regents, and their influence was exercised through the women of their clan, whom they strategically placed as consorts of the emperor and wives of members of the imperial family. The Fujiwara regents actively encouraged the further development of the rich, patterned society of the court, in which the emperor spent his life performing elaborate rituals and acting as the central figure in the equally elaborate religious festivals designed to assure the continued welfare of the state.

This highly artificial court society reached its zenith in the so-called Heian Age, from the tenth to the twelfth century. The daughters of the Fujiwara, as consorts of successive emperors and wives of other imperial figures, took a leading role. They surrounded themselves with other talented women who vied with one another in learning and religious observance, in poetic composition, and in fine writing.

Earlier Japanese writing had been completely dominated by Chinese influence, and all the serious literature and records of Japan— histories, chronicles, works of geography and law, and official documents—were written in a cumbersome, adapted Chinese script. Further, they were written exclusively by male scholars; women were not considered sufficiently intelligent to learn the Chinese script. Instead, the native Japanese language was relegated to the use of women, in a script called *Kana* that had been developed in the ninth century. It was even called "women's writing." Ironically, while the laborious and tedious works of their male contemporaries have virtually disappeared, the works of "women's writing" survive to depict for us their society and the activities of their lives in letters, diaries, poems, stories, and in *The Tale of Genji,* the masterpiece of the Heian court lady Murasaki Shikibu.

The Tale of Genji

MURASAKI SHIKIBU

In spite of the fame of *The Tale of Genji,* which was honored in its own time and has been ever since, its author remains stubbornly obscure. In part this is surely because of Murasaki's own reticence. It was simply not seemly for a lady of the court to flaunt the details of her personal life. For example, we have no portrait of her and no literary description. There was in Heian Japan a tradition of vigorous and realistic portraiture of men, especially of important men, but not of women. Even if women had been depicted, the depictions would not have been realistic. Women were typically swathed in so many layers of clothing that they often literally could not move. Their faces were painted with a dead-white face powder, presumably to conceal their features; their teeth were blackened at the dictate of high fashion. We do not even know Murasaki's real name. Murasaki is the name of one of the leading characters in her novel and probably was used to refer to the author indirectly. *Shikibu* was a title held by her father, who was Senior Secretary in the imperial Bureau of Ceremonial. Her father, though a member of the great Fujiwara clan, belonged to a lesser branch of the family and never rose to high office. He was a scholar, a poet, and a minor administrative functionary.

Murasaki was probably born in 973 in the provincial capital where her father was posted. We know almost nothing about her youth. In 998 she married Fujiwara no Nobutaka, an associate and distant relative of her father and an older man who already had three wives. In spite of this, Murasaki's marriage was apparently happy enough, and she had a daughter in 999. Her husband died of an epidemic in 1001.

To fill the emptiness of her widowhood, Murasaki is thought to have begun writing *The Tale of Genji* at some time during the next four or five years. In 1005 or 1006 she entered the service of the court. She may have been selected by the Fujiwara regent Michinaga as tutor and lady-in-waiting to his daughter, the young Empress Shoshi. Murasaki led a rather retiring life at court and seems never to have enjoyed a great court title. But her familiarity with the court and with its people and their manners is reflected in *The Tale of Genji,* which she substantially completed by 1010. She may have departed the court as early as the following year, when the Empress Shoshi retired to a private residence. We know that Murasaki was, by this time, deeply interested in Buddhism, and had contemplated becoming a Buddhist nun. The date of her death is unknown—it may have been as early as 1014 or as late as 1026, more likely the latter.

In contrast to the sketchy details of Murasaki's biography we have the teeming tapestry of her novel, with its endless details about the life of the court. One critic has called it "a great and sophisticated work of fictional history." *The Tale of Genji* is a rambling, episodic work spanning more than fifty years. Its central theme is the amorous adventures of Genji, "The Shining Prince." He is of noble birth, the son of the emperor. Genji is rich, wise, and witty, but his wit and wisdom are almost entirely expended on planning or concealing seductions and dwelling upon the liaisons of love. Yet this is not an erotic book. Murasaki is a woman of "discriminating and delicate taste, and a deep understanding of the emotions of the human heart. She is interested not in the details of her hero's conquests, but in the subtlest refinements of human intercourse; not in the lovers' embraces, but in their longings and their regrets."[1] And she is interested in the context in which the love affairs take place— the charming entertainments, the solemn ceremonies at shrines and monasteries, the archery and equestrian contests, the contests of poetry, painting, and perfume blending. She tells us of the delicacy of sentiment of the ladies and gentlemen of the court, the nuances of gesture and innuendo, the refinements of costume, rich beyond belief, with each color and fabric and pattern steeped in symbolism.

The modern reader is most affected by the incredible artificiality of this society and the equally incredible triviality of its concerns. There are almost no real intellectual interests. Even the Buddhism that played so prominent a part in the court society tended to be mainly a matter of external forms subscribed to with a bland disregard for the incompatibility of Buddhism with either the imported Confucianism or the native Japanese Shinto cult. Instead of meaningful spiritual or intellectual questions, the courtiers, nobles, and officials of the court were preoccupied with manners, taste, and empty formalism. However, one gains the distinct impression that Murasaki herself is dissatisfied with the emptiness of the court life that she describes so faithfully.

The Tale of Genji is in no sense an autobiographical novel. Yet, in an occasional passage, there is a shadowy reflection of the author and of her concerns. The following excerpt is one such passage. In it Genji makes fun of the romances that the court ladies love to

---

[1]George Sansom, *A History of Japan to 1334* (Stanford: Stanford University Press, 1958), p. 179.

read. But he is drawn up short by one of the ladies, Tamakazura, "the most avid reader of all," who insists that the romances are really a vehicle for the expression of truth. After a moment's half-ironic reflection, Genji agrees, and suggests that "the two of us set down our story and give them a really interesting one." It is a suggestion too ridiculous and amusing for Tamakazura even to imagine: "She hid her face in her sleeves."

The excerpt begins with one of those interminable entertainments that filled the life of the court, this one an equestrian archery contest.

Genji went out to the stands toward midafternoon. All the princes were there, as he had predicted. The equestrian archery was freer and more varied than at the palace. The officers of the guard joined in, and everyone sat entranced through the afternoon. The women may not have understood all the finer points, but the uniforms of even the common guardsmen were magnificent and the horsemanship was complicated and exciting. The grounds were very wide, fronting also on Murasaki's southeast quarter, where young women were watching. There was music and dancing, Chinese polo music and the Korean dragon dance. As night came on, the triumphal music rang out high and wild. The guardsmen were richly rewarded according to their several ranks. It was very late when the assembly dispersed.

Genji spent the night with the lady of the orange blossoms. . . .

They were good friends, he and she, and no more, and they went to separate beds. Genji wondered when they had begun to drift apart. . . . She had let him have her bed and spread quilts for herself outside the curtains. She had in the course of time come to accept such arrangements as proper, and he did not suggest changing them.

The rains of early summer continued without a break, even gloomier than in most years. The ladies at Rokujō amused themselves with illustrated romances. . . . Tamakazura was the most avid reader of all. She quite lost herself in pictures and stories and would spend whole days with them. Several of her young women were well informed in literary matters. She came upon all sorts of interesting and shocking incidents (she could not be sure whether they were true or not), but she found little that resembled her own unfortunate career. . . .

Genji could not help noticing the clutter of pictures and manuscripts. "What a nuisance this all is," he said one day. "Women seem to have been born to be cheerfully deceived. They know perfectly well that in all these old stories there is scarcely a shred of truth, and yet they are captured and made sport of by the whole range of trivialities and go on scribbling them down, quite unaware that in these warm rains their hair is all dank and knotted."

He smiled. "What would we do if there were not these old romances to relieve our boredom? But amid all the fabrication I must admit that I do find real emotions and plausible chains of events. We can be quite aware of the frivolity and the idleness and still be moved. We have to feel a little sorry for a charming princess in the depths of gloom. Sometimes a series of absurd and grotesque incidents which we know to be quite improbable holds our interest, and afterwards we must blush that it was so. Yet even then we can see what it was that held us. Sometimes I stand and listen to the stories they read to my daughter, and I think to myself that there certainly are good talkers in the world. I think that these yarns must come from people much practiced in lying. But perhaps that is not the whole of the story?"

She pushed away her inkstone. "I can see that that would be the view of someone much given to lying himself. For my part, I am convinced of their truthfulness."

He laughed. "I have been rude and unfair to your romances, haven't I. They have set down and preserved happenings from the age of the gods to our own. *The Chronicles of Japan* and the rest are a mere fragment of the whole truth. It is your romances that fill in the details.

"We are not told of things that happened to specific people exactly as they happened; but the beginning is when there are good things and bad things, things that happen in this life which one never tires of seeing and hearing about, things which one cannot bear not to tell of and must pass on for all generations. If the storyteller wishes to speak well, then he chooses the good things; and if he wishes to hold the reader's attention he chooses bad things, extraordinarily bad things. Good things and bad things alike, they are things of this world and no other.

"Writers in other countries approach the matter differently. Old stories in our own are different from new. There are differences in the degree of seriousness. But to dismiss them as lies is itself to depart from the truth. Even in the writ which the Buddha drew from his noble heart are parables, devices for pointing obliquely at the truth. To the ignorant they may seem to operate at cross purposes. The Greater Vehicle is full of them, but the general burden is always the same. The difference between enlightenment and confusion is of about the same order as the difference between the good and the bad in a romance. If one takes the generous view, then nothing is empty and useless."

He now seemed bent on establishing the uses of fiction.

"But tell me: is there in any of your old stories a proper, upright fool like myself?" He came closer. "I doubt that even among the most unworldly of your heroines there is one who manages to be as distant and unnoticing as you are. Suppose the two of us set down our story and give the world a really interesting one."

"I think it very likely that the world will take notice of our curious story even if we do not go to the trouble." She hid her face in her sleeves.

The Diary

MURASAKI SHIKIBU

With Murasaki's *Diary* we are on somewhat more solid ground concerning the details of her life than in *The Tale of Genji*. On the other hand, the *Diary* covers only some two years of her life, 1008–10. She had been a member of the empress's household for several years, and the excerpted passage comes near the end of her period of court service. Still, she dwells not so much on the facts of her life as on the reactions of others to her. She conveys very clearly her own increasing melancholy, the spitefulness of many of her female companions, her criticisms of their deportment, and, at the end, her own increasing attraction to Buddhism. We gain a powerful impression of a talented, learned woman who is both bound by the traditions of the court and disillusioned with them.

---

63. For instance, whenever the Master of Her Majesty's Household Tadanobu arrives with a message for Her Majesty, the senior women are so helpless and childish that they hardly ever come out to greet him, and, when they do, they seem unable to say anything in the least appropriate. It's not that they are at a loss for words, and it's not that they are lacking in intelligence; it's just that they feel so self-conscious and embarrassed that they are afraid of saying something silly, so they refuse to say anything at all and try to make themselves as invisible as possible. Women in other households cannot possibly act in such a manner! Once one has entered this sort of world even the highest born of ladies falls into line, but our women still seem to act as though they were little girls at home. If a woman of a lower rank comes out to

greet him, Major Counselor Tadanobu takes it in very bad grace, so there are even times when he leaves without seeing anyone, either because the right woman has gone home or because those women who are in their rooms refuse to come out. Other nobles, the kind who often visit Her Majesty with messages, seem to have secret understandings with particular women of their choice and retire somewhat crestfallen if they happen to be absent. It is hardly surprising that they take every opportunity they can to complain that the place is moribund.

The women in the High Priestess' household[2] must obviously look down on us for this. But, even so, it makes little sense to ridicule others by saying: "We are the only ones of note. Everyone else is as good as blind and deaf when it comes to taste." It is very easy to criticize people, but a far more difficult task to keep oneself in check, and it is while one forgets this truth, lauds oneself to the skies, treats everyone else as worthless and generally despises others, that one's true character is often clearly revealed. . . .

I criticize other women like this, but here is one who has managed to survive this far without having achieved anything of note and has nothing to rely on in the future that might afford her the slightest consolation. Yet, perhaps because I still retain the conviction that I am not the kind of person to abandon herself completely to despair, on autumn evenings, when nostalgia is at its most poignant, I go out and sit on the veranda to gaze in reverie. "Is this the moon that used to praise my beauty?" I say to myself, as I conjure up memories of the past. Then, realizing that I am making precisely that mistake which must be avoided, I become uneasy and move inside a little, while still, of course, continuing to fret and worry.

67. I remember how in the cool of the evening I used to play the koto to myself, rather badly; I was always worried lest someone were to hear me and realize that I was just "adding to the sadness of it all." How silly of me, and yet how sad! So now my two kotos, one of thirteen strings and the other of six, stand in a miserable little closet blackened with soot, ready tuned but idle. Through neglect—I forgot, for example, to ask that the bridges be removed on rainy days— they have accumulated the dust and lean there now against a cupboard, their necks jammed between that and a pillar, with a biwa standing on either side.[3]

There is also a pair of large cupboards crammed full to bursting

---

[2]Referring to the ladies of another, rival court, that of the High Priestess of the Kamo Shrines.—ED.

[3]The *biwa* was a flutelike instrument also popular with the court nobility.—ED.

point. One is full of old poems and tales that have become the home for countless silverfish that scatter in such an unpleasant manner that no one cares to look at them any more; the other is full of Chinese books which have lain unattended ever since he who carefully collected them passed away. Whenever my loneliness threatens to overwhelm me, I take out one or two of them to look at. But my women gather together behind my back. "It's because she goes on like this that she is so miserable. What kind of lady is it who reads Chinese books?" they whisper. "In the past it was not even the done thing to read sutras!"[4] "Yes," I feel like replying, "but I've never seen anyone who lived longer just because they obeyed a prohibition!" But that would be inconsiderate of me, for what they say is not unreasonable.

68. Everyone reacts differently. Some are cheerful, open-hearted, and forthcoming; others are born pessimists, amused by nothing, the kind who search through old letters, carry out penances, intone sutras without end, and clack their beads, all of which I find most unseemly. So aware am I of my women's prying eyes that I hesitate to do even those things a woman in my position should allow herself to do. How much more so at court, where I do have many things I wish to say but always think better of it. There would be no point, I tell myself, in explaining to people who would never understand, and as it would only be causing trouble with women who think of nothing but themselves and are always carping, I just keep my thoughts to myself. It is very rare that one finds people of true understanding; for the most part they judge everything by their own standards and ignore everyone else's opinion.

69. So I seem to be misunderstood, and they think that I am shy. There have been times when I have been forced to sit in their company, and on such occasions I have tried to avoid their petty criticisms, not because I am particularly shy but because I consider it all so distasteful; as a result, I am now known as somewhat of a dullard.

"Well, we never expected this!" they all say. "No one liked her. They all said she was pretentious, awkward, difficult to approach, prickly, too fond of her tales, haughty, prone to versifying, disdainful, cantankerous, and scornful. But when you meet her, she is strangely meek, a completely different person altogether!"

How embarrassing! Do they really look upon me as such a dull thing, I wonder? But I am what I am and so act accordingly. Her Majesty too has often remarked that she had thought I was not the kind of person with whom she could ever relax, but that now I have become closer to her than any of the others. I am so perversely

---

[4]Sutras were Buddhist scriptures.—Ed.

standoffish; if only I can avoid putting off those for whom I have genuine respect. . . .

71. There is a woman called Saemon no Naishi, who, for some strange reason, took a dislike to me, I cannot think why. I heard all sorts of malicious rumors about myself.

His Majesty was listening to someone reading the *Tale of Genji* aloud. "She must have read the Chronicles of Japan!" he said. "She seems very learned." Saemon no Naishi heard this and apparently jumped to conclusions, spreading it abroad among the senior courtiers that I was flaunting my learning. She gave me the nickname Our Lady of the Chronicles. How utterly ridiculous! Would I, who hesitate to reveal my learning in front of my women at home, ever think of doing so at court?

When my brother, Secretary at the Ministry of Ceremonial, was a young boy learning the Chinese classics, I was in the habit of listening to him and I became unusually proficient at understanding those passages which he found too difficult to grasp. Father, a most learned man, was always regretting the fact: "Just my luck!" he would say. "What a pity she was not born a man!" But then gradually I realized that people were saying, "It's bad enough when a man flaunts his learning; she will come to no good," and ever since then I have avoided writing even the simplest character. My handwriting is appalling. And as for those classics, or whatever they are called, that I used to read, I gave them up entirely. Still I kept on hearing these malicious remarks. Worried what people would think if they heard such rumors, I pretended to be unable to read even the inscriptions on the screens. Then Her Majesty asked me to read to her here and there from the Collected Works of Po Chü-i,[5] and, because she evinced a desire to know more about such things, we carefully chose a time when other women would not be present and, amateur that I was, I read with her the two books of Po Chü-i's New Ballads in secret; we started the summer before last. I hid this fact from the others, as did Her Majesty, but somehow His Excellency and the Emperor got wind of it and they had some beautiful copies made of various Chinese books, which His Excellency then presented to Her Majesty. That gossip Saemon no Naishi could never have found out that Her Majesty had actually asked me to study with her, for, if she had, I would never have heard the last of it. Ah what a prattling, tiresome world it is!

72. Now I shall be absolutely frank. I care little for what others say.

---

[5]Po Chü-i (772–846) was a Chinese poet of the T'ang dynasty whose works were very popular in Heian Japan.—ED.

I have decided to put my trust in Amitābha[6] and immerse myself in reading sutras. You might expect me to have no compunction in becoming a nun, for I have lost what little attachment I retained for the trials and pains that life has to offer, and yet still I hesitate; even if I were to commit myself to turning my back on the world, there might still be moments of irresolution before he came for me, trailing clouds of glory. The time too is ripe. If I get much older my eyesight will surely weaken to the point that I shall be unable to read the sutras, and my spirits will fail. It may seem that I am merely going through the motions of being a true believer, but I assure you that I can think of little else at the present moment. But then someone with as much to atone for as myself may not qualify for salvation; there are so many things that serve to remind one of the transgressions of a former existence. Ah the wretchedness of it all!

A Historical Appraisal

IVAN MORRIS

Given the scanty facts we have about Murasaki's life, how can we put together even a biographical sketch? The answer is to take those few facts we do have and extrapolate from them and from passages in her two most important books, the *Diary* and *The Tale of Genji*—in short, to find the author in her work.

This is a nearly irresistible temptation when dealing with the author of one of the world's greatest literary works, and many scholars have done it. One of the most successful was Ivan Morris, from whose *The World of the Shining Prince: Court Life in Ancient Japan* the following passage is taken.

'Pretty yet shy, shrinking from sight, unsociable, fond of old tales, conceited, so wrapped up in poetry that other people hardly exist, spitefully looking down on the whole world—such is the unpleasant opinion that people have of me. Yet when they come to know me they say that I am strangely gentle, quite unlike what they had been led to

---

[6]Amitābha (or Amida) was a Buddhist deity.—ED.

believe. I know that people look down on me like some old outcast, but I have become accustomed to all this, and tell myself, "My nature is as it is." '

This is one of the few parts of her diary in which Murasaki turns her acute power of description towards herself. It is a revealing passage. She was what would nowadays be labelled as an introvert and, typically, she was convinced that people misunderstood her. The diary suggests that Murasaki got little pleasure from the casual social relations, the gossip, and the badinage that occupied most of the other ladies at court. She had the reputation of being virtuous (an unusual one in her circle), and we have reason to believe that she was something of a prude. . . .

To what extent does Murasaki's life provide a clue to her character? Our fund of facts about Japan's first and greatest novelist is soon exhausted. She was born in the seventies of the tenth century into a minor, though very literary, branch of the Fujiwara family. From her earliest youth she lived in a cultured atmosphere among people well versed in the classics, whose pastime it was to compose elegant, if not very original, verses in Chinese. Her father, Tametoki, was an ambitious and fairly successful official, who started his career as a student of literature preparing for what roughly corresponds to a D.Lit. degree. He had slowly worked his way up the government hierarchy, largely thanks to the influence of his kinsman, the all-powerful Michinaga, to whom he regularly sent appeals in the form of stereotyped Chinese poetry. Tametoki's grandfather was a poet of some note and he in turn was the great-grandson of Fuyutsugu, an illustrious statesman and *littérateur,* who had greatly contributed to establishing the fortunes of the Fujiwara family in the early part of the preceding century. In short, Murasaki had the advantage of belonging to a family with a long tradition of scholarly and artistic interests.

Tametoki had great ambitions for his eldest son and made sure that he had all the benefits of a classical education. A knowledge of Chinese history and literature was essential for any worth-while political career, and in Murasaki's diary father and son are described poring over Ssu-ma Ch'ien's *Historical Records.* For women this type of study was far from being an asset. Many of the court ladies had a smattering of classical knowledge, but anything more serious might label a woman as being unconventional and, worse still, a bluestocking. This prejudice did not deter Murasaki, and we find her profiting from her brother's studies to learn what she could herself. Tametoki does not appear to have prevented his daughter from indulging in these odd pursuits, but it is doubtful whether he encouraged her. On one unfortunate occasion (mentioned in the diary) he observed his two children at their lessons and realized that Mura-saki was more adept at memorizing Chinese characters than her brother. This inspired the well-known lament, 'If only you were a boy, how happy I should be!' Nobunori, the brother in question, entered government service with a post in the Ministry of Ceremo-nial (where his father had also served); later he was attached to his father's staff in the province of Echigo, where he died in about 1013 at an early age. Like most well-bred young men of his time he wrote conventional poetry.

We know little about Murasaki's youth. It seems likely that a good deal of her time was devoted to reading and study; for she became familiar with the standard Chinese and Buddhist classics and was also widely read in the literature of her own country. This may well have deterred potential suitors. In any case she was not betrothed until about twenty, an advanced age for girls of her time. It was of course a *mariage de convenance:* her husband was a kinsman and appears to have been considerably older.

It did not last long. In 1001 (the first fairly definite date in Mura-saki's life) her husband died, probably in an epidemic. . . .

For five years after her husband's death Murasaki lived at home in retirement, and it was almost certainly during this period that she began work on her novel. In 1004 her father's poems finally pro-duced the desired effect and he was appointed governor of the province of Echizen, some eighty miles from the capital. Shortly thereafter he arranged for his daughter to enter court as maid-of-honour to Michinaga's daughter, the nineteen-year-old consort of the young Emperor Ichijō. Murasaki began her diary in 1008 and kept it for about two years. It gives a vivid picture of her life at court, but does not help us to fix any accurate chronology; for the Heian diary was an impressionistic literary form rather than a sys-tematic record of events.

Ichijō died in 1011 at the age of thirty-one and was succeeded by his first cousin. The Empress, accompanied by her suite (in which Murasaki was presumably included), moved to one of the 'detached palaces' and embarked on her sixty-year period of staid retirement. In the same year Murasaki's father was made governor of the large northern province of Echigo. His son joined him there, but died after a couple of years. . . .

During all this time we know absolutely nothing about the life of Murasaki Shikibu. There is little factual basis for the traditional view that she became a nun in 1015 and died in 1031. On the other hand, there is some evidence that she continued in the service of the Empress Dowager; for *Tales of Glory,* in an entry dated the eighth month of 1025, speaks of 'Echigo no Ben, daughter of Murasaki

Shikibu, a lady-in-waiting at court'. Six years later, however, Mura-saki's name is conspicuously absent from a list of ladies who are mentioned as having travelled in the Empress Dowager's suite on a flower-viewing expedition. It is probable, then, though by no means certain, that Murasaki either died or retired into the seclusion of a convent at some time between 1025 and 1031 at the age of about fifty.

While we have few facts about Murasaki's life, the diary and *The Tale of Genji* do provide ample evidence about her knowledge and her experience of the world. Even the most cursory reading of the novel will suggest how intimately she was acquainted with the aristocratic life of her time, not only at court, but in town mansions and in remoter houses beyond the limits of the capital. Murasaki had keenly observed how different kinds of men and women spoke and behaved, and she had tried to enter into their feelings and to know why they acted as they did. She was sensitive to the natural surroundings in which these people lived and to the subtle effects that these surroundings had on them. Possibly she deserved her reputation for being virtuous (though Michinaga, for one, doubted it); but this did not prevent her from being keenly interested in love between men and women and in all the conflicting emotions and other complexities that it involved. Indeed many people have regarded her novel as primarily a study of the varied manifestations of sexual and romantic love. . . .

We know from the diary that Murasaki's interest in Chinese literature was no youthful whim. Her husband was a specialist in the subject and at his death he appears to have left a substantial Chinese library. Murasaki mentions that she would occasionally read some of the volumes to while away the long days when she was on leave from court and living at her father's house. Since Chinese studies were socially taboo for her sex, Murasaki's maids expressed dismay, mingled with dire forebodings, when they observed their mistress at this unorthodox pastime: 'My women gather round me and say, "Madam, if you go on like this, there won't be much happiness in store for you. Why should you read books in Chinese characters? In the old days they wouldn't even let women read the sutras." '

At court Murasaki was at great pains to hide her knowledge of the foreign classics; and fear that the other ladies would find out about her interests (as of course they did) seems to have become a sort of complex. The young empress was also eager to explore these illicit realms, and Murasaki mentions that for some years she has clandestinely been teaching her mistress parts of Po Chü-i's collected works when no one else was present.

If Murasaki had a fair knowledge of Chinese literature—or rather, of that somewhat scattered selection of Chinese literature that circulated in Heian Kyō—she was well versed in the writing of her own country, and we can assume that she was familiar with the principal Japanese works until her time. The diary tells us that when *The Tale of Genji* was read to Emperor Ichijō he commented, 'The person who wrote this must have been reading *The Chronicles of Japan* and is surely very learned'. The Emperor's remark was no doubt well intentioned, but it was responsible for Murasaki's acquiring the nickname of 'the lady of the Chronicles' (*Nihongi no tsubone*), which she so greatly resented.

Apart from historical works and official court annals, Murasaki was well acquainted with the wealth of Japanese poetry beginning with the vast *Manyō Shū* anthology (*The Collection of Ten Thousand Leaves*) compiled in the eighth century. She was widely read in the vernacular *kanabun* literature, which had developed so brilliantly during the first two centuries of the Heian period—the diaries, the travel records, and the miscellaneous jottings, of which only a small portion has survived to the present day. Above all, she must have used her long leisure hours at home to steep herself in those voluminous tales or romances known as *monogatari*, the form in which she was to establish her own name.

Murasaki's diary throws considerable light on her knowledge of Buddhism and on her attitude to religion. Her writing shows that she knew a great deal about the intricate Buddhist ceremonial, its hierarchy, and its monastic orders; and we have evidence that she was familiar, not only with the official writings of Tendai (the sect with which she was mainly associated), but with the names, and to some extent the contents, of the other principal scriptures that were known in Japan. Above all, she shows herself to have been imbued with the underlying spirit of Buddhism common to all the sects—the sense of universal impermanence. This is reflected in the thoughts and words of her principal characters; and in the diary itself we find a direct and moving affirmation of faith:

> 'All the things of this world are sad and tiresome. But from now on I shall fear nothing. Whatever others may do or say, I shall recite my prayers tirelessly to Amida Buddha. And when in my mind the things of this world have come to assume no more importance or stability than the vanishing dew, then I shall exert all my efforts to become a wise and holy person.' . . .

Finally, what were the circumstances under which Murasaki wrote her novel? . . .

We know from references in the diary that at least part of the book was being circulated at court in 1008. In describing a party given to celebrate the birth of the Empress' first child, Murasaki mentions this incident: ' "Well, now," said the Captain of the Outer Palace Guards, "I expect that little Murasaki must be about here somewhere." "There's no one here like Genji," thought I to myself, "so what should Murasaki be doing in this place?" ' . . .

Some of the events in the novel seem to have been taken from things that actually happened at court in 1013 and 1017, but this cannot be accepted as positive evidence. The only other reliable date occurs in the *Sarashina Diary*.[7] I quote the passage at some length, since it gives a good idea of the impression that Murasaki's book made on one young girl at the time, and also of how hard it was to come by a copy:

> 'I read *Waka Murasaki* and a few of the other [early] books in *The Tale of Genji*, and I longed to see the later parts. . . . But we were still new to the capital and it was not easy to find copies. I was burning with impatience and curiosity, and in my prayers I used to say, "Let me see the whole!" When my parents went to the Kōryū Temple for a retreat, this was the only thing I asked for. Yet all my hopes were in vain.
>
> 'I was feeling most dejected about it when one day I called on an aunt of mine who had come up from the country. She received me very affectionately and showed the greatest interest in me. "What a pretty girl you've grown up to be!" said she. Then, as I was leaving, she asked, "What would you like as a present? I am sure you don't want anything too practical. I'd like to give you something that you will really enjoy."
>
> 'And so it was that she presented me with fifty-odd volumes of *The Tale of Genji* in a special case, together with [numerous other *monogatari*]. Oh, how happy I was when I came home with all these books in a bag! In the past I had only been able to have an occasional flurried look at parts of *The Tale of Genji*. Now I had it all in front of me and I could lie undisturbed behind my screen, taking the books out one by one and enjoying them to my heart's content. I wouldn't have changed places with the Empress herself.'

Since *The Tale of Genji* consists of fifty-four books, this would seem to be fairly good evidence that most of the novel, if not all, was completed and in circulation by 1022, the date to which this passage refers. It seems plausible that Murasaki started writing shortly after her husband's death when she was living at home, say in about 1002, and that she continued with occasional interruptions during her long period of service at court until about 1020, when she had completed some fifty books.

---

[7]This was another contemporary diary, that of a thirteen-year-old girl, also preserved, like Murasaki's.—Ed.

Review and Study Questions

1. How does Murasaki's writing reflect her society? How does it reflect her own private life?
2. What was the status of women in Heian Japan?
3. How did Murasaki's devout Buddhism affect her outlook on life?

Suggestions for Further Reading

The standard English translation of *The Tale of Genji* was done by Arthur Waley in 1935. See *The Tale of Genji: A Novel in Six Parts* by Lady Murasaki, tr. Arthur Waley (New York: Modern Library, 1960). It was the first English translation of the work and had come to be regarded as a classic of English literature. But it is limited in several serious ways. Waley was arbitrary and often followed his personal views rather than the text. He sometimes mistranslated passages or simply ignored sections of the text that he did not agree with. A better translation is Murasaki Shikibu, *The Tale of Genji*, tr. Edward G. Seidensticker (New York: Knopf, 1976), excerpted for this chapter. This stays much closer to the text and picks up its fundamental ironic undertones. Marian Ury, reviewing the book in *Harvard Journal of Asiatic Studies*, 37 (1977), 201, insists that this is the first true representation of the Genji in English. The best edition of the *Diary* is that excerpted for this chapter, Richard Bowring, *Murasaki Shikibu: Her Diary and Poetic Memoirs, A Translation and Study* (Princeton: Princeton University Press, 1982). There is an older edition of the *Diary*, among other works in *Diaries of Court Ladies of Old Japan*, tr. Annie Shepley Omori and Kochi Doi, intro. Amy Lowell (Tokyo: Kenkusha, 1935). This work, however, is somewhat inferior to Bowring's and has much less substantial editorial apparatus and notes.

The best interpretive work on Murasaki and her works is Ivan Morris, *The World of the Shining Prince: Court Life in Ancient Japan* (New York: Knopf, 1964), excerpted for this chapter. There are also several specialized studies that are useful for various aspects of her life and work. Two are in *Medieval Japan: Essays in Institutional History*, ed. John W. Hall and Jeffrey P. Mass (New Haven and London: Yale University Press, 1974): G. Cameron Hurst III, "The Structure of the Heian Court: Some Thoughts on the Nature of 'Familial Authority' in Heian Japan," and John W. Hall, "Kyoto as Historical Background." Another useful study is William H. McCullough, "Japanese Marriage Institutions in the Heian Period," *Harvard Journal of Asiatic Studies*, 27 (1967), 103–67. Another is *Ukifune: Love in The Tale of Genji*, ed. Andrew Pekarik (New York: Columbia University Press, 1982).

Among the historical studies of Murasaki's period, one of the best is George Sansom, *A History of Japan to 1334* (Stanford: Stanford University Press, 1958). Another is Robert Karl Reischauer, *Early Japanese History (c. 40 B.C.–A.D. 1167), Part A* (Princeton and Oxford: Princeton University Press and Oxford University Press, 1937). Especially recommended is the brief and readable Jonathan Norton Leonard, *Early Japan* (New York: Time–Life Books, 1968), a volume in the "Great Ages of Man" series. A respected general history that can be recommended is by Edwin O. Reischauer, *Japan: The Story of a Nation*, rev. ed. (New York: Knopf, 1974), the great American interpreter of things Japanese.

There are no full-scale biographies of Murasaki in English or in any other western language and only two in Japanese, both of them roundly criticized by western scholars.

ELEANOR OF AQUITAINE
AND THE
WRATH OF GOD

c. 1122	Born
1137	Married the future Louis VII of France
1147–1149	Second crusade
1152	Divorced from Louis VII and married to the future Henry II of England
1192–1194	Regent during captivity of Richard I
1204	Died

Eleanor of Aquitaine was one of the most remarkable and important figures in medieval history. In her own right, she was duchess of the vast domain of Aquitaine and countess of Poitou, the wife first of Louis VII of France and then of Henry II of England, the mother of "good King Richard" and "bad King John," patroness of poets and minstrels. Tradition remembers her as beautiful and passionate, headstrong and willful. But beyond that intriguing traditional reputation, she is a figure only imperfectly seen and, ironically enough, seen at all largely through the accounts of her enemies.

The sources of medieval history are scanty at best and tend, moreover, to record men's doings in a preponderantly man's world. Even the greatest of medieval women appear in the records of their time as conveyors of properties and channels for noble blood lines, and we know of them only that they were "good and faithful wives"—or that they were not. So it is with Eleanor. We do not even have a contemporary description of her. Troubadour poets sang rapturously of her "crystal cheeks," her "locks like threads of gold," her eyes "like Orient pearls." One even proclaims:

> Were the world all mine,
> From the sea to the Rhine,
> I'd give it all

　　　　　　　If so be the Queen of England
　　　　　　　Lay in my arms.

In sober fact, we do not know what color her eyes were, nor her hair, whether it was indeed "like threads of gold" or raven black. Even the few pictorial representations we have of her—including her tomb effigy at the Abbey of Fontevrault—are purely conventional.

　　But Eleanor's part in the great events of her time was real enough. It began with her marriage, at the age of fifteen, to Louis the young king, son of Louis VI (Louis the Fat) of France. Her father, the turbulent Duke William X of Aquitaine, had died suddenly and unexpectedly on pilgrimage to Spain, leaving Eleanor his heir. And, in feudal law, the disposition of both Eleanor and her fiefs was a matter to be decided by her father's overlord, Louis VI of France. Duke William had been Louis's most intractable vassal, and his death was a priceless opportunity not only to put an end to the contumaciousness of Aquitaine but to tie that large and wealthy duchy to the French realm. Louis decided that the interests of his house were best served by the marriage of Eleanor to his son. And so, it was done. There is no record of how either the young bride or the young groom responded, only an account of the brilliant assemblage that gathered to witness the ceremony in Bordeaux and to accompany the couple back by weary stages to Paris. In the course of this journey, the aged King Louis died. His son was now Louis VII, the Duchess Eleanor now queen of France. The year was 1137.

　　We must not imagine that Eleanor was a very happy bride in those first years of her marriage. Paris was a cold and gloomy northern city, very different from sunny Provence, and the Capetian castles in which she lived were dark and uncomfortable. The king—her husband— had an inexhaustible thirst for devotion and piety and surrounded himself with ecclesiastical advisers, confessors, theologians, and barren, quibbling scholars, so unlike the more robust and charming practitioners of the *gai savoir* (merry learning) with whom Eleanor had grown up at her father's court. Nor was Louis very happy, for he and his young wife had two daughters, Marie and Alix, but no son, no member of what was then considered "the better sex" to be groomed for the Capetian throne.

　　Then word reached Paris of the fall of Edessa in the distant Latin Kingdom of Jerusalem, one of those fortress principalities to secure the Holy Land dating from the first crusade almost half a century before. The resurgence of Muslim power was clearly seen to threaten the Holy Land, and the call for a second crusade went out. The pious King Louis took the cross—to the consternation of his more realistic advisers. And Eleanor insisted upon accompanying him. Whatever

Louis and his fellow crusaders may have thought about this matter, Eleanor's position as a great vassal who could summon a substantial host of warriors from her own lands made her support crucial: and her support was contingent upon her going in person. There is a persistent legend that the queen and her ladies decked themselves out as Amazons in anticipation of their role in the coming military adventure.

But the military adventure itself turned into a military disaster. The second crusade was a dismal failure. The French forces of Louis VII were seriously defeated by the Turks, and the German contingent led by the Emperor Conrad III was almost wiped out. Both the French and the Germans accused the Byzantine Greeks of treachery. There were disagreements among the Western knights, and many of them simply abandoned the crusade and returned home. There were divided counsels among those who remained and mistrust between them and the Christian lords of the Eastern principalities. And there were continued military blunders and defeats. Tempers were short, old quarrels flared, new ones commenced.

In this atmosphere, what had apparently been a growing estrangement between King Louis and Queen Eleanor became an open break. Their troubles were aggravated by what was then considered the boldness and outspokenness of the queen and in particular by her attentions to her handsome uncle, only eight years older than she, Raymond of Poitiers, Prince of Antioch. It may have been no more than an innocent flirtation. But Louis thought otherwise. He brooded not only on his queen's conduct but on what he perceived as her failure to produce a son for him, and his mind turned to divorce, the grounds for which were to be found in consanguinity, a marriage within the prohibited degree of blood relationship, which was the usual legal pretext for the dissolution of feudal marriages no longer bearable or profitable.

Eleanor and the Chroniclers

WILLIAM OF TYRE
AND JOHN OF SALISBURY

Eleanor's role in the second crusade is scarcely mentioned by the chroniclers who recorded the deeds of its other leading figures. Odo of Deuil, a monk of the French royal monastery of St. Denis and the chaplain of Louis VII, wrote the most detailed account of Louis's part in the crusade—*De profectione Ludovici VII in orientem*—but he makes only four passing references to the queen in the entire narrative. Odo clearly had reason to favor the cause of the king, his master. And, for one reason or another, so did the few other chroniclers who give any account at all of the estrangement between Louis and Eleanor. The most detailed is that of William, Archbishop of Tyre. William is generally regarded as the best of all the chroniclers of the crusades, but he was not present at the time of this crisis and we do not know what source he used. In any event, he regarded the behavior of the queen and the resulting breach with her husband as part of a cynical attempt by Raymond of Antioch to turn the crusade to his own advantage. Here is the account of William of Tyre.

For many days Raymond, prince of Antioch, had eagerly awaited the arrival of the king of the Franks. When he learned that the king had landed in his domains, he summoned all the nobles of the land and the chief leaders of the people and went out to meet him with a chosen escort. He greeted the king with much reverence and conducted him with great pomp into the city of Antioch, where he was met by the clergy and the people. Long before this time—in fact, as soon as he heard that Louis was coming—Raymond had conceived the idea that by his aid he might be able to enlarge the principality of Antioch. With this in mind, therefore, even before the king started on the pilgrimage, the prince had sent to him in France a large store of noble gifts and treasures of great price in the hope of winning his favor. He also counted greatly on the interest of the queen with the lord king, for she had been his inseparable companion on his pilgrimage. She was Raymond's niece, and eldest daughter of Count William of Poitou, his brother.

As we have said, therefore, Raymond showed the king every attention on his arrival. He likewise displayed a similar care for the nobles and chief men in the royal retinue and gave them many proofs of his great liberality. In short, he outdid all in showing honor to each one according to his rank and handled everything with the greatest magnificence. He felt a lively hope that with the assistance of the king and his troops he would be able to subjugate the neighboring cities, namely, Aleppo, Shayzar, and several others. Nor would this hope have been futile, could he have induced the king and his chief men to undertake the work. For the arrival of King Louis had brought such fear to our enemies that now they not only distrusted their own strength but even despaired of life itself.

Raymond had already more than once approached the king privately in regard to the plans which he had in mind. Now he came before the members of the king's suite and his own nobles and explained with due formality how his request could be accomplished without difficulty and at the same time be of advantage and renown to themselves. The king, however, ardently desired to go to Jerusalem to fulfil his vows, and his determination was irrevocable. When Raymond found that he could not induce the king to join him, his attitude changed. Frustrated in his ambitious designs, he began to hate the king's ways; he openly plotted against him and took means to do him injury. He resolved also to deprive him of his wife, either by force or by secret intrigue. The queen readily assented to this design, for she was a foolish woman. Her conduct before and after this time showed her to be, as we have said, far from circumspect. Contrary to her royal dignity, she disregarded her marriage vows and was unfaithful to her husband.

As soon as the king discovered these plots, he took means to provide for his life and safety by anticipating the designs of the prince. By the advice of his chief nobles, he hastened his departure and secretly left Antioch with his people. Thus the splendid aspect of his affairs was completely changed, and the end was quite unlike the beginning. His coming had been attended with pomp and glory; but fortune is fickle, and his departure was ignominious.

The only other substantial account of the events leading to the divorce of Louis and Eleanor is that of the great twelfth-century ecclesiastic and intellectual, John of Salisbury, in his *Historia Pontificalis*. In one respect, John was even further removed from the events than was William of Tyre. He had no direct knowledge of the East at all and was, at this time, in Rome on a mission from the see of Canterbury and attached to the papal court. We do not know what source he used for the events in Antioch. It is likely that he is simply repeating the story as he heard it from members of Louis's retinue, for the hostility against Eleanor that already animated Louis's close supporters is clearly present in John's account. It is also possible that the hostility of the account and its strong pro-French bias is related to the later time at which John's work was actually written, about 1163. At this time, John was involved in the growing bitterness between Thomas Becket, whom he supported, and Henry II of England, who had just sent John into exile for his support of Becket. John found refuge in France.

But in any event, the account in the *Historia Pontificalis* is strongly favorable to Louis, even to the extent of ascribing to Eleanor the initiative in the proposal for the divorce.

In the year of grace 1149 the most Christian king of the Franks reached Antioch, after the destruction of his armies in the east, and was nobly entertained there by Prince Raymond, brother of the late William, count of Poitiers. He was as it happened the queen's uncle, and owed the king loyalty, affection and respect for many reasons. But whilst they remained there to console, heal and revive the survivors from the wreck of the army, the attentions paid by the prince to the queen, and his constant, indeed almost continuous, conversation with her, aroused the king's suspicions. These were greatly strengthened when the queen wished to remain behind, although the king was preparing to leave, and the prince made every effort to keep her, if the king would give his consent. And when the king made haste to tear her away, she mentioned their kinship, saying it was not lawful for them to remain together as man and wife, since they were related in the fourth and fifth degrees. Even before their departure a rumour to that effect had been heard in France, where the late Bartholomew bishop of Laon had calculated the degrees of kinship; but it was not certain whether the reckoning was true or false. At this the king was deeply moved; and although he loved the queen almost beyond reason he consented to divorce her if his counsellors and the French nobility would allow it. There was one knight amongst the king's secretaries, called Terricus Gualerancius, a eunuch whom the queen had always hated and mocked, but who was faithful and had the king's ear like his father's before him. He boldly persuaded the king not to suffer her to dally longer at Antioch, both because "guilt under kinship's guise could lie concealed," and because it would be a lasting shame to the kingdom of the Franks if in addition to all the other disasters it was reported that the king had been deserted by his wife, or robbed of her. So he argued, either because he hated the queen or because he really believed it, moved perchance by widespread rumour. In consequence, she was torn away and forced to leave for Jerusalem with the king; and, their mutual anger growing greater, the wound remained, hide it as best they might.

In the next passage, John is on more familiar ground since he was in Rome, a familiar of the curia and of Pope Eugenius III, and perhaps even a witness to some of the events he describes.

In the year of grace eleven hundred and fifty the king of the Franks returned home. But the galleys of the Emperor of Constantinople lay in wait for him on his return, capturing the queen and all who were journeying in her ship. The king was appealed to to return to his Byzantine brother and friend, and force was being brought to bear on him when the galleys of the king of Sicily came to the rescue. Freeing the queen and releasing the king, they escorted them back to Sicily rejoicing, with honour and triumph. This was done by order of the king of Sicily, who feared the wiles of the Greeks and desired an opportunity of showing his devotion to the king and queen of the Franks. Now therefore he hastened to meet him with an ample retinue, and escorted him most honourably to Palermo, heaping gifts both on him and on all his followers; thereafter he travelled with him right across his territory to Ceprano, supplying all his needs on the way. This is the last point on the frontier between the principality of Capua and Campania, which is papal territory.

At Ceprano the cardinals and officials of the church met the king and, providing him with all that he desired, escorted him to Tusculum to the lord pope, who received him with such tenderness and reverence that one would have said he was welcoming an angel of the Lord rather than a mortal man. He reconciled the king and queen, after hearing severally the accounts each gave of the estrangement begun at Antioch, and forbade any future mention of their consanguinity: confirming their marriage, both orally and in writing, he commanded under pain of anathema that no word should be spoken against it and that it should not be dissolved under any pretext whatever. This ruling plainly delighted the king, for he loved the queen passionately, in an almost childish way. The pope made them sleep in the same bed, which he had had decked with priceless hangings of his own; and daily during their brief visit he strove by friendly converse to restore love between them. He heaped gifts upon them; and when the moment for departure came, though he was a stern man, he could not hold back his tears, but sent them on their way blessing them and the kingdom of the Franks, which was higher in his esteem than all the kingdoms of the world.

Eleanor, the Queen of Hearts

AMY KELLY

Despite "the lord pope's" good offices, his tears and his blessing, even his threat of anathema, the estrangement between Louis and Eleanor continued. Louis was adamant, and finally, in the spring of 1152 at a solemn synod in Beaugency on the Loire, Louis's representatives argued the case of the consanguinity of their lord and his queen, and the Archbishop of Sens proclaimed their marriage invalid. The Archbishop of Bordeaux, the queen's surrogate, sought only the assurance that her lands be restored. But this had already been arranged, as had all the other details of this elaborate royal charade. Eleanor was not even present. She had already returned to Poitou.

But Eleanor was not destined to reign as a dowager duchess in her own domains. Within two months, she married Henry, Duke of Normandy. He was not only the Norman duke but also the heir to the fiefs of his father, Geoffrey Plantagenet, Count of Maine and Anjou. These already substantial lands, when joined to those of his new bride, made Henry lord of a nearly solid block of territories that stretched from the English Channel to the Mediterranean and from Bordeaux to the Vexin, hardly a day's ride from Paris. At one stroke, Henry of Anjou had become the greatest feudatory of France, with lands and resources many times the size of those held by his nominal overlord, King Louis VII. Two years later, another piece of Henry's inheritance came into his hands. His mother, Matilda, was the daughter of the English King Henry I and had never ceased to press the claim of her son to the English throne. The reign of King Stephen was coming to an end, and he had no surviving heirs. At his death in 1154, Henry of Anjou claimed his crown, and there was none to deny him. Eleanor was a queen once more.

But this time, she had a very different king. Henry II was as godless as Louis had been pious, as flamboyant as Louis had been humble. Where Louis was stubborn and persistent, Henry was furiously energetic and decisive. The setting was at hand for one of the classic confrontations of medieval history that was to stretch into the following generation of the kings of both France and England.

As for Eleanor, the sources are once more almost silent. We do know that she and Henry produced a large family. The eldest son, William, born before the succession to England, died in childhood. But in 1155 came Henry; in 1156, their first daughter, Matilda; in 1157 came Richard, to be called the Lion Hearted; in 1158 came Geoffrey; in 1161, Eleanor; in 1165, Johanna; and in 1166, John. We know that through the early years of her marriage to Henry, Eleanor was often with him at court and sometimes presided in his absence, a fact attested by writs and seals. But her marriage was by no means serene. There were long periods of separation during which the king was known to be unfaithful. The incidents of his infidelity had grown more flagrant with the passing years. At about the time of Prince John's birth in 1166, Henry was involved with a paramour of spectacular beauty, Rosamond Clifford. Their affair was the object of such celebration by poets, balladeers, and wags alike that Eleanor may have decided that her bed and her dignity could no longer endure such an affront. But there may have been other matters at issue. The queen may have become alarmed at her husband's efforts to substitute his rule for hers in her dower lands.

In any case, about 1170 she returned to Poitou with her favorite son, Richard, whom she installed as her heir for the lands of Poitou and Aquitaine. For the next three or four years she lived in her old capital of Poitiers, separated from her husband. In these years of self-imposed exile, Eleanor not only reasserted her rights to her own lands, but created a center in Poitiers for the practice of the troubadour culture and *l'amour courtois* that had long been associated with her family.

The following passage, from Amy Kelly's *Eleanor of Aquitaine and the Four Kings*—the book that has come to be regarded as the standard work on Eleanor—is a brilliant reconstruction of this period of Eleanor's life.

When the countess of Poitou settled down to rule her own heritage, she took her residence in Poitiers, which offered a wide eye-sweep on the world of still operative kings. In the recent Plantagenet building program her ancestral city, the seat and necropolis of her forebears, had been magnificently enlarged and rebuilt, and it stood at her coming thoroughly renewed, a gleaming exemplar of urban elegance. The site rose superbly amidst encircling rivers. Its narrow Merovingian area had lately been extended to include with new and ampler walls parishes that had previously straggled over its outer slopes; ancient quarters had been cleared of immemorial decay; new churches and collegials had sprung up; the cathedral of Saint Pierre was enriched; markets and shops of tradesmen and artisans bore witness to renewed life among the *bourgeoisie;* bridges fanned out to suburbs and monastic establishments lying beyond the streams that moated the city. Brimming with sunshine, the valleys ebbed far away below—hamlet and croft, mill and vineyard—to a haze as blue as the vintage. . . .

When Eleanor came in about 1170 to take full possession of her newly restored city of Poitiers and to install her favorite son there as ruling count and duke in her own patrimony, she was no mere game piece as were most feudal women, to be moved like a queen in chess. She had learned her role as *domina* in Paris, Byzantium, Antioch, London, and Rouen, and knew her value in the feudal world. She was prepared of her own unguided wisdom to reject the imperfect destinies to which she had been, as it were, assigned. In this, her third important role in history, she was the pawn of neither prince nor prelate, the victim of no dynastic scheme. She came as her own mistress, the most sophisticated of women, equipped with plans to establish her own assize, to inaugurate a regime dedicated neither to Mars nor to the Pope, nor to any king, but to Minerva, Venus, and the Virgin. She was resolved to escape from secondary roles, to assert her independent sovereignty in her own citadel, to dispense her own justice, her own patronage, and when at leisure, to survey, like the Empress of Byzantium, a vast decorum in her precincts. . . .

The heirs of Poitou and Aquitaine who came to the queen's high place for their vassals' homage, their squires' training, and their courtiers' service, were truculent youths, boisterous young men from the baronial strongholds of the south without the Norman or Frankish sense of nationality, bred on feuds and violence, some of them with rich fiefs and proud lineage, but with little solidarity and no business but local warfare and daredevil escapade. The custom of lateral rather than vertical inheritance of fiefs in vogue in some parts of Poitou and Aquitaine—the system by which lands passed through a whole generation before descending to the next generation—produced a vast number of landless but expectant younger men, foot-loose, unemployed, ambitious, yet dependent upon the reluctant bounty of uncles and brothers, or their own violent exploits. These wild young men were a deep anxiety not only to the heads of their houses, but to the Kings of France and England and to the Pope in Rome. They were the stuff of which rebellion and schism are made. For two generations the church had done what it could with the problem of their unemployment, marching hordes out of Europe on crusade and rounding other hordes into the cloister.

It was with this spirited world of princes and princesses, of apprentice knights and chatelaines, at once the school and the court of young Richard, that the duchess, busy as she was with the multifarious business of a feudal suzerain, had to deal in her palace in Poitiers. . . .

Eleanor found a willing and helpful deputy to assist her in the person of Marie, Countess of Champagne, her daughter by Louis of France. Marie, now entrusted to Eleanor's tutelage, was a well-educated young woman and apparently well disposed to her mother's plans.

. . . The character of the milieu which Marie appears to have set up in Poitiers suggests a genuine sympathy between the queen and her daughter who had so long been sundered by the bleak fortuities of life. Old relationships were knit up. Something native blossomed in the countess, who shone with a special luster in her mother's court. The young Count of Poitou learned to love particularly his half sister Marie and forever to regard the Poitiers of her dispensation as the world's citadel of valor, the seat of courtesy, and the fountainhead of poetic inspiration. Long after, in his darkest hours, it was to her good graces he appealed. The countess, having carte blanche to proceed with the very necessary business of getting control of her academy, must have striven first for order. Since the miscellaneous and high-spirited young persons in her charge had not learned order from the liturgy nor yet from hagiography, the countess bethought her, like many an astute pedagogue, to deduce her principles from something more germane to their interests. She did not precisely invent her regime; rather she appropriated it from the abundant resources at her hand.

The liberal court of Eleanor had again drawn a company of those gifted persons who thrive by talent or by art. Poets, *conteurs* purveying romance, ecclesiastics with Latin literature at their tongues' end and mere clerks with smatterings of Ovid learned from quotation books, chroniclers engaged upon the sober epic of the Plantagenets, came to their haven in Poitiers. The queen and the countess, with their native poetic tradition, were the natural patrons of the troubadours. It will be seen that the Countess Marie's resources were rich and abundant, but not so formalized as to afford the disciplines for a royal academy nor give substance to a social ritual. The great hall was ready for her grand assize; the expectant court already thronged to gape at its suggestive splendors. . . .

At least one other important source Marie employed. She levied upon the social traditions of her Poitevin forebears. Nostredame relates that in Provence chatelaines were accustomed to entertain their seasonal assemblies with so-called "courts of love," in which, just as feudal vassals brought their grievances to the assizes of their overlords for regulation, litigants in love's thrall brought their problems for the judgment of the ladies. André in his famous work[1] makes reference to antecedent decisions in questions of an amatory nature by "les dames de Gascogne," and the poetry of the troubadours presupposes a milieu in which their doctrines of homage and deference could be exploited. Thus we have in Andre's *Tractatus* the framework of Ovid with the central emphasis reversed, the Arthurian code of manners, the southern ritual of the "courts of love," all burnished with a golden wash of troubadour poetry learned by the queen's forebears and their vassals in the deep Midi, probably beyond the barrier of the Pyrenees. Marie made these familiar materials the vehicle for her woman's doctrine of civility, and in so doing, she transformed the gross and cynical pagan doctrines of Ovid into something more ideal, the woman's canon, the chivalric code of manners. Manners, she plainly saw, were after all the fine residuum of philosophies, the very flower of ethics. . . .

With this anatomy of the whole corpus of love in hand, Marie organized the rabble of soldiers, fighting cocks, jousters, springers, riding masters, troubadours, Poitevin nobles and debutantes, young chatelaines, adolescent princes, and infant princesses in the great hall of Poitiers. Of this pandemonium the countess fashioned a seemly and elegant society, the fame of which spread to the world. Here was a woman's assize to draw men from the excitements of the tilt and the hunt, from dice and games to feminine society, an assize to outlaw boorishness and compel the tribute of adulation to female majesty. . . .

While the ladies, well-accoutered, sit above upon the dais, the sterner portion of society purged, according to the code, from the odors of the kennels and the highway and free for a time from spurs and falcons, range themselves about the stone benches that line the walls, stirring the fragrant rushes with neatly pointed shoe. There are doubtless preludes of music luring the last reluctant knight from the gaming table, *tensons* or *pastourelles*, the plucking of rotes, the "voicing of a fair song and sweet," perhaps even some of the more complicated

---

[1]André, simply known as the Chaplain, a scholar of this court whose work *Tractatus de Amore* is referred to here, one of the basic works on medieval chivalry and the courts of love.—Ed.

musical harmonies so ill-received by the clerical critics in London; a Breton *lai* adding an episode to Arthurian romance, or a chapter in the tale of "sad-man" Tristram, bringing a gush of tears from the tender audience clustered about the queen and the Countess of Champagne.

After the romance of the evening in the queen's court, the jury comes to attention upon petition of a young knight in the hall. He bespeaks the judgment of the queen and her ladies upon a point of conduct, through an advocate, of course, so he may remain anonymous. A certain knight, the advocate deposes, has sworn to his lady, as the hard condition of obtaining her love, that he will upon no provocation boast of her merits in company. But one day he overhears detractors heaping his mistress with calumnies. Forgetting his vow in the heat of his passion, he warms to eloquence in defense of his lady. This coming to her ears, she repudiates her champion. Does the lover, who admits he has broken his pledge to his mistress, deserve in this instance to be driven from her presence?

The Countess of Champagne, subduing suggestions from the floor and the buzz of conference upon the dais, renders the judgment of the areopagus. The lady in the case, anonymous of course, is at fault, declares the Countess Marie. She has laid upon her lover a vow too impossibly difficult. The lover has been remiss, no doubt, in breaking his vow to his mistress, no matter what cruel hardship it involves; but he deserves leniency for the merit of his ardor and his constancy. The jury recommends that the stern lady reinstate the plaintiff. The court takes down the judgment. It constitutes a precedent. Does anyone guess the identity of the young pair whose estrangement is thus delicately knit up by the countess? As a bit of suspense it is delicious. As a theme for talk, how loosening to the tongue!

A disappointed petitioner brings forward a case, through an advocate, involving the question whether love survives marriage. The countess, applying her mind to the code, which says that marriage is no proper obstacle to lovers (*Causa coniugii ab amore non est excusatio recta*), and after grave deliberation with her ladies, creates a sensation in the court by expressing doubt whether love in the ideal sense can exist between spouses. This is so arresting a proposition that the observations of the countess are referred to the queen for corroboration, and all wait upon the opinion of this deeply experienced judge. The queen with dignity affirms that she cannot gainsay the Countess of Champagne, though she finds it admirable that a wife should find love and marriage consonant. Eleanor, Queen of France and then of England, had learned at fifty-two that, as another medieval lady put it, "Mortal love is but the licking of honey from thorns."

Eleanor the Regent

MARION MEADE

During the years of Eleanor's dalliance at Poitiers, her husband's larger world had been turned upside down by his quarrel with Thomas Becket. It had not ended even with the martyrdom of that troublesome prelate at the altar of Canterbury in 1170. The question of whether Henry ordered Becket's murder or not—and he probably did not—is quite immaterial. For he bore its consequences. And its principal consequence was to give to the French king a priceless justification to move against Henry and his fiefs. What is more, Henry's own sons were as often as not in league with the French king. With some of them, Henry had been too hard, with others too soft. And when he favored one, the others feared and plotted against the favorite of the moment. Even Henry's proposed disposition of his estates and titles served only to further their quarrels with each other and with him. These quarrels reached their first climax in the great rebellion of 1173, in which Henry the young king, Richard, and Geoffrey were in open alliance with Louis of France against their father. To the alliance flocked rebellious barons from Scotland to Aquitaine. Henry charged Eleanor with sedition and with embittering their sons against him. As the rebellion faltered and then was quelled, Henry was reconciled, however fitfully, with his sons but not their mother. With Eleanor, Henry was unyielding. She was imprisoned, first at Salisbury Castle, later at Winchester and other places, for the next sixteen years. One must imagine that the captivity was genteel, but it was nonetheless real. From time to time, she was released for a holiday visit to court or to participate in some stormy family council.

In the last years of Eleanor's imprisonment, two of her sons, Henry and Geoffrey, died, but the surviving sons, Richard and John, could still intrigue against their father. They did so in league with a new and more dangerous Capetian enemy, Philip II Augustus, the able and energetic son of Louis VII, who had followed him to the throne in 1180. Henry II's final years were filled with his sons' rebellion, and he died in 1189 shamed by defeat at their hands. It was only after Henry's death and the succession of Richard that Eleanor was released from her captivity.

With none of her ardor dimmed, the queen, now almost seventy, set about to serve her favored son, now king at last. While Richard was still on the Continent, Eleanor assumed the regency and on her own authority convoked a court at Westminster to demand the oaths of loyalty from the English feudality to their new king. She then traveled to other centers to take similar obeisances and to set the affairs of the kingdom in order. Her son arrived for an undisputed coronation in the summer of 1189.

But Richard's thoughts in that triumphal summer season were not upon the affairs of England or any of his other lands. He had already taken the cross almost two years before, and the third crusade was about to begin. The Lion Hearted was to be its greatest hero.

The third crusade, despite Richard's heroics, was as unsuccessful as the second. And, after three years, during which most of his fellow crusaders had declared their vows discharged and returned to their own lands—including his Capetian rival, Philip Augustus— Richard started for home.

We pick up the story of his return—with its delays and betrayals —and of Eleanor's role in it from her recent biography, by Marion Meade, *Eleanor of Aquitaine: A Biography.* Meade's book is broadly revisionist, and the basis of her revisionism is her feminism. Meade observes that "the historical record, written to accommodate men" has judged Eleanor ". . . a bitch, harlot, adultress, and monster" and that this is not surprising "for she was one of those rare women who altogether refused to be bound by the rules of proper behavior for her sex; she did as she pleased, although not without agonizing personal struggle" (p. ix). In Meade's account, as in any other account of Eleanor, there is much latitude for interpretation, given the pervasive silence of contemporary chronicles. Meade further argues that even these are "riddled with lies since monks and historians—in the twelfth century one and the same—have always abhorred emancipated women" (p. xi). Meade intends to redress the balance. And she does so, in no part of her account more forcefully than in the following passage.

In England, Eleanor was expecting her son home for Christmas. All through November and early December companies of Crusaders had begun arriving in the kingdom; in the ports and marketplaces there were firsthand reports of the king's deeds in Palestine and plans for celebrations once he arrived. But the days passed without news, and newly arrived contingents of soldiers expressed astonishment that they had beaten the king home although they had left Acre after Richard. Along the coast, lookouts peered into the foggy Channel in hope of sighting the royal vessel, and messengers waited to race over the frozen roads toward London with the news of the king's landing. Eleanor learned that Berengaria and Joanna[2] had safely reached Rome, but of her son, weeks overdue, there was an alarming lack of information. She held a cheerless Christmas court at Westminster, her apprehension mounting with each day, her silent fears being expressed openly in the ale houses along the Thames: The king had encountered some calamity, a storm along the Adriatic coast no doubt, and now he would never return.

Three days after Christmas, the whereabouts of the tardy Richard Plantagenet became known, not at Westminster but at the Cité Palace in Paris. On December 28, Philip Augustus received an astounding letter from his good friend Henry Hohenstaufen, the Holy Roman emperor:[3]

> We have thought it proper to inform your nobleness that while the enemy of our empire and the disturber of your kingdom, Richard, King of England, was crossing the sea to his dominions, it chanced that the winds caused him to be shipwrecked in the region of Istria, at a place which lies between Aquila and Venice. . . . The roads being duly watched and the entire area well-guarded, our dearly beloved cousin Leopold, Duke of Austria, captured the king in a humble house in a village near Vienna. Inasmuch as he is now in our power, and has always done his utmost for your annoyance and disturbance, we have thought it proper to relay this information to your nobleness.

Shortly after the first of the new year, 1193, the archbishop of Rouen was able to send Eleanor a copy of the letter, accompanied by a covering note in which he cited whatever comforting quotations he could recall from Scripture to cover an outrage of this magnitude.

Eleanor's most imperative problem—finding the location where Richard was being held prisoner—she tackled with her usual energy and resourcefulness. From all points, emissaries were dispatched to find the king: Eleanor herself sent the abbots of Boxley and Pontrobert to roam the villages of Bavaria and Swabia, following every lead and rumor; Hubert Walter, bishop of Salisbury, stopping in Italy on his way home from the Crusade, changed course and hastened to Germany; even William Longchamp, the exiled chancellor, set out at once from

---

[2]Berengaria was Richard's wife—a Spanish princess he had married, at Eleanor's urging, on his way to the crusade. Joanna was Richard's sister, the widowed Queen of Sicily, whom he had taken under his protection to Palestine.—ED.

[3]The Plantagenet kings were related by marriage to the great German feudal family, the Welfs, who were the most dangerous rivals to the imperial house of Hohenstaufen. The Angevins, including Richard, had frequently supported the Welfs, hence the emperor's hostility.—ED.

Paris to trace his master. It was not until March, however, that Richard's chaplain, Anselm, who had shared many of the king's misadventures, arrived in England, and Eleanor was able to obtain authentic details [including the fact that Richard was being held in a remote castle of Durrenstein in Austria].

Treachery was rife not only in Germany but in Paris and Rouen; it even percolated rapidly in the queen's own family. Before Eleanor could take steps to secure Coeur de Lion's release, she was faced with more immediate catastrophes in the form of Philip Augustus and his newest ally, her son John. These two proceeded on the assumption that Richard, king of England, was dead. Or as good as dead. But before Eleanor could take her youngest son in hand, he fled to Normandy, where he declared himself the king's heir, an announcement the Norman barons greeted with disdain. John did not wait to convince them, proceeding instead to Paris, where he did homage to Philip for the Plantagenet Continental domains and furthermore agreeing to confirm Philip's right to the Vexin.[4] . . . In the meantime, Eleanor, "who then ruled England," had taken the precaution of closing the Channel ports and ordering the defense of the eastern coast against a possible invasion, her hastily mustered home guard being instructed to wield any weapon that came to hand, including their plowing tools.

At this point, Eleanor's dilemma in regard to her sons would have taxed the most patient of mothers. John, returning to England, swaggered about the countryside proclaiming himself the next king of England—perhaps he sincerely believed that Richard would never be released alive—and, never known for his sensitivity, constantly regaled Eleanor with the latest rumors concerning the fate of her favorite son. Her actions during this period indicate clearly that she failed to take John seriously. Although he was twenty-seven, she thought of him as the baby of the family, always a child showing off and trying to attract attention. Her attitude was probably close to that of Richard's when, a few months later, he was informed of John's machinations: "My brother John is not the man to subjugate a country if there is a person able to make the slightest resistance to his attempts." With one hand, Eleanor deftly managed to anticipate John's plots and render him harmless; with the other, she worked for Richard's release. After Easter, the king had been removed from Durrenstein Castle and the hands of Duke Leopold and, after some haggling, had been taken into custody by Leopold's suzerain, the Holy Roman emperor. As the

---

[4]The Vexin was an area at the juncture of Normandy, Anjou, and the Île de France, long disputed by the English and French kings.—ED.

emperor's prisoner, Richard found himself the object of high-level decisions. His death, it was decided, would achieve no useful purpose; rather the arrogant Plantagenets, or what remained of them, should be made to redeem their kin, but at a price that would bring their provinces to their knees: 100,000 silver marks with two hundred hostages as surety for payment. The hostages, it was specified, were to be chosen from among the leading barons of England and Normandy or from their children.

Relieved as Eleanor must have felt to learn that her son could be purchased, she could only have been appalled at the size of the ransom. The prospect of collecting such an enormous sum, thirty-five tons of pure silver, seemed impossible after Henry's Saladin tithe[5] and Richard's great sale before the Crusade.[6] Where was the money to be found? Where were two hundred noble hostages to be located? At a council convened at Saint Albans on June 1, 1193, she appointed five officers to assist with the dreaded task. During the summer and fall, England became a marketplace to raise the greatest tax in its history. The kingdom was stripped of its wealth: "No subject, lay or clerk, rich or poor, was overlooked. No one could say, 'Behold I am only So-and-So or Such-and-Such, pray let me be excused.'" Barons were taxed one-quarter of a year's income. Churches and abbeys were relieved of their movable wealth, including the crosses on their altars. The Cistercians, who possessed no riches, sheared their flocks and donated a year's crop of wool. Before long, the bars of silver and gold began slowly to pile up in the crypt of Saint Paul's Cathedral under Eleanor's watchful eyes. But not quickly enough to comfort her. Even more painful was the job of recruiting hostages from the great families, their lamentations and pleadings rising like a sulphurous mist all over the kingdom and providing constant agony for the queen.

From Haguenau, where Richard was incarcerated, came a flood of letters to his subjects and most especially to his "much loved mother." He had been received with honor by the emperor and his court, he is well, he hopes to be home soon. He realizes that the ransom will be difficult to raise but he feels sure that his subjects will not shirk their duty; all sums collected should be entrusted to the queen. . . .

It is said that in her anguish she addressed three letters to Pope

---

[5]A tax that Henry had levied for a crusade, hence called after the great Muslim leader Saladin.—Ed.

[6]A sale not only of movable property of the crown but that of such protected folk as foreign and Jewish merchants, and what could be extracted from the nobility.—Ed.

Celestine III imploring his assistance in securing Richard's re-lease and in her salutation addressed the pontiff as "Eleanor, by the wrath of God, Queen of England." . . . Why, she demands, does the sword of Saint Peter slumber in its scabbard when her son a "most delicate youth," the anointed of the Lord, lies in chains? Why does the pope, a "negligent," "cruel" prevaricator and sluggard, do nothing?

These letters, supposedly written for her by Peter of Blois, are so improbable that it is surprising that many modern historians have accepted them as authentic. While preserved among the letters of Peter of Blois, who is undoubtedly their author—they are characteristic of his style and use his favorite expressions—there is no evidence that they were written for Eleanor or that they were ever sent. Most likely they were rhetorical exercises. No contemporary of Eleanor's mentioned that she wrote to the pope, and not until the seventeenth century were the letters attributed to her. From a diplomatic point of view, they are too fanciful to be genuine; Eleanor, clearheaded and statesmanlike, was never a querulous old woman complaining of age, infirmities, and weariness of life. On the contrary, her contemporaries unanimously credit her with the utmost courage, industry, and political skill. A second point to notice is that the details of the letters misrepresent the facts of Richard's imprisonment. He was never "detained in bonds," and as both she and the pope knew, Celestine had instantly, upon receiving news of Richard's capture, excommunicated Duke Leopold for laying violent hands on a brother Crusader; he had threatened Philip Augustus with an interdict if he trespassed upon Plantagenet territories; and he had menaced the English with interdict should they fail to collect the ransom. Under the circumstances, Celestine had done all he could. In the last analysis, the letters must be viewed as Peter of Blois's perception of Eleanor's feelings, a view that may or may not be accurate.

In December 1193, Eleanor set sail with an imposing retinue of clerks, chaplains, earls, bishops, hostages, and chests containing the ransom. By January 17, 1194, the day scheduled for Richard's release, she had presented herself and the money at Speyer, but no sooner had they arrived than, to her amazement, Henry Hohenstaufen announced a further delay. He had received letters that placed an entirely new light on the matter of the king's liberation. As the gist of the problem emerged, it seemed Philip Augustus and John Plantagenet had offered the emperor an equivalent amount of silver if he could hold Coeur de Lion in custody another nine months, or deliver him up to them. These disclosures, and Henry's serious consideration of the counteroffer, provoked horror from the emperor's own vassals, and after two days of argument, Henry relented. He would liberate

Richard as promised if the king of England would do homage to him for all his possessions, including the kingdom of England. This request, a calculated humiliation, would have made Richard a vassal of the Holy Roman emperor, a degradation that the Plantagenets were hard put to accept. Quick to realize the meaninglessness, as well as the illegality, of the required act, Eleanor made an on-the-spot decision. According to Roger of Hovedon, Richard, "by advice of his mother Eleanor, abdicated the throne of the kingdom of England and delivered it to the emperor as the lord of all." On February 4, the king was released "into the hands of his mother" after a captivity of one year six weeks and three days.

Seven weeks later, on March 12, the king's party landed at Sandwich and proceeded directly to Canterbury, where they gave thanks at the tomb of Saint Thomas. By the time they reached London, the city had been decorated, the bells were clanging furiously, and the Londoners ready to give a rapturous welcome to their hero and champion. Her eldest son "hailed with joy upon the Strand," Eleanor looked in vain for the remaining male member of her family, but the youngest Plantagenet was nowhere to be found. Once Richard's release had been confirmed, he had fled to Paris upon Philip Augustus's warning that "beware, the devil is loose." . . .

According to the chronicles, "the king and John became reconciled through the mediation of Queen Eleanor, their mother." In the circumstances, it seemed the safest course as well as the wisest. There was no doubt in Eleanor's mind that the boy, now twenty-eight, could not be held responsible for his actions, that he was, as Richard of Devizes termed him, "light-minded." But at that moment, he was the last of the Plantagenets. With luck, Richard might reign another twenty-five years or more. Who was to say that he would not produce an heir of his own? Thus the queen must have reasoned in the spring of 1194 when her son, after so many adversities, had come home to her.

Review and Study Questions

1. What were Eleanor's motives in her indiscreet flirtation with Raymond of Antioch?

2. What role did Eleanor play in the evolution of medieval chivalric culture?

3. What role did Eleanor play in European political affairs?

4. To what extent should Eleanor be considered a feminist heroine?

Suggestions for Further Reading

As we have seen, despite her importance and inherent interest, there are virtually no contemporary source materials for Eleanor. Thus, whether hostile or sympathetic, the treatments of Eleanor have had to be not so much biographies as life-and-times books. This is true even of the best modern works. Two of them, Amy Kelly, *Eleanor of Aquitaine and the Four Kings* (Cambridge, Mass.: Harvard University Press, 1950), and Marion Meade, *Eleanor of Aquitaine: A Biography* (New York: Hawthorn, 1977), are excerpted in this chapter, and students are encouraged to read further in them. Two additional works are also recommended: Curtis H. Walker, *Eleanor of Aquitaine* (Chapel Hill: University of North Carolina Press, 1950), and Regine Pernoud, *Eleanor of Aquitaine*, tr. P. Wiles (New York: Coward-McCann, 1967), both well written, lively, and fast moving. *Eleanor of Aquitaine: Patron and Politician*, ed. Wm. W. Kibler (Austin: University of Texas Press, 1976), is a series of specialized papers on aspects of Eleanor's life and reign.

Of Eleanor's contemporaries, the best, most comprehensive, and up-to-date work on Henry II is W. L. Warren, *Henry II* (London: Eyre Methuen, 1973). Somewhat less intimidating are the smaller but entirely competent Richard Barber, *Henry Plantagenet* (Totowa, N.J.: Rowman and Littlefield, 1964), and John Schlight, *Henry II Plantagenet*, "Rulers and Statesmen of the World" (New York: Twayne, 1973). Probably the best biography of Richard I is Philip Henderson, *Richard Coeur de Lion: A Biography* (New York: Norton, 1959), but students are also encouraged to read James A. Brundage, *Richard Lion Heart* (New York: Scribners, 1974), largely a study of Richard as soldier and crusader, and a tough, realistic work. The standard work on John is Sidney Painter, *The Reign of King John* (Baltimore: Johns Hopkins University Press, 1949). W. L. Warren, *King John* (Berkeley: University of California Press, 1978), is a somewhat revisionist treatment of John showing him as a hard-working monarch and more the victim than the causer of his troubles—but he still is a far from attractive figure. For Eleanor's French royal contemporaries, see R. Fawtier, *The Capetian Kings of France*, tr. Lionel Butler and R. J. Adam (London: Macmillan, 1960). There are a handful of studies of important nonroyal figures whose lives intertwined with Eleanor's: Sidney Painter, *William Marshall: Knight Errant, Baron, and Regent of England* (Baltimore: Johns Hopkins University Press, 1933); Charles R. Young, *Hubert Walter: Lord of Canterbury and Lord of England* (Durham, N.C.: Duke University Press, 1968); and a number of books on the durable subject of Henry and Becket—the best are Richard Winston, *Thomas Becket* (New York: Knopf, 1967), a tough, skeptical, but solidly source-based work; Dom David Knowles, *Thomas Becket* (London: A. and C. Black, 1970), a scrupulously objective account by a great ecclesiastical historian, but, naturally, most occupied with the arguments of Thomas and the church; and finally, Alfred L. Duggan, *My Life for My Sheep* (New York: Coward-McCann, 1955), a lively novelized account by an experienced historical novelist.

Two special topics relate to Eleanor throughout her life—chivalry and courtly love and the crusades. Both have been much studied and written about. On chivalry and courtly love, see two excellent and well-written background works—John C. Moore, *Love in Twelfth-Century France* (Philadelphia: University of Pennsylvania Press, 1972), and Jack Lindsay, *The Troubadours and Their World of the Twelfth and Thirteenth Centuries* (London: Frederick Muller, 1976), and two equally interesting ones dealing with the actual operation of knightly chivalry as well as its romanticized literary aspects—Sidney Painter, *French Chivalry: Chivalric Ideas and Practices in Medieval France* (Baltimore: Johns Hopkins University Press, 1940), and the more comprehensive Richard Barber, *The Knight and Chivalry* (New York: Scribners, 1970). But the definitive work on chivalry in all its aspects is Maurice Keen, *Chivalry* (New Haven: Yale University Press, 1984). The standard work on the crusades is now *The History of the Crusades* (Philadelphia: University of Pennsylvania, 1955–1962), a great multiauthored work under the general editorship of Kenneth M. Setton: vol. 1, *The First Hundred Years*, ed. M. W. Baldwin, and vol. 2, *The Later Crusades, 1189–1311*, ed. R. L. Wolff. Steven Runciman, *A History of the Crusades*, 3 vols. (Cambridge, England: Cambridge University Press, 1951–1954), may, however, still be the best account. Students may prefer Zoé Oldenbourg, *The Crusades*, tr. Anne Carter (New York: Pantheon, 1966), somewhat less successful than her famous historical novels but still excellent and exciting. For the warfare of the period, students should look at the recent and comprehensive Philippe Contamine, *War in the Middle Ages*, tr. Michael Jones (Oxford: Blackwell, 1984), especially the sections on the Feudal Age and Medieval Society at its prime.

元太祖
鐵木真

GENGHIS KHAN: THE FLAIL OF GOD

c. 1162	Born
1206	Named Genghis Khan
1207	Invaded North China
1215	Defeated the Chinese Chin Dynasty
1215–23	War against the Khwarwzm
1227	Died

In the year 1206, at the great assembly of the Mongol clans by the Onan river, the clan chieftain Temujin was proclaimed Genghis Khan, universal ruler. It was an event that Temujin had been preparing for for more than twenty-five years.

Temujin had been born, probably in 1162, the son of a royal Mongol clan leader who died while Temujin was still a boy. Largely on the basis of his promise and the force of his personality Temujin was given support by the Mongol leaders and put in command of a formidable army. With this force he attacked rival Mongol clans, and his success led other clan leaders to gather around him. He systematically eliminated all his rivals and consolidated the Mongols into a single people. Temujin had created a unified and powerful nation as a personal instrument of world conquest.

The Secret History of the Mongols: The Young Genghis Khan

In the lifetime of Genghis Khan the Mongols were still a preliterate people who kept their tribal traditions alive in oral sagas. *The Secret History of the Mongols* is such a saga. It was probably written down in the thirteenth century within a few years of Genghis Khan's death as the official account of the ruling clan of the Mongols and the life history of its late, great leader. The original Mongol version is no longer extant. The text exists in a Chinese version dating from the Ming Dynasty, after the Mongols had been driven out of China, from which the present translation into English by Francis W. Cleaves is made.

The excerpt begins with an account of the battles against the Tatars, fought by Temujin's father.

It was during one of these battles
that Yesugei captured a Tatar chief named Temujin Uge.
Yesugei's people were camped at Deligun Hill on the Onan then,
and Hogelun Ujin was about to give birth to her first child.
It was here that Chingis Khan was born.
As he was born
he emerged clutching a blood clot the size of a knucklebone die in
    his right hand.
They gave him the name Temujin, saying:
"He was born when his father had captured the Tatar, Temujin
    Uge." . . .

[The] year, when Temujin was nine,
Yesugei decided to take him to visit his mother's tribe, saying:
"I'll ask for a girl from his mother's tribe to marry him."
On their way to the Olkhunugud tribe they met an Ungirad man,
    Dei the Wise,
camped between Mount Chegcher and Mount Chikhurkhu.
Dei the Wise addressed Yesugei as if they were related by marriage:
"My friend Yesugei, travelling so far,
who are you going to see?"

"I'm on my way to the Olkhunugud,
the tribe of this son of mine's mother,
to find a girl for him there," he replied.
Dei the Wise said to him:
"I look at your son and I see
his eyes contain fire,
his face fills with light.
My friend Yesugei, I had a dream last night.
A white falcon holding the Sun and the Moon in its claws
flew down from the sky and lit on my hand.
I told my family this, saying:
'Whenever I saw the Sun or the Moon in my dreams before
it was always from a distance.
Now this falcon, taking them in his claws,
has brought them both into my hand.
The bird was all white and it brought them to me.' "
The next morning Yesugei asked Dei for his daughter. . . .

The narrative then moves to the history of the mature Temujin. Temujin's wife,
Borte, has been captured by a rival clan.

As Temujin moved out his people
Toghoril Khan, commanding ten thousand men,
and Jakha Gambu, Toghoril's younger brother, commanding ten
   thousand,
had nearly reached Burgi cliff.
The two camps moved together and united their forces.
Temujin, Toghoril Khan, and Jakha Gambu brought their forces to
   Botoghan Bogorji,
at the head of the Onan as they'd been instructed.
Jamugha was already there with his army
and had been waiting three days.
Jamugha stood at the head of his army of twenty thousand men
and Temujin, Toghoril Khan, and Jakha Gambu rode up at the
   head of their army.
As the leaders recognized each other
Jamugha spoke first, saying:
"Didn't we say to each other,
'Even if there's a blizzard,
even if there's a rainstorm,
we won't arrive late'?
Aren't the Mongol a people whose word is sacred?
Haven't we said to each other,

'Let's get rid of anyone who can't live up to his word'?"
Toghoril Khan answered Jamugha's criticism by saying:
"We've arrived three days late, you're correct.
Let Younger Brother Jamugha decide who he'll punish and who
    he'll blame."
Having settled this score
they moved their forces from Botoghan Bogorjin to the Kilgho
    River
where they built rafts to cross over to the Bugura Steppe,
into Toghtoga Beki's land.
They came down on him as if through the smoke-hole of his tent,
beating down the frame of his tent and leaving it flat,
capturing and killing his wives and his sons.
They struck at his door-frame where his guardian spirit lived
and broke it to pieces.
They completely destroyed all his people
until in their place there was nothing but emptiness.
But while Toghtoga Beki lay sleeping before the attack
fishermen, trappers, and hunters who lived by the Kilgho River
    came to warn him.
Running through the night
they brought news that the army was coming.
"Our enemies have thrown themselves across the river!" they cried.
And hearing this Toghtoga and Dayir Usun gathered a few
    followers,
with nothing but the clothes on their backs,
and escaped down the Selenge River to the Barghujin region.
As the Merkid people tried to flee from our army
running down the Selenge with what they could gather in the
    darkness,
as our soldiers rode out of the night capturing and killing the
    Merkid,
Temujin rode through the retreating camp shouting out:
"Borte! Borte!"
Borte Ujin was among the Merkid who ran in the darkness
and when she heard his voice,
when she recognized Temujin's voice,
Borte leaped from her cart.
Borte Ujin and Old Woman Khogaghchin saw Temujin charge
    through the crowd
and they ran to him,
finally seizing the reins of his horse.
All about them was moonlight.
As Temujin looked down to see who had stopped him

he recognized Borte Ujin.
In a moment he was down from his horse
and they were in each other's arms, embracing.
There and then Temujin sent off a messenger
to find Toghoril Khan and Anda Jamugha, saying:
"I've found what I came for.
Let's go no further and make our camp here."
When the Merkid who ran from us in the night saw our army had
    halted
they halted as well and spent the night where they'd stopped.
This is how Temujin found Borte Ujin,
saving her from the Merkid. . . .

Temujin thanked Toghoril Khan and Jamugha for their help,
    saying:
"Because I was joined by my father the Khan and Anda Jamugha
my strength was increased by Heaven and Earth.
In the name of Eternal Blue Heaven
with the aid of Our Mother the Earth
we've torn out the hearts of the Merkid warriors,
we've emptied their beds and killed all their sons,
we've captured all the rest of their women.
Now that we've scattered the Merkid we should go back." . . .

So the forces of Temujin, Toghoril Kahn, and Jamugha,
who'd united to attack the Merkid clans,
who'd thrown open the Merkid's locked tents,
who'd reduced the Merkid's noblest women to slaves,
withdrew from Talkhun Island where the Orkhon joins the Selenge.
Temujin and Jamugha kept their forces together
riding back to the Khorkhonagh Valley to camp.
Toghoril Khan's army rode to the far side of Burkhan Khaldun
down the Hokortu Valley.
They rode on through Khachaguratu and Huliyatu Subchid
hunting as they went,
and finally returned to their camp
near the Black Forest on the Tula River.
After travelling all that night
they halted at dawn to see who had followed them.
Camping circles from nearly all of the clans had chosen to follow
    Temujin. . . .

Then in came Khorchi of the Bagarin.
When Khorchi arrived he spoke with Temujin, saying:

"My people are descended from the woman Holy Ancestor
    Bodonchar captured
and took for his wife.
Because of this, we're such close kin to Jamugha
that we're just like people who share the same mother's belly,
like people who come from the waters of the same mother's womb.
We'd never have left Jamugha's camp.
But a sign from Heaven came to me in a dream
and told me that Temujin was meant to be our leader.". . .

Once Chingis had been elected
Ogele Cherbi, Bogorchu's young kinsman,
was named as his archer.
Soyiketu Cherbi promised him:
"I'll see to it
you'll never miss your morning drink,
you'll never miss your evening meal,"
and he became head cook.
Degei promised him:
"I'll see to it
that a lamb is brought in for the morning broth,
that another's brought in for the evening.
I'll herd the speckled sheep

and see that your carts are filled with their wool.
I'll herd the yellow sheep
and see that your flocks are filled with their number,"
and he became head shepherd.
Then his younger brother, Guchugur, promised:
"I'll see to it
that the lynch-pins are always tight on the wheels of your carts,
that the axletree doesn't break when the carts are on the road.
I'll be in charge of the tent carts."
Dodai Cherbi promised:
"I'll be in charge of the men and women who serve in your tents."
Then Chingis appointed three men,
along with his brother Khasar,
to be his personal swordsmen, saying:
Anyone who thinks they are stronger,
you'll strike off their heads.
Anyone who thinks they're more courageous,
you'll cut them in two.
My brother Belgutei will bring the geldings in from the pasture.
He will be in charge of the horses.

Mulkhalkhu will be in charge of the cattle.
Arkhai Khasar, Taghai, Sukegei, and Chakhurkhan,
these four warriors will be like my arrows,
like the arrows I shoot near and far."
Then Subetai the Brave promised him:
"I'll be like a rat and gather up others,
I'll be like a black crow and gather great flocks.
Like the felt blanket that covers a horse,
I'll gather up soldiers to cover you.
Like the felt blanket that guards a tent from the wind,
I'll assemble great armies to shelter your tent."
Then Chingis Khan turned to Bogorchu and Jelme, and said:
"You two,
from the time when there was no one to fight beside me but my own
     shadow,
you were my shadow and gave my mind rest.
That will always be in my thoughts.
From the time when there was nothing to whip my horses with but
     their own tails,
you were their tails and gave my heart peace.
That will always be in my heart.
Since you were the first two who came to my side
you'll be chiefs over all the rest of the people."
Then Chingis Khan spoke to the people, saying:
"If Heaven and Earth grant me their protection so that my powers
     increase,
then each of you elders of the clans
who've chosen to leave Anda Jamugha and follow me
will be happy with the choice that you've made.
I'll give you each your position and office." . . .

Just then a messenger arrived, saying:
"When the Tatar chief, Megujin,
disobeyed the commands of the Golden King of Cathay,
the Golden King sent his general, Prince Hsiang,
with an army against them.
Prince Hsiang and his army are driving the Tatar
up along the Ulja River.
They are coming this way with all their herds and possessions."
Chingis Khan spoke to the people, saying:
"The Tatar have been our enemies
since the days when they killed our grandfathers and fathers.
Now is our chance to attack them."
He sent a messenger off to Toghoril Khan at once, saying:

"I've just heard that Prince Hsiang is marching
up the Ulja River with a great army,
driving the Tatar this way.
Let's attack these Tatar together,
since they're the ones who killed our grandfathers and fathers.
Let my father Toghoril Khan send his troops quickly."
Toghoril Khan agreed, saying:
"My son, Temujin, speaks wisely.
We'll attack them together." . . .

Chingis and Toghoril ordered their armies to attack,
and overrunning the Tatar defense,
they captured Megujin and killed him.
Chingis took the Tatar chief's silver cradle
and a blanket covered with pearls.
When Prince Hsiang found out
that Chingis Khan and Toghoril Khan had defeated the Tatar,
killing Megujin,
he was ecstatic.
As a reward he honored his new allies with Chinese titles.
To Chingis he gave the title Ja'ud Khuri, meaning Pacifier.
To Toghoril he gave the title Ong, meaning Prince.
So it's because Prince Hsiang gave Toghoril this name
that he was known from that time as Ong Khan. . . .

Chingis Khan gathered all the people back in the camp
and pitched his tents there for the night.
At the evening meal he had Khadagan sit beside him
and the following day Sorkhan Shira and Jebe,
both men who had served the leaders of the Tayichigud clan,
came to offer themselves to Chingis.
When Chingis saw Sorkhan Shira he said:

"You and your sons took the wood from my neck,
took the cangue from my collar.[1]
Why have you taken so long to come join me?"
Sorkhan Shira answered him:
"I often thought about the situation I was in
and said to myself, 'Don't be too quick.
If I go off to join Temujin the Tayichigud will kill all my family,
make them blow away like the ashes of an abandoned fire.

---

[1]This is a reference to a large wooden collar Genghis was forced to wear when he
was a prisoner of these people.—ED.

They'll take my wife and my sons, everything I leave behind.'
So I was patient
and now that the right moment's here we've come to join our khan."
When he'd finished this speech Chingis Khan nodded and said:
"You've done the right thing." . . .

At the end of that winter
in the autumn of the Year of the Dog,
Chingis Khan assembled his army at Seventy Felt Cloaks
to go to war with the four Tatar clans.
Before the battle began
Chingis Khan spoke with his soldiers and set down these rules:
"If we overcome their soldiers
no one will stop to gather their spoils.
When they're beaten and the fighting is over
then there'll be time for that.
We'll divide their possessions equally among us.
If we're forced to retreat by their charge
every man will ride back to the place where we started our attack.
Any man who doesn't return to his place for a counterattack will be
    killed."
Chingis Khan met the Tatar at Seventy Felt Cloaks
and made them retreat. . . .

During that same Dog Year that Chingis Khan defeated the Tatar,
Ong Khan went to war with the Merkid.
He followed Toghtoga Beki all the way to the lowlands of Barghujin
and in the battle there Ong Khan killed the Merkid chief's eldest
    son,
captured his two daughters as well as his wives,
and took for himself Toghtoga's younger sons, Khudu and
    Chilagun,
as well as all of their possessions and people.
But Ong Khan offered none of his spoils to Chingis.

Then together Chingis Khan and Ong Khan
went to war with the Naiman led by Buyirugh Khan.
When they came on his forces at Ulugh Tagh,
Buyirugh Khan had no time to gather his army for a fight,
so he retreated back through a pass in the Altai mountains.
Chingis and Ong Khan followed him through the Altai,
riding down the Urunggu River valley.
Yedi Tublugh, a Naiman chief, hung back to spy on us,
but when he tried to escape our men by riding over the mountain

his saddle-strap broke and we captured him.
So without warning,
Chingis Khan and Ong Khan overtook the Naiman at Lake Kishil
    Bashi
and they destroyed Buyirugh Khan's army. . . .

In the fall of that same Year of the Rat
Chingis Khan led his armies against the remaining followers of
    Toghtoga Beki,
who had fled to the Kharadal Forest.
He forced Toghtoga to retreat,
driving his people out onto the Donkey-back Steppe,
capturing all his herds and possessions.
Toghtoga, along with his sons Khudu and Chilagun,
with a few followers and nothing but the clothes on their backs,
escaped from the battle and got away. . . .

And so in the Year of the Tiger,
having set in order the lives
of all the people whose tents are protected by skirts of felt,
the Mongol clans assembled at the head of the Onan.
They raised a white standard of nine tails
and proclaimed Chingis Khan the Great Khan.

A Russian Near-Contemporary

BERTOLD SPULER

The proclamation of Temujin as Genghis Khan in 1206—"the Year
of the Tiger"—was the most significant division point in his career.
The wars for the securing of Mongolia were over: All the native
tribes of fellow Asiatic nomads had come under the horsetail banner of the Great Khan. He now turned to the outer world. This was
probably not a new goal for Genghis Khan. But prior to this time
he could not risk leaving potential enemies at his back to march to
distant frontiers. The events of 1206 changed all that and the building of a Mongol world empire began.

Under Genghis Khan and his generals Mongol armies spread out
east and west. In the east, by 1215, the Chinese Chin Empire was

defeated and in that year Peking fell to the Mongols. The westward expansion brought the Mongols across the borders of the emerging states of eastern Europe. As a result, a more or less permanent relationship was established with those states. And this meant envoys appointed to the Mongol court, envoys who would make regular reports to their governments, keep notes and records, and write memoirs.

The following selection, from Bertold Spuler's *History of the Mongols,* is probably taken from the reminiscenses of such an envoy, in this case from the Duchy of Moscovy, whose name is not recorded. His lifetime, or at least his diplomatic career, seems to have carried a generation or two beyond Genghis Khan himself. But he was well enough informed about the Great Khan to leave us an instructive account of the government and society Genghis had set in place. His account begins with the completion of Genghis Khan's outer conquests, within a year or so of his death.

Then Chinggiz Khan returned to his own country. Here he enacted his laws and promulgated orders to which the Tatars[2] strictly adhere. Only two of them shall be mentioned here. The first order says: Anybody who puffed by pride and on his own authority without election by the princes aspires to Imperial dignity, shall be executed without grace or pardon. Consequently, before the present Emperor Göyük Khan was elected, one of the princes, an actual grandson of Chinggiz Khan, was executed for this crime, since he wanted to make himself Emperor without election by the princes.

The other order says they must subjugate the whole world, and must not live in peace with any people who has not first surrendered to them; and this will apply until the time when they themselves are annihilated. For they had already made war for forty-two years and have still to rule for another eighteen [before their destruction]; then, so they say, according to some prophesy made to them, they are to be conquered by another nation; but they do not know themselves which nation that will be. And those who are able to escape will, so they say, have to observe that law which their future conquerors will also observe. (That means: Both the victors and the defeated will have to observe the commandments of Chinggiz Khan.)

Further he ordered that there should be commanders for every thousand men, for every hundred, for every ten men, and for the

---

[2]This author uses the term *Tatar* as synonymous with Mongol.—Ed.

darknesses, that is, for ten thousand men,[3] and on this pattern he built the whole army organization. He gave many other orders, but it would take us too far beyond the scope of our subject to list them all here; moreover, they are not known to us. After he had completed giving his laws and orders, he was struck by lightning and died. . . .

The Great Khan of the Tatars has extraordinary power over all his subjects; nobody dares to settle in any part of his empire without his express direction. In fact he determines the places of residence for the dukes, the dukes in their turn those of the commanders of a thousand, they in turn those of the commanders of a hundred, and the last those of the commanders of ten. If, moreover, at any time or any place he gives them an order, be it for war [or for peace], be it for life or for death, they obey without question.

Even when he demands somebody's unmarried daughter or sister for a wife, she is given to him [instantly] without argument. Actually, every year, or at any rate every few years, he orders the maidens from everywhere throughout the Tatar lands to be assembled, so that he may choose and keep those he likes; the others he gives to those around him as he sees fit.

If he sends any envoys, however great their number may be, to any place, his subjects must provide them with post horses without delay and supply them with the necessary provisions; and if there come to him from anywhere people bringing tribute or envoys, they have equally to be provided with horses, carts, and provisions. If, on the other hand, envoys come to them from elsewhere, they have to suffer great deprivations and shortage of food and clothing, for their provisions are poor and scanty, especially if they come to see princes [rather than the Khan], and if their stay here is drawn out; in that case what is provided for ten people is hardly enough for two. Both at the courts of the princes and on the journey they are given food only once a day, and then very little. Even so, they have little opportunity to make even a modest complaint, if they are wronged; they just have to bear it patiently.

And as if this were not enough, everyone, including princes and noblemen, and even people of a more lowly status, continually demand presents from the envoys, and if they do not get what they want, they look down on them with disdain, and in fact treat them as though they were not there. If, in fact, the envoys should have been sent by a powerful lord, they are not satisfied with an ordinary gift, but say: 'You come from such a powerful lord, why then, do you offer such trifling gifts?' And they refuse to accept [such a meager gift]. If,

---

[3]*Tümen* = 10,000; here connected with Russian *t'ma* = darkness.—ED.

therefore, the envoys hope to succeed with their business they are forced to give more. In this way we ourselves could not avoid using for presents a large portion of the donations given to us by the faithful to defray our expenses.

Further, it is important one should know that all property is in the hands of the Great Khan so that nobody dares to say: 'This belongs to me and that belongs to the other.' But everything, household chattels, cattle and people, is the property of the Khan. Only recently he issued an express order to this effect.

The dukes, in their turn, enjoy the same absolute power over their [subordinate] people. In fact, men and women, Tatars as well as others, are distributed among the dukes [as their property]. If a duke sends his envoys anywhere, the people, the Khan's men just as all the other people, are equally obliged to provide without argument post horses, the necessary provisions and servants, both to look after the horses and to wait on the envoys personally. The dukes [beys], like everyone else, are under an obligation to provide the Great Khan with mares as dues, for one, two, or three years, as he may see fit, so that he may have the benefit of their milk. The subjects of the dukes have to provide precisely the same for their lords; for nobody is free among them. In short, the Khans and the dukes take from the property of the subjects whatever and however much they like, and also have unlimited rights to dispose of their persons as they wish. . . .

The Conduct of War: The Organization of the Army

Of this we can report as follows: Chinggiz Khan laid down that there should be one man in charge of every ten soldiers, called a commander of ten [corporal]; in charge of ten such units there should be a commander of a hundred, in charge of ten of these a commander of a thousand, and finally in charge of ten of these a high commander. In their language, this latter number [ten thousand] is called darkness. At the head of the whole army are then two or three dukes (*duces* or holders of a *tugh*, i.e., of a commander's standard), but again, one of them has the supreme command.

In the event of war, should one or two or three or more of these ten men flee, they [those who fled] are all punished by death. Moreover, should all of these ten flee, unless all the other men belonging to their unit of a hundred flee, then they are all punished by death. In short, unless there is a general retreat, all those fleeing are punished by death. If, on the other hand, one or two or three throw themselves boldly into battle and the rest of the ten they belong to do not follow, the latter must pay for it with their lives, and if one or more of the ten soldiers are taken prisoner, then unless their other comrades free them, they equally must pay with their lives. . . .

The Tyranny of the Tatars over Their Vassals

In those countries whose princes they allow to return home, they install their own *basqaqs* or governors, to whose beck and call the princes and the common people are all equally subject. If the inhabitants of a city or a country do not do what they require, these *basqaqs* brand them as disloyal toward the Tatars, and as a result the city or region in question is laid waste and the inhabitants killed. For, at the order of the prince to whom that country is subject, the Tatars arrive in strength and completely without warning, and pounce upon the unsuspecting people, as happened recently while we were still in the land of the Tatars, to a city that they themselves had founded in the land of the Cumans and had populated with Ruthenes. And not only the Tatar prince who has possessed himself of the land, or his governor, but any Tatar passing through this town or region gives himself, as it were, the airs of a lord there, and above all those among them who have a somewhat higher rank. Furthermore, they demand and receive without more ado, gold and silver and anything they want, at any time and in any amount they like.

If quarrels break out between the vassal princes they have to go to the Great Khan to present their case there, as happened recently with the two sons of the King of Georgia. One of them, called Melik,[4] was the son of a legal union; the other, called David, an illegitimate son. Now the dying father had bequeathed part of his kingdom to the bastard. Upon this, the other one who was younger set out with his mother for the court of the Great Khan, since the previously mentioned David had also gone there. In the course of the journey Melik's mother died. She had been the real queen of Georgia, and her husband had ascended the throne only on marriage to her, since in that country succession along the female line is also valid.

When the two rivals arrived, they presented magnificent gifts, particularly the legitimate son who laid claim to the land which his father had bequeathed to his son David, who as a bastard had no right to it. The other argued against this: Although I am the son of a concubine, I still demand to be given my right according to the traditional law of the Tatars who do not distinguish between the son of the legitimate wife and the son of the servant. As a consequence, judgment was given against the son of the legitimate marriage. David, as the elder

---

[4]Melik in Arabic (and Persian) means "King."—Ed.

brother, was set even above the legitimate son, and he was allowed to retain the land given to him by his father peacefully and without further challenge. In this way, the other son lost both the gifts which he had made in vain, and his case against his brother David.

They also exact tribute from those nations who live at some distance from them, and who are in alliance with other nations whom they still somehow fear and who have not yet been conquered by them. They treat them gently, as it were, so as not to incur the wrath of the army [of the nation whom they fear], and also so that others should not be afraid of submitting to them.

That was the case with the Obesians or Georgians from whom, as was mentioned before, they receive a tribute of fifty thousand or forty thousand hyperpera.[5] Yet other nations are at present left in peace by them; but as we gathered from them, they do intend to make war against them.

A Modern Assessment of Genghis Khan

LEO DE HARTOG

Genghis Khan died in mid-autumn of the year 1227. By his own orders his death was to be kept secret. The entire court was dispersed save only for his faithful old guard numbering about a thousand men. They were to accompany the body, which was placed on a wagon. The procession began toward Inner Mongolia. As they traveled every living thing they encountered was killed. On the Mongolian frontier they were met by his five wives and their children, his 500 concubines, and other members of the royal clan. The procession then proceeded into the mountain fastness not far from the source of the Onan river, where the Great Khan had once rested beneath a spreading tree and said, "This place is fit for my last rest. Let it be noted."[6] It had been noted and his body was buried under that tree, but with no markers. Its exact location is still unknown.

---

[5]The Byzantine unit of currency.—ED.

[6]Michael Prawdin, *The Mongol Empire, Its Rise and Legacy,* tr. Eden and Cedar Paul (New York: Free Press, 1961), p. 229.

In the years following the death of Genghis Khan the imperial expansion was continued under his son Ogedei as Great Khan and subsequently under his grandsons. But within two centuries the decline and decentralization of the Mongol Empire had begun. In 1368 the Mongols were driven out of China by the Ming Dynasty. In 1380 the Russian Prince Dmitri Donskoi defeated the last significant Mongol force in the west, the Khanate of the Golden Horde.

Nevertheless, the memory of Genghis Khan, the founder of the Mongol Empire, remained alive. And it remains alive today. Much work of historical scholarship has been done on Genghis Khan and his Mongols in the last generation. And, while no definitive consensus has emerged, various scholars have begun to present their own summary judgments. Such a one is the Dutch Orientalist Leo de Hartog in his book *Genghis Khan, Conqueror of the World*. David Morgan, writing in the *Times Literary Supplement*, calls it "the most recommendable biography . . . at present available in English."[7]

There are only sporadic references to be found to Genghis Khan's personal appearance. The most detailed information on this subject was obtained from people who saw Genghis Khan during the war in Khwarazm. The world conqueror was then about sixty. He was remarkable for his distinguished figure and his strong constitution. He had cat's eyes and his hair was only partially grey.

A judgment about Genghis Khan can only be made if he is seen in the context of his times and surroundings. In the twelfth and thirteenth centuries the Mongols were far more barbarous than their neighbouring tribes. For this reason Genghis Khan, as the cultivated Chinese put it, was nothing more nor less than a barbarian. However, this barbarian possessed a number of qualities that enabled him to become one of the greatest conquerors in the history of the world.

His unusual self-control and his ability to keep his temper were striking. Although he never permitted himself to behave treacherously in his private life and in his personal relationships, he was certainly cunning and calculating. In his conduct of warfare he was even deceitful. He hated traitors: servants of opponents who betrayed their masters to win his favour were immediately ordered to be executed. We may assume that this attitude was adopted only partly for reasons of idealism. In those times it was not unusual to desert to the strongest. Genghis Khan must have believed that such opportunists would abandon him also if fortune turned. To make clear what a

[7]*Times Literary Supplement*, Nov. 24, 1989, p. 1293.

traitor in his army might expect if he were to fall again into his hands, he showed no mercy to deserters from the enemy. Supporters who remained loyal to him in difficult circumstances were richly rewarded; while those who served their leaders faithfully to the last in a defeated army he often spared, even giving them the opportunity of entering his service.

Another characteristic was his suspicious nature. . . . This suspicion resulted in Genghis Khan's refusal to allow anyone but himself to wield any authority. As his power increased he became more and more anxious to protect his own position.

As was the case with all his contemporaries, Genghis Khan worked exclusively for himself, his descendants and his closest companions. There is no evidence that he entertained any ideas about the welfare of the whole nation, not even in the form that such ideas were expressed in the Yasa.[8] Nor did Genghis Khan see himself as the head of a people: he was the head of the Mongol aristocracy, to which he had given first unity and then power and wealth. It is characteristic of Genghis Khan that, although he won submission from a great part of the world and in other countries aroused fear and alarm, his giddy success never went to his head. Each such a cultured people as the Chinese were astonished at the noble bearing of this so-called barbarian.

Like his fellow countrymen, Genghis Khan was fond of a drink; and hunting was his favourite sport. Although this world conqueror was undoubtedly drunk at certain times, he was not guilty of excessive use of alcohol. Ögödei and Tolui, who were both the slaves of drink, had to be regularly rebuked for their weakness. Drunkenness was regarded by the Mongols as a manly virtue. . . . It was therefore difficult to prohibit this widespread vice in the Yasa.

Women played a great part in his private life. The four most important wives of Genghis Khan were Börte, Qulan, Yesüi and Yesügen. He kept an ordu for each of them. In addition to these women there were a few others, such as the daughter of the Chin emperor, the daugher of the king of Hsi-Hsia, and Gübersü, the former wife of the conquered tayang of the Naiman. He also had a number of concubines. Whenever he rested, Genghis Khan loved to have attractive women around him and always liked to see girls who were busy at all kinds of work. During long campaigns he took one of his chief wives with him. He enjoyed being entertained by an orchestra consisting of 17 or 18 beautiful girl performers.

Although Genghis Khan in his youth showed that he possessed courage and daring and often took risks, he never distinguished him-

---

[8]The Mongol law codified by Genghis Khan.—ED.

self later as a military commander by personal bravery. In his eyes the leader of the battle was always more important than the fighter; all forms of romantic heroism were foreign to his nature. In this respect he differs greatly from the later Asiatic conqueror Timur Lenk (Tamerlan). Genghis Khan directed military operations personally; but he did not think fighting in the front ranks of the cavalry was the job of the supreme commander.

In his later years, however, he cannot be accused of any lack of daring. From the way in which he progressed from a simple tribal chief to one of the mightiest overlords in world history, he did indeed show a great measure of personal courage. He never forced a decision but bided his time, realizing that he ran the danger of losing the opportunities among his supporters. Although he always approached a task with great circumspection, Genghis Khan took great risks when he and his small army attacked the powerful Chin empire and afterwards the vast Khwarazm sultanate. His successful conduct of these wars clearly reveals his military genius.

Genghis Khan did not use any original techniques of warfare. He simply perfected the methods of his predecessors in the steppes. Discipline guaranteed that his orders were strictly carried out. Not even the basic organization of the Mongol army was originated by the world conqueror. There is no doubt, however, that he played a unique role in making this organization faultless.

His profound knowledge of men enabled Genghis Khan to select efficient subordinate commanders. Usually origin and age played no part in his choice. The generals he picked were often given tasks they had to carry out independently, far removed from the Mongol main forces. Not one of the generals, entrusted with the confidence of the world conqueror, ever let him down.

This was the result of his absolute authority and the respect that he inspired everywhere. His choice of civil advisers also shows his gifts for shrewd assessment of human character. They were, without exception, able intelligent and loyal servants. He had, moreover, the good sense to listen carefully to what these ministers had to say. In this connection it is typical that, although he was illiterate and could only speak the Mongol language, he recognized the need for and value of introducing the Uighur script as the official alphabet of the Mongols, who themselves had no alphabet.

Before the rule of Genghis Khan, Mongol society was dominated by complete licence. To obtain law and order in his state, rules of conduct were necessary. By his compilation of the Yasa and his demand for unquestioning obedience, Genghis Khan exerted a tremendous influence upon the morals of the Mongol people, who hitherto had lived in utter anarchy. It is significant that the Franciscan monk John of Plano Carpini, who visited Mongolia 19 years after the death of Genghis Khan, noticed that the Mongols followed the Yasa much more closely than European priests observed their regimen.

Naturally, the genius of Genghis Khan had limitations. The attempt to reconcile two opposing cultures—nomad and urban—was the weakest link in his system, and later it was one of the chief causes of the disintegration of the Mongol Empire. But the organization he imposed upon his dominions was such that it remained in operation for 40 years after his death. This is a remarkable achievement; the more so because not one of his sons or grandsons inherited his genius. That the Genghisids were able to maintain their rule over the member states after the partition of the Mongol Empire derived partly from Genghis Khan's enormous authority, which remained operative long after his death. During his lifetime this indisputable authority was the force that bound together the various camps in his world empire. The religious basis, which was the fundamental strength of his authority, was an important factor particularly in Central Asia. . . .

Genghis Khan has often been portrayed as a monster whose progress was marked by bloody deeds; in the places through which he passed, it is said, rose piles of corpses of murdered peace-loving people and the ruins of towns which, before his arrival, had been prosperous and busy centres. In Islam especially, he was thought to be an odious killer, spreading the silence of the grave over half the world.

It is true that various sources speak of bloodthirsty deeds committed by the Mongol conqueror. The present-day impartial investigator, however, must reach the conclusion that neither as Temüjin, nor later as khan of the Mongols, did he exceed his contemporaries in cruelty or destructiveness. However considerable his genius may have been, Genghis Khan was a child of his times and his country. The outrages must be viewed in the context of the times and the prevailing social conditions; it would be unfair to judge such events by different criteria. That the names of many other rulers, whose brutality was not much less than that of Genghis Khan, are hardly known, is because they are of no historical significance. During the Mongol conquest inconceivable numbers of people died and destruction was enormous, but this was the consequence of the extent of Genghis Khan's campaigns which covered vast areas of Eurasia. Numerically Genghis Khan's army was always smaller than those of his opponents. As all tribes had done in the steppes, the Mongols controlled subjected countries not with occupation troops but by terror. Genghis Khan's Mongols had hardly outgrown their primitive origins and this affected their methods of warfare. These nomads and forest-hunters had no idea how a sedentary people functioned. Nor did they recognize the importance of agriculture.

Genghis Khan was never guilty, during his great campaigns, of barbarities over and above those which were accepted in his day as normal features of war. But like conquerors of any period, Genghis Khan was able (if it was necessary to reach his goal) coldly to do whatever was necessary, to sacrifice countless human lives and to order widespread devastation. . . .

The Mongol conquests were not only the most far-reaching in world history; they also had the most radical consequences. At Genghis Khan's death the Mongol Empire embraced approximately half of the then known world. The slaughter of people and the destruction of towns were not, however, the only features of Genghis Khan's operations. In the huge areas that he united under his rule, close contacts occurred between countries that had hitherto hardly known of each other's existence, on account of their geographical situation and the unsafe conditions that had formerly prevailed. The empire included two old cultural centres, China and Persia, which now associated more intensively as member states. The whole of Asia was opened up; trade in particular benefited from the new order. This was possible because after the conquests the disciplines embodied in the Yasa were introduced in the subjected countries. These rules were undoubtedly harsh, but they brought about a large measure of security and peace, named the *Pax Mongolica*. A contemporary Persian historian wrote that in the region between Persia and Turfan public safety was so widespread that a traveller could journey without interference from the Levant to Central Asia with a gold plate on his head.

The commander of a large military unit was also responsible for the protection of the mounted courier service (Yam). This benefited not only efficient military and governmental communications, trade also profited with the Yam. Along the protected routes flowed an exchange of products, information, discoveries and ideas. After the violence and their defeat, came the activity of travellers dedicated to the spirit of enterprises or to peaceful undertakings. Multicoloured throngs of messengers, merchants and missionaries during the coming years would move along the opened communication routes between Southwest Asia and China. Thanks to the *Pax Mongolica*, commerce especially was able to develop vigorously.

Although the Mongol conqueror was well aware of the value of this international trade, the Mongols themselves did not participate in it. For centuries their activities had been limited to barter with China; in exchange for furs and skins they obtained clothing, food and metal goods from the vast neighbouring country. There was particularly busy commerce between the mediterranean countries and China. The profits from this trade remained long one of the chief financial pillars of the Mongol Empire.

The opinion that the Mongols wished to convert all conquered territories into steppes is not borne out by the facts. The account of the travels of the Chinese philosopher Ch'ang-ch'un relates that the Mongols strove to restore the prosperity of the defeated countries very soon after the battles were over. Influenced by his advisers Ta-ta-T'ong-a, Yeh-lü Ch'u-tsai and the two Yalavachs, Genghis Khan was convinced that he could obtain more income from a prosperous country, run on a municipal and agricultural basis, than from nomads. In order to govern his enormous empire, with its various nationalities and religions, Genghis Khan relied upon the knowledge and experience of the more sophisticated countries. The Mongols had the upper hand, but they were not really the ruling class. For most of their administrative work they had to rely on foreign co-operators recruited from the conquered populations. As nomads they were not well adapted to regular work. The number of Mongols engaged in the higher governmental departments was therefore very small. For such functions it was usually the Uighurs, the Khitans, the Chinese and Persians who were appointed.

Until the end of his life Genghis Khan remained convinced that the Uighur civilization was the one that was best suited to his empire. Nor was this conviction shaken after the world conqueror had gained some experience of the Chinese and Persian cultures. Even his close association with Yeh-lü Ch'u-ts'ai failed to change his ideas. The Chinese and Persian civilizations naturally exerted an influence upon Mongol society, but Genghis Khan wanted the ruling Genghisids to adhere to their nomad life and the teachings of the Yasa, even after his death. For this purpose the Uighur culture was the most acceptable. Genghis Khan, who assumed that his clan would remain overlords for ever, demanded that his descendants and the Mongol aristocracy should not abandon the life of the steppes. It was a simple life and was not restricted by a fixed location. The Yasa, which he thought should be followed for all eternity, was attuned to this way of life. By so doing, the imperial clan could continue to dominate the settled peoples.

Even after gaining control of the territories of the more developed countries, Genghis Khan applied the policies used when uniting all tribes of Central Asia. Whatever the real social and economic causes of the Mongol conquests were, Genghis Khan himself motivated his wars of conquest in terms of an order received from Tengri (Eternal Heaven). His successors followed his example and further elaborated on this scheme. In their eyes the Mongol Empire was not merely a state among states but a 'world empire in the making.' The building of it was the will of Tengri. According to this conception, the right to rule over the world was conferred by the Eternal Heaven on Genghis Khan and his successors. Orders of submission were therefore sent out to inform other states that they had to conform with the orders of the representative of the god of the Mongols. Refusal to surrender was regarded as rebellion.

Genghis Khan regarded the state as a possession belonging to his clan. His empire's constitution was formulated in such a way that he, his family and his loyal associates could derive from it as large an income as possible, with a view to guaranteeing for themselves a grand life-style. In Genghis Khan's time no moral justification of rule seems to have been current. To rule over others was a pleasure and therefore the Genghisids called the throne the seat of joy. Dwellers in the civilized countries were to Genghis Khan the permanent slaves of his empire, whose job it was to see to it that their nomad masters lived an agreeable life. . . .

Genghis Khan's wishes were eventually forgotten. His empire collapsed and the Mongols, who had been compelled by the military and administrative genius of their greatest son to enter the world arena, were unable to maintain their position. They were absorbed or driven back by the countless educated peoples among whom they lived. Later, many of them relapsed into the circumstances in which they had lived at the time of the birth of their brilliant leader. The hope that his clan would remain intact and would for ever continue to rule his empire proved vain. The Yasa, which was to exert the rule of law for all time, was not influential enough to preserve the solidarity of the Genghisids.

Review and Study Questions

1. How does the saga-like *Secret History of the Mongols* differ from more modern historical writing?

2. In your opinion is the account of the anonymous Russian envoy to the Mongol court a hostile or a sympathetic account? Explain.

3. How do you account for the traditional negative assessment Genghis Khan and his Mongols have received, especially in the West?

4. Is Genghis Khan truly a "maker" of world history? Have his contributions endured? Discuss.

Suggestions for Further Reading

There are several collections of sources tangential to the history of the Mongols in the age of Genghis Khan, such as Mouradja d'Ohsson's compilation of Persian and Arabic sources dating from mid-thirteenth century or Etienne Quatremère's translation of Rashid ad-Din's *History of the Reign of Hülegü*, from Persian sources; but almost nothing in the way of Mongol sources existed until very recently. The most important such source is *The Secret History of the Mongols: The Origin of Chingis Khan*, excerpted for this chapter. But this work had to await the translation of Francis Woodman Cleaves in the 1950s. The only other important Mongol source is the *Yasa*, the compilation of Mongol law ordered by Genghis Khan, which does not exist in a comprehensive collection, but only in later citations.

For this reason definitive narrative works on Genghis Khan and his age have had to wait for the painstaking work of scholarship in anthropology, archaeology, and linguistic studies, largely in the twentieth century. Thus the older general histories such as Jeremiah Curtin, *The Mongols: A History* (Boston: Little, Brown and Co., 1908) or Jacob Abbot, *History of Genghis Khan* (New York: Harper and Bros., 1860) are almost useless.

Among the biographies of Genghis Khan, the best is probably René Grousset, *Conqueror of the World*, tr. Marian McKeller and Denis Sinor (New York: Orion Press, 1966), although excellent also are Leo de Hartog, *Genghis Khan: Conqueror of the World* (New York: St. Martin's Press, Inc., 1989), excerpted for this chapter and Peter Brent, *Genghis Khan* (New York et al.: McGraw-Hill, 1976).

On the history of the Mongols in the age of Genghis Khan there are several good books. Walter Heissig, *A Lost Civilization: The Mongols Rediscovered*, tr. D. J. S. Thomson (London: Thames and Hudson, 1966) is an authoritative survey of the whole of Mongol history by a great specialist, as is Michael Prawdin, *The Mongol Empire: Its Rise and Legacy*, tr. Eden and Cedar Paul (New York: Free Press, 1961). Three attractive popular works are James Chambers, *The Devil's Horsemen: The Mongol Invasion of Europe* (New York: Atheneum, 1979), David Morgan, *The Mongols* (London: Blackwell, 1986), and *The Mongol Conquests*, by the editors of Time-Life Books (Alexandria, Va.: Time-Life Books, n.d.). See also E. D. Phillips, *The Mongols* (New York and Washington: Praeger, 1969) in the popular "Ancient Peoples and Places" series.

On the Mongol conquests specifically see J. J. Saunders, *The History of the Mongol Conquests* (London: Routledge and Kegan Paul, 1971), the standard work. An attractive up-to-date popular survey is Robert Marshall, *Storm from the East: From Genghis Khan to Khubilai Khan* (Berkeley and Los Angeles: University of California Press, 1993). Dealing specifically with Russia see Charles J. Halperin, *Russia and the Golden Horde: The Mongol Impact on Medieval Russian History* (Bloomington: Indiana University Press, 1985).

JOAN OF ARC: MAID AND MARTYR

c. 1412   Born
1429   Raised the siege of Orléans
1430   Captured by the Burgundians
1431   Trial and execution

When Joan of Arc was born, probably about 1412, in the village of Domrémy in the duchy of Lorraine in eastern France, the Hundred Years' War had already been going on for more than seventy years. France had been devastated by foreign invasion and civil war. Even the remote province of Lorraine had not been spared the marauding bands of soldiers burning and looting towns, ravaging the country-side, robbing and killing the helpless peasantry. The French royal cause was in ruins, what leadership it had in the hands of the Dauphin Charles, the still uncrowned heir presumptive to the vacant throne.

In 1428, when Joan was about sixteen, she came to believe that the patron saints of her village were speaking to her, telling her to go to the Dauphin and secure his coronation. She made her way to the nearby castle of Vaucouleurs, which was held by Robert de Baudricourt, a royal partisan. She won him over, and he provided her with an escort of six men-at-arms. After traveling through enemy-held territory for eleven days, she reached Chinon and the Dauphin. She found him living like a servant in his own court, robbed and bullied by the nobles who surrounded him. Joan told him that she wanted to go to battle against the English and that she would have him crowned at Rheims. The superstitiously religious Charles believed her and provided her with a modest military staff, sword and armor, a muster of a few hundred soldiers, and a banner blazoned with the name of Jesus.

Thus equipped, Joan and her small force joined the royal army raggedly attacking the stronghold of Orléans, a key city besieged by the English and their Burgundian allies. Her presence infused new spirit into the discouraged French army. Orléans was relieved. Other military successes followed, and the course of the war began to turn. On July 17, 1429, Joan secured the coronation of the Dauphin as Charles VII in the liberated city of Rheims, the traditional site of French royal investiture.

Less than a year later Joan was captured by the Burgundians and sold to the English. For a year she was held in prison and subjected to repeated and persistent questioning. Neither her faith nor her simplicity could save her: she was found guilty of witchcraft and executed in the Old Marketplace of the English-held town of Rouen. An English witness standing near the stake said in awe, "We have burned a saint."

The Documentary Sources

The records of the life and martyrdom of Joan of Arc are more complete and extensive than for any other medieval saint. They were collected by the French scholar Jules Quicherat in the mid-nineteenth century and published in five heavy volumes as *Procès de condamnation et de réhabilitation de Jeanne d'Arc, dite la Pucelle*.[1] This work contains not only the complete texts of her trial and of the review of that trial—the *Réhabilitation*, some twenty years later—but virtually every other document pertaining to her: excerpts from chronicles, literary works, letters, state papers, and eyewitness testimony.

The following excerpt from the *Réhabilitation* is the account of Joan's final hearing and execution given by the two friars who assisted her on the scaffold, Martin Ladvenu and Isambart de la Pierre.

MARTIN LADVENU

. . . Many appeared at the trial rather for their love of the English and their partiality toward them than out of zeal for justice and the Catholic faith. This I would particularly say of the zeal and excessive partisanship shown by Messire Pierre Cauchon, then Bishop of Beauvais. I would accuse him of two signs of partiality. Firstly, when the Bishop appointed himself judge he ordered that Joan should be kept in a secular prison and in the hands of her mortal enemies, although he could easily have had her kept and guarded in an ecclesiastical prison. Nevertheless, from the beginning of the trial to its conclusion he permitted her to be tormented and ill-treated in a secular prison. Moreover, at the first hearing or instance, the said Bishop asked for and demanded the opinions of everyone present as to which was the more suitable, to keep her in a secular prison or to hold her in the prisons of the Church. On this point it was decided that it was more proper to keep her in the Church prison than in

---

[1]The Report of the Condemnation and Rehabilitation of Joan of Arc, Called the Maid.—ED.

any other. But the Bishop answered that he would not do that for fear of displeasing the English. The second sign is that on the day when the Bishop and some others declared her a heretic, lapsed and returned to her sin because she had resumed male clothing in prison, as he left the prison he said to the Earl of Warwick and a great crowd of Englishmen around him: "Farewell, farewell, it is done. Be of good cheer!" This, or something like it, he said in loud and intelligible tones, and laughed as he did so.

They put questions to her which were too difficult in order to catch her out by her own words and opinions. For she was a poor, rather simple woman who scarcely knew her Pater Noster and Ave Maria.

This simple Maid revealed to me that after her abjuration and renunciation she was violently tormented, worried, beaten, and ill-treated in her prison, and that an English lord had done her violence. She openly said that this was the reason why she had resumed male clothing; and toward her end she said to the Bishop of Beauvais: "Alas, it is through your fault that I am to die. For if you had had me kept in a Church prison, I should not be in this plight."

When her last sermon was preached to her in the Vieux Marché[2] and she was handed over to the secular arm, although the secular judges were seated on the platform she was not sentenced by any of those judges. Without sentence, she was compelled by two sergeants to come down from her scaffold, and she was led by these sergeants to the place where she was to be burnt, and there handed over by them to the executioner. . . . After the burning, at about four hours after nones, the executioner said that he had never been so much afraid in officiating at the death of any criminal as he had been at Joan's, and this for several reasons:

Firstly because of her great name and reputation.

Secondly, because of the cruel way in which she was tied and made a show of. For the English had a tall scaffold of stone built, so that, as the executioner reported, he could not easily reach her or hasten her end. This grieved him greatly, for he was much upset by the cruel form and manner in which she was brought to her death.

As for her great and wonderful contrition, repentance, and re-peated confessions, she called continuously on the name of Jesus, and devotedly invoked the aid of the Saints, male and female, in Paradise, as Friar Isambart, who accompanied her to her death and spoke to her of her salvation on the way, has testified above.

---

[2]The Old Market in Rouen.—ED.

ISAMBART DE LA PIERRE

. . . On one occasion I and several others were admonishing and begging Joan to submit to the Church. She replied that she would willingly submit to the Holy Father, to whom she asked to be led, but that she would not submit to the judgment of her enemies. And at that time I advised her to submit to the Council of Basle, and Joan asked me what a general council was. I replied that it was an assembly of the whole universal Church and of Christendom, and that in this council there were as many of her party as of the English. When she heard and understood this she began to cry out: "Oh, if there are some of our party there, I will willingly surrender and submit to the Council of Basle." Then suddenly, in a great fury and indignation, the Bishop of Beauvais began to shout: "Be quiet, in the devil's name!" And he told the notary to be sure not to record the submission she had made to the Council of Basle. On this account and for several other reasons, the English and their officers threatened me horribly that if I did not keep quiet they would throw me in the Seine.

After her renunciation and abjuration, when she had put on male clothes again, she excused herself for having done so in the presence of myself and several others. She said and publicly affirmed that when she put on women's clothes the English had done her great wrongs and violence in her prison. And indeed I saw her weeping, with her face running with tears, and so outraged and disfigured that I felt pity and compassion for her.

When she was labeled an obstinate and relapsed heretic, she publicly answered before the whole court: "If you, lords of the Church, had taken me and kept me in your own prisons, perhaps things would not be like this with me."

After the final conclusion of that session and of the suit, the lord Bishop of Beauvais said to the English: "Farewell, be of good cheer. It is done."

They put such difficult questions to poor Joan, and framed such subtle and tricky interrogatories that the great clerks and men of learning there present would have found it very hard to know how to answer. Several of those present grumbled about this.

As for myself, I was summoned in person before the Bishop of Avranches, a good cleric but very old, who had been asked and entreated to give an opinion on the case. The Bishop asked me, therefore, what the worthy Saint Thomas said on the subject of the proper form of submission to the Church. I gave the Bishop Saint Thomas's ruling in writing. It says: "In all doubts as to faith, one should always resort to the Pope and the General Council." The Bishop subscribed to this opinion, and seemed most unhappy at the decision which had been reached in defiance of it. This opinion of his was not recorded, but omitted out of malice.

After her confession and her taking of the sacrament of the Host, sentence was pronounced on her, and she was declared an excommunicated heretic.

I well saw and clearly perceived—for I was present throughout and watched the whole summing up and conclusion of the case— that the secular judge did not condemn her to death or to be consumed by the fire. And although the lay and secular judge appeared and was present at the very place of her last sermon and her transfer to the secular arm, nevertheless she was handed over to the executioner and burnt without any judgment or conclusion by that judge. The executioner was told: "Do your duty." She received no other sentence.

Joan showed such great contrition and such a fine repentance in her death as was a wonder to see. The words she uttered were so devout, pious, and Christian that all who watched her—and they were a great multitude—wept warm tears. Even the Cardinal of England (the Bishop of Winchester) and several other Englishmen were constrained to weep and were moved to compassion.

The pious woman asked, commanded, and begged me, since I was near her at the end, to go into the nearby church and bring her the Crucifix. This she made me hold up, right before her eyes, until the moment of her death, so that the Cross upon which God hung should be continually before her eyes so long as her life lasted. Moreover, when she was surrounded by flames she continued to cry aloud and acknowledge the sacred name of Jesus, and ceaselessly to implore and invoke the aid of the Saints in Paradise. And, what is more, as she gave up the ghost and bowed her head, she pronounced the name of Jesus. This was a sure sign that she fervently believed in God, as we read in the case of Saint Ignatius and many other martyrs.

Immediately after the execution, the executioner came up to me and my companion, Friar Martin Ladvenu. He was struck and moved by a marvelous repentance and terrible contrition; and he was desperate with fear that he would never be able to obtain God's pardon and indulgence for what he had done to that saintly woman. He said and affirmed that, notwithstanding the oil, sulphur, and charcoal that he had applied to Joan's entrails and heart, he had not found it possible to burn them or reduce them to ashes. He was astonished at this as at a patent miracle.

A Nationalist View of Joan

JULES MICHELET

The story of Joan of Arc was largely the subject of poems and legends until the 1840s and the appearance of Jules Michelet's monumental *History of France*. The fifth volume of this work, devoted to
the reign of Charles VII, contains three chapters on Joan of Arc.
They were later republished as a separate volume and are generally
regarded as Michelet's masterpiece. Like most of his fellow French
intellectuals of the time, Michelet was an ardent nationalist and a
critic of the traditional French Catholic church. He tended to see
religion as properly the service of man through the service of
God—a thoroughly liberal, humanitarian, and democratic interpretation. Thus, he depicted Joan of Arc as a champion of French nationalism brought down by the functionaries of the church, as corrupt
in her century as in his own. One critic has called Michelet's Joan of
Arc "a hymn to patriotism."[3]

On Friday and Saturday the wretched prisoner, deprived of her male
garments, had much to fear. Brutal nature, furious hatred, ven-
geance, everything would urge the cowards to degrade her before she
perished, to sully the victim they were going to burn. . . . They might
be tempted to cover their infamy with a *raison d'état*, according to the
ideas of the time; by ravishing her virginity, they would destroy the
occult power of which they were so horribly afraid; it might restore
their courage to realize that after all she was but a woman. According
to her confessor, to whom she had revealed the fact, an Englishman,
not a common soldier, but a gentleman, a lord, had patriotically assumed the task; he had bravely attempted to rape a girl in chains; and
when he did not succeed, he had showered her with blows.

When Sunday morning came, Trinity Sunday, and she had to rise,
as she reported to a witness, she told her English guards, "Take off
my shackles, so that I may get up." One of them took off the woman's
garments she wore, emptied a bag containing man's clothing, and

---

[3]Frances Gies, *Joan of Arc: The Legend and the Reality* (New York: Harper & Row,
1981), p. 253.

said to her, "Arise."—"Gentlemen," she said, "you know I am forbidden to wear this; excuse me, but I will not put it on." The discussion went on until noon; finally, a bodily necessity compelled her to go out, and to take the clothes given her. When she came back, they would not give her any other, in spite of all her entreaties.

It was not actually to the advantage of the English that she should resume the wearing of man's clothing, thus canceling the recantation that had been so hard to obtain. But at that moment their rage knew no bounds. Saintrailles had boldly attempted a raid on Rouen. It would have been a splendid stroke to snatch the judges right from their tribunal, to take Winchester and Bedford to Poitiers; Bedford had another narrow escape on his way back from Rouen to Paris. The English felt insecure so long as the accursed woman was alive; undoubtedly, she kept weaving her evil spells in her prison. She must perish.

The assessors, summoned at once to the castle to certify that she had changed to man's clothes again, found in the courtyard some hundred Englishmen who barred their way; they thought that these doctors, if allowed to enter, would spoil the game; they raised their battle-axes and their swords against them and chased them away, calling them *Armagnac traitors.* Cauchon managed with great difficulty to be admitted; he affected gaiety in order to please Warwick, and said with a laugh, "She is caught."

On Monday he returned with the inquisitor and eight assessors to question the Maid and asked her why she had resumed those garments. She offered no excuse, but, bravely facing her peril, she said that this garb was more suitable, so long as she had men as her keepers, and that besides the judges had failed to keep their word to her. Her saints had told her that "it was a great pity she had abjured in order to save her life." However, she was not refusing to wear woman's clothes. "Give me a safe and mild prison," she said, "and I shall be good, and obey the Church in everything."

The bishop, as he left, met Warwick, and to show his loyalty to the English cause he said in English, "Farewell, farewell." This cheerful good-bye meant something like "it is all over."

On Tuesday the judges summoned to the archbishop's palace a hotchpotch assembly, some assessors who had been present only at the first meetings, some who had never attended at all; men of all sorts, clerics, jurists, and even three medical men. The judges reported to the assembly what had taken place and requested its opinion. The opinion, very different from what had been expected, was that the prisoner should be summoned once more, and that her act of abjuration should be read over to her. It is doubtful whether the judges had any authority to do this. In reality, in the tumult of the raging soldiery and the clanking of swords there were no judges any more, and no judicial process was possible. The mob was howling for blood; perhaps the judges would have been the first victims. They drew up in haste a summons to be delivered on the morrow at eight o'clock; she was not to appear again, save to be burnt.

In the morning, Cauchon sent her a confessor, Brother Martin l'Advenu, "to apprise her of her coming death and induce her to penitence. . . ." When he told the poor woman what manner of death was awaiting her, she cried out most piteously, flung her arms about and tore her hair, "Alas! Am I to be treated with such horrible cruelty, that my body, wholly pure and never sullied, should be consumed today and turned into ashes! Ah! I should prefer to be beheaded seven times over than to be burnt in this wise! . . . Oh! I appeal to God, the great judge, to right the wrongs and grievances done to me!"

After this outburst of grief, she recovered herself, made confession, and asked to receive communion. The friar was in a predicament; but the bishop, whom he consulted, answered that she might be given communion, "and anything she might desire." Thus, at the very moment he had pronounced her a heretic and a backslider, and as such cut off from the Church, he was granting her that which the Church gives to the faithful. Perhaps a last sentiment of humanity rose in the heart of the wicked judge; he may have thought he had done enough in having the poor creature burnt, without casting her into despair and damnation. Perhaps the bad priest, with the indifferent levity of a skeptic, was allowing her the sacraments as something of little consequence, which might simply soothe the victim, and induce her to hold her peace. At first they attempted to go through with the ceremony surreptitiously, the host was brought without stole and without tapers. But the monk complained, and the churchmen of Rouen, duly informed, took advantage of this to express their opinion of Cauchon's judgment; they sent the body of Christ by the light of many torches, escorted by numerous priests who chanted litanies and told the people kneeling along the streets, "Pray for her."

After receiving communion with abundant tears, she caught sight of the bishop and said to him, "Bishop, my death is your doing. . . ." And again, "If you had placed me in a Church prison and in the keeping of ecclesiastics, this would not have happened. . . . That is why I appeal against you before God!"

Then, noticing among those in attendance Peter Morice, one of those who had preached to her, she said to him, "Ah! Master Peter, where shall I be tonight?"—"Do you not have a firm hope in the Lord?"—"Oh! yes, with God's help, I shall be in Paradise."

It was nine. They had clothed her in woman's garb and put her on a cart. By her side stood her confessor, Brother Martin l'Advenu;

Massieu, the usher, was on her other side. The Augustinian monk, Brother Isambart, who had already shown such charity and such courage, would not relinquish her. It was asserted that the wretched Loyseleur[4] also climbed onto the cart, to beg her forgiveness; the English would have killed him but for the Earl of Warwick's intervention.

Up to that moment the Maid had never despaired, except perhaps in her hour of temptation during Holy Week. While saying as she sometimes did, "These English people will put me to death," at bottom she did not believe it. She did not imagine that she would be abandoned. She had faith in her king, in the good people of France. She had said it expressly, "There will be in the prison, or at the time of the judgment, a great commotion whereby I shall be freed . . . delivered through a great victory! . . ." But even if king and people failed her, she had another support, infinitely more powerful and more assured, that of her friends from on high, her kind and beloved saints. . . . When she was besieging St. Peter,[5] and her soldiers abandoned her at the moment of the assault, the saints sent an invisible army to her aid. How could they now forsake their obedient daughter, they who so often had promised her rescue and deliverance!

What must have been her thoughts then, when she saw that of a certainty she was going to die, when she was carried in the cart through a quivering multitude, under the guard of eight hundred Englishmen armed with spears and swords? She wept and mourned; yet she accused neither her king nor her saints. . . . Only these words escaped her lips: "O Rouen, Rouen! Is it here that I must die?"

The end of this sorrowful journey was the Old Market Place, the fish market. Three platforms had been erected. On the first was the episcopal and royal chair, the throne of the English cardinal, and beside it the seats of his prelates. On the second were to figure the characters in the somber drama, the preacher, the judge, the bailiff, and the condemned. Apart from these, there rose a huge mass of plaster heaped high with wood; they had not been niggardly with the pyre: its height filled the spectators with awe. This was not done merely to give the execution a more solemn character: there was another motive. The pyre had been made so high, so that the executioner could only reach its base; he would not be able to shorten the torture, and mercifully to dispatch the victim, as he usually did, and so to spare her the flames. In this case, they wanted to make sure that

---

[4]Loyseleur was a church canon on the trial commission who had volunteered to serve as Joan's confessor and then revealed her spiritual confidences to the commission.—ED.

[5]The site of an action in one of the battles in which Joan took part.—ED.

justice would not be cheated, that the fire would not simply devour a corpse; they wanted her to be literally burnt alive; they wanted her, hoisted atop this mountain of fuel, above the encircling spears and swords, to be in plain sight for everyone in the market place. The slow, protracted burning under the eyes of the watchful crowd would probably expose at last some flaw, would wrench from her some cries that might be given out as a recantation, at the very least some confused, barely articulate words that could be so twisted; perhaps some craven prayer, some humiliating appeal to mercy, such as one would expect from a woman demented with terror.

A chronicler, a friend of the English, here lays a heavy charge against them. If we are to believe him, they wanted her dress to be consumed first, revealing her nakedness, "so as to remove all doubts from the minds of the people"; the fire being brushed aside for a moment, everyone could draw nigh and stare at her, "and all the secrets which may or should be in a woman's body"; after this immoral and ferocious exhibition, the executioner was to make the flames blaze anew on her poor carcass.

The horrible ceremony began with a sermon. Master Nicholas Midy, one of the lights of the University of Paris, preached on the edifying text: "When one limb of the Church is sick, the whole Church is sick." The poor Church could be healed only by cutting off the limb. He concluded with the formula: "Joan, go *you* in peace, the Church can no longer defend *thee*."

Then the ecclesiastical judge, the bishop of Beauvais, exhorted her with benignity to care for her soul and to remember all her transgressions, so as to rouse herself to contrition. The assessors had ruled that according to the law her abjuration should be read over to her; the bishop omitted this. He was afraid she would give him the lie, raise a protest. But the poor girl had little thought of thus haggling for her life; her mind was fixed on very different things. Even before she had been exhorted to contrition, she had fallen on her knees, invoking God, the Virgin, St. Michael and St. Catherine, forgiving everyone and asking forgiveness; begging of the crowd that they pray for her. Above all, she entreated every one of the priests present to say a mass for her soul. All this in such a devout, humble and touching fashion that all were moved and could not repress their feelings; the bishop of Beauvais began weeping, the bishop of Boulogne was sobbing, and now even the English were in tears, Winchester like the rest.

Might it be that in that moment of universal tenderness, of tears, of contagious weakness, the hapless girl, softened, relapsing into mere womanhood, did confess that now she could see clearly she had been wrong, that they had deceived her who had promised deliverance?

On this point, we cannot accept with implicit faith the biased testimony of the English. But it would betray scant knowledge of human nature to doubt that, frustrated as she was in her hope, her faith may have wavered. Did she actually utter the words? The thing is not certain; but I dare to affirm that the thought was there.

Meanwhile, the judges, dismayed for a moment, had rallied and were their stern selves again; the bishop of Beauvais, wiping his eyes, began reading the sentence. He rehearsed for the culprit all her crimes—schism, idolatry, invoking demons; how, after being admitted to penitence, she was "seduced by the Prince of lies and had relapsed, O grief! *like the dog returning to his vomit!* . . . Therefore, we pronounce you a rotten limb, and as such cut off from the Church; we deliver you over to the secular power, *begging it however to be mild in dealing with you, and to spare you death and bodily mutilation.*"

Thus rejected by the Church, she committed herself in full confidence to God. She asked for a cross. An Englishman made a wooden one out of a stick, and handed it to her; she received it devoutly, crude as it was, and placed it under her garments, next to her skin. . . . But she desired a regular Church crucifix to keep before her eyes until the moment of death. The kindly usher, Massieu, and Brother Isambart pleaded so earnestly that a cross was brought to her from the parish church of St. Saviour. As she was clasping the cross, and as Isambart was comforting her, the English began to grow weary of the delay; it must have been past noon; the soldiers were grumbling; the captains growled, "What's all this, you priests? Do you mean us to stay here till dinner time? . . ." Then, losing patience, and without waiting for the order of the bailiff, who alone had the authority to send her to death, they had two sergeants climb the platform and snatch her from the hands of the priests. At the foot of the tribunal, she was seized by men-at-arms, who dragged her to the executioner, and told him, "Do your office. . . ." The fury of the soldiers roused a feeling of horror; many in the crowd, and even some of the judges, ran away, unable to bear the sight any more.

When she was brought down from the platform to the market place, roughly handled by the English soldiers, nature broke down, and the flesh in her was perturbed; she cried anew, "O Rouen, so thou art to be my last abode! . . ." She said no more, and *did not sin with her lips*, in this hour of terror and agony.

She accused neither her king, nor her saints. But when she had reached the top of the pyre, and saw the vast city, the motionless and silent crowd, she could not help saying, "Ah! Rouen, Rouen, I sadly fear thou wilt suffer because of my death!" She who had saved the people, and whom the people were forsaking, in the admirable sweetness of her soul, had only words of compassion for the people, as she was about to die.

She was tied under the placard of infamy; a miter placed on her head with the words: "Heretic, backslider, apostate, idolater. . . ." The executioner lit the fire. She saw it from her high station and uttered a cry. Then, as the friar who was exhorting her was paying no heed to the flames, she, forgetting herself, was afraid for him and bade him descend.

The proof that up to that moment she had made no formal recantation is that the wretched Cauchon felt obliged (impelled no doubt by the supreme satanic will which presided over the whole) to come to the foot of the pyre, forced to confront his victim once more, in a last effort to wrest from her some damning admission. He drew but these words, fit to rack his soul—words that she had told him before, and which she repeated with gentleness, "Bishop, my death is your doing. . . . If you had placed me in a prison of the Church, this would not have come to pass." They may have hoped that, believing herself abandoned by her king, she would accuse him at last, and speak against him. But even then, she was defending him still: "Whether I have done well or ill, my king is not at fault; it was not he who counseled me."

Meanwhile the flames were rising. At the moment they reached her she shivered and in her agony cried for holy *water; water,* it was probably a cry wrenched by terror. But soon conquering herself, she had only the names of God, her angels and her saints on her lips, "Yes, my voices came from God, my voices did not deceive me! . . ." All doubt vanished in the flames; this leads us to believe that she had accepted death as the promised *deliverance,* that she no longer understood *salvation* in the Judaic, literal, material sense, as she had done hitherto, that she saw the light at last, and that, as she emerged from the dark shadows, her gifts of illumination and sanctity were fully purified and attained their supreme perfection.

These great words of hers are vouched for by the one who was the official and sworn witness of her death—the Dominican who went with her up the pile, whom she requested to go down, and who, from below, spoke to her, listened to her, held the cross before her eyes.

We have another testimony on her holy death, a witness of the most unimpeachable authority. This man, whose name history must preserve and honor, was the Augustinian monk we have mentioned before, Brother Isambart de la Pierre; during the trial, he came near being put to death because he had advised the Maid; yet, although so clearly exposed to the hatred of the English, he insisted on climbing into the cart with her; he had the parish crucifix brought to her; he comforted her in the midst of the raging multitude, both on the platform and at the stake.

Twenty years later, the two religious, plain monks, who had espoused poverty, without anything to gain or to fear in this world, testified to the scene we have just described, "We could hear her," they said, "in the fire, invoking her saints, her archangel; she kept repeating the name of our Saviour. . . . Finally, her head dropped, and she uttered a great cry: 'Jesus!' "

"Ten thousand men were weeping. . . ." Only a few Englishmen laughed, or were trying to laugh. One of them, among the most furious, had sworn he would lay a faggot on the pyre; she was expiring at the time he put it, and he swooned; his comrades took him to a tavern, to make him drink and revive his spirits; but he could not recover. "I saw," he said, beside himself, "I saw with her last breath a dove fly out of her mouth." Others had read in the flames the name she was repeating: "Jesus!" The executioner that evening sought Brother Isambart; he was terror-stricken; he made confession, but he could not believe that God would ever forgive him. A secretary of the king of England, as he returned, said aloud, "We are lost, we have burnt a saint."

Joan of Arc in Context

MALCOLM G. A. VALE

For the following selection, we have turned not to one of the hundreds of works on Joan of Arc but to a modern biography of the king she served so faithfully, Charles VII, by the English historian Malcolm G. A. Vale. Vale deals with his subject through "a series of episodes" (p. ix), one of which is the episode of Joan of Arc. His version of Joan is rather more complex than that of Michelet— indeed of many other more recent biographers—in that he sees her neither as an innocent nor as a committed champion of French nationalism, but as the archetype of the medieval visionary, dedicated not to human causes but to the voices of her saints. Further, he sets Joan in the context of both fifteenth-century historical events and twentieth-century historical scholarship.

Joan of Arc was born about 1412, at the village of Domrémy, on the borders of the duchies of Bar and Lorraine. She was the daughter, not of a peasant, but of a fairly substantial tenant farmer. There is no subsequent surviving record of her existence from the time of her childhood until May 1428, when she arrived at the castle of Vaucouleurs, where Robert de Baudricourt was captain. He held the castle in the name of the uncrowned Charles VII. Baudricourt, initially sceptical, was eventually won over and dispatched Joan with an escort to see Charles at Chinon. She claimed that she would raise the siege of Orléans which the English, under the earl of Salisbury, had begun on 12 October 1428. She arrived at Chinon probably on 23 February 1429, saw Charles two days later, and evidently impressed him deeply. A month later, after an examination at Poitiers, she began her campaign against the English and their Burgundian allies by sending them a letter, calling upon them to surrender outside Orléans in God's name. On 29 April she arrived with an army to raise the siege, and on 8 May she entered the town in triumph. The following two months saw a series of French military successes, ending with a thrust to Rheims—then in Anglo-Burgundian hands—where, on 17 July 1429, Charles was crowned and anointed.

There Joan's successes ended. On 23 May 1430 she was captured by Burgundian troops at the siege of Compiègne, and two days later the University of Paris, acting in Henry VI of England's name, demanded that she be tried as a heretic. She was sold by her Burgundian captors to the English administration, and was delivered into the hands of the Inquisition. As she had been captured within the diocese of Beauvais, a common Inquisitorial practice was followed and Pierre Cauchon, bishop of Beauvais—although exiled from his see because it was in territory then occupied by Charles—was appointed to judge the case by Jean Graverent, Inquisitor of France. With Cauchon sat Jean Lemaître, a preaching friar, vicar of the Inquisition in the diocese of Rouen, where the trial was held. It began with preliminary investigations and interrogation of witnesses lasting from 9 January until 26 March 1431. This was followed by the trial itself, which ended with Joan's abjuration on 24 May. On Sunday 27 May she relapsed into heresy, and the swift series of interrogations which followed this relapse ended with her being delivered to the secular power for execution. Three days later she was burnt at the stake in the Old Market Place of Rouen.

Joan of Arc has received more attention than any other female visionary of the later Middle Ages. Despite (or perhaps because of) this, the Saint has tended to oust the girl from Domrémy from serious historical investigation. It is appropriate that her canonisation in 1920 should have been in part a result of pressure from France upon the

Holy See. She was one of the most valuable of Saints politically. Her arrival at Chinon in February 1429 was, arguably, a political act. Her execution as a heretic at Rouen in May 1431 was also, allegedly, a political act. John, duke of Bedford, could announce that she was "a disciple and lyme of the feende called the Pucelle, that used fals enchauntments and sorcerie." Her beliefs were not strictly orthodox, at least in fifteenth-century terms. She was no friend of the earthly Church Militant. Like other mystics and visionaries, she posed a threat to the hierarchy of the Church. If men were able to communicate so directly with God—through visions or "voices"—what need was there for the clergy? Mediation between God and Man, except through the Saints, was therefore redundant. Shaw could point to this aspect of her "voices" when he made Pierre Cauchon, bishop of Beauvais, exclaim:

> A faithful daughter of the Church! The Pope himself at his proudest dare not presume as this woman presumes. She acts as if she herself were The Church.

The fictitious Cauchon was merely being made to voice an objection which had already been made in fact—but by the other side. After her capture, Charles's adviser, Regnault de Chartres, archbishop of Rheims, told the inhabitants of the town that "she raised herself in pride." Her pride and presumption—that *superbia* which was noted by her interrogators—was her downfall. Her answers to the tribunal which tried her at Rouen served to indict her. Similarly, her avowed ability to predict and prognosticate the future course of events placed her in a very dangerous position. The line dividing permissible astrology from sorcery was thin and was becoming thinner. Her trial may have been in some respects irregular, but there were many fifteenth-century men—even among those who were on the side of Charles VII—who were not unduly disturbed by her fate. It was dangerous to have so unorthodox a *fille du régiment* in your camp. Her interrogator, Guillaume Erard, could voice the views of many when he said to her on 24 May 1431: "I'm talking to you, Joan, and I tell you that your king is a heretic and schismatic." The trial at Rouen was in part a device to discredit Charles VII as a heretic by association. It was conducted largely by Frenchmen, born in France. Of the 131 judges, assessors and other clergy concerned with her trial and condemnation, only eight were Englishmen. Of those eight, only two attended more than three sessions of the trial. One of France's patron Saints was thus condemned by Frenchmen. She was a victim as much of a civil war within France as of a war with the English. . . .

Joan's career still poses many unanswered (and perhaps unanswerable) questions. What was the "sign" given by her to Charles which, it was alleged, so effectively convinced him of his legitimacy? How was Joan able to win his confidence so quickly, and so easily? What was the king's "secret"? Why was the trial of rehabilitation so long delayed? Many answers have been given to these questions. Some are ludicrous and many are unconvincing. Among the latter stands a recent contribution to the literature on Joan of Arc, entitled *Histoire Véridique et Merveilleuse de la Pucelle d'Orléans.*[6] Its author, M. David-Darnac, attempts to argue that she was not the daughter of a substantial tenant farmer at Domrémy, but the illegitimate child of Louis, duke of Orléans, and Isabella of Bavaria. She was born, not at Domrémy in about 1412, but in Paris on the eve of Orléans's murder in 1407. She was then (for reasons which are by no means clear) transported to Lorraine and left there in the care of the d'Arc family. David-Darnac's account of the story is fairly orthodox from this stage until her capture and trial in 1430–1. But he sees Cauchon as being concerned throughout the trial to have her released. At the very last moment, Cauchon, it is asserted, allowed her to escape by way of a secret tunnel under the walls of the castle at Rouen. To introduce such Gothic novelist's nonsense into a work which purports to be history, albeit popular history, seems inexcusable. Joan is then said to have gone into hiding and reappears (for reasons which are again unclear) as the wife of one Robert des Armoises, a minor noble of Lorraine. A substitute has therefore to be conjured up and burned at Rouen in her stead. Undeterred by the sheer improbability of all this, David-Darnac concludes his book with an account of the activities of Joan, identified as "la Pucelle de France," between 1436 and her supposed death in 1449.

The grounds for objection to this version of events are basically twofold. First, Joan's date of birth has to be put back by at least four years if David-Darnac's assertions are to be entertained. A child was born to Isabella of Bavaria in 1407, but it was male and died soon after birth. Joan herself said in 1431 that she was about eighteen or nineteen years old. This would put her date of birth at about 1412 or 1413, at least five years after the death of her pretended father Louis of Orléans. David-Darnac also demands that the evidence of the rehabilitation process of 1455–6 is ignored. On this argument, about 150 witnesses must have perjured themselves to a man in giving evidence on Joan's early life and subsequent career. Secondly, both the thesis of Joan's bastardy and her escape from burning have been long discredited. In 1805 the thesis of bastardy was first put forward. David-Darnac

---

[6]The True and Marvelous History of the Maid of Orleans.—Ed.

adduces no new documentary evidence to support that contention. Nor has the "survival" of Joan received further documentation. A woman calling herself "la Pucelle de France" certainly appeared in Lorraine, at Orléans and in the South-West between 1436 and 1449. A document referring to her was published by Dom Calmet, in his *History of Lorraine,* in the early eighteenth century. The "false" Joan of Arc, moreover, confessed before Charles VII and the Paris *Parlement* to being an impostor, a piece of evidence which David-Darnac chooses to ignore. There seems no reason to suppose either that Joan was not burnt by the English administration at Rouen in 1431 (as every witness at the inquiries of 1450, 1452 and 1455–6 deposed), or that she was not a girl from the borders of the duchies of Bar and Lorraine.

Review and Study Questions

1. What did Joan actually accomplish in her brief public career?
2. What were the real reasons why Joan was tried and executed?
3. Describe the execution of Joan of Arc.
4. What was the basis on which Joan was canonized as a saint, according to the readings in this chapter?
5. In your opinion, what were the motives of Joan of Arc?

Suggestions for Further Reading

Although Quicherat's monumental five-volume collection of the documentary sources for Joan of Arc remains untranslated, several selections from that collection are available. One of them, Régine Pernoud, *The Retrial of Joan of Arc: The Evidence at the Trial for Her Rehabilitation, 1450–1456,* tr. J. M. Cohen (New York: Harcourt, Brace, 1955), is excerpted for this chapter. Much of the rest of Joan's earlier trial is presented in another book by Pernoud, *Joan of Arc by Herself and Her Witnesses* (New York: Stein and Day, 1966). Another such selection is *Joan of Arc: Self-Portrait, Compiled and Translated from the Original Latin and French Sources,* ed. Willard Trask (New York: Stackpole Sons, 1936). Yet others are Wilfred T. Jewkes and Jerome B. Landfield, *Joan of Arc: Fact, Legend, and Literature* (New York: Harcourt, Brace, 1964), which also includes some selections from modern writers about Joan, and *The First Biography of Joan of Arc with the Chronicle Record of a Contemporary Account,* ed. and tr. Daniel S. Rankin and Claire Quintal (Pittsburgh: University of Pittsburgh Press, 1964).

From the mid–nineteenth century on, there has been a steady

stream of biographies and special studies of Joan of Arc. Of the more recent works, Frances Gies, *Joan of Arc: The Legend and the Reality* (New York: Harper & Row, 1981) is not only a biography but an extensive review of the scholarly material on the subject. Marina Warner, *Joan of Arc: The Image of Female Heroism* (New York: Knopf, 1981) is a complex and difficult work of psychohistory that relates Joan to a number of themes of feminist criticism.

Many literary figures, including George Bernard Shaw and Anatole France, have been attracted by the Joan of Arc story. Among the best of these is Victoria Sackville-West, *Saint Joan of Arc* (Garden City, N.Y.: Doubleday, Doran, 1936), a vivid and sensitive biography by a distinguished British novelist. Edward Lucie-Smith, *Joan of Arc* (New York: Norton, 1976) is again a general account by a literary writer, much in the same vein as Sackville-West's, but less well done. Lucien Fabre, *Joan of Arc,* tr. Gerard Hopkins (London: Odhams Press, 1954), is a sensitive and moving account by a great French man of letters.

Of the many straightforward historical biographies, two can be especially recommended: John Holland Smith, *Joan of Arc* (New York: Scribner's, 1973) and Pierre de Sermoise, *Joan of Arc and Her Secret Missions,* tr. Jennifer Taylor (London: Robert Hale, 1973).

CHRISTOPHER COLUMBUS: ADMIRAL OF THE OCEAN SEA

c. 1451	Born
1492–93	First voyage
1493–96	Second voyage
1498–99	Third voyage
1502–04	Fourth voyage
1506	Died

Every schoolchild knows the name Christopher Columbus, the date 1492, and the fact that in that year Columbus "discovered" the New World. This alone assures Columbus a secure niche in history, for his was the most stupendous accomplishment of any discoverer-explorer. Never before had two entirely new and unsuspected continents been discovered by Europeans. It is true that medieval Vikings touched the shores of North American and that Bristol fishermen may have worked the outer banks off Newfoundland. But neither left a permanent European mark on the New World. That was the accomplishment of Christopher Columbus, who established the first permanent European settlement in the New World that quickly led to long-term colonization and conquest.

Yet, the supreme irony of the story of Columbus is that he himself never knew what he had discovered. He continued to believe, to the end of his life, that he had sailed to the coast of Asia. He was led to this conviction by the calculation of the circumference of the earth by contemporary cosmologists—ultimately going back to the ancient geographer Ptolemy—which was underestimated by some 25 percent. This shortfall was confirmed by the fact that Columbus's computation of a degree of longitude at the equator was 56.86 miles when in fact it is 69 miles. Moreover, Columbus had studied the works of Marco Polo, which indicated that the continent of Asia

285

extended much farther to the east than it actually does. By Columbus's own calculations, then, when he made his first landfall on October 12, 1492, he had sailed 3,200 miles in just over 33 days and should have been off the coast of Japan. If he had even suspected the true distance to Asia, he probably would never have undertaken his great "enterprise."

The Ship's Log

CHRISTOPHER COLUMBUS

Columbus was a native-born Genoese but most of his mature life had been spent in Portugal, where he came to be involved in various Portuguese maritime adventures out of which grew his plan to reach Asia by sailing to the west. For almost a decade, Columbus had tried to interest various European governments in supporting his plan. He had approached the Portuguese, the English, and the court of Spain, without success. Then, in 1492, he appealed again to Spain. This time he gained the ear of a great court official, Luis de Santangel, who not only interested the king and queen in Columbus's proposal but who himself provided a considerable part of the money to finance it. Under these circumstances, Ferdinand and Isabella agreed to underwrite the expedition, providing the ships, paying for the crews and supplies, setting out generous rewards for Columbus, and conferring upon him the title Admiral of the Ocean Sea. They also provided him with a letter of credence to the Great Khan.

The expedition sailed from Palos on Friday, August 3, 1492. It consisted of three vessels, the *Niña*, the *Pinta*, and the *Santa Maria*, Columbus's flagship. After a brief stop in the Canary Islands for fresh water and for rerigging the *Niña*, he sailed out to the west on his epochal voyage of discovery.

In the course of that voyage Columbus, like the good sea captain he was, kept a detailed ship's log. On his triumphant return this log was presented to Queen Isabella. It has not survived. But the queen immediately had a copy made for Columbus, the "Barcelona copy," which remained among the papers of the Columbus family. This copy has also disappeared, but at some point before the disappearance, it came into the hands of Fray Bartolomé de las Casas. Las Casas was a great admirer of Columbus, a friend of the Columbus family, and the first major historian of the New World. In the course of collecting the materials for his own history, las Casas prepared an abstract of the "Barcelona copy" that seems to have been copied directly from "the formal words of the Admiral." This is the only surviving version of the Columbus log. Excerpts from it follow.

Wednesday, 10 October 1492

I held course to the WSW, running 7½ knots, and at times 9 knots, and for awhile 5¼ knots. Between day and night I made 177 miles. I told the crew 132 miles, but they could stand it no longer. They grumbled and complained of the long voyage, and I reproached them for their lack of spirit, telling them that, for better or worse, they had to complete the enterprise on which the Catholic Sovereigns had sent them. I cheered them on as best as I could, telling them of all the honors and rewards they were about to receive. I also told the men that it was useless to complain, for I had started out to find the Indies and would continue until I had accomplished that mission, with the help of Our Lord.

Thursday, 11 October 1492

I sailed to the WSW, and we took more water aboard than at any other time on the voyage. I saw several things that were indications of land. At one time a large flock of sea birds flew overhead, and a green reed was found floating near the ship. The crew of the *Pinta* spotted some of the same reeds and some other plants; they also saw what looked like a small board or plank. A stick was recovered that looks man-made, perhaps carved with an iron tool. Those on the *Niña* saw a little stick covered with barnacles. I am certain that many things were overlooked because of the heavy sea, but even these few made the crew breathe easier; in fact, the men have even become cheerful. I sailed 81 miles from sunset yesterday to sunset today. As is our custom, vespers were said in the late afternoon, and a special thanksgiving was offered to God for giving us renewed hope through the many signs of land He has provided.

After sunset I ordered the pilot to return to my original westerly course, and I urged the crew to be ever-vigilant. I took the added precaution of doubling the number of lookouts, and I reminded the men that the first to sight land would be given a silk doublet as a personal token from me. Further, he would be given an annuity of 10,000 maravedies from the Sovereigns.

About 10 o'clock at night, while standing on the sterncastle, I thought I saw a light to the west. It looked like a little wax candle bobbing up and down. It had the same appearance as a light or torch belonging to fishermen or travellers who alternately raised and lowered it, or perhaps were going from house to house. I am the first to admit that I was so eager to find land that I did not trust my own senses, so I called for Pedro Gutiérrez, the representative of the King's household, and asked him to watch for the light. After a few moments, he too saw it. I then summoned Rodrigo Sánchez of Segovia, the comptroller of the fleet, and asked him to watch for the light. He saw nothing, nor did any other member of the crew. It was such an uncertain thing that I did not feel it was adequate proof of land.

The moon, in its third quarter, rose in the east shortly before midnight. I estimate that we were making about 9 knots and had gone some 67½ miles between the beginning of night and 2 o'clock in the morning. Then, at two hours after midnight, the *Pinta* fired a cannon, my prearranged signal for the sighting of land.

I now believe that the light I saw earlier was a sign from God and that it was truly the first positive indication of land. When we caught up with the *Pinta*, which was always running ahead because she was a swift sailer, I learned that the first man to sight land was Rodrigo de Tríana, a seaman from Lepe.

I hauled in all the sails but the mainsail and lay-to till daylight. The land is about 6 miles to the west.

Friday, 12 October 1492
(Log entry for 12 October is combined with that of 11 October)

At dawn we saw naked people, and I went ashore in the ship's boat, armed, followed by Martín Alonso Pinzón, captain of the *Pinta*, and his brother, Vincente Yáñez Pinzón, captain of the *Niña*. I unfurled the royal banner and the captains brought the flags which displayed a large green cross with the letters F and Y at the left and right side of the cross. Over each letter was the appropriate crown of that Sovereign. These flags were carried as a standard on all of the ships. After a prayer of thanksgiving I ordered the captains of the *Pinta* and *Niña*, together with Rodrigo de Escobedo (secretary of the fleet), and Rodrigo Sánchez of Segovia (comptroller of the fleet) to bear faith and witness that I was taking possession of this island for the King and Queen. I made all the necessary declarations and had these testimonies carefully written down by the secretary. In addition to those named above, the entire company of the fleet bore witness to this act. To this island I gave the name *San Salvador*, in honor of our Blessed Lord.

No sooner had we concluded the formalities of taking possession of the island than people began to come to the beach, all as naked as their mothers bore them, and the women also, although I did not see more than one very young girl. All those that I saw were young people, none of whom was over 30 years old. They are very well-built people, with handsome bodies and very fine faces, though their appearance is marred somewhat by very broad heads and foreheads, more so than I have ever seen in any other race. Their eyes are large and very pretty, and their skin is the color of Canary Islanders or of sunburned peasants, not at all black, as would be expected because we were on an east-west line with Hierro in the Canaries. These are tall people and their legs, with no exceptions, are quite straight, and none of them has a paunch. They are, in fact, well proportioned. Their hair is not kinky, but straight, and coarse like horsehair. They wear it short over the eyebrows, but they have a long hank in the back that they never cut. Many of the natives paint their faces; others paint their whole bodies; some, only the eyes or nose. Some are painted black, some white, some red; others are of different colors.

The people here called this land *Guanahaní*[1] in their language, and their speech is very fluent, although I do not understand any of it. They are friendly and well-dispositioned people who bare no arms except for small spears, and they have no iron. I showed one my sword, and through ignorance he grabbed it by the blade and cut himself. Their spears are made of wood, to which they attach a fish tooth at one end, or some other sharp thing.

I want the natives to develop a friendly attitude toward us because I know that they are a people who can be made free and converted to our Holy Faith more by love than by force. I therefore gave red caps to some and glass beads to others. They hung the beads around their necks, along with some other things of slight value that I gave them. And they took great pleasure in this and became so friendly that it was a marvel. They traded and gave everything they had with good will, but it seems to me that they have very little and are poor in everything. I warned my men to take nothing from the people without giving something in exchange.

This afternoon the people of San Salvador came swimming to our ships and in boats made from one log. They brought us parrots, balls of cotton thread, spears, and many other things, including a kind of

---

[1]The exact location of this first landfall is a subject of controversy. Following Morison, most modern scholars say it was Watling's Island in the Bahamas. But Fuson, following Dunn and Kelley, prefers Samana Cay.—ED.

dry leaf[2] that they hold in great esteem. For these items we swapped them little glass beads and hawks' bells.

Many of the men I have seen have scars on their bodies, and when I made signs to them to find out how this happened, they indicated that people from other nearby islands come to San Salvador to capture them; they defend themselves the best they can. I believe that people from the mainland come here to take them as slaves. They ought to make good and skilled servants, for they repeat very quickly whatever we say to them. I think they can easily be made Christians, for they seem to have no religion. If it pleases Our Lord, I will take six of them to Your Highnesses when I depart, in order that they may learn our language. . . .

If the weather permits, I shall depart this Cabo del Isleo and sail around Isabela until I find the king and see if I can get from him the gold which I hear that he wears. Then I shall sail for another great island which I strongly believe should be Japan, according to the signs made by the San Salvador Indians with me. They call that island *Colba*, where they say there are many great ships and navigators. And from that island I intend to go to another that they call *Bohío*, which is also very large. As to any others that lie in between, I shall see them in passing, and according to what gold or spices I find, I will determine what I must do. But I have already decided to go to the mainland and to the city of Quisay, and give Your Highnesses' letters to the Grand Khan and ask for a reply and return with it. . . .

Tuesday, 25 December 1492—Christmas Day

I sailed in a light wind yesterday from La Mar de Santo Tomás to Punta Santa, and at the passing of the first watch, 11 o'clock at night, I was 3 miles east of the point. I decided to lie down to sleep because I had not slept for two days and one night. Since it was calm, the sailor who was steering the ship also decided to catch a few winks and left the steering to a young ship's boy, a thing which I have always expressly prohibited throughout the voyage. It made no difference whether there was a wind or calm; the ships were not to be steered by young boys. . . .

Our Lord willed that at midnight, when the crew saw me lie down to rest and also saw that there was a dead calm and the sea was as in a

---

[2]This is the earliest reference to tobacco.—ED.

bowl, they all lay down to sleep and left the helm to that boy. The currents carried the ship upon one of these banks. Although it was night, the sea breaking on them made so much noise that they could be heard and seen at a 3-mile distance. The ship went upon the bank so quietly that it was hardly noticeable. When the boy felt the rudder ground and heard the noise of the sea, he cried out. I jumped up instantly; no one else had yet felt that we were aground. Then the master of the ship, Juan de la Cosa, who was on watch, came out. I ordered him to rouse the crew, to launch the small boat we carry on our stern, and to take an anchor and cast it at the stern. The master and many others jumped into the small boat, and I assumed they were going to follow my orders. Instead, their only thoughts were to escape to the *Niña*, which was 1½ miles to the windward. The crew of the *Niña* would not receive them, which was correct, and therefore they returned to the ship. But the boat from the *Niña* reached the ship before my own boat did!

When I saw that some of my own crew were fleeing and that the sea was becoming more shallow, with my ship broadside to it, I did the only thing I could. I ordered the mast cut and the ship lightened as much as possible, to see if it could be refloated. But the water became even more shallow, and the ship settled more and more to one side. Although there was little or no sea, I could not save her. Then the seams opened, though she remained in one piece.

I took my crew to the *Niña* for their safety, and as there was a light land breeze and still half the night ahead of us, and since I did not know how far the banks extended, I beat about till daybreak and then went inside the bank to the ship. I also dispatched Diego de Arana, master-at-arms of the fleet, and Pedro Gutiérrez, representative of the Royal Household, to take the small boat and go directly to the King that had last Saturday invited me to his village. I instructed them to beg the King to come to this harbor with his boats.

The village of this King is about 5 miles beyond this bank. My men told me that the King wept when he heard of the disaster. He sent all his people from the village with many large canoes to help us unload the ship. The King displayed great haste and diligence, and everything was unloaded in a very brief space of time. He himself personally assisted the unloading, along with his brothers and relatives, and guarded what was taken ashore in order that everything might be completely secure.

From time to time the King sent one of his relatives to me, weeping, to console me, and they said that I was not to be troubled or annoyed, for the King would give me whatever he possessed. I certify to Your Highnesses that in no part of Castile could things be so secure; not even a shoe string was lost! The King ordered everything placed near the houses, even emptying some in order that everything could be stored and guarded. He ordered armed men placed around the houses to guard everything all night. He, with all his people in the village, wept a great deal. They are an affectionate people, free from avarice and agreeable to everything. I certify to Your Highnesses that in all the world I do not believe there is a better people or a better country. They love their neighbors as themselves, and they have the softest and gentlest voices in the world and are always smiling. They may go naked, but Your Highnesses may be assured that they have very good customs among themselves, and the King maintains a most marvelous state, where everything takes place in an appropriate and well-ordered manner. It is a pleasure to see all of this. These people have good memories and want to see everything; they ask what things are and for what purpose they are used. . . .

The King was delighted to see me happy, and he understood that I desired a great deal of gold. He indicated by signs that he knew where there was a lot of it nearby and that I should be of good cheer, for he would give me as much of it as I desired. He told me all about this gold, specifically, that is found in Japan, which they call *Cibao*. The people there have so much of it that they place no value on it and will bring it here. Also, the King told me, there is much gold here in the Isla Española, which they call Bohío, and in the province of Caribata. . . . I derived a great deal of pleasure and consolation from these things, and when I realized that this mitigated the trouble and affliction I had experienced by losing the ship, I recognized that Our Lord had caused me to run aground at this place so that I might establish a settlement here. And so many things came to hand here that the disaster was a blessing in disguise. Certainly, if I had not run aground here, I would have kept out to sea without anchoring at this place because it is situated inside a large bay containing two or three banks of shoals. Neither would I have left any of my people here on this voyage; even if I had desired to leave them, I could not have outfitted them well enough, nor given them enough ammunition, provisions, and materials for a fort. It is quite true that many of the people with me have pleaded with me to permit them to remain here.

Now I have ordered that a tower and a fortress be constructed, very well built, with a large moat. This is not because I believe this to be necessary with these Indians, for I am sure that I could subjugate the entire island—which I believe is larger than Portugal with twice the population—with the men that I have in my company. These Indians are naked, unarmed, and cowardly beyond help. But it is right that this tower be built, and what must be, must be. Since these Indians are so far from Your Highnesses, it is necessary that the people here know your people and what they can do, in order that the Indians may obey Your Highnesses with love and fear. The men remaining have timbers with which to construct the fortress and provisions of bread and wine for more than a year, as well as seeds for sowing, and the ship's boat. I am leaving a caulker, a carpenter, a gunner, and a caskmaker among the many who desire zealously to serve Your Highnesses and who will please me greatly if they find the mine where the gold comes from. Thus, everything that has happened was for this purpose, that this beginning may be made. . . .

I hope to God that when I come back here from Castile, which I intend on doing, that I will find a barrel of gold, for which these people I am leaving will have traded, and that they will have found the gold mine, and the spices, and in such quantities that within three years the Sovereigns will prepare for and undertake the conquest of the Holy Land. I have already petitioned Your Highnesses to see that all the profits of this, my enterprise, should be spent on the conquest of Jerusalem, and Your Highnesses smiled and said that the idea pleased them, and that even without this expedition they had the inclination to do it. . . .

Tuesday, 8 January 1493

Because of a strong east and SE wind I did not start today, but I ordered the ships supplied with wood and water and everything necessary for the voyage. Although I wanted to sail this entire coast of the Isla Española, which I could do maintaining my course, my captains on the caravels are brothers, that is to say, Martín Alonso Pinzón and Vincente Yáñez Pinzón, and their followers are greedy and untrustworthy. They do not respect the honor I have shown them, and they have not and do not obey my commands. Rather, they have done and said many unjust things against me, and Martín Alonso left me from 22 November to 6 January, without cause or reason, but from disobedience. All this I have endured in silence, in order to finish my voyage succcessfully. On account of this, in order to escape such bad company, which I have to ignore, I have decided to return with the greatest possible haste and not to stop longer. Although there are many disobedient people among the crew, there are also many good men. Now is not the time to think about their punishment. . . .

Three hours before dawn I departed the gulf, which I have named the *Golfo de las Flechas*, first with a land breeze and then with a west wind. I turned the prow to the east by north, in order to go to the Isla de Caribe, where the people are whom the inhabitants of all these islands and countries fear so greatly. This is because the Caribes cross all these seas in their countless canoes and eat the men they are able to capture. One of the four Indians I took yesterday in the Puerto de las Flechas has shown me the course. After we had gone about 48 miles, the Indians indicated to me that the islands lay to the SE. I wanted to follow that course and ordered the sails trimmed, but after we had gone 6 miles the wind again blew very favorably for going to Spain. I noted that the crew were becoming dismayed because we had departed from a direct course for home; and as both ships were taking in a great deal of water, they had no help save that of God. I was compelled to abandon the course that I believe was taking me to the island; I returned to the direct course for Spain, NE by east, and held it until sunset, 36 miles. The Indians told me that on this course I would find the island of Matinino, which is inhabited only by women. I would like to carry five or six of them to the Sovereigns, but I doubt if the Indians know the course well, and I am not able to delay because of the danger with the leaking caravels. . . .

The danger was further increased by the fact that the ship was short of ballast, since the load has been lightened by the consumption of the provisions, water, and wine. I had not provided these in sufficient quantity, having hoped for favorable weather like I found in the islands, and having planned to take on ballast at the Island of Women. The solution I found for this problem, when I was able to do it, was to fill the empty water and wine casks with sea water; by this means I corrected the problem. . . .

Last night, after sunset, the skies commenced to clear toward the west, indicating that the wind was about to blow from that direction. I had the bonnet placed on the mainsail. The sea was still very high, although it was subsiding a little. I sailed to the ENE at a speed of 3 knots, and in 13 hours of the night I went 39 miles. After sunrise we saw land, off the prow to the ENE. Some said it was the island of

Madeira; others, the Rock of Sintra in Portugal, near Lisbon. The wind changed and blew ahead from the ENE, and the sea came very high from the west. The caravel must have been 15 miles from land. According to my navigation I think we are off the Azores and believe the land ahead is one of those islands. The pilots and sailors believe that we are already off Castile.

From Success to Failure

BARTOLOMÉ DE LAS CASAS

Before the year was out Columbus had sailed on his second voyage, this time with a much larger and better provisioned fleet— seventeen ships carrying tools, seed, livestock, and more than a thousand colonists. His purpose was to settle the island of Hispaniola.

The expedition found the site of the first settlement deserted and its buildings destroyed. Columbus established a second settlement, which he named Isabela. He left his brother Diego in charge. Diego shortly abandoned Isabela for a more favorable location and the new town of Santo Domingo. Meanwhile Columbus himself had continued his exploration of the south coast of Cuba and discovered Jamaica. Early in 1496 he returned to Spain.

The king and queen were becoming somewhat disillusioned. Columbus had found only trifling amounts of gold and no spices, and there was muttering against him from the colony he had founded. Nevertheless, they supported a third voyage. This time Columbus discovered the coast of South America, which he took to be the mainland of Asia. But he found his colony in turmoil. To pacify the settlers, he was forced to parcel out the land—with the Indians as slave labor. Thus Columbus introduced into the New World the terrible *repartimiento* system of plantation-slave agriculture, which had originally been developed in the Canary Islands.

In the meantime the king and queen, disturbed by reports from the settlers in the New World, sent a new governor, Francisco de Bobadilla, to replace Columbus. When Columbus challenged his authority, Bobadilla had him arrested and sent back to Spain in irons.

Columbus had great difficulty in regaining the confidence of the king and queen, but they finally consented to support a fourth voyage, on the condition that he stay away from Santo Domingo. He left in the spring of 1502, with four ships; with him sailed his son Fernando, his brother Bartholomew, and many old shipmates. He did not, however, stay away from Santo Domingo, as ordered, but was refused permission to land by the new governor, Nicolas de Ovando, even in the face of an approaching hurricane. Columbus rode out the storm at sea and continued with his explorations. He explored the coast of Central America and lost two of his ships in battles with the native people, whom he called Indians. On the way back to Hispaniola Columbus's ships landed in Jamaica. After more than a year at sea the two remaining ships were rotting away and sinking under them; Columbus ordered them beached.

It is at this desperate juncture in his fourth voyage that we turn to the account of the final failure of what Columbus had called his *alto viaje,* "high voyage," that he was sure would rescue his fortunes.

The account is from the *History of the Indies* by Fray Bartolomé de las Casas. As we have seen, it was las Casas who abstracted and preserved the log of Columbus's first voyage. In addition to admiring Columbus himself and knowing Columbus's son Fernando, las Casas was present in the New World and an eyewitness to many of the events he describes. He had come to Hispaniola with Governor Ovando in 1502 and remained in the West Indies until 1516, the first of several periods of residence in the New World, culminating in his appointment as Bishop of Chiapas in Guatemala in 1544. He went on to become a major figure of both the Spanish church and court.

Las Casas began to write his history about 1527 and worked on it for most of the rest of his life. His primary purpose was to defend the native people from slavery and persecution by his fellow Spaniards. This became the great work of las Casas's life and the theme not only of his history but of all his voluminous writings. Despite his passion, however, las Casas remained a reliable reporter of historical events. His is the best contemporary account of the later voyages of Columbus.

We pick up his narrative of the *alto viaje* as Columbus beached his ships on the coast of Jamaica.

———————————

Since the holds of the ships were drawing water, the admiral ran aground safely away from the surf. The crew had orders to stay on board and the Indians, a gentle people (don Hernando,[3] who was there, actually said this), came in canoes to exchange food and other objects for Castilian trinkets. To avoid inequities, disputes and

———————————

[3]This is Columbus's son Fernando.—ED.

grudges, Columbus placed two persons in charge of trading and distributing the goods equally among everyone, since all the food supplies were gone, either eaten, rotten or lost in the hustle of departure from the Belén river. Don Hernando says the Lord guided them to this island, then heavily populated and fertile, whose inhabitants flocked from all the villages in their eagerness to trade with the Spaniards.

For this reason, and to avoid Spanish misdemeanor on the island, the admiral decided to rest and recover at sea because, as don Hernando says, we are an uncouth lot of people and no manner of order or punishment could prevent our men from stealing and molesting women if they went ashore, and this would greatly endanger our friendly relations with the Indians. We would be forced to fight for food and would find ourselves in a scrape. This was avoided because all the men remained assigned to their posts and could not leave ship except by special permission, which pleased the Indians. They brought us essential things at a very low cost to us: we traded an end strip of brass for one or two *hutías*, a rabbit-like animal; a handful of green or yellow glass beads for cassava bread, made of grated edible roots; and a rattle bell for something of more value. Sometimes, kings and nobles would receive a small looking glass, a colorful cap or a pair of scissors; thus these gifts relieved their misery and left them in good spirits. The admiral bought ten canoes for the crews of the grounded ships. In this manner the Spaniards were very well provided for and the Indians communicated with them.

The admiral held councils with his officers to discuss how the ships would be put to sail and at least reach Hispaniola. They were deprived of all human help and all hope of a rescue ship except by miracle, since everything, especially qualified officers, was lacking to start that journey again. They weighed advantages and disadvantages, ways and means and dangers involved over and over again for many days and concluded, by resolution of the admiral, to inform the governor general as well as Columbus's manager on Hispaniola of their plight and ask that a ship be sent to Jamaica with all the necessary equipment and a food supply. For this difficult enterprise, he named two persons whose faithfulness, courage and common sense could be relied upon. It was indeed a dangerous matter to cross a gulf which measures twenty or twenty-five leagues between Jamaica and Hispaniola without counting the thirty-five leagues they had to navigate along the coast of Jamaica from its eastern point, all this in frail canoes that are nothing but hollowed-out tree trunks.

There is a large rock called Navasa in that gulf, eight leagues from Hispaniola. Crossing the gulf was an exploit demanding great prowess and courage. Canoes are so shallow they turn over like pumpkins.

This presents no danger to the Indians because they can swim and empty their canoes with gourds and climb in again; canoes do not sink when they are overturned. Of the men Columbus named, I knew one personally, Diego Méndez de Segura, chief clerk of the fleet and a very prudent, honorable, well-spoken man he was; the other was Bartolomé de Flisco, a Genoese worthy of this mission. Each took a canoe, six Spaniards and ten Indian oarsmen. Diego Méndez was told to embark for Castile from Santo Domingo and present letters and an account of the voyage to the King; Bartolomé Flisco was told to return to Jamaica with news of Diego Méndez's progress. Two hundred full leagues separated the admiral's ships from Santo Domingo.

I have a copy of the long letter Columbus wrote to the monarchs, in which he relates the anguish and the many adversities of his voyage, the new lands he had discovered, the richness of the Veragua[4] mines. He repeats the list of services he had rendered to the Spanish Crown by discovering the New World at the cost of much hardship, and he laments his fate and that of his brothers now made prisoners, their property confiscated, deprived of their honor and titles. Honor and titles he well deserved and well earned, for no services so famous were ever rendered to any other earthly King. The admiral did not write the last sentence; I am adding it because he is owed the praise.

Further in his letter, he asks for the restitution of his titles and satisfaction of his claims as well as for punishment of his accusers. He implores Heaven and earth to share his grief, saying: "Up to now I have cried alone; may Heaven take pity and may those on earth who are acquainted with charity, truth and justice cry with me!" and so on. He stresses his poverty, saying he has no roof of his own over his head, but instead must take to an inn when he needs to eat and sleep. After twenty years of extraordinary services, he and his brothers have acquired very little benefit. He misses the sacraments of the Church, especially since he is ill with the gout and fears death will overtake him in exile and isolation. He declares that he did not make this last voyage for personal fame and gains, as if to say he had these already, but sailed instead to serve the Crown with devotion and good intentions. Finally, he ends the letter by asking that, once back in Castile, he may be allowed to make a pilgrimage to Rome and other places and entrusting the King of God, he signs his letter July 7, 1503, from Jamaica in the Indies.

Columbus also wrote a letter to the governor general of Hispaniola

---

[4]A site in Central America, near Panama, where substantial amounts of gold were indeed mined by the Indians. But it was never successfully exploited by the Spaniards.—ED.

to notify him of his plight and recommend his two messengers for assistance in their mission, and not to forget the rescue ship. With these and others letters for Castile, Columbus dispatched Diego Méndez and Bartolomé Flisco with two canoes, with water, *ajes* and cassava bread for the Indians, and water, bread, and *hutías* or rabbits for the Spaniards which, though certainly not much, was all the canoes could hold. The ocean is always furiously rough near these islands; therefore, it was necessary to await the calming of the waves to enter the great gulf in such frail craft which, as I said, offer less danger to the Indians than our larger ships do to us. The admiral accompanied them to the tip of Jamaica, thirty leagues from where the ships had anchored, taking a few soldiers with him for the safety of his men in case of trouble with the Indians on the way. Then he returned slowly to his ships, visiting villages along his path and conversing joyfully with their inhabitants and leaving many friends behind.

A year later, the ship Diego Méndez had chartered arrived in Jamaica with a smaller caravel. Diego de Salcedo sailed it: he was Columbus's financial administrator I believe; and he brought with him a letter from the governor. Columbus complained a great deal about the governor's tardiness in sending help, accusing him of the deliberate intent to let him die there, since a whole year had passed without a sign of assistance. He said the governor finally relented only because people were talking in Santo Domingo and missionaries there were beginning to reprehend him in their sermons. Everyone, including Columbus, sailed from Jamaica on June 27, 1504. . . .

Columbus arrived in Santo Domingo on August 13, 1504. The governor and the whole city came to welcome him with great respect and celebration. The governor made Columbus a guest in his house and gave him excellent service. But Columbus was unhappy with the governor because underneath the friendliness and benevolence, there was a will at work to humiliate him, which made him believe that the governor's kindness was false. For example, the governor sent for Francisco de Porras,[5] whom Columbus kept imprisoned in the ship, unfettered him and freed him in the presence of Columbus. Also, the governor took it upon himself to punish those who had taken arms to defend the admiral, had participated in Porras's imprisonment, and had killed or wounded others, and he attempted to receive a full account from them of what had taken place in Jamaica. This right belonged only to the admiral since he was in general com-

---

[5]Francisco de Porras and his brother Diego instigated a mutiny while the ships were beached in Jamaica, took the Indian canoes and tried to return to Santo Domingo. But rough seas forced them to return, and Columbus put them in irons.—ED.

mand of the fleet. Columbus gave advice and sentences that were not accepted or carried out because they said no one could understand him and all this I am told took place behind the admiral's back in mockery.

These vexations lasted until the ship they brought from Jamaica was repaired and they had equipped another for the return to Castile of Columbus, his brother, his son and his servants. The others stayed here and some went to San Juan to settle it or, rather, destroy it. They sailed September 12, 1504, losing a mast just as they came out of the river, which caused the admiral to proceed alone. They had good weather for one-third of their journey over the gulf, then a terrible storm broke out that greatly endangered them. On Saturday, the nineteenth of October, when the storm had ceased, the mast fell and broke into four pieces. But the admiral was a great sailor; despite an attack of gout, he repaired it by using the yard of a lateen sail, strengthening it in the middle with material from the forecastles undone for that purpose. Later, another storm broke the mizzenmast; indeed, it seemed the Fates were against the admiral, pursuing him relentlessly throughout his life with hardship and affliction. He navigated this way another 700 leagues until God willed he reach the port of San Lúcar de Barrameda, whence he went to Seville to rest a few days.

The End of the Admiral

SAMUEL ELIOT MORISON

For an account of Columbus's last years and an assessment of his achievements we turn to the greatest of modern authorities on him, the eminent American historian Samuel Eliot Morison. Morison not only mastered the sources and bibliography of Columbus research, he actually navigated and sailed the routes of all Columbus's voyages. His *Admiral of the Ocean Sea: A Life of Christopher Columbus*, 2 vols. (1942) is the definitive biography. An abbreviated version is *Christopher Columbus, Mariner* (1955). The selection that follows is from his last major work touching the life and career of Columbus, *The European Discovery of America: The Southern Voyages A.D. 1492–1616* (1974).

The narrative begins with Columbus's return from his last voyage.

After this long and distressing voyage, Columbus expected at least to be summoned to court to tell his story, a favor accorded to almost every captain of an overseas voyage, however insignificant. But the report he had sent home by Diego Méndez did not make a good impression. This *Lettera Rarissima* is rambling and incoherent. It contains some interesting information, together with a superfluity of self-justification and numerous unconvincing "proofs" that he had been sailing along the Malay Peninsula or somewhere in the Far East.

By the time the Admiral reached Seville, 8 or 9 November, the Sovereigns were holding court at Segovia and the Queen was suffering an illness that turned out to be her last. She died on 26 November 1504, greatly to Columbus's grief and loss. Isabella had never sneered at him. She understood what he was trying to do, respected his rights, and protected him from envy and detraction. Ferdinand, too, had supported him, but the Indies were the Queen's overseas kingdom, not his.

The Admiral, now living in a hired house in Seville, was sick in heart and body, but not badly off in this world's goods. He retained a share of the gold acquired on the Fourth Voyage, and Carvajal had brought home a substantial sum for him in *Aguja,* which survived the hurricane of 1502. Two years later, Ovando delivered to him a chest of gold, and he claimed about $180,000 more, still at Hispaniola with his mark on it. But Columbus felt that he had been defrauded and repeatedly besought his son to obtain confirmation of what he called his tithes, eighths, and thirds. The tithe meant 10 per cent of the net exports from all lands that he discovered, as guaranteed by the original contract of 1492. Columbus complained that the government allowed him only a tenth of their fifth of the gold; that is, 2 instead of 10 per cent. The eighth meant the Admiral's guaranteed investment in one-eighth part of the lading of any vessel trading with the Indies. He complained that Bobadilla or Ovando impounded his eighth in sundry cargoes without payment. The third was preposterous. Columbus's grant as Admiral of the Ocean Sea stated that it carried "preëminences and prerogatives . . . in the same manner as . . . the Grand Admiral of Castile." Having ascertained that this Grand Admiral collected 33⅓ per cent tax on trade between Spain and the Canary Islands, Columbus claimed a similar cut on the entire inward and outward trade between Spain and the Indies! Obviously, if the crown had admitted that, little profit would have been left for anyone. As it was, even by collecting a mere 2 per cent of the gold, the Admiral was a rich man according to the standards of his day, and able to leave substantial legacies to his sons.

There is no evidence known to me to indicate that Columbus ever changed his cosmographical ideas, or realized the vast extent of the continent which he had discovered. Peter Martyr very early and Rodrigo Fernández de Santaella (the editor of the first Spanish edition of Marco Polo) in 1503, among others, questioned whether Columbus's Indies were the real Indies, but the Discoverer ignored them. He died believing that his *Otro Mundro* was but an extension of the Malay Peninsula for several hundred miles.

Even on his deathbed Columbus planned to finance a new crusade, and tried to provide for it in his last will and testament. He spent practically nothing on himself or on keeping up appearances, and he always intended to use the profits of his discoveries to recover the Holy Sepulchre from the infidel. But he also concerned himself over collecting pay for his seamen on the Fourth Voyage who had returned with him. Poor men with no other means of support, they now had two years' wages due. Thrice the Admiral begged the treasurer of Castile to pay them off, without result. They even sent a delegation to court to demand their back pay, with letters from the Admiral to his son and to other persons of influence backing them up, but for years nobody received anything.

Columbus now wisely concluded it was hopeless to expect to be sent back to Hispaniola as viceroy and governor; his poor health and "advanced age" of fifty-three made that impractical. So he concentrated on having the viceroyalty and admiralty conferred on his son Diego. That boy, a clever courtier, had made himself solid by marrying a lady of royal blood, Doña Maria de Toledo. And, three years after his father's death, Diego was appointed governor of Hispaniola and confirmed in some of his father's hereditary titles.

By the spring of 1505 Columbus felt well enough to travel, provided he could ride a mule; a horse's gait was too rough for him. The crown, under pressure by the horse breeders of Andalusia, had forbidden the use of mules for riding, so the Admiral had to beg for a special permit. That the King granted, and in May 1505 the Admiral started on his long journey to the court at Segovia, north of Madrid.

Ferdinand received him graciously and proposed that an arbitrator be appointed to settle his claims against the crown. Columbus refused because the King insisted that his viceroyalty and admiralty be adjudicated as well as the pecuniary claims, and he was too proud to arbitrate anything to which he had a clear legal title. The King then hinted that if he would renounce all titles, offices, and revenues, he would be granted a handsome estate with a fat rent roll. Columbus rejected that absolutely. He considered it dishonorable. He would have all or nothing, and nothing he got.

As the court moved to Salamanca and on to Valladolid, the Admiral painfully followed. A year passed, nothing happened, and in the meantime his arthritis grew worse, and he became bedridden. But he felt so certain of justice being done that he made a will providing legacies out of his expected revenues, such as a sinking fund for the crusade, a house in Genoa to be kept open perpetually for his descendants, a chapel in Hispaniola so endowed that daily Masses might be said for his soul forever. In his simplicity he seemed to feel that these pious bequests would attract the attention of the Almighty, who would compel the King to make them practicable.

Almost at the last moment of his life, Columbus had his hopes raised by the arrival in Spain of the Infanta Doña Juana to claim her mother's throne of Castile. She had been at court when Columbus first returned from the Indies, and looked wide-eyed at his artifacts and his Indians, so he hoped that she might confirm the favors granted by her sainted mother. He was too ill to move, so he sent brother Bartholomew to kiss the young sovereign's hands and bespeak her favor.

During Bartholomew's absence, the Admiral failed rapidly. On 19 May 1506 he ratified his final will, creating son Diego his principal heir and commending to his benevolence all other relatives, including Ferdinand's mother Beatriz de Harana. Next day he suddenly grew worse. Both sons, brother Diego, and a few faithful followers such as Diego Méndez and Bartolomeo Fieschi gathered at his bedside. A priest, quickly summoned, said Mass, and everyone in the devoted circle of relatives, friends, and domestics received the sacrament. After the concluding prayer, the Admiral, remembering the last words of his Lord and Saviour, murmured as his own, *In manus tuas, Domine, commendo spiritum meum*—"Into Thy hands, O Lord, I commend my spirit."

A poor enough funeral followed for the "Admiral of the Ocean Sea, Viceroy and Governor of the Islands and Mainlands in the Indies." The court sent no representative; no bishop, no great dignitary attended, and the official chronicle failed to mention either death or funeral. Columbus had the ill fortune to die at the moment when his discoveries were slightly valued and his personal fortunes and expectations were at their lowest ebb.

Little by little, as his life receded into history and the claims of others to be the "real" discoverers of America faded into the background, his great achievements began to be appreciated. Yet it is one of the ironies of history that the Admiral himself died ignorant of what he had really accomplished, still insisting that he had discovered a large number of islands, a province of China, and an "Other World"; but of the vast extent of that Other World, and of the ocean that lay between it and Asia, he had neither knowledge nor suspicion.

Now, more than five hundred years after his birth, when the day of Columbus's first landfall in the New World is celebrated throughout the length and breadth of the Americas, his fame and reputation may be considered secure, despite the efforts of armchair navigators and nationalist maniacs to denigrate him. A glance at a map of the Caribbean may remind you of what he accomplished: discovery of the Bahamas, Cuba, and Hispaniola on the First Voyage; discovery of the Lesser Antilles, Puerto Rico, Jamaica, and the south coast of Cuba on his Second, as well as founding a permanent European colony; discovery of Trinidad and the Spanish Main, on his Third; and on the Fourth Voyage, Honduras, Nicaragua, Costa Rica, Panama, and Colombia. No navigator in history, not even Magellan, discovered so much territory hitherto unknown to Europeans. None other so effectively translated his north-south experience under the Portuguese flag to the first east-west voyage, across the Atlantic. None other started so many things from which stem the history of the United States, of Canada, and of a score of American republics.

And do not forget that sailing west to the Orient was his idea, pursued relentlessly for six years before he had the means to try it. As a popular jingle of the 400th anniversary put it:

> What if wise men as far back as Ptolemy
> Judged that the earth like an orange was round,
> None of them ever said, "Come along, follow me,
> Sail to the West and the East will be found."

Columbus had his faults, but they were largely the defects of qualities that made him great. These were an unbreakable faith in God and his own destiny as the bearer of the Word to lands beyond the seas; an indomitable will and stubborn persistence despite neglect, poverty, and ridicule. But there was no flaw, no dark side to the most outstanding and essential of all his qualities—seamanship. As a master mariner and navigator, no one in the generation prior to Magellan could touch Columbus. Never was a title more justly bestowed than the one which he most jealously guarded—*Almirante del Mar Océano*— Admiral of the Ocean Sea.

Review and Study Questions

1. Why did Columbus never realize that he had discovered a new world?

2. How did Columbus characterize the native Americans he first met?

3. Why did Columbus lose the confidence of the Spanish monarchs in the years following his first voyage?
4. Is Bartolomé de las Casas sympathetic to Columbus in his account?
5. What does Morison consider to be Columbus's greatest asset as an explorer?

Suggestions for Further Reading

There is a considerable body of Columbus's own writings—letters, journals, and the like. There are two comprehensive Spanish editions of these materials, but only two smaller collections available in English: *Select Documents Illustrating the Four Voyages of Columbus*, 2 vols., ed. Cecil Jane (London: Hakluyt Society, 1930–33) and *Journals and Other Documents on the Life and Voyages of Christopher Columbus*, ed. and tr. Samuel Eliot Morison (New York: Heritage, 1964). There are several modern English translations of Columbus's log of his first voyage. For many years the standard edition was *The Journal of Christopher Columbus* (*During His First Voyage, 1492–93*), tr. and ed. Clement R. Markham (London: Hakluyt Society, 1893). Then there appeared *The Journal of Christopher Columbus*, tr. Cecil Jane, rev. by L. A. Vigneras (London: A. Blond, 1960), and a version of the log translated by Morison in his collection of documents (1964). The definitive contemporary edition is *The Diario of Christopher Columbus' First Voyage to America, 1492–1493*, ed. and tr. Oliver Dunn and James E. Kelley, Jr. (Norman, Okla.: University of Oklahoma Press, 1987). This edition contains the Spanish text along with the translation and comprehensive notes. The text used for this chapter is based on the foregoing edition but is written in colloquial English and with some further refinements of terminology and extended notes: *The Log of Christopher Columbus*, tr. and ed. Robert H. Fuson (Camden, Maine: International Marine Publishing Co., 1987).

Columbus's achievements were described in detail by four contemporary writers who knew him well—Peter Martyr Anghiera, Gonzalo Fernández de Oviedo y Valdés, Fernando Colon (Columbus's son), and las Casas. Peter Martyr's *De orbe novo*, tr. and ed. F. A. MacNutt, 2 vols. (New York: Putnam, 1912) and *The Life of the Admiral Christopher Columbus by His Son Fernando*, tr. and ed. Benjamin Keen (New Brunswick, N.J.: Rutgers University Press, 1959) are translated into English. There is no definitive English translation of la Casas's *History of the Indies*. But Bartolomé de las Casas, *History of the Indies*, tr. and ed. Andrée Collard (New York, Evanston, and London: Torchbooks, 1971), excerpted for this chapter, is a partial translation.

The best modern biography of Columbus is Samuel Eliot Morison, *Admiral of the Ocean Sea: A Life of Christopher Columbus* (Boston: Little, Brown, 1942), in both one-volume and two-volume editions. Morison's *Christopher Columbus, Mariner* (Boston and Toronto: Little, Brown, 1955) is an abridged edition of the foregoing. His *The European Discovery of America: The Southern Voyages A.D. 1492–1616* (New York: Oxford University Press, 1974) was his last major book dealing with Columbus and the one excerpted for this chapter.

The treatments of Columbus since Morison do not, on the whole, represent much of an improvement. Gianni Granzotto, *Christopher Columbus,* tr. Stephen Sartarelli (Garden City, N.Y.: Doubleday, 1985), is a fictionalized biography full of errors and misjudgments. Paolo Emilio Taviani, *Christopher Columbus: The Grand Design* (London: Orbis, 1985), while a larger book than Granzotto's, is not much more reliable: it is comprehensive without being critical. G. R. Crone, *The Discovery of America,* in the series "Turning Points in History" (New York: Weybright and Talley, 1969), is a competent but pedestrian survey. Hans Koning, *Columbus: His Enterprise* (New York and London: Monthly Review Press, 1976), starts out as a straightforward biography but quickly becomes a polemic against the Spanish exploitation of the New World and its people, which can hardly be blamed entirely on Columbus. There is one book that can be read with both pleasure and profit, Björn Landström, *Columbus* (New York: Macmillan, 1966), a handsome book and popularized account of the best modern Columbus scholarship.

Two books of somewhat larger scope can be recommended: Carl Ortwin Sauer, *The Early Spanish Main* (Berkeley and Los Angeles: University of California Press, 1966), an account by a famous geographer of the conquest of the Caribbean rim, and *First Images of America: The Impact of the New World on the Old,* ed. Fredi Chiappelli (Berkeley: University of California Press, 1976).

MONTEZUMA: THE LAST GREAT SPEAKER OF THE AZTECS

1467	Born
1480	Succession of Montezuma's uncle Tizoc as Great Speaker
1480–84	Montezuma trained as priest and warrior
1485	Succession of another uncle, the war leader Axayacatl
1497	Appointed commander of the Aztec army
1502	Elected Great Speaker
1519	First meeting with Cortés
1520	Died

The Spaniards who flocked to the New World in the wake of Columbus's discoveries were after not only land but the gold that was persistently rumored to be had there in such abundance. Among the seekers was an impoverished *hidalgo*[1] named Hernán Cortés. He made himself useful to Don Diego Velásquez, the Deputy Admiral of the Islands and Governor of Cuba, and was entrusted with an expedition to the mainland of Mexico. With only a bare handful of men and horses and a few cannon and shotguns, this man, who would shortly become the greatest of the *conquistadores,* set out on an incredible journey of conquest. He won the support of native people near the coast, including an invaluable woman, Doña Marina, who became his interpreter and mistress. And he began to hear of the great and wealthy empire of the Aztecs, the Mexica. He allied himself with the

---

[1]A *hidalgo* was a Spanish nobleman of secondary rank, below that of a grandee.— ED.

Tlaxcalans, another native people, who were bitter enemies of the Aztecs, and with some Tlaxcalan support and his own small force Cortés pressed inland toward the Aztec capital of Tenochtitlan, the later site of Mexico City, entering the city on November 8, 1519. He was met by a large delegation of high officials sent out by the Emperor Moctezuma—or Montezuma, as he was more commonly called by the Spaniards—and at last by the emperor himself.

What sort of man was Montezuma, and what sort of state and culture did he represent? He was in his early fifties. He had been Great Speaker, the ruler of the Aztec Empire, for nearly twenty years, having been elected to succeed his uncle as Great Speaker in 1502. Long before that he had been a powerful figure in the ruling Mexica nobility. As he is characterized by one of his modern biographers, "In his own world Montezuma was considered a wise man and one with prophetic gifts which were of great value to his nation. One may say that he was regarded as the ideal of a noble ruler by his own people and that in their fear and reverence for the Great Speaker there was mingled not a little love."[2]

His state comprised the Aztec Empire, which had been put together over the past two centuries by the conquests of his aggressive, warlike people. The Aztecs had subjugated the many indigenous peoples of central Mexico in a closely controlled imperial state that claimed between a million and a million and a half people, ruled from the capital city of Tenochtitlan. Tenochtitlan itself had some 400,000 people and spread out from its central temple, with its towering twin pyramids and spacious temple compound, to cover more than five square miles. It included religious structures, government buildings, and residences of the nobility, all built of stone and coated in glistening white and painted stucco, and the more modest homes of craftsmen and artisans. It had an enormous market where all the products of Meso-America were available for purchase. It was supplied with fresh water by aqueducts from Chapultapec and surrounded by the waters of Lake Texcoco, entered by an elaborate system of elevated causeways that also acted as dikes and breakwaters.

But the Aztec state was also a religious community. The Aztecs worshipped many gods, but the all-powerful "Lord of the World" was the sun god Huitzilopochtli, the Blue Hummingbird. It was mainly this god whose worship accounted for the most arresting feature of Aztec religion—mass human sacrifice and cannibalism. The practice of human sacrifice had grown over recent years until by the time of Montezuma thousands of persons were sacrificed every year—their

---

[2]C. A. Burland, *Montezuma, Lord of the Aztecs* (New York: Putnam, 1973), p. 144.

chests slashed open by priests in ceremonies that took place atop the temple pyramids, their blood and still-beating hearts consecrated to the god, and their flesh cooked and eaten by the priests and the people. One of the main motives of Aztec wars was to capture prisoners to serve as sacrifices; they were called, ironically, "flower wars." Montezuma, as Great Speaker, was the chief priest of Huitzilopochtli, the servant of the god on behalf of his subjects.

But conquest tradition claimed that Montezuma was also devoted to the god Quetzalcoatl, the Feathered Serpent, the special deity of an earlier warrior people, the Toltecs, to whom the Aztec nobility traced their own ancestry. This tradition also recounted how Quetzalcoatl had returned to find his people so contented with their way of life and so intermingled with the native inhabitants that they refused to follow him. So he returned to the East once more, whence he had come. But the Aztecs were convinced that he would come again to reclaim their loyalty or that he would send someone in his stead.

On that November day of 1519 the stage was set for the most important confrontation in the entire story of the Spanish conquest of the New World.

The Second Letter to Emperor Charles V

HERNAN CORTÉS

There are several contemporary Spanish accounts of the first meeting and subsequent relations between Cortés and Montezuma. The most interesting and authoritative is that of Cortés himself, in the form of one of several detailed dispatch letters that he sent to Spain, to the Emperor Charles V, in whose name he claimed his conquests. The Second Letter, describing his dealings with Montezuma, was written less than a year after the events, and was dated October 30, 1520.

When we had passed this bridge Muteczuma himself came out to meet us with some two hundred nobles, all barefoot and dressed in some kind of uniform also very rich, in fact more so than the others. They came forward in two long lines keeping close to the walls of the street, which is very broad and fine and so straight that one can see from one end of it to the other, though it is some two-thirds of a league in length and lined on both sides with very beautiful, large houses, both private dwellings and temples. Muteczuma himself was borne along in the middle of the street with two lords one on his right hand and one on his left, being respectively the chief whom I described as coming out to meet me in a litter and the other, Muteczuma's brother, ruler of Iztapalapa, from which only that day we had set out. All three were dressed in similar fashion except that Muteczuma wore shoes whereas the others were barefoot. The two lords bore him along each by an arm, and as he drew near I dismounted and advanced alone to embrace, but the two lords prevented me from touching him, and they themselves made me the same obeisance as did their comrades, kissing the earth: which done, he commanded his brother who accompanied him to stay with me and take me by the arm, while he with the other lord went on a little way in front. After he had spoken to me all the other lords who were in the two long lines came up likewise in order one after the other, and then re-formed in line again. And while speaking to

Muteczuma I took off a necklace of pearls and crystals which I was wearing and threw it round his neck; whereupon having proceeded some little way up the street a servant of his came back to me with two necklaces wrapped up in a napkin, made from the shells of sea snails, which are much prized by them; and from each necklace hung eight prawns fashioned very beautifully in gold some six inches in length. The messenger who brought them put them round my neck and we then continued up the street in the manner described until we came to a large and very handsome house which Muteczuma had prepared for our lodging. There he took me by the hand and led me to a large room opposite the patio by which we had entered, and seating me on a daïs very richly worked, for it was intended for royal use, he bade me await him there, and took his departure. After a short time, when all my company had found lodging, he returned with many various ornaments of gold, silver and featherwork, and some five or six thousand cotton clothes, richly dyed and embroidered in various ways, and having made me a present of them he seated himself on another low bench which was placed next to mine, and addressed me in this manner:

"Long time have we been informed by the writings of our ancestors that neither myself nor any of those who inhabit this land are natives of it, but rather strangers who have come to it from foreign parts. We likewise know that from those parts our nation was led by a certain lord (to whom all were subject), and who then went back to his native land, where he remained so long delaying his return that at his coming those whom he had left had married the women of the land and had many children by them and had built themselves cities in which they lived, so that they would in no wise return to their own land nor acknowledge him as lord; upon which he left them. And we have always believed that among his descendants one would surely come to subject this land and us as rightful vassals. Now seeing the regions from which you say you come, which is from where the sun rises, and the news you tell of this great king and ruler who sent you hither, we believe and hold it certain that he is our natural lord: especially in that you say he has long had knowledge of us.[3] Wherefore be certain that we will obey you and hold you as lord in place of that great lord of whom you speak, in which service there shall be neither slackness nor deceit: and throughout all the land, that is to say all that I rule, you may command anything you desire, and it shall be obeyed and done, and all that we have is at your will and

---

[3]This "knowledge" on the part of the Spanish emperor was, of course, simply made up by Cortés.—ED.

pleasure. And since you are in your own land and house, rejoice and take your leisure from the fatigues of your journey and the battles you have fought; for I am well informed of all those that you have been forced to engage in on your way here from Potonchan, as also that the natives of Cempoal and Tlascala have told you many evil things of me; but believe no more than what you see with your own eyes, and especially not words from the lips of those who are my enemies, who were formerly my vassals and on your coming rebelled against me and said these things in order to find favour with you: I am aware, moreover, that they have told you that the walls of my houses were of gold as was the matting on my floors and other household articles, even that I was a god and claimed to be so, and other like matters. As for the houses, you see that they are of wood, stones and earth." Upon this he lifted his clothes showing me his body, and said: "and you see that I am of flesh and blood like yourself and everyone else, mortal and tangible."

Grasping with his hands his arms and other parts of his body, he continued: "You see plainly how they have lied. True I have a few articles of gold which have remained to me from my forefathers, and all that I have is yours at any time that you may desire it. I am now going to my palace where I live. Here you will be provided with all things necessary for you and your men, and let nothing be done amiss seeing that you are in your own house and land."

I replied to all that he said, satisfying him in those things which seemed expedient, especially in having him believe that your Majesty was he whom they had long expected, and with that he bade farewell. On his departure we were very well regaled with great store of chickens, bread, fruit, and other necessities, particularly household ones. And in this wise I continued six days very well provided with all that was necessary and visited by many of the principal men of the city. . . .

Having passed six days, then, in the great city of Tenochtitlan, invincible Prince, and having seen something of its marvels, though little in comparison with what there was to be seen and examined, I considered it essential both from my observation of the city and the rest of the land that its ruler should be in my power and no longer entirely free; to the end that he might in nowise change his will and intent to serve your Majesty, more especially as we Spaniards are somewhat intolerant and stiff-necked, and should he get across with us he would be powerful enough to do us great damage, even to blot out all memory of us in the land; and in the second place, could I once get him in my power all the other provinces subject to him would come more promptly to the knowledge and service of your Majesty, as indeed afterwards happened. I decided to capture him and place him in the lodging where I was, which was extremely strong. . . .

Cortés's stratagem was to accuse Montezuma of an attack on his men that had occurred earlier, along the way, at the hands of some of his subject chiefs. Montezuma immediately summoned those chiefs to account for themselves, but in the meantime, Cortés insisted that Montezuma accompany him to the quarters provided for him, under house arrest. Amazingly, Montezuma agreed! A few days later the guilty chiefs were taken and executed.

Muteczuma proclaimed an assembly of all the chiefs of the neighbouring towns and districts; and on their coming together he sent for me to mount to the platform where he already was and proceeded to address them in this manner: "Brothers and friends, you know well that for many years you, your fathers and your grandfathers have been subjects and vassals to me and to my forefathers, and have ever been well treated and held in due esteem both by them and me, as likewise you yourselves have done what it behoves good and loyal vassals to do for their lords; moreover I believe you will recollect hearing from your ancestors that we are not natives of this land, but that they came to it from another land far off, being led hither by a powerful lord whose vassals they all were; after many years he returned to find our forefathers already settled in the land married to native wives and with many children by them in such wise that they never wished to go back with him nor acknowledge him as lord of the land, and upon this he returned saying that he would come again himself or send another with such power as to force them to re-enter his service. And you know well that we have always looked to this and from what the captain has told us of the king and lord who sent him hither, and the direction from which he came I hold it certain as ye also must hold it, that he is the lord whom we have looked to, especially in that he declares he already had knowledge of us in his own land. Therefore while our ancestors did not that which was due to their lord, let us not so offend now, but rather give praise to the gods that in our times that which was long expected is come to pass. And I earnestly beg of you, since all that I have said is notorious to everyone of you, that as you have up till now obeyed and held me as your sovereign lord, so from henceforth you will obey and hold this great king as your natural lord, for such he is, and in particular this captain in his place: and all those tributes and services which up to this time you have paid to me, do you now pay to him, for I also hold myself bound to do him service in all that he shall require me: and over and above doing that which is right and necessary you will be doing me great pleasure."

All this he spoke to them weeping, with such sighs and tears as no man ever wept more, and likewise all those chieftains who heard him wept so that for a long space of time they could make no reply. And I can assure your Majesty that there was not one among the Spaniards who on hearing this speech was not filled with compassion. After some time when their tears were somewhat dried they replied that they held him as their lord and had promised to do whatever he should bid them, and hence that for that reason and the one he had given them they were content to do what he said, and from that time offered themselves as vassals to your royal Majesty, promising severally and collectively to carry out whatever should be required of them in your Majesty's royal name as loyal and obedient vassals, and duly to render him all such tributes and services as were formerly rendered to Muteczuma, with all other things whatsoever that may be commanded them in your Majesty's name. All this took place in the presence of the public notary and was duly drawn up by him in legal form and witnessed in the presence of many Spaniards. . . .

From this point, however, the situation began to deteriorate. The Spaniards had discovered vast treasuries of gold in the city. There was an incident in which they attacked the Aztecs during a religious festival and killed a large number of priests and nobles. The Aztec nobility, now led by Montezuma's brother, turned against the Spaniards and besieged them in their quarters.

Muteczuma, who was still a prisoner together with his son and many other nobles who had been taken on our first entering the city, requested to be taken out on to the flat roof of the fortress, where he would speak to the leader of the people and make them stop fighting. I ordered him to be brought forth and as he mounted a breastwork that extended beyond the fortress, wishing to speak to the people who were fighting there, a stone from one of their slings struck him on the head so severely that he died three days later: when this happened I ordered two of the other Indian prisoners to take out his dead body on their shields to the people, and I know not what became of it; save only this that the fighting did not cease but rather increased in intensity every day.

Cortés and his men at this point were forced to withdraw from the city with many casualties, but he recovered and, against impossible odds, defeated the Aztec army sent after him. After enlisting more

Tlaxcalan allies, he returned and besieged the city of Tenochtitlan, which finally surrendered on August 13, 1521. There was never again to be serious native resistance to Spanish rule.

The Aztec Account

TEXTS FROM THE *CODEX FLORENTINO*

The incredible events of the Spanish conquest, including the incredible behavior of Montezuma, are described in the surviving Aztec documents as well as in Spanish sources, and in suspiciously similar terms. The most comprehensive Aztec account is that contained in the so-called *Codex Florentino*. It was written in Nahuatl, the Aztec language, by native students in the school founded by the Franciscan missionary Bernardino de Sahagún. He had worked out a way of writing Nahuatl in Latin characters with Spanish sound values and taught the method to his native pupils. They used it to record much of their Aztec culture and to describe historical events, such as the conquest. For their account they depended on the recollections of aged natives who had witnessed the events, on traditional songs and orations transmitted orally, and on contemporary Spanish sources. The first version of the account was done in about 1555 but does not survive. Brother Bernardino made a résumé of it in Spanish and later, about 1585, reconstructed the original text in Nahuatl.

Our excerpt begins after the first reports of the Spaniards' arrival have reached Montezuma. He has sent messengers to them and anxiously awaits their return.

While the messengers were away, Motecuhzoma could neither sleep nor eat, and no one could speak with him. He thought that everything he did was in vain, and he sighed almost every moment. He was lost in despair, in the deepest gloom and sorrow. Nothing could comfort him, nothing could calm him, nothing could give him any pleasure.

He said: "What will happen to us? Who will outlive it? Ah, in other times I was contented, but now I have death in my heart! My heart burns and suffers, as if it were drowned in spices . . . ! But will our lord come here?"

Then he gave orders to the watchmen, to the men who guarded the palace: "Tell me, even if I am sleeping: 'The messengers have come back from the sea.'" But when they went to tell him, he immediately said: "They are not to report to me here. I will receive them in the House of the Serpent. Tell them to go there." And he gave this order: "Two captives are to be painted with chalk."

The messengers went to the House of the Serpent, and Motecuhzoma arrived. The two captives were then sacrificed before his eyes: their breasts were torn open, and the messengers were sprinkled with their blood. This was done because the messengers had completed a difficult mission: they had seen the gods, their eyes had looked on their faces. They had even conversed with the gods!

When the sacrifice was finished, the messengers reported to the king. They told him how they had made the journey, and what they had seen, and what food the strangers ate. Motecuhzoma was astonished and terrified by their report, and the description of the strangers' food astonished him above all else.

He was also terrified to learn how the cannon roared, how its noise resounded, how it caused one to faint and grow deaf. The messengers told him: "A thing like a ball of stone comes out of its entrails: it comes out shooting sparks and raining fire. The smoke that comes out with it has a pestilent odor, like that of rotten mud. This odor penetrates even to the brain and causes the greatest discomfort. If the cannon is aimed against a mountain, the mountain splits and cracks open. If it is aimed against a tree, it shatters the tree into splinters. This is a most unnatural sight, as if the tree had exploded from within."

The messengers also said: "Their trappings and arms are all made of iron. They dress in iron and wear iron casques on their heads. Their swords are iron; their bows are iron; their shields are iron; their spears are iron. Their deer carry them on their backs wherever they wish to go. These deer, our lord, are as tall as the roof of a house."

"The strangers' bodies are completely covered, so that only their faces can be seen. Their skin is white, as if it were made of lime. They have yellow hair, though some of them have black. Their beards are long and yellow, and their moustaches are also yellow. Their hair is curly, with very fine strands. . . ."

When Motecuhzoma heard this report, he was filled with terror. It was as if his heart had fainted, as if it had shriveled. It was as if he were conquered by despair. . . . Motecuhzoma listened to their report and then bowed his head without speaking a word. For a long time he remained thus, with his head bent down. And when he spoke at last, it was only to say: "What help is there now, my friends? Is there a mountain for us to climb? Should we run away? We are Mexicanos: would this bring any glory to the Mexican nation?

"Pity the old men, and the old women, and the innocent little children. How can they save themselves? But there is no help. What can we do? Is there nothing left us?

"We will be judged and punished. And however it may be, and whenever it may be, we can do nothing but wait." . . .

The Spaniards arrived in Xoloco, near the entrance to Tenochtitlan. That was the end of the march, for they had reached their goal.

Motecuhzoma now arrayed himself in his finery, preparing to go out to meet them. The other great princes also adorned their persons, as did the nobles and their chieftains and knights. They all went out together to meet the strangers. . . .

Thus Motecuhzoma went out to meet them, there in Huitzillan. He presented many gifts to the Captain and his commanders, those who had come to make war. He showered gifts upon them and hung flowers around their necks; he gave them necklaces of flowers and bands of flowers to adorn their breasts; he set garlands of flowers upon their heads. Then he hung the gold necklaces around their necks and gave them presents of every sort as gifts of welcome.

When Motecuhzoma had given necklaces to each one, Cortes asked him: "Are you Motecuhzoma? Are you the king? Is it true that you are the king Motecuhzoma?"

And the king said: "Yes, I am Motecuhzoma." Then he stood up to welcome Cortes; he came forward, bowed his head low and addressed him in these words: "Our lord, you are weary. The journey has tired you, but now you have arrived on the earth. You have come to your city, Mexico. You have come here to sit on your throne, to sit under its canopy.

"The kings who have gone before, your representatives, guarded it and preserved it for your coming. The kings Itzcoatl, Motecuhzoma the Elder, Axayacatl, Tizoc and Ahuitzol ruled for you in the City of Mexico. The people were protected by their swords and sheltered by their shields.

"Do the kings know the destiny of those they left behind, their posterity? If only they are watching! If only they can see what I see!

"No, it is not a dream. I am not walking in my sleep. I am not seeing you in my dreams. . . . I have seen you at last! I have met you face to face! I was in agony for five days, for ten days, with my eyes fixed on the Region of the Mystery. And now you have come out of the clouds and mists to sit on your throne again.

"This was foretold by the kings who governed your city, and now it has taken place. You have come back to us; you have come down from the sky. Rest now, and take possession of your royal houses. Welcome to your land, my lords!"

When Motecuhzoma had finished, La Malinche[4] translated his address into Spanish so that the Captain could understand it. Cortes replied in his strange and savage tongue, speaking first to La Malinche: "Tell Motecuhzoma that we are his friends. There is nothing to fear. We have wanted to see him for a long time, and now we have seen his face and heard his words. Tell him that we love him well and that our hearts are contented."

Then he said to Motecuhzoma: "We have come to your house in Mexico as friends. There is nothing to fear."

La Malinche translated this speech and the Spaniards grasped Motecuhzoma's hands and patted his back to show their affection for him. . . .

When the Spaniards entered the Royal House, they placed Motecuhzoma under guard and kept him under their vigilance. . . .

Then the Spaniards fired one of their cannons, and this caused great confusion in the city. The people scattered in every direction; they fled without rhyme or reason; they ran off as if they were being pursued. It was as if they had eaten the mushrooms that confuse the mind, or had seen some dreadful apparition. They were all overcome by terror, as if their hearts had fainted. And when night fell, the panic spread through the city and their fears would not let them sleep. . . .

When the Spaniards were installed in the palace, they asked Motecuhzoma about the city's resources and reserves and about the warriors' ensigns and shields. They questioned him closely and then demanded gold.

Motecuhzoma guided them to it. They surrounded him and crowded close with their weapons. He walked in the center, while they formed a circle around him.

When they arrived at the treasure house called Teucalco, the riches of gold and feathers were brought out to them: ornaments made of quetzal feathers, richly worked shields, disks of gold, the necklaces of the idols, gold nose plugs, gold greaves and bracelets and crowns.

The Spaniards immediately stripped the feathers from the gold shields and ensigns. They gathered all the gold into a great mound and set fire to everything else, regardless of its value. Then they melted down the gold into ingots. As for the precious green stones, they took only the best of them; the rest were snatched up by the Tlaxcaltecas. The Spaniards searched through the whole treasure house, questioning and quarreling, and seized every object they thought was beautiful. . . .

---

[4]Another name for Cortés's translator, Doña Marina.—ED.

The Aztec sources, like the Spanish, then tell of the massacre of the Aztec priests and nobles by the Spaniards—but in greater detail.

When the news of this massacre was heard outside the Sacred Patio, a great cry went up: "Mexicanos, come running! Bring your spears and shields! The strangers have murdered our warriors!"

This cry was answered with a roar of grief and anger: the people shouted and wailed and beat their palms against their mouths. The captains assembled at once, as if the hour had been determined in advance. They all carried their spears and shields.

Then the battle began. The Aztecs attacked with javelins and arrows, even with the light spears that are used for hunting birds. They hurled their javelins with all their strength, and the cloud of missiles spread out over the Spaniards like a yellow cloak.

The Spaniards immediately took refuge in the palace. They began to shoot at the Mexicans with their iron arrows and to fire their cannons and arquebuses. And they shackled Motecuhzoma in chains. . . .

On the third day, Motecuhzoma climbed onto the rooftop and tried to admonish his people, but they cursed him and shouted that he was a coward and a traitor to his country. They even threatened him with their weapons. It is said that an Indian killed him with a stone from his sling, but the palace servants declared that the Spaniards put him to death by stabbing him in the abdomen with their swords.

On the seventh day, the Spaniards abandoned the city along with the Tlaxcaltecas, the Huexotzincas and their other allies. They fled down the causeway that leads out to Tlacopan. But before they left, they murdered King Cacama of Tezcoco, his three sisters and two of his brothers.

A New Explanation

J. H. ELLIOTT AND ANTHONY PAGDEN

In the whole account of the conquest of Mexico, nothing is more puzzling than the behavior of Montezuma. He was in the prime of life, in secure and undisputed control of an aggressive, warlike empire that could field hundreds of thousands of soldiers on his order alone. He had a considerable reputation for military leadership himself. Yet he was virtually paralyzed by the course of events.

The explanation that is presented both in the Spanish and the Aztec sources—as we have seen—is that Montezuma profoundly believed that Cortés was the agent of the Aztec god Quetzalcoatl and that Cortés acted on behalf of the god, incarnate in the person of his sovereign, Charles V.

But was this the case? In the critical notes to the latest and best edition of the Cortés letters, the editor, Anthony Pagden, and the author of the introduction, J. H. Elliott, offer an alternative explanation. Elliott argues that Cortés's letters were not only reports on the events of the conquest but carefully crafted political apologies as well. He notes, quite correctly, that Cortés was operating without any real official authorization. He had been sent by Don Diego Velásquez, the Governor of Cuba, to investigate the loss of a small exploration fleet and to rescue any Spaniards being held captive in Yucatan. He was also authorized to explore and trade—but he had no permission to colonize. Yet he had founded the town-settlement of Vera Cruz, in large part so that he could be authorized by the town government (which was himself) to undertake an expedition to the interior. He had set out on that expedition on the basis of this contrived and specious authority.

Cortés had therefore defied his own immediate superior, Velázquez, and had potentially antagonized Velázquez's powerful friends at Court. He knew well enough the grave risks he was running. But to Cortés and his friends . . . the risks paled before the attractions of the anticipated prize. Nothing could more quickly obliterate the stigma of treachery and rebellion than a brilliant military success and the acquisition of fabulous riches. If new peoples were won for the Faith, and rich new lands won for the Crown, there was reason to hope that the original defiance of Velázquez would be regarded as no more than a peccadillo, and that Velázquez's friends and protectors would be silenced by a *fait accompli*. . . .

Success in arms, and resort to the highest authority of all, that of the king himself—these were the aims of Cortés and his fellow conspirators as they prepared in April, 1519, to compound their defiance of Velázquez by a landing which would mark the real beginning of their attempt to conquer an empire. They were concerned, like all conquistadors, with fame, riches and honor. But behind the willful defiance of the governor of Cuba there existed, at least in Cortés's mind, a philosophy of conquest and colonization which made his action something more than an attempt at self-aggrandizement at the expense of Velázquez. He entertained, like so many Castilians of his generation, an exalted view of the royal service, and of Castile's divinely appointed mission. Both the divine and the royal favor would shine on those who cast down idols, extirpated pagan superstitions, and won new lands and peoples for God and Castile. . . .

But what seemed plausible enough in Mexico was bound to seem highly implausible in Cuba and at the Spanish Court. Clearly it was essential to win support in Spain for an action which Fonseca[5] and his friends would certainly represent to the king as an act of open rebellion. . . .

Everything now depended on the successful presentation of his case at Court, where the Fonseca group would certainly do all in its power to destroy him. If possible, Charles and his advisers must be reached and won over before they had time to learn from Velázquez himself of Cortés's act of rebellion. . . .

The first letter from Mexico, then, was essentially a political document, speaking for Cortés in the name of his army, and designed to appeal directly to the Crown over the heads of Velázquez and his friends in the Council of the Indies. Cortés was now involved in a desperate race against time. Montejo and Puertocarrero[6] left for Spain on July 26, 1519, with their bundle of letters and the gold; and unless, or until, they could persuade Charles to sanction retrospectively the behavior of Cortés and his men, Cortés was technically a traitor, liable to arrest and persecution at the hands of an irate governor of Cuba, fully empowered to act in the royal name. The danger was acute, and the blow could fall at any time, perhaps even from within Mexico itself. For there was still a strong group of Velázquez partisans in the expedition, and these men would do all they could to sabotage Cortés's plans. But Cortés, who had his spies posted, was well aware of the dangers. The friends of the governor of Cuba appear to have been plotting to send him warning of the mission of Montejo and Puertocarrero, so that he could intercept their ship. The plot was discovered, the conspirators arrested, and two of them, Juan Escudero and Diego Cermeño, put to death. . . . As long as Cortés could command the loyalties of his army—and this would ultimately depend on his ability to capture and distribute the fabulous riches of Motecuçoma's empire—he was now reasonably safe from subversion within the ranks. . . .

Velázquez began to organize an army to be sent to Mexico against

---

[5]Juan Rodríguez de Fonseca, Bishop of Burgos, was Velásquez's relative and patron at the Spanish court and the royal councillor principally responsible for the affairs of the Indies during the previous reign.—ED.

[6]Cortés's agents.—ED.

Cortés. . . . At a time when a smallpox epidemic was raging in Cuba, Velázquez felt unable to lead his army in person, and handed over the command to one of his more reliable but less intelligent friends, Pánfilo de Narváez. The army, twice the size of that of Cortés, set sail from Cuba on March 5, 1520. . . . During the autumn and winter of 1519, therefore, at the time when Cortés was securing the submission of Motecuçoma and had established himself precariously in Tenochtitlan, he was faced with the prospect of a military confrontation with his immediate superior, the governor of Cuba. . . .

The outcome was likely to be determined on the battlefield, in an internecine struggle of Spaniard against Spaniard, which could well jeopardize and even destroy Cortés's uncertain hold over the Aztec empire. But in the Spanish monarchy of the sixteenth century a military solution could never be final. Legality was paramount, and the key to legality lay with the king.

Everything therefore turned on the success of Montejo and Puertocarrero in Spain. They duly reached Seville at the beginning of November, 1519, only to find their country on the verge of revolt. Charles had been elected Holy Roman Emperor on June 28. Once elected, his immediate aim was to extract the largest possible subsidies from the Cortes[7] of the various Spanish kingdoms, and then to leave for Germany. When the procuradores[8] arrived in Seville, the emperor was still in Barcelona, heavily preoccupied with plans for his departure; and the Castilian cities were beginning to voice their dissatisfaction at the prospect of heavy new fiscal demands and an absentee king.

At this particular moment the chances of winning the emperor's support for a still-unknown adventurer on the other side of the world hardly looked very promising. . . . From Barcelona they [Montejo and Puertocarrero] moved across Spain in the tracks of the emperor, finally catching up with him at Tordesillas, near Valladolid, early in March. Here, seven months after leaving Vera Cruz, they could at last petition the emperor in person to confirm Cortés in his position as captain general and *justicia mayor.* . . .

Meanwhile, in Mexico, Cortés had seized the initiative, divided his forces, and moved to intercept Narváez's army. This was his situation at the time of the massacre of the Aztec lords at the religious

---

[7]The *Cortes* were the legislative bodies of the Spanish kingdoms.—ED.

[8]The *procuradores* were the "agents" whom Cortés had sent from Mexico to the Spanish court.—ED.

festival. He defeated Narváez, conscripted the bulk of Narváez's
men to his own cause, and returned to Tenochtitlan.

Narváez's defeat left the governor of Cuba a ruined and broken man.
Cortés had defeated Velázquez—geographically his nearest enemy—
but he was still without news from the Spanish Court. Moreover, his
march to the coast to defeat Narváez had fatally weakened the Spanish position in Tenochtitlan. When Cortés got back to the capital on
June 25 it was already too late. The behavior of Alvarado and his men
in Tenochtitlan during Cortés's absence had precipitated an Indian
uprising, and neither Cortés's troops, nor the diminished authority of
Motecuçoma, proved sufficient to quell the revolt. Motecuçoma, rejected by his own subjects, died his strange death on June 30. During
the course of the same night, the *noche triste*, the Spaniards made their
famous retreat from Tenochtitlan. Cortés might have defeated the
governor of Cuba, but he had also lost the empire he had promised to
Charles.

It was during the autumn months of 1520, while Cortés was preparing for the siege and reconquest of Tenochtitlan, that he wrote the
Second Letter. This letter, like its predecessor from Vera Cruz, is both
more and less than a straightforward narrative of events, for it, too,
has an essentially political purpose. Cortés, when writing it, was influenced by three major considerations. In the first place, he still did not
know what decision, if any, had been reached in Spain on his plea for
retrospective authorization of his unconventional proceedings. In the
second place, he had by now heard the news of Charles's election to
the imperial throne. Finally, he had won a new empire for Charles
and had proceeded to lose it. His letter, therefore, had to be so angled
as to suggest that, at the most, he had suffered no more than a
temporary setback . . . and that he would soon be in a position to
render the most signal new services to a king who had now become
the mightiest monarch in the world.

With these considerations in mind, Cortés carefully contrived his
letter to convey a predominantly "imperial" theme. Its opening para-
graph contained a graceful allusion to Charles's new empire in Germany, which was skillfully coupled with a reference to a second empire across the Atlantic, to which he could claim an equal title. This
reference set the tone for the document as a whole. The fact that
Cortés was no longer at this moment the effective master of the
Mexican empire was no doubt inconvenient, but could be played
down as far as possible. For the thesis of the letter was that Charles
was already the *legal* emperor of this great new empire, and that
Cortés would soon recover for him what was rightfully his.

The entire story of the march to Tenochtitlan and the imprisonment of Motecuçoma was related in such a way as to support this general thesis. Motecuçoma, by his speeches and his actions, was portrayed as a man who voluntarily recognized the sovereignty of Charles V, and voluntarily surrendered his empire into his hands. Whether Motecuçoma did indeed speak anything like the words which Cortés attributes to him will probably never be known for certain. Some passages in his two speeches contain so many Christian overtones as to be unbelievable coming from a pagan Aztec. Others, and in particular the identification of the Spaniards with the former rulers of Mexico wrongly banished from their land, may be an ingenious fabrication by Cortés, or may conceivably reflect certain beliefs and legends, which Motecuçoma himself may or may not have accepted. Whatever its origins, the story of the expected return of lords from the east was essential to Cortés's grand design, for it enabled him to allege and explain a "voluntary" submission of Motecuçoma, and the "legal" transfer of his empire—an empire far removed from the jurisdiction of the Audiencia of Santo Domingo and from the Caribbean world of Diego Colón[9] and Velázquez—to its rightful ruler, Charles V.

Motecuçoma's death at the hands of his own subjects left Charles the undisputed master of the field. It was unfortunate that the Mexicans were now in open rebellion—a situation which could only be ascribed to the nefarious activities of the governor of Cuba, acting through his agent Pánfilo de Narváez. But although Narváez's invasion had nearly brought disaster, the tide had now been turned, because God was on the emperor's side. With divine help, and through the agency of that most loyal of lieutenants, Hernán Cortés, the land would soon be recovered; and what better name could be bestowed upon it than that of New Spain?

Anthony Pagden, the editor of the text, turns more specifically to the inexplicable behavior of Montezuma. He begins with the speech that Montezuma made as soon as Cortés and his men had been settled in their quarters in Tenochtitlan.

Both this speech and the one that follows . . . would seem to be apocryphal. Motecuçoma could never have held the views with which Cortés accredits him. Eulalia Guzmán (*Relaciones de Hernán Cortés*, I:

---

[9]The son of Christopher Columbus, who had inherited the title of Admiral from his father.—Ed.

279 ff.) has pointed out the Biblical tone of both these passages and how their phraseology reflects the language of the *Siete Partidas*.[10] Cortés is casting Motecuçoma into the role of a sixteenth-century Spaniard welcoming his "natural lord," who in this case has been accredited with a vaguely Messianic past. Indeed the whole setting has a mythopoeic ring: Motecuçoma is made to raise his garments and to declare, "See that I am flesh and blood like you and all other men, and I am mortal and substantial," words reminiscent of those of Jesus to his disciples, "A spirit hath not flesh and bones as ye see me have" and of Paul and Barnabas to Lystra, "We also are men of like passions with you." (J. H. Elliott, "The Mental World of Hernán Cortés," pp. 51–53). There is evidence, however, that Motecuçoma did believe himself to be the living incarnation of Huitzilopochtli (see Durán, chaps. LIII–LIV; and Sahagún, bk. IV, chap. 10), and certainly such an identification would not have been alien to Mexica religious thought. Despite the absurdity of attributing such words and gestures to an Amerindian, it seems likely that Cortés's account of the events is based on partially understood information about the native mythologies. A number of modern commentators seem to believe the thesis of Motecuçoma's speeches, namely, that the Mexica lived in fear of a vengeful Messiah, who would one day return from the east, and mistook Cortés for his captain. Later this Messiah, who in the words attributed to Motecuçoma is only a legendary tribal chieftain, becomes Quetzalcoatl, the "Plumed Serpent" lord of Tula, whose story as told by Sahagún bears some resemblance to the Cortés-Motecuçoma version of Mexica prehistory. There is, however, no preconquest tradition which places Quetzalcoatl in this role and it seems possible therefore that it was elaborated by Sahagún . . . from informants who themselves had partially lost contact with their traditional tribal histories.

The identification of Cortés with Quetzalcoatl is also the work of Sahagún (see bk. XII, chap. 4, pp. 11 ff.). Don Antonio de Mendoza, first viceroy of New Spain, however, said that Cortés was mistaken for Huitzilopochtli (Elliott, *op cit.*, p. 53), traditionally associated with the south, and about whom no Messianic legend is known to exist. It is possible that Mendoza was told this by Cortés himself, and "Uchilobos" was the only Mexica deity Cortés could name.

Cortés may have picked up a local legend and embellished it in an attempt to prove that Motecuçoma was himself an usurper and therefore had no right to the lands he ruled (cf. the Third Letter, n. 3). . . .

Where Cortés first heard the story is uncertain. Cervantes de Sala-

---

[10]This is a thirteenth-century compilation of Castilian law.—ED.

zar (bk. 111, chap. 49) and Bernal Díaz (chap. 79) both say that it was in Tlaxcala but both are very vague (see also Muñoz Camargo, pp. 184–185). Professor Guzmán says that a similar legend was common in the Antilles. But perhaps the first contact was made in Yucatán, where a foliated cross appears on a number of Mayan buildings and seems to have been associated with Quetzalcoatl, called Kukulcan in Maya. . . . If it is unlikely that Motecuçoma took the Spaniards to be the vicars-on-earth of the "Plumed Serpent," it is even more unlikely that it would have in any way affected his attitude toward Cortés. Besides the improbability of any leader acting on a prophecy, Quetzalcoatl's cult was largely confined to the lowland regions beyond Popocatepetl and Iztaccihuatl and appears to have held little sway in central Mexico itself (*Códice Borgia,* 1: 67). Its cult center was Cholula, which, when it came under Mexica rule, was granted no special respect and even forced to venerate Huitzilopochtli. Nor, it might be added, did Cholula accord to Cortés the welcome he might be expected to receive as Quetzalcoatl's lieutenant. Motecuçoma was himself a priest of Huitzilopochtli; and, secure in the power of the tutelary deity of his race, it does not seem likely that he would have resigned his powers to the supposed avatars of an apotheosized Toltec chieftain.

The attitude of the Mexica toward the Spaniards can best be explained by the traditional immunity from harm enjoyed by all ambassadors—and Cortés claimed to be an ambassador albeit without an embassy. It is also possible that once Motecuçoma had realized Cortés's intentions, he deliberately drew him inland, not understanding that the sea could be a supply route for the Spaniards. . . . Motecuçoma may well have underestimated the Spanish powers of diplomacy and the state of unrest within his own empire. It was unfortunate for him . . . that the Spaniards were in a position to play one Indian against another. . . .

Pagden next turns to the puzzle of Montezuma's death.

There are two versions of Motecuçoma's death. The first, that given by Cortés, is corroborated by most of the Spanish writers. Bernal Díaz (chap. 126) and Vázquez de Tapia, both witnesses, say that there were a large number of Spanish soldiers on the roof guarding the *Uei Tlatoani;*[11] if this was so, it is possible that the Mexica were

---

[11]The Great Speaker.—ED.

aiming at them rather than at Motecuçoma. Gómara (p. 365) suggests that the Mexica did not see him, and Juan Cano told Oviedo (bk. XXXIII, chap. 54) that "Motezuma died from a stone which those outside threw at him, which they would not have done had not a buckler been placed in front of him, for once they had seen him they would not have thrown." Bernal Díaz says that Motecuçoma died because he refused to eat or to have his wound attended, a story repeated by Herrera (dec. 11, bk. X, chap. 10). If the Mexica did attack him on the roof, this might be true. Bernal Díaz then goes on to say that Cortés and the other soldiers wept at Motecuçoma's death as though they had lost a father, which seems somewhat unlikely.

The second theory is that Motecuçoma was stabbed to death shortly before the Spaniards fled the city. This idea is advanced by most of the native writers, though some of them agree that Motecuçoma had been discredited and would therefore be open to attack if he appeared in public. The *Anales Tolteca-Chichimeca* (quoted by Orozco y Berra, IV: 425) even say that it was Cuauhtemoc who threw the stone. Durán (chap. LXXVI) also mentioned the wound but says that when Motecuçoma was found it was almost healed, and that he had been stabbed five times in the chest. Ixtlilxóchitl (I:341), who is largely pro-Spanish, repeats the Spanish version of the killing but adds, "his vassals say that the Spaniards killed him by stabbing him in the bowels." The *Codex Ramirez* (p. 144) also says that he was killed by a sword thrust in the bowels. Torquemada (bk. IV, chap. 70), following Sahagún, says that Motecuçoma and Itzquauhtzin, lord of Tlatelolco, were found garroted. There is little evidence to support this: garroting was for formal executions, not assassination.

Review and Study Questions

1. What were Cortés's hidden motives in his letter to Charles V detailing his conquest of Montezuma's empire?

2. How much credence do you place in the story that Montezuma and the Aztecs believed Cortés to be the agent of the god Quetzalcoatl? Explain.

3. How do you account for the submissive tone of the Aztec account of the conquest?

4. Regardless of the motives and actions of Montezuma himself, how do you account for the surprising ease with which Cortés accomplished the conquest of Mexico?

Suggestions for Further Reading

In addition to *Hernando Cortés: Five Letters,* tr. and ed. J. Bayard Morris (New York: Norton, 1960), excerpted for this chapter, there are two other editions: *Conquest: Dispatches of Cortéz from the New World,* intro. and commentary Irwin R. Blacker, ed. Harry M. Rosen (New York: Grosset and Dunlap, 1962), and *Hernán Cortés: Letters from Mexico,* tr. and ed. A. R. Pagden, intro. J. H. Elliott (New York: Grossman, 1971), also excerpted for this chapter. There are two more contemporary Spanish accounts of the conquest. One is Francisco López de Gómara, *Cortés: The Life of the Conqueror by His Secretary,* tr. and ed. Lesley Byrd Simpson (Berkeley and Los Angeles: University of California Press, 1964). Although Gómara never actually visited the New World, he had access to Cortés's own papers and recollections. The other account is by one of the soldiers on the expedition, written many years later from his recollections: *The Bernal Díaz Chronicles: The True Story of the Conquest of Mexico,* tr. and ed. Albert Idell (Garden City, N.Y.: Doubleday, 1957) and another edition, Bernal Díaz del Castillo, *The Discovery and Conquest of Mexico, 1517–1521,* ed. and tr. A. P. Maudslay, intro. Irving A. Leonard (New York: Farrar, Straus and Cudahy, 1956). In addition to *The Broken Spears: The Aztec Account of the Conquest of Mexico,* ed. and intro. Miguel Leon-Portilla (Boston: Beacon Press, 1962), excerpted for this chapter, another contemporary Indian work is Fray Bernardino de Sahagún, *1547–1577, A History of Ancient Mexico,* tr. Fanny R. Bandelier (Glorieta, N. M.: The Rio Grande Press, 1976). This is actually not a history but an account of the Aztec religion; it is, furthermore, largely a series of selections from the much more comprehensive edition of Fray Bernardino de Sahagún, *Florentine Codex: General History of the Things of New Spain,* ed. Arthur J. O. Anderson and Charles E. Dibble (Santa Fe, N. M., and Salt Lake City, Utah: The School of American Research and The University of Utah, 1955–1982), a massive work in thirteen parts. The account of Cortés and Montezuma occurs in Part XIII, No. 14.

Of the modern accounts of the dramatic confrontation between Aztec and Spaniard, Cortés and Montezuma, the best is R. C. Padden, *The Hummingbird and the Hawk: Conquest and Sovereignty in the Valley of Mexico, 1503–1541* (Columbus: Ohio State University Press, 1967). A much less substantial and analytical popular work is Maurice Collis, *Cortés and Montezuma* (New York: Harcourt, Brace, 1954). An earlier work that tried to make some of the same analyses that Padden did is Charles S. Braden, *Religious Aspects of the Conquest of Mexico* (Durham, N.C.: Duke University Press, 1930).

The standard modern biography of Cortés is Salvador de Madariaga, *Hernán Cortés, Conqueror of Mexico* (New York: Macmillan, 1941).

There is also a 1955 edition of this work, published by Henry Regnery Co., Chicago. A brief, popular, but competent biography is William Weber Johnson, *Cortés* (Boston: Little, Brown, 1975). The only substantial modern biography of Montezuma is C. A. Burland, *Montezuma, Lord of the Aztecs* (New York: Putnam, 1973); this is a brilliantly written if somewhat fictionalized account, but solidly based on the standard sources. The masterwork on the entire history of the period is William H. Prescott, *History of the Conquest of Mexico*, 3 vols. (Philadelphia: Lippincott, 1843, and five later editions). There is a one-volume abridgement of this work, dealing only with the career of Cortés: *A History of the Conquest of Mexico*, ed. Harry Block (New York: Heritage Press, 1949).

Of the many works on the Aztecs themselves, probably the best general history is Nigel Davies, *The Aztecs: A History* (London: Macmillan, 1973). Rudolf A. M. van Zantwijk, *The Aztec Arrangement: The Social History of Pre-Spanish Mexico* (Norman: University of Oklahoma Press, 1985) is a detailed but somewhat difficult book on Aztec social organization by a great European anthropologist. Inga Clendinnen, *Aztecs: An Interpretation* (Cambridge: Cambridge University Press, 1991) is an attempt to reconstruct the social life and customs of the Aztecs on the eve of the Spanish conquest.

Aquitaine and the Four Kings by Amy Kelly, Cambridge, Mass.: Harvard University Press. Copyright © 1950 by the President and Fellows of Harvard College. From *Eleanor of Aquitaine* by Marion Meade, pages 316–325. Copyright © 1977 by Marion Meade. Used by permission of Dutton Signet, a division of Penguin Books USA, Inc.

Ghengis Khan: From *The Secret History of the Mongols: The Origin of Chingis Khan.* Copyright © 1984 by Paul Kahn. Reprinted by permission of the author. From *History of the Mongols: Based on Eastern and Western Accounts of the Thirteenth and Fourteenth Centuries,* by Bertold Spuler, trans./ed. by Drummond & Drummond, pages 81–86. Copyright © 1972 Routledge Kegan & Paul. Reprinted by permission of University of California Press. From "A Modern Assessment of Genghis Khan" from *Genghis Khan, Conqueror of the World* by Leo de Hartog. Copyright © 1989. Reprinted with permission of St. Martin's Press, Inc., Scholarly & Reference Division.

Joan of Arc: From *The Retrial of Joan of Arc: The Evidence of the Trial for her Rehabilitation, 1450–1456* by Regine Pernoud, tr. J. M. Cohen (originally published by Harcourt Brace & Co., 1955, pp. 239–243). From *Joan of Arc* by Jules Michelet, trans. by Albert Guerard, pp. 110–122. Copyright © 1957 The University of Michigan Press, renewed 1985 in name of Albert Guerard. Reprinted by permission of The University of Michigan Press. From M. G. A. Vale, *Charles VII,* pp. 45–49. Copyright © 1974 M. G. A. Vale. Reprinted by permission of University of California Press.

Christopher Columbus: Reprinted, with permission, from *The Log of Christopher Columbus,* by Robert H. Fuson. Copyright © 1987 by Robert H. Fuson. Published by International Marine/TAB Books, a Division of McGraw-Hill, Inc., Blue Ridge Summit, PA 17294-0850 (1-800-233-1128). From *History of the Indies* by Bartoleme de las Casas, translated and edited by Andrée Collard. Copyright © 1971 Joyce Contrucci. Reprinted by permission. From *The European Discovery of America: The Southern Voyages 1492–1616* by Samuel Eliot Morison. Copyright © 1974 by Samuel Eliot Morison. Reprinted by permission of Oxford University Press, Inc., New York.

Montezuma: From *Five Letters* by Hernando Cortes, translated and edited by J. Bayard Morris. Reprinted by permission of Routledge Kegan & Paul Ltd. From *The Broken Spears* by Miguel Leon-Portilla. Copyright © 1962, 1990 by Beacon Press. Reprinted by permission of Beacon Press. From *Hernando Cortes: Letters from Mexico,* edited and translated by Anthony Pagden. Copyright © 1986 by Yale University. Reprinted by permission of Yale University.